# CONVERTIBLE SECURITIES

**Other books in The Irwin Library of Investment and Finance**

*Pricing and Managing Exotic and Hybrid Options* by Vineer Bhansali
*Risk Management and Financial Derivatives*, edited by Satyajit Das

# CONVERTIBLE SECURITIES

## The Latest Instruments, Portfolio Strategies, and Valuation Analysis

**JOHN P. CALAMOS**

Revised Edition

**McGraw-Hill**
New York  San Francisco  Washington, D.C.  Auckland  Bogotá
Caracas  Lisbon  London  Madrid  Mexico City  Milan
Montreal  New Delhi  San Juan  Singapore
Sydney  Tokyo  Toronto

**Library of Congress Cataloging-in-Publication Data**

Calamos, John P.
   Convertible securities : the latest instruments, portfolio
strategies, and valuation analysis / John P. Calamos.
     p.   cm.
   Rev. ed. of: Investing in convertible securities. ©1988.
   Includes bibliographical references.
   ISBN 1-55738-921-7
   1. Convertible preferred stocks.  2. Convertible bonds.
3. Convertible securities.  I. Calamos, John P.  Investing in
convertible securities.  II. Title.
HG4661.C32    1998
332.63′2044—dc21                       97-51242

# *McGraw-Hill*

*A Division of The **McGraw·Hill** Companies*

The sponsoring editor for this book was Stephen Isaacs and the production
supervisor was Suzanne W. B. Rapcavage. It was set in Palatino by Judy Brown.

Printed and bound by R. R. Donnelley & Sons Company.

This publication is designed to provide accurate and authoritative information in regard
to the subject matter covered. It is sold with the understanding that neither the author or
the publisher is engaged in rendering legal, accounting, or other professional service. If legal advice or other expert assistance is required, the services of a competent professional
person should be sought.

> —*From a Declaration of Principles jointly adopted by a Committee
> of the American Bar Association and a Committee of Publishers.*

McGraw-Hill books are available at special quantity discounts to use as premiums and
sales promotions, or for use in corporate training programs. For more information, please
write to the Director of Special Sales, McGraw-Hill, Professional Publishing, Two Penn
Plaza, New York, NY 10121-2298. Or contact your local bookstore.

# CONTENTS

# PREFACE

This book is designed to introduce investors to the rewarding world of convertible securities. Convertible investing was once considered by many as special situations niche market. That is no longer the case. Convertible securities investment strategies are use by many investors. Some use convertibles as a separate asset class with the goal of achieving higher risks adjusted returns for the total fund. Others investors use convertibles as a lower risk equity alternative. Still others, as a means to further diversify fixed income investments. The versatility of convertible securities allows a variety of investors with differing objectives to benefit from their use.

The purpose of this book is to provide a guide to investing in convertible securities. It does not presume to predict the direction of long-term interest rates, bond or stock prices. It does seek to develop the most appropriate and effective ways in which investors can control risk and return through the use of convertible securities. So versatile are convertible securities—employed either alone or in connection with other financial instruments—that in many cases the investor may be able to gain above-average returns while reducing risk. The most attractive strategy for one investor at a particular time may involve simply purchasing convertibles; for another it may be the writing of call options against convertibles or the use of put options with convertibles. The use of warrants or various convertible-hedging techniques might be another consideration. Alternative convertible strategies differ at times, depending on their opportunity for reward and their associated risks.

The discussion that follows was adapted from the original book "Investing In Convertible Securities" published in 1988. This book updates that material and presents new information on convertible structures and the expanding Global Convertible Market. It is designed to provide a reference guide to various convertible strategies, each with its own risk/reward characteristics. The applications in this guide are not meant to be all-inclusive or directed exclusively toward any one category of investor; some of the strategies are appropriate for conservative investors, while others would be better suited to speculators or hedgers.

The techniques and strategies discussed herein have evolved over the years and are dynamic in nature. They will continue to change, as do the capital markets in which they compete. An ancillary goal of this reference guide is to develop a decision-making mechanism by which the reader assembles a frame of reference to evaluate convertible opportunities. This book is not simply about the development of mathematical formulas to describe complex relationships—although these calculations are important and must be done properly. My goal is to provide the reader with insight into how the decision-making process of a convertible specialist can be used with flexibility and success.

Lastly, the reader must recognize how difficult it is to compete in our complex capital markets. Therefore, I have included past examples to bridge the gap between theory and reality. This is done to illustrate the contribution of theoretical analysis and to show its limits in the real world. Formula-type investment strategies often seem foolproof, except when applied with dollars. If it were not so, I'm sure there would be many more wealthy mathematicians than there are.

The capital marketplace can be compared to Socrates' parable of the cave. Each market player makes decisions based on how he or she views the world. Each, locked into position in the cave, views only the shadows on the cave wall in front of him, never being able to turn and see the fire outside the cave and the real figures that make the distorted images on the cave's wall. Each player has to determine reality but sees only distorted shadows. The number of variables that influence the capital markets is so immense that, even with computers, statistics, macroeconomics and microeconomics and capital pricing theory, we can quantify only a fraction of them. Like the parable of the cave, investors do not know all factors that influence the market, but we know some things. In the end, our insight—derived from education and experience—becomes a crucial factor in the decision-making process. The more knowledge we can obtain by quantifying as many variables as possible, the better equipped we will be to decipher the distorted figures on the wall of Wall Street.

Thus, the successful convertible strategist, or any serious investor, does not just apply neat mathematical formulas, but instead meshes accurate theoretical analyses with critical thought. I hope that this book will contribute to the reader's understanding of the convertible segment of the capital markets, because the greater the understanding derived through experience and thought, the greater the probability of success.

# ACKNOWLEDGMENTS

This book has evolved from practical day-to-day experience as a portfolio manager of convertible securities and from the academic theories that help explain the complexity of our capital markets. The goal is to continually seek better tools that allow for the proper evaluation of investment opportunities and thereby manage money effectively. The book details and explains these tools as they apply to convertibles, many of which have not previously been published.

To the extent that we have accomplished that, I want to acknowledge Nick P. Calamos, Director of Research at Calamos Asset Management, for the fundamental contributions he has made to the development of convertible price theory and its applications as outlined in this book. His probing curiosity in the employment of academic theories to our decision-making process, along with the critical thought necessary to fully develop an idea into a useful investment management tool have provided an invaluable contribution without which this book could not have accomplished its purpose.

The book could not have been completed without the dedication, patience, and direct and indirect help from others and the support of the staff at Calamos Asset Management, Inc.®. The main benefit of running your own firm is to help create an environment that is interesting, challenging, and productive. It is gratifying to be associated with people who not only share your enthusiasm for an idea, or a goal, but who also are instrumental in achieving that goal.

# PART ONE

# INTRODUCING CONVERTIBLE SECURITIES

# Introduction

## BACKGROUND AND REVIEW

Convertible securities are both appealing and unusual in that they have both fixed-income and equity characteristics. Investors familiar with stocks for growth and bonds for income and safety will find the convertible's hybrid features very attractive as an investment alternative. In a single security, investors can obtain the safety of a bond and the capital gains opportunity of common stocks. These hybrid features have proved over the years to be beneficial to holders of these unique securities.

Investors have overlooked convertible securities for many years, partly because they are less widely discussed in the financial press than stocks and bonds and partly because they are very complex. At one time, the relatively small size of the public convertible market kept it from attaining the depth necessary to develop complete investment strategies. Those individual investors who were knowledgeable in convertible evaluation have used convertible investments effectively for many years. The private convertible market, which uses convertible securities to structure venture capital investments, has been in widespread use for decades.

The public convertible market changed significantly in the 1980s, and investors' use of convertible securities has grown significantly since then. There has been a dramatic increase in the number of new corporate bond offerings, and this in turn has sparked interest among the larger institutional investors. This interest is spilling over to pension funds and individual investors. A number of mutual funds invest primarily in convertible securities, and other types of mutual funds have allocated a significant portion of fund assets to convertibles. Investment managers and bank trust departments have set up separate departments to manage convertible portfolios. Furthermore, Wall Street's recent introduction of equity-linked securities, which have been derived from classic convertible bonds, has sparked additional interest in convertible securities and introduced many new investors to the investment characteristics of convertibles.

The current interest in convertibles can be traced back to the increased volatility of the stock and bond markets of the early 1970s. The great bull market of the 1950s and 1960s came to an end in 1969, and the economic consequences of those times threw traditional ways of managing portfolios into disarray. Bonds became as volatile as stocks; investors could not simply buy bonds for safety and stocks for growth. To achieve financial success, investors sought ways to control volatility. The defensive characteristics of convertibles made them increasingly attractive as a means to achieve higher risk-adjusted returns.

This quote from *Forbes,* 25 years ago (February 15, 1972), illustrates the point perfectly: "Some experts are predicting that the Dow will thrust past the magic 1000 mark this year. Others warn that stubborn economic problems may again cause deep trouble in the stock market. In the current period of market uncertainty, the convertible debenture market is once again starting to boil. " [1]

As the markets recovered from the disastrous early 1970s, volatility did not subside. The occasional disruptions of the bull markets of the 1980s caused many investors to rethink traditional investment strategies. Buy-and-hold strategies did not automatically result in capital growth. Pension funds and conservative investors were dismayed by the volatility in their fixed-income holdings, as valuations reacted to extreme changes in interest rates. The interest in convertible securities increased in response to the continuing volatility of the financial markets. Since the first edition of this book was published, the stock market experienced a meltdown in 1987, and the 1994 bond market was one of the worst of the century.

Even with the lower-interest-rate environment of the mid-1990s, volatility has not subsided. In fact, individual stock volatility continues to be as high now as at any time in history. Given the internationalization of the financial markets, it is unlikely that volatility will be reduced any time soon. The vast promise of our financial markets rests on the increasing acceptance of free markets in the emerging world. The opportunities are greater now than at any time in our history. It is exciting to watch the world being recreated by the driving force of free markets. No doubt there is great opportunity for investors. However, the flip side of opportunity is volatility. As Mexico's stock market collapse in 1994 starkly illustrated, volatility in the financial markets can occur swiftly, and it is likely to occur frequently.

Of course, increasing interest in convertibles was not the only result of the volatile financial markets. The demands on portfolio managers to control risk in volatile times led to an increasing number of other new investment vehicles and strategies. The opening of the Chicago Board Options Exchange (CBOE) in 1973 and the passing of the Employees Retirement Income Security Act (ERISA) in 1974 both fostered the growth of nontraditional investment strategies. The CBOE showed investors different ways to reduce market volatility by using stock options, index options, and other investment vehicles. Professors Black and Scholes developed their option price theory, which helped provide a solid academic framework for options strategies and fostered the growth of additional types of derivative securities. Undoubtedly some investors paid dearly as they learned to use these new vehicles, even before the derivatives debacle lost Orange County, California, billions in 1994.

Other factors made convertibles more attractive as an investment strategy. ERISA became law in 1974 and challenged the traditional prudent man rule and legal lists of the past by recognizing modern techniques of portfolio management. In response, plan sponsors began to diversify their assets and search for complementary investment strategies. Pension plan funding exploded as modern portfolio theory became more widely accepted. The unexpected volatility of the stock and bond markets meant plan sponsors searched for more than portfolio performance alone; risk-adjusted performance became key.

The volatility of the markets created an atmosphere of evaluation, and investors began to test the paradigms of the past. As investors became more knowledgeable, they were no longer convinced that the traditional mix of stocks and bonds was the optimum strategy, nor were they willing to ride the performance roller coaster. Investing today requires a continual search for ways to control risk and protect assets while still achieving above-average returns on investment. It is therefore not surprising that convertible securities are gaining advocates in many parts of the financial community as a specific investment strategy to be used throughout the market cycle.

The purpose of this book is to show the serious investor how to use convertibles in pursuing investment strategies that can achieve above-average returns at below-average risk. Evaluating convertible securities is complex, and it will take time for the serious investor to learn to use convertibles profitably. However, before we begin the process of explanation, analysis, and evaluation, we should place convertibles into their historic perspective.

## HISTORICAL REVIEW OF CONVERTIBLE SECURITIES

In general, when corporations use the capital markets to raise capital, they issue either stocks or bonds. It is relatively simple to organize a corporation and provide for the issuance of common stocks and corporate bonds. It is quite another matter to sell these securities to the investing public. Convertible securities came into being as a way to make securities more attractive to investors. Convertible bonds are not new; issuers and investors have been using them since the 1800s.

During the nineteenth century, the United States was what we would now classify as an emerging market. It was not easy to gain access to capital in a rapidly growing country. The convertible clause was added to first mortgage bonds to entice investors to finance the building of the railroads. The Chicago, Milwaukee & St. Paul Railway, for example, used many convertible issues for financing between 1860 and 1880. In 1896, that company had 12 separate convertible issues outstanding, most bearing a 7 percent coupon. As the country and its railroads grew, it became easier to market new bonds. Thus the convertible clause virtually disappeared as a feature in new issues for a period of 20 years.

At the turn of the century, the convertible clause reappeared with the Baltimore & Ohio Railroad's issuance of $15 million of 4 percent, 10-year debentures, convertible into common stock at par. In that same year (1901), the Union Pacific Railroad issued $100 million 4 percent mortgage bonds convertible into common stock at par. Many others followed, including both the Pennsylvania and the Erie Railroad. Besides the railroads, convertibles were issued during this era by the Brooklyn Rapid Transit, Distillers Securities Corporation, Lackawanna Steel Company, International Steam Pump Co., Consolidated Gas Company of New York, Brooklyn Union Gas Co., International Paper, and Western Union Telegraph. Westinghouse Electric & Manufacturing Co. brought convertible issues to the market in 1906, and General Electric offered its stockholders the right to subscribe to a convertible bond issue in 1907.[2]

The American Telephone & Telegraph Co. first authorized $150 million 4 percent convertible bonds in 1906. Over the years, AT&T has sold at least nine separate issues of convertible bonds, most of them through subscription rights to stockholders. Companies like AT&T issued convertible bonds because they brought in a wider class of shareholders than would have been available with a stock offering. Due to business practices at the time, many financial institutions with available funds were not allowed to buy common stock.[3] Bonds, however, were approved, so buying convertible bonds was a way around the "no common stock" rules.

During the favorable economic environment of the 1950s, many growth companies issued convertibles. Avco, General Dynamics, Martin, and others were growing faster than the Dow Industrials. During this period an increasing share of preferred and bond issues were in the form of convertibles. Even with the relatively low interest rates at the time, the "equity kicker" enabled companies to sell these fixed-income securities with lower yields.

Many convertibles were issued during the bull market of the 1960s, as mergers and acquisitions became the means to create the megaconglomerates of the time. International Telephone & Telegraph (ITT) purchased many companies by issuing convertible preferreds. In the financial pages under ITT, there were convertible preferred issues I, J, K, L, and M, each separate issue the result of ITT purchasing a company. LTV and others issued many convertibles during this period. Many small- and mid-sized companies also issued convertibles as the economy expanded and the convertible became a means to access capital. This created the myth that convertibles were issued only by companies with lower-quality credit.

It is interesting to note that AT&T used the convertible market quite extensively in its early years. Similarly, MCI Communications Corp. (MCI), a fledgling company in 1975, was also able to make good use of the convertible markets. MCI had two public stock offerings, in 1972 and 1975. It came to the public market with its first convertible preferred offering in December 1978, raising $25.8 million. A second convertible preferred, in September 1979, raised $63.1 million; a third, in October 1980, raised $46.7 million. MCI continued to need capital: Between December 1978 and December 1982, MCI issued a total of $842.3 million in straight and convertible bonds and convertible preferred stock. Settlement of the antitrust suit between AT&T and the U. S. Department of Justice in January 1982 provided an important growth opportunity, and in March 1983, MCI brought a $400 million convertible bond to the market. Although MCI did issue straight debt in the first 10 years of its existence, convertible securities provided the majority of the capital raised over its formative years.

The 1980s saw the United States in the midst of one of its greatest periods of corporate creation and corporate restructuring. There were large increases in all types of debt financing, including convertibles. Growth companies such as Home Depot, Compaq Computer, A. L. Williams Corp., Price Company, Cray Research, Seagate Technology, Thermo Electron, Columbia Pictures, Wendy's International, and Avnet financed much of their dramatic growth by issuing convertible bonds; for many of these companies, the convertibles were issued at a time when their ratings were below investment grade. A record number of new issues in the emerging-growth sector was brought to the market in 1986. This portion of the market has expanded so much that a whole new sector was created, called by some the "junk-bond" or "high-yield" market.

IBM issued a convertible bond late in 1984. This new issue alone seemed to change institutional investors' perceptions about the convertible market. If IBM could issue a convertible bond rated AAA, then convertible bonds were not just for emerging-growth companies. Other large companies soon followed with investment-grade issues. Interest rates were high at the time, and investors believed that equity prices were undervalued. Since convertible debt can be issued at rates that are slightly lower than those on regular corporate debt, issuing convertible securities allowed companies to lower their fixed-income costs.

During this time, Thermo Electron Corporation (TMO) provided an excellent example of how to use convertible financing effectively. In the 1970s and 1980s, TMO's growth was being constrained by its ability to finance innovation. Promising projects had to wait as divisions competed for scarce capital. A spin-off strategy was developed to take advantage of market opportunities to raise capital for the parent and subsidiaries. Figure 1–1 indicates the many convertible issues TMO brought to market by placing bonds in Europe and the United States.

In November 1995, Thermo again accessed the convertible market with a $400 million-144A offering. TMO's effectiveness in raising capital via the convertible market has helped make it a technology leader and a major, diversified technology company.

The expansion of the global market has encouraged blue-chip companies to issue convertibles in the expanding Eurobond market. Many large, well-known companies seeking worldwide distribution of their securities offer convertible bonds to foreign investors. In addition to taking advantage of favorable financial terms in other markets, issuing convertibles widens the shareholder base—one reason AT&T used convertibles some 60 years ago. American Brands issued three Eurobond convertibles; IBM issued a convertible in French francs; and Disney issued a French-franc convertible to finance EuroDisney. This practice will continue to grow with the continued internationalization of the securities markets.

**F I G U R E  1–1**

Thermo Electron's Corporate Financings Using Convertibles

| Thermo Entity | Debenture Type | Coupon | Issue Date | Year Due |
|---|---|---|---|---|
| Thermo Process Systems, Inc. | Subord. Conv. | 6.50% | Jul-89 | 1997 |
| Thermedics, Inc. | Subord. Conv. | 6.50% | Jun-90 | 1998 |
| Thermo Electron Corporation | Subord. Conv. | 6.75% | Feb-91 | 2001 |
| Thermo Instrument Systems, Inc. | Subord. Conv. | 6.63% | Jul-91 | 2001 |
| Thermo Electron Corporation | Senior Conv. | 4.63% | Jul-92 | 1997 |
| Thermo Electron Corporation | Subord. Conv. | 4.88% | Dec-92 | 1997 |
| Thermo Cardiosystems, Inc. | Subord. Conv. | 5.50% | Jul-93 | 2002 |
| Thermo Instrument Systems, Inc. | Senior Conv. | 3.75% | Sep-93 | 2000 |
| Thermo Voltek Corporation | Subord. Conv. | 3.75% | Nov-93 | 2000 |
| Thermo Cardiosystems, Inc. | Subord. Conv. | 0.00% | Dec-93 | 1997 |
| Thermo Electron Corporation | Senior Conv. | 5.00% | Apr-94 | 2001 |

Other industries added significantly to the convertible universe in the late 1980s and early 1990s. The banking industry required new equity capital both as a result of the saving and loan crises of the late 1980s and early 1990s and because the Federal Reserve mandated increased equity requirements for banks. NationsBank used a private placement convertible preferred with a government guarantee to take over the failing Texas Commerce Bank. This was the beginning of the tremendous growth for this well-run regional bank. Dozens of other banks issued convertible preferreds to add equity to their balance sheet. Citicorp, BankOne, Northern Trust, First Chicago, BankAmerica, and Great Western Financial, among others, added a significant number of issues to the convertible universe.

The private placement market also expanded during the 1980s. Private placement convertibles are used extensively in the venture capital market with small issues that are not very liquid. The institutional private placement market also grew as investment bankers brought issues from seasoned companies to the market. Such private placement issues could be brought to market quickly without the voluminous disclosure that a public offering required. The companies were already well known to the institutional buyers, so underwriting costs could be significantly reduced by the use of private placements. Since private placements were restricted securities, the Securities and Exchange Commission (SEC) established a means to trade them.

The SEC introduced rule 144A, effective April 30, 1990. This rule provided a safe-harbor exemption from the Securities Act of 1933's registration requirements for resales of certain restricted securities to certain qualified institutional buyers. Convertible issues constituted a significant portion of this institutionally dominated market. Similar to shelf registrations, rule 144A allows issuers to come to the market quickly. It also improved secondary trading in the private placement market. By February 1995, 59 convertibles had been issued under the rule, including such well-known companies as Apache, Grand Met, Thermo Electron, AMR Corp., Browning Ferris, Cellular Communications, Chemical Bank, Chrysler, Ciba Geigy/Alza, Citibank, Ivax, Medical Care, Turner Broadcasting, and others. The overall effect has been to contribute to the market's expansion.

Many cyclical companies with high debt-to-equity ratios continue to need capital and therefore issue convertible preferreds. They have participated in the convertible markets for many years, but even more so after rule 144A was introduced. The issuance of convertible preferreds provides the additional capital as equity instead of debt. It also allows the conversion to common stock in the future. Ford Motor Company issued a convertible preferred in the U. S. market, and Chrysler issued a 144A convertible preferred in the highly liquid, institutional private-placement market. General Motors added a twist by issuing a convertible preferred against the cash flow of its wholly owned subsidiary, Electronic Data Systems, Inc., which it purchased some years ago.

In the 1990s, Wall Street innovation adapted the classic convertible bond, producing new types of securities with acronyms such as MIPS, DECS, ELKS, PERCS, and PRIDES. These securities also expanded the size of the convertible market. The many different variations of convertible securities have slightly different risk characteristics, allowing investors to choose an instrument that is tailor-made for their portfolio needs. Similarly, the use of synthetic convertibles—combining a warrant with a fixed-income instrument such as a U. S. government note—has also been a great boon to the convertible market. Constructing a synthetic allows investment access to companies that have not issued regular convertible securities.

Technology companies became the growth sector of the equity market in the 1990s. Companies such as Motorola, Ericsson, Oracle, Silicon Graphics, Lam Research, and Automatic Data Processing have made good use of convertible securities. Other technology companies include National Semi-Conductor, VLSI Technology, LSI Logic, Arrow Electronics, TRW Inc., Control Data, Wang Labs, Inc., Texas Instruments, 3COM Corporation, Cisco Systems, Adaptec Inc., Iomega Corporation, Quantum Corporation, Seagate Technology, EMC Corporation, C-Cube Microsystems, Inc., and Western Digital. Technology companies continue to make use of the convertibles, as witnessed for example by the large Microsoft issue that came to market in early 1997.

It's clear that the convertibility feature has been used over the years as a sweetener, to entice investors to buy securities that might not otherwise be attractive. This added kicker is not needed when markets are less volatile, so the issuance of convertibles diminishes with the volatility. A number of factors have caused record growth in the convertible market in recent years. The fact that bond markets have become almost as volatile as stock markets has played an important role. The poor bond markets of the late 1970s and early 1980s, not to mention 1994, have not gone unnoticed. The uncertainty of the financial markets and the volatility it has fostered has forced companies to add the convertible option as an additional feature to their preferred stock or bond issuance to make it more attractive to buyers.

However, the dramatic growth of the capital markets is also a factor. The convertible issue provides an incentive to buy the unseasoned securities of the many new companies coming to the market. The technological developments of our age provide a fertile field for new ideas; companies need capital to develop those ideas. Smaller-cap companies are often riskier and more volatile than more established companies. The convertibility feature makes the risk of such companies much more palatable for investors, who retain the upside potential of the stock but still receive the bond income while waiting for the stock to increase in value.

Economic growth is the most important contributor to the growth of the convertible market. These periods of dramatic growth are a result of entrepreneurial capitalism. The great expansion of business in the 1980s created a $100 billion convertible market. Both new companies with innovative ideas and old companies restructuring for the future need access to capital. We are in the midst of another great wave of emerging growth; the convertible market has and will continue to be a significant contributor of capital to these companies.

## CONVERTIBLE PERFORMANCE IN VOLATILE MARKETS

Convertibles have performed extremely well over the past 20 years when compared to both the equity and fixed-income markets. A little-known Ibbotson study[4] showed that convertibles achieve returns competitive with those of stocks, but with lower volatility. Risk, as measured by standard deviation, is 25 percent lower on convertibles than on the S&P 500 (standard deviation of 12.75 percent on convertibles versus 17.50 percent for the S&P), while returns are comparable (11. 75 percent compounded annual return for the convertibles and 11.33 percent for the S&P). In other words, convertibles achieve equity-like returns with less risk. Figure 1–2 shows these figures in table form. Convertibles could no longer be ignored and began to emerge as a separate asset class.

## F I G U R E  1–2

Performance of Various Asset Classes, 1973–1995[1]

|  | Compound Annual Return | Standard Deviation |
|---|---|---|
| Convertible bonds | 11.70% | 12.47% |
| S&P 500 | 11.84% | 17.27% |
| Long-term corporate bonds | 9.66% | 12.44% |
| Intermediate-term corporate bonds | 9.91% | 8.93% |

[1]Scott L. Lummer and Mark W. Riepe, "Convertible Bonds as an Asset Class: 1957–1992," *The Journal of Fixed Income*, Vol. 3, No. 2 (September 1993). With updated data completed by Ibbotson Associates, as published by Goldman Sachs Global Convertible Research, 1996, "Convertibles as an Asset Class."

During the volatile stock and bond market of the late 1970s and early 1980s, convertibles benefited from their hybrid characteristics. Although convertibles are influenced to a degree by interest-rate fluctuations, they are also affected by the price movements of their underlying stock, a factor that tends to soften the negative effects of rising interest rates. Figure 1–3 illustrates

## F I G U R E  1–3

Convertibles Outperformed Other Asset Classes 1979–1984

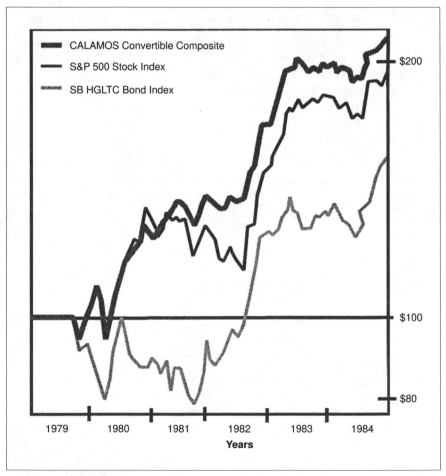

Source: The Carmack Group, Alhambra, California. Used with permission.

the performance of convertible securities (as represented by the Calamos Convertible Composite) compared to that of the S&P 500 and the Salomon Brothers High-Grade Bond Index from 1979 to 1984. During that period, when the bond market declined because of double-digit inflation and interest rates, convertibles appreciated in value, unlike other fixed-income vehicles. As a result, convertibles outperformed both the stock and bond markets over that period.

Investors fear a repeat of the experience of the Japanese markets of the late 1980s and 1990s. Over the years 1986 through 1996, convertible bonds outperformed other asset classes, including equities, long- and short-term Japanese government bonds, gold, and residential property. This experience is shown in Figure 1–4.

In the late 1980s, as the Japanese stock market experienced extraordinary performance, Japanese convertibles performed well but lagged the stock market. However, as the Japanese stock market began its slide—which it has still not recovered from—the Japanese convertible market's losses were small because bond values cushioned declining equity values.

Over the 10-year period, Japanese convertibles ended up outperforming all asset classes considered because bond values held up well as their maturity dates approached. Notice how well convertibles preserved capital over those volatile stock market years, while equity investors experienced significant capital losses. This is an excellent display of the defensive characteristics of convertibles.

An asset allocation decision made in the late 1980s that included Japanese convertibles would have resulted in a portfolio that preserved capital better than the Japanese equity markets and showed returns competitive with those of the fixed-income markets. The experience of other developed markets should not go unheeded when developing the criteria by which to make asset allocation decisions.

The nonlinear upside and downside risks of convertible securities are among their most important features, and we will discuss them at length later. We have found that, on average, convertible securities have two-thirds of the upside potential and one-third of the downside potential of common stocks. This varies depending on market conditions.

## FIGURE 1-4

The Japanese Convertible Market

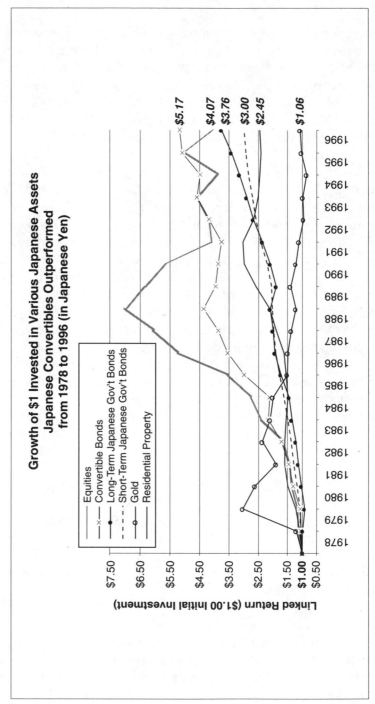

**Growth of $1 Invested in Various Japanese Assets**
**Japanese Convertibles Outperformed**
**from 1978 to 1996 (in Japanese Yen)**

Legend:
—— Equities
—×— Convertible Bonds
—●— Long-Term Japanese Gov't Bonds
--- Short-Term Japanese Gov't Bonds
—○— Gold
—— Residential Property

$5.17
$4.07
$3.76
$3.00
$2.45
$1.06

Linked Return ($1.00 Initial Investment)

$7.50
$6.50
$5.50
$4.50
$3.50
$2.50
$1.50
**$1.00**
$0.50

1978 1979 1980 1981 1982 1983 1984 1985 1986 1987 1988 1989 1990 1991 1992 1993 1994 1995 1996

## MARKETS OF THE LATE 1990s AND BEYOND

Despite periods of turbulence, many conservative investors have been spoiled by the investment climate of the last 15 years. Consider the bond market, which has experienced a bull market since interest rates hit the highs of the century in 1981. Bond investors have experienced double-digit total return for most of the period since, first from double-digit interest rates and then from the capital appreciation that came from declining interest rates.

Most market participants expect interest rates to remain relatively stable for the next few years. Investors will either have to become accustomed to much lower rates of total return, or they will have to seek out alternative investments such as convertible securities. With few exceptions, convertible securities are the one fixed-income instrument that offers investors significant upside potential—and the potential to generate the kind of returns that will help investors achieve their long-term investment objectives.

In general, the last 15 years have also been very profitable for the equity markets. Investors have become aware of the importance of investing in equities for the long term, but are wary of their volatility and the downside risk of equities. These investors, too, will find convertible securities to be a suitable investment. The fixed-income part of convertibles generates a stream of income that the investor receives no matter what happens to the underlying stock. The investment value of the convertible also acts as a floor value to the investment. Together these factors decrease the volatility of equity investing to make it more attractive for the conservative investor. This is particularly true for investments in small- to mid-cap companies and companies in emerging markets, whose stocks tend to be particularly risky.

In this chapter, we have provided a brief overview of the convertible market to illustrate how convertibles have evolved. Because of my involvement with convertibles since the early 1970s, I have observed these phenomena for nearly 30 years. It has been exciting to witness the market's growth as well as the growing interest in convertible investing, It is not easy to evaluate convertibles because they are complex; the techniques needed to evaluate them properly have undergone continuous serious study.

The remainder of the book is devoted to an in-depth analysis of convertible securities and how they can be used effectively to achieve above average returns at lower risk.

# E N D   N O T E S

1. Dero A. Saunders, ed. , "Flashback," *Forbes* Vol. 159, No. 3, February 10, 1997, p. 221.
2. Thomas Gibson, Special Market Letter, 1908 (New York: Gibson, 1908).
3. Benjamin Graham, *The Intelligent Investor: A Book of Practical Counsel* (New York: Harper, 1954), p. 121.
4. Scott L. Lummer and Mark W. Riepe, "Convertible Bonds as an Asset Class: 1957–1992," *The Journal of Fixed Income,* September 1993.

CHAPTER

# Overview of Convertible Evaluation: The Basics

This chapter presents an overview of convertible securities. We introduce the basics of convertible valuation factors, with more detail to follow in subsequent chapters.

Convertible evaluation involves numerous, complicated mathematical equations. The hybrid nature of a convertible bond lends itself to the use of various equity and fixed-income techniques to analyze a convertible security. Before we begin to delve into that process in detail, it will be useful to review some of the most important principles as well as definitions. Convertible securities consist of debt instruments (bonds or debentures) or preferred stock of a corporation that may be exchanged at the holder's option for a specified number of shares of the common stock over a specified time period under terms defined by the issuing corporation at the time of the security's issuance.

## INTRODUCING CONVERTIBLE SECURITIES

Convertible securities are relatively simple in concept: A convertible bond is a regular corporate bond that has the added feature of being convertible into a fixed number of shares of common stock.

Conversion terms and conditions are defined by the issuing corporation at issuance. (A convertible security may also be preferred
stock, but convertibles are best understood by studying convertible bonds.)

Convertible bonds are a specific type of corporate bond issued by corporations but having the same characteristics as other
bonds. The actual terms can vary significantly, but the bond pays
a fixed interest rate and has a fixed maturity date. The issuing
company guarantees to pay the specified coupon interest, usually
semiannually, and the par value, usually $1,000 per bond, upon
maturity. Like other nonconvertible bonds, a corporation's failure
to pay interest or principal when due results in the first step toward company bankruptcy. Therefore, convertible bonds share
with nonconvertible bonds the feature that bond investors consider most precious: principal protection.

Convertibles are senior to common stock but may be junior to
other long-term debt instruments. Convertibles have one important feature that other corporate bonds do not have: At the
holder's option, the bond can be exchanged for the underlying
common stock of the company. This feature completely changes
the investment characteristics of the bond.

Convertible bonds are governed under the Trust Indenture
Act of 1939. The bond indenture associated with each convertible
bond offering is designed to control the conflicts of interest between the shareholders of a company and its bondholders. The
terms of the covenants to any individual bond indenture are an
important part of it, and violation of such covenants can lead to a
technical default. Specific covenants apply to seniority, call provisions, sinking fund requirements, restrictions on sale/leasebacks
of assets, limitations of shareholder distributions (dividend restrictions), and debt limitation.

The convertible bond has three main parts: Its value as a
straight bond, called the investment value; its value as a stock,
called the conversion value; and the theoretical fair value. The
investor must dissect the convertible security to understand the
valuation process. The three factors are interdependent, and each
must be considered for a proper valuation of a convertible security. In this chapter we begin the process of evaluating convertibles
by dissecting the convertible bond into its various parts.

## Investment Value

A convertible bond's investment value is its value as a bond. This is the fixed-income component of the convertible. (Keep in mind that investment value refers to this one aspect of convertible valuation and is not the same as the convertible security's market value.) Conceptually speaking, it is the value of the bond without the conversion feature. It is calculated by determining what the value of the bond would be if it were not convertible, according to standard fixed-income analysis—company fundamentals, type of bond (collateral or debenture), coupon and maturity date, sinking fund requirements, call features, and yield to maturity. The market value of a straight bond fluctuates with any changes in these factors. However, since the investment value of a convertible bond is embedded and is a component of the total market value of the convertible, changes in fixed-income determinants may not directly affect its market price.

The investment value of a bond remains stable over a wide range of stock prices if interest rates stay stable and drops only as the stock price approaches zero (meaning that the company is likely to be in financial distress). It is theoretically extremely unlikely for the value of a convertible to fall below its investment value, although in reality slight discounts to investment value do occur.

Figure 2–1 shows the relationship between the common stock price and market price of the bond investment value graphically as a horizontal line for normal price fluctuations. With the convertible value shown on the vertical axis and the stock price shown on the horizontal axis, the effect of changes in the variables is easily determined.

The investment value of a bond remains stable over a wide range of stock prices, if we assume stable interest rates for the sake of simplicity. The financial stability of the company and most of the other bond quality factors change slowly, if at all. Since investment value, therefore, remains constant over relatively short periods of time, it appears as a horizontal line on the graph. The bond investment value is not affected by increases in value of the common stock, although the market price of the convertible will be affected. In situations of deteriorating creditworthiness, the stock

## F I G U R E  2–1

A Convertible's Investment Value

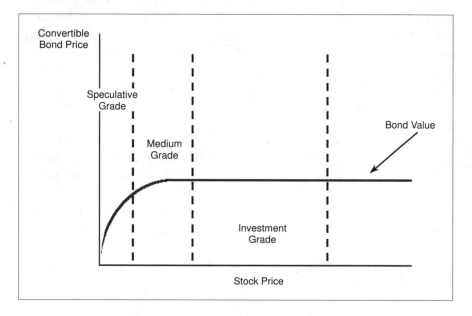

price begins to sink to zero. The obvious probable cause for this is a not-so-normal deterioration of company financial fundamentals, which causes the expected recovery of full principal to come into question. As shown in Figure 2–1, the value of the convertible bond must also approach its bankruptcy value.

The decline of a particular stock due to overall negative market sentiment should not influence the investment value, especially in the short run. The investment value will continue to provide an investment floor below the convertible market price, and the convertible bond should not fall below its investment value as long as the creditworthiness of the issuer remains unchanged. This provides the essential safety element in convertible bonds. Furthermore, the convertibility feature should ensure that convertible securities will always be more valuable than income-equivalent nonconvertible bonds.

However, there are a number of factors that do influence the investment value of a convertible security. If the common stock declines due to company factors (unsystematic risk), poor earnings, or other causes, the bond's investment value will be influenced, similar to the way the value of a straight bond is influenced by a rating downgrade. In fact, deterioration of company fundamentals should cause a rating downgrade. A stock decline caused by such factors will also cause the investment value to decline, reflecting the possibility that the company may not be able to pay the coupon or principal of the bond. In the ultimate case, both the value of the firm and the bond investment value would approach zero. Studies have shown that dramatic changes in the fundamentals of a company will have an immediate effect on bond investment value. Investors who ignore these fundamentals in evaluating convertibles will be at a distinct disadvantage in the marketplace. Rating agencies assist with this effort, but may not always be timely enough.

In approaching the mathematical analysis of convertible securities, it's convenient to assume a stable investment value over the short term and that stock price fluctuation is due to general market sentiment. The investment value does fluctuate over the longer term, and it must increase to par value by the time the bond matures, regardless of how the common stock is changing.

Of course, changing interest rates affect the investment value of convertibles like they affect the value of straight bonds. As interest rates increase, the investment value will decline; as interest rates decrease, the investment value will rise. The investment value fluctuates in tandem with the price of straight corporate bonds of similar quality.

However, due to the unique nature of convertibles, a change in the investment value of the convertible bond may not necessarily mean a change in the market price. The investment value may fluctuate, but the market price of the convertible bond remains relatively stable because changes in interest rates are just among many factors that may be affecting the market price at any given moment. A bond that is trading close to its investment value will be relatively more affected by changes in interest rates than one that is trading close to its conversion value and well above its investment value. If the underlying stock is increasing in value as interest rates are rising, the convertible bond will be driven by its equity component rather than by its fixed-income component and will increase in value.

It is important to recognize that the investment value of a convertible bond at issuance is rarely near par. The convertible bond is not discounted at its coupon rate, but rather must be discounted at a rate appropriate for the issuing company's nonconvertible debt. For example, if the company has issued a convertible with a 5 percent coupon and its nonconvertible debt is at 8 percent, then the investment value of the convertible will be discounted at 8 percent. On a 10-year bond, the investment value will be $798.70 for a bond with a $1,000 par value.

Arriving at a proper estimate of the investment floor is critically important in evaluating a convertible bond; it constitutes the minimum value below which the convertible bond should not fall, regardless of common stock fluctuations, and influences all other calculations in the mathematical analysis of convertibles. Because investment value is the hinge on which all other calculations depend, it's important to understand how the various factors affect it. Chapter 8 discusses this topic in detail.

## Investment Premium

The convertible bond's investment premium is the difference between the convertible's market price and its investment value, expressed as a percentage.

An important measure of the basic value of the convertible is its premium over investment value. At this point, we determine the convertible's market value by calculating the difference between the convertible's market price and its investment value, expressed as a percentage. This value is important because it indicates the level of downside risk and can be monitored as market prices change. For example, in the case of a bond with a par value of $1,000 and an investment value of $798.70, the investment premium is ([1,000 − 798.70]/ 798.70), or 25.2 percent.

The higher the investment premium, the more sensitive the market price of the convertible is to a decline in the underlying common stock. A high market price relative to investment value is caused by increases in the value of the underlying stock such that the convertible's market value depends on the value of the stock. There is less downside protection because the stock would have to decrease in value by a significant amount before the market price of the convertible would approach the investment value and offer protection.

Similarly, when the investment premium is small, a small decrease in the value of the underlying stock would result in the market price reaching the investment value. At that time, the investment value floor serves as significant downside protection. Furthermore, when the investment premium is small, the convertible is more interest-rate sensitive rather than equity sensitive and will typically be vulnerable to changes in market interest rates.

## Conversion Price

The convertible's conversion price is the effective price for conversion into stock with the bond at par. At the time of issue, the offering prospectus indicates the common-stock price equivalent to the value of the bond at par. This price in turn determines the number of shares of stock into which each bond at par can be converted; this is the conversion ratio.

Confusion often arises among investors because the conversion price is specified in the bond documents, but the conversion ratio is not; it must be calculated. The conversion price is meaningful only when the bond is at par, and it can be calculated by dividing the par value by the conversion price, as shown in Figure 2–2. For example, if the common stock price at which the bond can be converted is $50, then each convertible bond represents 20 shares of stock (par value of $1,000 divided by stated conversion price of $50 = 20).

Investors often focus on the conversion price when they should be paying attention to the conversion ratio. From the moment the bond is brought to market, it trades either above or below par value, depending on the market forces. Since the

**F I G U R E  2–2**

$$\frac{\text{Par Value}}{\text{Conversion Price}} = \text{Conversion Ratio}$$

conversion ratio remains the same whether the bond is at par or not, it is the more important number for investors.

## Conversion Ratio

The conversion ratio determines the number of shares of common stock a convertible bondholder would receive if the bond were converted into stock. The conversion ratio is set at the issuance of the security and is typically protected against dilution. It may well specify partial shares (i.e., 21.3 shares).

The conversion ratio is usually adjusted for stock splits and stock dividends. The initial conversion ratio in our example was 20 shares of stock per each convertible bond. The conversion ratio would be adjusted to 22 following a 10 percent stock dividend. Although convertible bondholders are not protected against normal cash dividends, in some cases they are protected against dividends that result from a spin-off of assets. (Cash or stock dividends paid out to stockholders might reduce the value of the stock and result in a convertible bond with a lower value.)

## Conversion Value

Conversion value represents the equity portion of the convertible bond. It is what the convertible bond would be worth if it were converted into common stock at current market prices. In Figure 2–3, the diagonal line indicates the conversion value. For any stock price, the conversion value is found by multiplying the given stock price times the stated number of common shares received per bond. For example, if a bond can be converted into 20 shares of stock and the stock currently sells at $42 per share, the conversion value of the convertible bond is $840. As we have said previously, the number of shares each bond can be converted into is the conversion ratio and is set at the time the bond is issued.

Like bond investment value, conversion value is a minimum value or price at which the security is expected to sell. If the market price fell below the conversion value, specialists and market makers would quickly take advantage of the situation; the arbitrageur would buy the bond and simultaneously sell an equivalent number of shares of the underlying common stock. The difference

**F I G U R E  2–3**

A Convertible's Equity Value

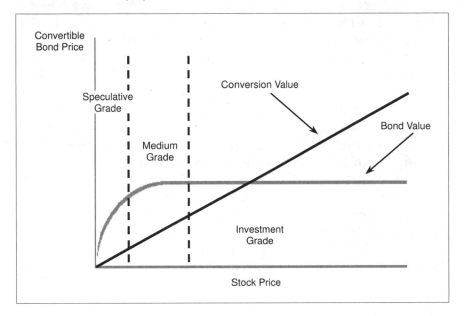

between these two values would be a risk-free profit to the arbitrageur. Because of this, conversion value, like investment value, becomes a minimum value, below which the convertible's market price should not fall.[1]

## Conversion Premium

The equity value of a convertible bond was determined to be its conversion value. Conversion premium can be calculated easily by simply taking the difference between the current market price of the convertible and the conversion value and expressing it as a percentage. Since the convertible bond is more secure than common stock and generally pays higher interest than the stock dividend, the convertible bond buyer is willing to pay a premium over conversion value. Market forces determine the amount of premium that a particular convertible may command in the marketplace. Determining whether the premium is high or low depends upon other variables to be discussed in later chapters. However, it should make sense that, as a convertible bond price increases above its investment value, its fixed-income attributes give way to equity characteristics, decreasing the conversion premium. On the other hand, if the stock price declines, the convertible bond price approaches its fixed-income value and the conversion premium increases. Convertible bonds that are trading near their fixed-income values with substantial conversion premiums are called "busted converts." Their equity component is of little value, and they trade mainly on their fixed-income characteristics.

Figure 2–4 depicts a typical convertible price curve, with the shaded area denoting conversion premium. Notice that as the stock increases in value, conversion premium gradually decreases until it becomes zero. At that point, the convertible market price and conversion value are equal. As the common stock declines in value, the convertible gains conversion premium because it is approaching its investment value.

From another perspective, the market value of the convertible should always be higher than either the conversion value or the

**F I G U R E  2–4**

A Convertible's Conversion Premium

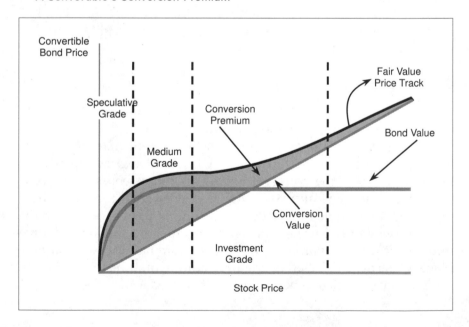

investment value. If we were to hypothesize a convertible with a market value that exactly equaled its investment value, the investment premium would have a value of zero and the convertible would be trading as if it were a straight nonconvertible bond. However, a convertible security has an implicit option, and as long as there is time remaining before the option expires—thereby providing the holder with equity potential—the option will have some value in itself.

The convertible price curve can be either an estimate of how much conversion premium a particular convertible security would command at various stock prices or an historical depiction of how a convertible has actually traded as the common stock has fluctuated over time. It is an extremely important consideration in evaluating convertible securities because it determines the upside potential versus the downside risk. Detailed mathematical formulae are needed to estimate the convertible price curve accurately. It is inadequate to rely on simple historical price relationships to properly analyze the fairness of the conversion premium level. That process is examined in detail beginning in Chapter 8.

## THE IDEAL CONVERTIBLE BOND

To illustrate the relationship between the conversion value and the investment value of the convertible bond, we will disregard many of the realities of the marketplace. Figure 2–4 shows the relationship between movements in stock price (horizontal axis) and their effect on the convertible bond's market price (vertical axis). The arrow indicates the ideal price at which this convertible bond may be purchased. At this price, if the stock increases in value, the convertible bond value will increase at the same percentage. On the other hand, if the common stock were to decline in value, the convertible bond would be supported by its investment value and would maintain its market value. The price movement is indicated by the hatched area in Figure 2–5.

In this simplified example, when the convertible bond is priced at this ideal point, it is obviously a superior buy because it offers the same upside potential as the common stock with none of the downside risk. The real world, of course, will not allow investors such easy profit opportunities. In the financial marketplace there exists a trade-off between the safety of the bond investment

**F I G U R E  2–5**

Ideal Convertible Bond

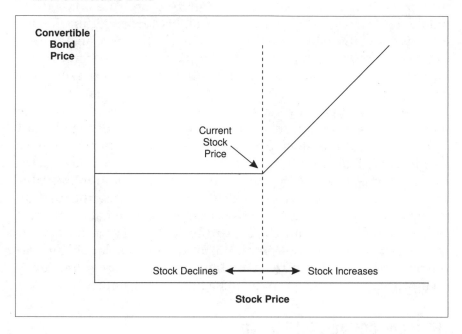

value and the opportunity of the conversion value. How much an investor is willing to pay for that trade-off creates a premium above conversion value, as well as a premium above investment value, and it becomes the most complicated aspect of convertible investing. A measure of that value is the convertible security's conversion premium.

There are two basic scenarios for holding a convertible bond. First, if the company stock does well, the convertible increases in value—and can increase greatly in value as a bond without equity conversion. Many investors who are new to convertibles don't realize that it is not necessary to convert to the underlying common stock to realize a profit. The market price of a convertible varies with changes in the stock price, and the bond can be sold at any time. The increased value of the stock will be reflected in the market price of the convertible. Of course, the bondholder also has the option to convert the bond into stock, although that is not necessary. Conversion occurs only at the request of the holder.

Second, if the stock does not do well, the bondholder retains the bond and collects the coupon interest (which is almost always higher than the stock dividend), and par value is repaid at maturity. When the stock stays flat or falls, the bondholder still retains the investment value of the bond, which constitutes a floor value for the security; in an adverse equity market, the bond will not decline in price as much as the underlying stock because of this investment value. Furthermore, if interest rates rise, the bond principal is protected to some extent by the convertibility feature.

Although simple in principle, convertibles can be complex to manage. The dual nature of convertibles—i.e., they have characteristics of both bonds and stocks—is part of what makes them so difficult to analyze, and the evaluation process must take both parts into consideration. However, their dual nature is also what makes them so attractive as an investment.

The investor can calculate the value of both the bond and the equity portions of the convertible security, but that still doesn't give the entire story. The final piece of the evaluation might be the hardest: pricing the security itself. The investor must determine the bond's theoretical fair value or normal expected price, the value at which it is fairly valued in the marketplace, taking into consideration both its bond and its equity value, as well as its call terms, volatility, and the term structure of interest rates. This theoretical fair value is then compared to the market price to determine profit opportunity and market advantage. The convertible can be over- or underpriced relative to the stock.

The investor must also evaluate how much the bond will rise or fall under different market scenarios. The risk/reward characteristics of the individual security depend on its value relative to its equity and bond values. This in turn determines the performance of both the security and the portfolio it is part of.

Since the concept of a convertible bond is easy for investors to grasp, some investors have tried to rely on simple rules of thumb in selecting convertibles. Examples of such rules are: "Buy converts only when the conversion premium is below 20 percent," or "Buy only when the time to break even is less than three years." However, the analysis of convertibles is not this simple. Strategies based on simplistic rules can only result in disappointing performance. The proper selection of convertibles requires careful analysis.

## AN EXAMPLE

To help clarify some of these concepts, we present a hypothetical example in the table below and graphically in Figure 2–6. Assume that a new-issue convertible has come to market. It has a 5 percent coupon and 10 years to maturity. The issuing company has other 10-year debt that carries an 8 percent yield, and the company's stock is currently trading at $42.

**XYZ Company**
Convertible Bond

| | |
|---|---|
| Coupon | 5% |
| Maturity | 10 years |
| Straight bond yield to maturity | 8% |
| Conversion price | $50/share |
| Current stock price | $42/share |
| Conversion ratio | 20 shares per bond |

**F I G U R E  2–6**

Hypothetical Convertible Bond

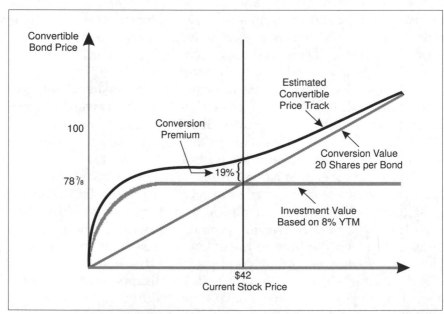

The bond indenture specifies a conversion price of $50. Since we know that the conversion price is the effective price for conversion into stock with the bond at par, we divide the par value of the bond ($1,000) by $50, resulting in a conversion ratio of 20 shares. To calculate the current conversion value, we know that the stock price is currently $42. Multiplying $42 by 20 shares, we get a current conversion value of $840. If the issue is sold at par, then the conversion premium would be 19 percent ([$1,000 – 840]/840). The investment value of the convertible at issuance would be the security with the 5 percent coupon discounted at a yield to maturity of 8 percent. The result, according to standard bond calculations, is 79.87, or a dollar value of $798.70. The investment premium would be 25.20 percent ([$1,000 – 798]/798).

# E N D N O T E S

1. Upon conversion, any accrued interest is lost. The arbitrageur must take that into account in determining the profit opportunity.

# 3

## CHAPTER

# Types of Convertible Securities

## CONVERTIBLE BONDS

In the first two chapters, we presented a brief overview of convertible securities, including their history, and discussed their general features. Chapters 3 through 7 will remain in this descriptive mode, as we consider the characteristics of convertible securities, including the various kinds of convertibles, certain legal characteristics and features, and characteristics of the global convertible markets. The analytic discussion that dissects the mathematics of convertibles begins in Part II with Chapter 8.

In this chapter, we describe some of the most common and basic types of convertible securities. However, even the most sophisticated and innovative Wall Street convertible derivatives discussed later in the book rely on an understanding of the general types of convertibles presented here. Like straight corporate bonds, convertible bonds can take the form of a coupon bond, a zero-coupon bond, or a discount bond.

## TRADITIONAL OR CLASSIC CONVERTIBLE BONDS

The conventional convertible bond is a coupon bond issued at par with a fixed-dollar amount of interest. It closely resembles a traditional bond and has a maturity date, coupon interest usually payable semiannually, principal repayment at maturity, and a credit rating. The one important difference is that the bond is convertible into stock at the bondholder's option. However, there are a number of variations on the most conventional type of convertible bond, and it is important to understand the characteristics and resulting advantages/disadvantages of each. We will talk about a few of them here and will discuss some of the more recent Wall Street innovations in later chapters.

## ORIGINAL-ISSUE DISCOUNT BONDS (OID)

Since 1980, the bond market has experienced a degree of innovation unprecedented in history. An outgrowth of that innovation is the original-issue discount (OID) bond, a bond issued at a discount well below its par value that gives investors a built-in capital gain if the bond is held to maturity. The return to the holder comes from the increase in principal value. The most extreme case of this issue is the zero-coupon bond, which is originally issued at 25, pays no interest, and matures at 100.

Corporations lost some of their incentive to issue OID bonds when the Internal Revenue Service and Congress closed the tax loopholes. When they were first used, the investors did not have to pay annual taxes on the increase in value (which was the imputed interest rate); rather, if the bond was held until maturity, the investor could choose to defer paying taxes until the bonds matured in 10 or 20 years, or until the investor sold or redeemed it prior to their final maturity date. Firms continue to issue OID bonds because they reduce the annual interest cost for the company, which in effect pays interest only at maturity when it redeems the bond. With a convertible, the interest rate associated with the discount may never have to be paid if the common stock increases above its conversion price and it becomes more advantageous to convert rather than to redeem the bond.

OID bonds have an additional complication for taxable investors. Since they are issued at a discount from par, the Internal

Revenue Service allows the corporation to deduct the discount amortized over the life of the bond even though the payment will not be made until maturity. This obviously gives corporations an incentive to issue discount bonds: The corporation essentially borrows money at no current cost because the whole payment is deferred into the future. However, individual investors do not fare as well with the IRS, which assumes the bond appreciates by a certain amount every year until maturity and requires the taxable investor to pay income taxes on the amortized amount even though no cash payments have been made. Adding to the confusion, the amortized amount has no relationship to the purchase price paid by the investor, but rather is determined at the time the bond is issued. If the investor sells the bond prior to maturity and for an amount greater than the cost basis, he or she must pay a capital gains tax or a tax at the ordinary income rate.

## CONVERTIBLE BONDS WITH PUT FEATURES

A further innovation of the 1980s was the convertible bond with a put. Under the terms of the offering, the holder can "put"[1] the bonds back to the corporation at a stated price on a specific date. This essentially means that the holder can be assured of the value of the bond on that date. The put is at the option of the holder and is for a much shorter time period than maturity date of the bond. It protects the holder against rising interest rates by effectively reducing the years to maturity. The issuer bases the put price on the cost of financing from the issue date to the date the bond can be put back to the company.

A good example of a security that is both an OID and a put bond is provided by a Liquid Yield Options Note (LYON), introduced by Merrill Lynch in 1985. To create LYONs, Merrill Lynch altered the standard convertible bond in two ways. First, the bonds were recreated as zero coupon bonds offered at a deep discount to face value. Second, investors were given a put option, which is exercisable on one or more future dates at a price equal to the original offering price of the LYONs plus the interest that accrues to the date of the put. The put or sell-back price is determined and listed in a schedule at the time of issue. Merrill Lynch's main purpose in creating LYONs was to reduce the downside risk of the security while at the same time keeping the equity participation of traditional convertible bonds. The issuer typically has the right to call the bonds for cash or stock in five years. From the corporation's point of view, the main reason to issue LYONs is to take advantage of a steep yield curve. The put price is based on a yield-to-maturity consistent with the time frame of the put. Therefore, companies can issue what is essentially longer-term debt at rates equivalent to those of short to intermediate time intervals.

For example, Motorola issued a LYON in September 1993 at a price of $639.23 with a final maturity date of September 2013. This bond is illustrated in Figure 3–1. The put feature allowed the holder to first put the bond back to the company at $714.90 after five years, which is an annualized yield of 2.26 percent—this put price was determined by a yield calculation based on the market's 5-year rate rather than the 20-year rate. This made the yield-to-first-put competitive with those of shorter-term money market instruments at that time, which saw the lowest rates since the inflation of the early 1980s. This bond would have a particularly low cost for the issuing company but also allows the bondholder to buy what might be viewed as a short-term convertible.

The risk/reward table in the lower half of the figure shows the investment potential of the Motorola zero coupon bond over the next 12 months. For example, for a 32 percent decline in the stock price, it is estimated that the bond price will decline only 1.4 percent, thereby demonstrating downside convertible participation of 4.3 percent. On the other hand, if the stock price rises 47.3 percent, the bond is expected to increase 23.4 percent in value, demonstrating upside participation of 49.4 percent.

Because of the put option at three or five years after issuance, the price of a LYON tends to be less sensitive to changes in interest rates than a long-term bond. This can provide substantial support to the security's price if the underlying stock's price declines or if interest rates rise (which would otherwise cause a long-term, zero coupon bond to fall in value). An investor can expect to earn at least a positive yield to the put date, assuming only that the issuer of the LYON remains solvent. The investment value of a LYON must take the put feature into account.

Although put features are used on convertibles in both the United States and international markets, they have become par-

**F I G U R E  3–1**

Motorola Inc. 0% Due 2013 LYON (Liquid Yield Option Notes)

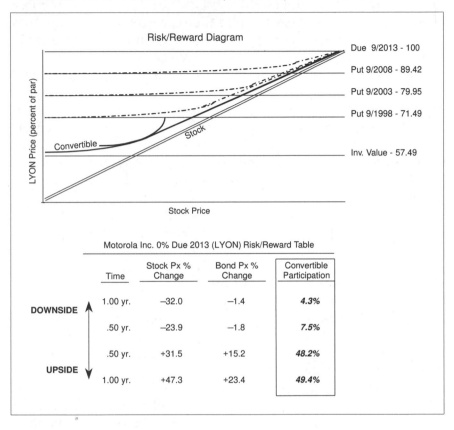

Risk/Reward Diagram

Due  9/2013 - 100

Put 9/2008 - 89.42

Put 9/2003 - 79.95

Put 9/1998 - 71.49

Inv. Value - 57.49

LYON Price (percent of par)

Convertible

Stock

Stock Price

Motorola Inc. 0% Due 2013 (LYON) Risk/Reward Table

|  | Time | Stock Px % Change | Bond Px % Change | Convertible Participation |
|---|---|---|---|---|
| **DOWNSIDE** | 1.00 yr. | −32.0 | −1.4 | *4.3%* |
|  | .50 yr. | −23.9 | −1.8 | *7.5%* |
|  | .50 yr. | +31.5 | +15.2 | *48.2%* |
| **UPSIDE** | 1.00 yr. | +47.3 | +23.4 | *49.4%* |

ticularly widely used in the Euroconvertible market. Several examples of put bonds are discussed later in this chapter in the section on Eurodollar convertibles.

## EXCHANGEABLE CONVERTIBLE BONDS

Convertible bonds may be issued by one company and converted into stock of another company. Such bonds are called exchangeable convertible bonds. This situation can occur if a company has acquired a large block of another company's common stock and wants to sell. By issuing a convertible bond on that block of stock, the corporation receives the proceeds immediately and may dispose of the stock at a premium above the current market value. The corporation does not establish a taxable event because in most cases it still owns the stock while the convertible is outstanding and therefore postpones any tax liability until the convertible bonds are actually converted. This may take a number of years, during which time the corporation has the full use of the proceeds.

Corporations issue exchangeable convertible bonds to postpone tax payments. The risk to the corporation is that the stock may stay below the conversion price and not be sold. However, the investor may be able to take advantage of some unusual convertible opportunities. The convertible bond rating depends on the credit of the issuing corporation rather than on the common stock into which it can be converted.

For example, IBM owned a block of Intel common stock for which it issued an exchangeable convertible bond. The investor purchasing this bond had a credit obligation guaranteed by IBM, but the value of the bond was determined by the stock performance of Intel Corporation, at the time a volatile growth company in the microchip industry. This convertible bond carried a coupon of 6.375 percent, was convertible into 26.143 shares of Intel common stock, and was rated AAA by Standard & Poor's. When Intel's common stock rose to $60 per share in October of 1987, the convertible had an intrinsic value of $1,568.86.

Exchangeable convertibles have offered some interesting investment opportunities. Investors often fail to notice such situations because the bonds are identified by the issuing company rather than the stock they can be converted into. Two good examples of exchangeables are General Motors Corporation (GM) and Pennzoil.

GM created a stock linked to Electronic Data Systems (EDS, a GM subsidiary) called GM class E stock (GME). Unlike regular common stock, which gives holders ownership in a company's assets, GME carried no ownership stake in EDS. GME was a GM common stock that paid a dividend based on EDS's profits. GM created the stock to give EDS employees and stockholders the opportunity to participate in something that looked like a growth company rather than a dull automaker. GME has been a resounding success for the company: It has increased over 700 percent since it was issued in 1984. It was finally called in early 1996.

1993 saw a good example of an exchangeable convertible bond. Pennzoil owned over 18,000,000 shares of Chevron common stock. Using this stock as collateral, Pennzoil issued over $902,000,000 worth of bonds convertible into Chevron. At issuance, Pennzoil immediately received the proceeds for selling the issues at a 21 percent premium over Chevron's current stock price, yet there was no taxable event until conversion. Furthermore, while waiting for the conversion, Pennzoil received $33.4 million annually in dividends from Chevron, of which 70 percent was excluded from taxes under the dividend received deduction (discussed in the next chapter). Each year, Pennzoil makes tax-deductible interest payments of approximately $48.75 million on the bonds of approximately $48.75 million per year.

In the case of the IBM bonds mentioned above, the issuer possessed the stronger credit rating than the company into which the bonds were convertible. In the Pennzoil transaction, Pennzoil's credit was weaker than Chevron's, which had an AA rating. The credit risk of the deal was that of Pennzoil, which was BBB, rather than that of Chevron, into which the bonds were convertible.

## CONVERTIBLES WITH RESET FEATURES

Reset features are used as sweeteners to help troubled companies sell their bonds. The reset feature allows for the adjustment of the coupon rate, conversion ratio, or maturity date if certain stipulated events occur. For example, this feature could be used to protect the bondholder's value if the stock has not performed as well as expected. Increasing the conversion ratio or the coupon would bolster the value of the bond. These bonds are often lower-grade, speculative issues.

A deal structured by Drexel Burnham Lambert for United Artists Communications in 1987 gave investors the protection of a reset and guaranteed long-term financing for the issuer. After a fixed period of time, the bonds were evaluated by an independent investment banker to determine a coupon rate that would allow the bonds to trade at 101 plus accrued interest. This adjustment to the coupon rate prevented the investor from losing principal if the stock price didn't perform as expected. It also prevented losses due to rising long-term interest rates because the reset occurred in only three years. However, since many companies that issue these types of bonds are highly leveraged, the investor should consider the financial status of the corporation.

The issuer finds reset features advantageous because they can help save interest costs and maintain long-term financing. This is important to an emerging company because its financing remains secure while allowing the terms of the financing to float with market conditions. In the case of United Artists, the company's cost of financing would have been 6⅜ percent for three years. It could have chosen instead to maintain fixed-rate financing with a higher coupon for the life of the maturity. The conversion premium on this issue was a high 31 percent, which also benefited the company.

In October 1995, Mitsubishi Bank issued a convertible with a reset feature. Mitsubishi brought to market $2 billion of seven-year bonds with a conversion feature that would make it difficult for them to trade below the offering price of par. The conversion ratio is reset annually, and it will offer investors more shares if the stock declines, with the goal of keeping the bonds' equity value at par. In contrast, the typical convertible falls in value if the underlying stock drops in price.

Mitsubishi Bank offered these terms because it wanted the convertible to be exchanged for stock, but the Japanese Ministry of Finance didn't want the company to issue stock. The deal was arranged with the underwriters to create a security that would, in the long run, almost certainly be converted. The risk/reward on the security was very favorable. The bank would certainly benefit from a strengthening Japanese economy. Meanwhile, the convertibles retained their value, even if the bank stock did not do well. This deal was seen as such a good one that it was significantly oversubscribed. Therefore it also sold out in one day—which is a big change from the much longer periods of time underwriters used to require to sell out a deal. The strength of interest also allowed the bank to lower the coupon rate to 3 percent.

## CONVERTIBLE BONDS WITH PREMIUM PROTECTION

Premium protection bonds, among the most recent innovations in the convertible market, were introduced by McMahan Securities Co., L.P. The holder who converts the security after a specified date will generally receive half of the coupon payments still remaining under call protection.

The premium protection preserves the value of the initial premium paid at issuance by making it very unlikely that the issuer will give an early call. It also addresses the fear that the conversion premium could evaporate as a result of the stock being unavailable for hedgers. Hedging provides liquidity in the marketplace and often keeps the convertibles trading at or near their fair value. If market makers and hedgers cannot borrow stock, issues often become illiquid. Protection against corporate actions is an additional feature of this convertible: The conversion premium is likely to retain its value even in the face of merger, acquisition, tenders, or other unforeseen events that can diminish the returns of convertible securities.

This works for both issuers and investors. The investor who converts before call protection expires will receive half of the coupons remaining, which halves the interest expense for the issuer. The issuer should be able to obtain advantageous terms at issuance because investors will find this feature attractive—it provides significant value protection for the investor. The premium protection convertible is likely to enhance returns for the convertible investor and make the issuer's financing even more cost-effective.

Although we are pleased to see this innovation, it has not been widely accepted in the marketplace. It will most likely be used by relatively small companies that need to offer investors additional incentive to provide capital.

## CONVERTIBLE PREFERRED STOCK

Convertible preferred stock, like nonconvertible preferred stock, is a class of the corporation's capital stock. Convertible preferred stocks have characteristics very similar to those of convertible bonds. The holder of a convertible preferred stock has the right to convert to a specified number of shares of the underlying common stock at any time. The relationship between changes in the stock price and the convertible price is the same for both convertible bonds and convertible preferred stocks. The convertible preferred has a specified dividend rate that is declared by the board of directors, usually quarterly. After the call protection expires, the company has the option of redeeming the issue at the stated par value or call price. Although the convertible preferred stock does not have a maturity date, it does grant the preference on earnings over that of the common stockholder. Also, preferred stocks are usually cumulative—the convertible preferred dividend will accumulate in arrears should the corporation be unable to make the payment. Convertible preferred shareholders often have the added protection of participating on the board of directors should any interest payments be missed. Warren Buffet's use of convertible preferreds allowed him to be active in the management of Salomon Brothers when it experienced financial difficulties.

## EXCHANGEABLE CONVERTIBLE PREFERRED STOCK

Exchangeable convertible preferred stock gives the company the additional option of exchanging the convertible preferred stock for convertible bonds. The terms of the exchange are stated at the time of issue and are at the original dividend rate of the preferred stock. It is advantageous for the company to exchange non-tax-deductible dividend cost for tax-deductible interest expense. The company may have issued the preferreds at a time when its balance sheet would not allow it to take on more debt without jeopardizing its credit rating. Exchangeable preferreds give the company additional flexibility to exchange preferred equity for debt at some point in the future.

For example, in February 1991, Cooper Industries, Inc. issued convertible exchangeable preferred stock. The issue had call protection through January 1, 1995. The holder could convert the preferred shares into common stock at a predetermined rate at any time. However, the issue was subject to call starting January 1, 1995, at which point a stockholder could either redeem the shares for cash or convert to stock. In addition, the company had the option of exchanging the preferred stock for convertible subordinated debentures.

## CONVERTIBLE MONEY MARKET PREFERREDS

Convertible money market preferreds are not of interest to convertible investors because they are not convertible into common stock. Corporations use them as an alternative to money market instruments. They are converted to a fixed number of dollars by varying the number of shares received by the holder. This is a fail-safe method for the holder to receive par value. Corporate investors use this vehicle as a short-term money market instrument to take advantage of the 70 percent dividend exclusion rule. (See Chapters 4 and 13.)

## EURODOLLAR CONVERTIBLE BONDS

The third-largest convertible market in the world is the Eurobond market, which consists of dollar-denominated bonds issued outside the United States. (We introduced the Eurobond market in Chapter 1.) Many of the largest domestic companies have issued convertible bonds in the Eurobond market. These bonds are dollar denominated and similar to the convertible bonds issued in the United States. For example, although the issues have generally been smaller in size than domestic issues, Texaco raised $1.5 billion by issuing two convertible Eurobonds in 1984. Because the bonds are not registered with the Securities and Exchange Commission, they cannot be purchased by U.S. investors until they become seasoned; the seasoning period is usually 90 days. A great many U.S. domestic companies have issued Eurodollar convertibles over the last 25 years, most of them since 1981.

Many of these issues are offered by foreign finance subsidiaries that are set up to market them. The parent company guarantees the payment of interest and principal, making the Eurobonds as safe as domestic issues.

However, investors should be aware that there are some differences. Eurodollar convertibles generally pay interest annually instead of semiannually. At issuance, both the coupon and the conversion premium may be lower than those of their U.S. counterparts, and many carry special features. In the past, Eurodollar convertibles were generally issued with shorter maturities and without the sinking funds that longer term issues might have. Many issues still have put features that allow investors to sell the bond back to the company at a price above par in five years. Others carried absolute call protection and short maturities, which, at that time, were unavailable in the domestic market. Today, Euros look very much like domestic issues because U. S. and European yield curves have tended to converge in recent years. Since many Eurodollar convertibles are issued by companies that do not have corresponding domestic issues, the Eurodollar convertible market offers wider investment alternatives.

Investing in Eurodollar convertibles used to be difficult for investors because many brokers were not equipped to handle the transaction. Brokers that are members of Euroclear (a European clearing firm) handle such trades as routinely as any domestic issue. It's easy for investors to overlook Eurodollar convertibles because of the difficulty in executing the transaction and the difference in terms, yet they are often attractively priced.

Investing in the international market has become such an important feature of the global convertible market that we have devoted Chapter 7 to a discussion of its characteristics.

## EUROBOND CONVERTIBLES WITH PUT FEATURES

In the past, investors in the Eurobond convertible market often seemed hesitant to purchase bonds with long maturities. This was undoubtedly due to the European experience of inflation and the disastrous effect it can have on long-term bond investments. To allay this fear, many convertibles are issued with a put feature that allows the bondholder to sell the bonds back to the company at par or a premium above par prior to maturity. Issuers in the Euro market have used the put features more extensively than those in the U.S. domestic market, and put features are very characteristic of some foreign markets.

Euroconvertibles can usually be put back to the company in three to seven years, so if the company's common stock does not rise in value over the life of the put, the investor is guaranteed a minimum return on investment. These minimum returns are usually in line with those on short-term money instruments at the time of issue.

An example of this was the Wyse Technology Eurobond offering on February 12, 1987, of $45 million, 6 percent convertible subordinated debentures due February 25, 2002. The prospectus stated that "each debenture may be redeemed, as a whole or in part, in increments of $1,000 on February 25, 1994, at the option of holders thereof at 100 percent of the principal amount to be redeemed plus interest accrued to the redemption date."[2]

Another popular structure is a bond with a put above par value. Renong Berhad, a Malaysian company, issued a bond with a 2.5 percent coupon with a yield-to-put at 7.5 percent and a put price of 129.7. The bond was issued in October 1994, and the first put was in October 1999. By issuing a 2.5 percent coupon, the company lowered its ongoing cost of debt. In the long run, the company is counting on bondholders converting their bonds to stock and not redeeming the bonds at the put price. The issue is attractive to bondholders because, even if the conversion turns out to be unprofitable, they are guaranteed a 7.5 percent return to the time of the put.

Another kind of put bond is known as a premium redemption; at maturity, the bond is redeemed for a price higher than par. Aegon N.V., an investment-grade insurance company based in the Netherlands, issued such a bond in October 1994. Maturity was 10 years. The coupon was 4¾ percent, paying annually, which is common in the Euro market. The redemption price was 138.9, rather than par. The uneven price was a result of the pricing process, where the underwriters wanted to set the price at 150 basis points over a Treasury bond of the same maturity. This is a common feature in emerging market convertible debt.

What is the point of issuing this kind of bond? It has several advantages for the company, among them a tax advantage should it have to redeem the bond at maturity. But the company fully expects that the bonds will be converted, not redeemed. The relatively low coupon on the Aegon issue is sweetened considerably by the yield-to-redemption, which at issuance was 7.5 percent. The high redemption value results in increased downside protection and lower downside risk since the higher redemption value keeps the bond's investment value high.

This structure can also be particularly useful in cases where stock dividends are high, which means the bond interest has to be even higher to maintain the income differential between the two instruments. If a stock is paying 4 percent, then a convertible bond at that rate or lower is less attractive. If the convertible offers a premium redemption above par, bondholders will be guaranteed a higher yield to maturity even if the coupon interest is as low as, or lower than, the dividend on the stock.

## CONVERTIBLE STOCK NOTES

Convertible stock notes are another variation of the convertible theme. Instead of paying interest and principal in cash, these notes pay in common stock or cash, at the issuer's option. They are sometimes referred to as pay-in-kind (PIK) securities and are designed to give issuers flexibility in managing cash flow. In cases where these issues are subordinated, most senior lenders view them as equity alternatives. Convertible stock notes are typically issued by troubled companies, so their yield cannot be readily compared to yields on other convertibles. As a group, these bonds trade flat—without accrued interest—and their market prices usually reflect an amount representing accrued interest since the last payment date. Even though this type of security is generally deeply subordinated, issuers are highly motivated to retire them because they are usually the most costly form of capital. They are found most often in private placements.

Companies facing bankruptcy often ask creditors to exchange debt for convertible stock notes. Since a company is in dire financial condition when negotiating these options, the bondholder often has little choice but to accept. Still, offers are made in an attempt to achieve a settlement that will be acceptable to the bondholders. It is important that the convertible investor evaluate the terms in detail before arriving at a decision to accept the offer.

One case in point is Anacomp. Facing bankruptcy in the mid-1980s, the company proposed to exchange the convertible 13⅞ percent bonds for convertible bonds with a higher conversion ratio and give the company the option of paying the interest in either common stock or cash. The conversion ratio on the new bonds was increased to 250 shares per bond from 57.143. As financial conditions improved and the stock recovered from $2 per share to $4, the new convertible bond with the higher conversion ratio increased from 50 to 100. In fact, as the stock recovered to $8 a share in mid-1987, the new convertible bonds had an intrinsic value of $2,000, or 200% of par. The common stock was still well below its former high. This points out the advantage of being a creditor rather than a shareholder when a company's fortunes change.

The original convertible bondholder of the Anacomp 13⅞ percent bond who did not accept the exchange offer did not fare as well. As the company's financial condition improved, the bond price returned to par; however, the high conversion premium and a conversion price of $17.50 left little room for much equity participation. However, the convertible investor in either case still fared a great deal better than the common stockholder.

As a general rule, exchange offers allowing for increased equity participation should be accepted by convertible bondholders, while offers to exchange convertible bonds for nonconvertible fixed-income securities should be declined. The latter usually have a higher yield factor to entice investors to accept the offer and give up equity participation.

While most convertible stock notes are negotiated as part of bankruptcy hearings, Bear, Stearns and Company managed the first public offering of convertible stock notes in August 1987. The offering for Tosco Corporation was part of the restructuring of $411 million in debt the troubled company owed to a group of banks. Structured as a private deal in December 1986, it carried registration rights that allowed investors to demand the securities be registered with the Securities and Exchange Commission and offered to the public after a certain period of time. The public offering occurred in August 1987 with a face value of $58.5 million, discounted to $640 per $1,000 note. The notes were convertible into 250 shares of common stock at a conversion price of $4. The notes paid 4 percent interest a year in stock, or 10 shares a year, so that upon maturity they would represent 300 shares. The issuer could call the issue for redemption at any time at 120 percent of principal plus accrued interest.

## ASSET-LINKED CONVERTIBLES

In the late 1970s and early 1980s, concerns about inflation became so pronounced that investors looked to metals to preserve their capital. Convertibles linked to metals combined the security of fixed income with convertibility into precious metal instead of common stock. These asset-linked convertibles were an extension of gold-linked certificates used in the past.

Commodities such as gold, silver, crude oil, and real estate were linked with a fixed-income instrument to provide the asset-

linked convertible issue. Each issue carried very specific requirements for converting to the commodity. For example, Sunshine
Mines issued a convertible bond with a 15-year maturity and an
8½ percent coupon, convertible into silver at $20 an ounce.[3] This
represented a 25 percent premium above the then-current market
price of silver. Others were issued by companies linked to oil and
real estate.

In Europe on June 10, 1987, Eastman Kodak Company issued
$130,000,000 of 9 percent notes, due in 1990, with 130,000 gold
warrants attached. Since this offering was not registered with the
Securities and Exchange Commission, U.S. investors could not
participate. The warrant entitled the holder to receive an amount
in U.S. dollars equal to the excess of the price of one troy ounce of
gold over the $470.60 strike price.

These securities were much more popular in the Eurobond
market than in the domestic market. As inflation leveled off from
its peak in the early 1980s, interest in asset-linked convertibles also
faded. A few of them are still available, most notably silver and
gold preferred issues from Freeport-McMoRan Copper and Gold
Inc., a subsidiary of an Indonesian company that engages in the
exploration, development, mining, and processing of copper, gold,
and silver. The gold issue came to market in 1993 with a 10-year
maturity, and at mandatory redemption in 2003, each share is convertible into the dollar-equivalent value of 0.10 ounces of gold.
Cumulative cash dividends are payable quarterly in an amount
equal to the dollar equivalent value of 0.000875 ounces of gold per
share. Similarly, the silver shares were issued in 1994 and also had
a 10-year maturity. Each share is convertible into the dollar-
equivalent value of 0.50 ounces of silver at the first call, beginning
in 1999, and cumulative cash dividends are payable quarterly in an
amount equal to the dollar equivalent value of 0.04125 ounces of
silver per share. The two issues between them have approximately
$332 million in shares outstanding.

## CONVERTIBLE MORTGAGES

A variation of the convertible theme has been applied to the real
estate market. In an attempt to entice investors to finance real estate projects, syndicators often package mortgages with equity

participation. Like public Real Estate Investment Trusts (REITs), these private issues hold little appeal for convertible investors. Although it hints at the hybrid nature of convertible securities, this investment tends to be illiquid, and equity participation in the real estate partnership is usually so slight as to be meaningless. Investors should compare and evaluate such limited partnerships units as they would any convertible issue. The most likely finding will be that the issue is extremely overvalued, with little chance for equity participation.

## E N D N O T E S

1. In this circumstance, to put a bond means to present it to the issuer for redemption, according to the terms of the bond indenture.
2. Prospectus dated February 12, 1987. Wyse Technology, $45,000,000, 6 percent convertible subordinated debentures due 2002. These securities were not offered in the United States or to any person who was a citizen, national, or resident thereof. U.S. citizens may purchase bonds after the seasoning period.
3. When convertible securities are linked to commodities, payouts (either coupon payments or conversion values) can be in either the commodity or its cash equivalent, depending on the structure of the particular convertible. It is more common to have the payout in cash.

# 4 CHAPTER

# Characteristics of Convertible Bonds

## CALL TERMS AND PROVISIONS

The call provision, which is standard in most bond indentures, is one of the most important features affecting the price of a convertible security. The issuing corporation retains the right to call the bond for redemption prior to final maturity. A call option gives the issuer a certain amount of control over the convertible issue. Call terms and provisions are outlined in the securities indenture and determined at or prior to issuance. The call terms typically indicate the circumstances under which the security can be called, the date, and the price. Call protection can be either hard or soft. Hard (or absolute) call protection protects the issue from being called for a certain period of time, no matter the circumstances. Soft (or provisional) call protection allows the issuer to call the security immediately under certain circumstances. Convertibles can be issued with either or both types of call protection.

When interest rates decline, issuers like to have the flexibility to be able to call an issue if they think they can refinance it more cheaply. This is true in general for all corporate bond issuers. Convertible issuers have other reasons for wanting a call option: Calling an issue forces bondholders to convert debt into equity, which can reduce debt levels and have a beneficial effect on the balance sheet.

While a corporation's preference is for the shortest possible call protection, giving it the maximum amount of control over the convertible bond, it is just the opposite for investors. Call protection acts to increase the value of the warrant feature of the convertible bond since it allows a longer period of time for the stock to increase in value and for the bondholder to convert the bond to stock at a profit. While waiting for the stock to increase in value, convertibles typically provide more income than the stock. Without call protection, this income stream could be called away at any time, making the convertible much less attractive. Provisional call protection helps ensures that the investor will receive a certain level of capital gain before the issue can be called.

There are trade-offs among all the features of a convertible bond issue: call protection, convertible premium, and yield. A bond with longer call protection will have a yield slightly below that of an otherwise comparable bond with shorter call protection because the bondholder will have a longer period of time to profit by an increase in stock value. An investor would expect a convertible with a higher conversion premium to have longer call protection, all else being equal, because the bond will need a longer period of time to become profitable for the bondholder. If a bond has relatively short call protection, the bondholder will demand a higher yield on the convertible to make sure the investment is profitable for the shorter period of time. Call protection helps ensure that a bond will retain its conversion premium no matter how much the price rises. In a sense, the call protection preserves the value of the equity option: As long as call protection is in force, no matter what the current level, the bond can still rise further. For example, the HFS convertible still had a 3 percent conversion premium even when its market price was 200 percent of par.

Before 1970, most convertibles did not have call protection. Wang issued a convertible in 1970 and called the issue before it paid a single interest payment. Institutional investors were furious. Although the convertible had increased in value due to the sharp increase in the value of the common stock, many felt that the 20 percent premium they paid at the time of issue entitled them to at least a few interest payments. This case and others brought enough pressure on underwriters to demand call protection. Initially, this was similar to call protection on straight corporate bonds, typically two to three years of full or absolute call protection, which guaranteed the holder at least two to three years of income, or absolute call protection, which guaranteed against a call for the life of the bond.

Soft call protection was introduced in 1982. This variation provided that the bond could not be called unless the underlying common stock increased to a certain level for 20 or 30 consecutive trading days. This level is typically defined as 140 to 150 percent above the conversion price. The underlying common stock would have to increase somewhere between 60 and 100 percent before the call could be effected. Most convertibles issued since 1982 have provisional call protection for two to three years, typically after hard call protection has expired.

## ANTIDILUTION CLAUSE

The antidilution clause protects convertible security holders by allowing the conversion ratio to be raised or lowered under certain conditions. Stock dividends and splits are the most common occurrences that result in an adjustment to the conversion ratio via the antidilution clause.

Since a large part of the value of a convertible is determined by the conversion feature, antidilution protection against corporate maneuvers to jeopardize this value is important. Most convertibles provide for protection against stock splits by adjusting the conversion ratio for the amount of the stock dividend in the proportional amount. For example, if the convertible had a conversion ratio of 30 shares per bond prior to a two-for-one split, the conversion ratio would become 60 shares per bond after the split. Convertibles with full dilution protection are protected against small stock dividends in the event of spin-offs if the company is acquired by another corporation. In other cases, investors are protected from a company diluting its value by issuing stock below book value.

In the 1970s, Commonwealth Edison issued a $1.96 convertible preferred with this type of protection. During the 1970s it issued stock below book value, so it had to increase the conversion ratio of the convertible preferred stock. The convertible preferred increased in value while the common stock fluctuated in a narrow range.

## TAKEOVER CLAUSES

Takeover clauses are notably missing from most convertible offerings. Although there is no particular reason that investors should be concerned about takeovers, there is always the possibility that a takeover could negate the convertibility feature if the takeover price were below the conversion price. An unexpected takeover bid can have the effect of eliminating any conversion premium.

## BONDHOLDER PROTECTION

The issue of bondholder protection has recently diminished somewhat in importance. It was extremely important during the merger mania of the 1980s, when negating the conversion value of convertibles became a common practice. Convertible bondholders pay for the right to convert to the common stock for a period of time. There have been a few alarming cases where the convertibility feature has been lost far short of the time stipulated in the trust indenture. Figure 4–1 shows a number of issues in which corporate managers negated the convertibility feature. Given the tremendous growth of the convertible market and the level of activity in mergers and takeovers at that time, it's not surprising that bondholders' rights were an important issue. Full dilution protection is not guaranteed;. the degree of protection varies widely from issue to issue, depending upon the ingenuity of corporate attorneys. Still, we should note that convertible bondholders generally fared well in takeovers. Furthermore, convertible bonds fared much better than their straight bond counterparts because most takeovers were accomplished by offering the takeover target shareholders a premium over the current market price, thus placing convertibles well above par.

A trust indenture, like many legal documents, is read most carefully by someone trying to evade its terms. This practice,

## F I G U R E  4–1

### Convertible Holders Hard-Hit in Takeovers during the 1980s

| Issue | Coupon/ Maturity | Conversion Price | Takeover Price/ Takeover Co./Date | $1,000 Bond Worth/ Convertible into % of Debentures | Bond Price Prior to Takeover Announcement |
|---|---|---|---|---|---|
| Knoll International | 9.88%* 8/15/2003 | $19.20 | $12.00 General Felt, Winter 1987 | $625.00 | $880.00 |
| Lieberman Enterprises | 7.62% 8/15/2005 | $21.00 | $20.50 Carolco Pictures in negotiations | $976.19 | NA |
| Big Three Industries | 8.50% 4/15/2006 | $43.50 | $29.00 Air Liquids, Fall 1986 | $666.70 | $980.00 |
| Energy Factors | 8.25% 12/15/2005 | $24.75 | $17.25 Silthe Energies proposal terminated, Summer 1987 | $696.96 | $870.00 |
| Miles Laboratories | 5.25% 4/01/1994 | $65.00 | $47.00 Rhinechen Labs, Winter 1979 | $722.86 | NA |
| Dorchester Gas | 8.50% 12/01/2005 | $34.48 | $22.50 Damson Oil, Summer 1984 | $625.55 | $720.00 |
| Healthcare USA | 8.2500 6/30/2003 | $19.80 | $13.50 Maxicare, Fall 1986 | $681.82 | $765.00 |
| Fibreboard | 6.75% 10/15/1998 | $18.50 | $17.00 Louisiana Pacific, June 1978 | $918.15 | NA |
| Fibreboard | 4.75% 10/15/1993 | $31.25 | $17.00 Louisiana Pacific, June 1978 | $544.00 | NA |
| Sprague Electric | 4.25% 10/01/1992 | $45.50 | $27.50 G.F. Technologies, Spring 1979 | $604.40 | NA |
| H.J. Wilson | 10.50% 5/15/2002 | $21.00 | $20.00 Service Merchandise, Spring 1985 | $952.38 | $950.00 |
| Van Dusen Air | 10.50% 8/01/2005 | $20.00 | $21.00 APL Limited Partnership, Winter 1986 | $1,050.00 | NA |
| Fruehauf** | 8.50% 4/15/2011 | $50.00 | $49.50 Asher Edelman, Fall 1986 | $1,085.00 | NA |
| Grunthal Financial | 7.50% 6/05/2011 | $10.00 | $9.50 Home Group, Summer 1987 | $950.00 | $1,000.00 |
| Mayflower | 7.88% 3/15/2006 | $32.50 | $29.25 Laidlaw Transportation, Summer 1986 | $900.00 | $1,000.00 |
| Crazy Eddie | 6.00% 6/15/2011 | $23.13 | $8.00 Entertainment Marketing pending | $345.94 | $620.00 |

* Bondholders' coupon raised to 9.875% from 8.12546.

** Bonds would have been convertible into $990 of debt, but poison pill raised value to $1,085

Source: Froley Revy Asset Management, Los Angeles, California; Calamos Asset Management, Inc., Naperville, Illinois. Reprinted with permission. *Pensions & Investment Age*, July 27, 1987.

which convertible traders aptly refer to as looking for the "screw" or "weasel" clause, has been at times alarmingly popular in corporate finance. For example, in 1983, Wal Mart called a large convertible issue for redemption on the day the full call protection expired, which was also the date on which the last coupon was to be paid. The call made sense since because the stock had risen dramatically over the past three years. Wal Mart may have a fine reputation for handling customers but with this episode, did not endear itself to the stockholders who provided capital for its expansion.

However, the enterprising treasurer informed holders that, based on a careful reading of the prospectus, the last coupon would not be paid. Obviously, bondholders would not redeem since conversion to stock was worth more than the redemption price plus interest. The prospectus stated that "conversion rights expire 15 days before the redemption date." Investors generally believed that the purpose of this clause was to limit the corporation's exposure to a sharp drop in the stock price, which would cause a redemption instead of a forced conversion. The prospectus also stated that "any debenture surrendered for conversion between a record date and the next interest payment date must be accompanied by an amount equal to the interest payable on that date." In effect, in order to convert, the holder had to give up the six-month interest payment.

There are several ways to prevent this problem from recurring. The most important is to constantly remind investors to read all the clauses of the bond indenture extremely carefully—as carefully as the attorneys of the issuer. A prospectus is the most convenient source of information on the specific terms of a convertible bond.

Institutional investors are the major purchasers of new issue convertibles, and they can put pressure on investment bankers to add protective clauses to the indenture to provide protection in the case of a leveraged buyout or other takeover. This protection could take the form of having the bond called immediately at the next call price plus some conversion premium. This would offer some protection to the bondholder who had, in good faith, accepted a lower coupon for equity participation. A takeover or leveraged buyout that eliminates the bondholders' equity participation cheats those bondholders; stockholders benefit without compensating the bondholders. After all, the bond was issued by the corporation with a conversion premium of 20 to 30 percent. The conversion premium could be amortized to the first call price, and a schedule easily provided for in the prospectus. This would be appropriate for a leveraged buyout or other takeover. The group assuming control should accept the cost of paying fair value for the convertibles regardless of the takeover details.

This type of protection was offered in a convertible bond underwritten by McMahan Securities in June 1996. The Keg Energy Group 7 percent of 2003 bond provides for payment of half of the remaining call-protected coupons to the holder who converts the security after a specified date. Thus it protects the investor from having the initial premium that he paid evaporate during the first few years of issuance. This addressed the convertible investor's concern about premium contractions caused by the potential difficulty in borrowing the underlying shares of common stock, tender offers, mergers, and a host of other unforeseen events that can diminish the returns of convertible securities.

In recent years, the change-of-control clause called the "poison put" was added as protection. This feature is triggered as a result of a hostile takeover and would allow the holder of the convertible bond to put the bonds back to the company at par. This would offer some safety for bonds trading at a discount from par.

Increased protection for bondholders could be provided through changes to the Trust Indenture Act, although one imagines the difficulty of passing that kind of technical legislation. Nonetheless, those of us involved with convertibles should pursue this avenue as part of our long-term commitment to the convertible market. If these changes were made, would they decrease the number of new issues coming to the market? A corporate treasurer who decided not to issue a convertible because of this added protection would be admitting that the corporation might be interested in trying to negate the conversion rights in the future, and we doubt that there are many who would do that.

Unfortunately for bondholders, U.S. courts interpret their rights as a contract and reject the position that corporations owe a fiduciary duty to bondholders. In fact, one could argue that the firm's fiduciary duty to shareholders is to maximize their value, and taking advantage of the bondholders, or at least minimizing the value delivered to them, serves that purpose. However, in the long run, shareholders do not serve their own interests by cheating bondholders who might be needed to buy more debt at some point in the future. In any event, it is to be hoped that sufficient protection can be assured to bondholders while also allowing corporations to meet their financing needs through the use of convertible debt. Chapter 17 discusses the use of convertibles from the issuer's point of view.

## SENIORITY STATUS

Since a convertible bond is considered to be a fixed-income instrument, it is senior to common stock on the books of the issuing company. It may or may not be junior to other debt, depending on the structure of the issuer. Typically, convertible bonds are debentures and junior to other debt on the books of the corporation.

## PAR VALUE

Par value is the face value of the security. Bonds are typically issued at $1,000 par value, and interest on bonds is stated as a percentage of par value (for example, 6 percent). Eurobonds often trade in denominations of $5,000 and often pay only annual interest. Preferred stocks also have par values, and their dividends are also expressed as a percentage of par value.

## CONVERTIBLE SECURITIES QUOTATIONS

Convertible bonds and convertible preferred stocks are quoted in the financial journals. Unlike the European financial press, which lists convertibles in a separate section, convertibles in the United States are mixed in with other securities, making it a bit difficult for investors to locate specific securities. Convertible bonds can be listed on the New York Stock Exchange, American Stock Exchange, regional exchanges, or traded in the NASDAQ over-the-counter market. In *The Wall Street Journal* and other financial publications, convertible bonds listed on the exchanges are distin-

*The Wall Street Journal,* Bond Listings—Monday, March 11, 1996

# New York Exchange Bonds

| Bonds | Curr Yld | Vol | Close | Net Chg |
|-------|------|-----|-------|-----|
| AMR 61/824 | cv | 10 | 111 | - 1/2 |
| ATT 43/498 | 4.8 | 73 | 98 | - 3/4 |
| ATT 43/899 | 4.6 | 30 | 961/4 | - 1/8 |
| ATT 6s00 | 6.1 | 182 | 991/8 | - 3/4 |
| ATT 71/802 | 6.9 | 16 | 1023/4 | - 17/8 |
| ATT 63/404 | 6.7 | 137 | 1001/2 | - 11/2 |
| ATT 7s05 | 6.9 | 135 | 1013/8 | - 23/8 |
| ATT 71/206 | 7.1 | 5 | 1061/8 | - 1 |
| ATT 73/406 | 7.2 | 20 | 107 | - 23/4 |
| ATT 81/822 | 7.9 | 914 | 1023/4 | - 21/8 |
| ATT 81/824 | 7.8 | 160 | 1041/8 | - 15/8 |
| ATT 85/831 | 8.0 | 283 | 1073/4 | - 11/2 |
| Aames 101/202 | 10.1 | 12 | 104 | - 1 |
| Advst 9s08 | cv | 21 | 102 | - 1/2 |
| AirbF 63/401 | cv | 16 | 102 | - 13/4 |

guished from nonconvertible corporate bonds by the designation of "cv" in the current yield column. Figure 4–2 shows *The Wall Street Journal* listing for bonds on Monday, March 11, 1996. It identifies the specific issue along with the name of the company, the coupon rate, and maturity date. Also listed is the current yield, the sales volume for that day, the closing price, and the net change from the previous day. Like all corporate bonds, convertible bonds are quoted as a percentage of par. Therefore, the $1,000 par value is always quoted as 100. The AMR convertible bond closed at 111, or $1,110.00 per bond. This book uses the convention of pricing bonds as a percentage of par.

The fact that Investor's Business Daily lists convertible bonds separately makes it much easier to find and price them. A section from that publication for Monday, March 11, 1996, is reproduced

F I G U R E  4–3

**F I G U R E  4–3**

*Investor's Business Daily,* Listing of Convertible Bonds—Monday, March 11, 1996

## Super Convertible Bond Tables

| S&P Rates | Convertible Bond | Exch | Coupon Rate | Mat- ures | Curr. Yld. | Yld. to Mat. | Vol. | Bond Close | Chg. | Conv. Price | Stk. Close | %Prem (Disc) |
|---|---|---|---|---|---|---|---|---|---|---|---|---|
| BBB- | Leucadia | NY | 5.500 | 02/03 | 5.3 | 5.0 | 10 | 103 | -1/4 | 28.75 | 251/4 | 17.3 |
| NR | MacNeal | Am | 7.875 | 08/04 | 7.3 | 6.7 | 10 | 1071/2 | -21/2 | 15.15 | 137/8 | 17.4 |
| B | Magnetek | NY | 8.000 | 09/01 | 8.9 | 10.4 | 8 | 90 | -1/2 | 16.00 | 71/4 | 98.6 |
| B | MarshMkt | O | 7.000 | 02/03 | 7.0 | 7.1 | 44 | 991/2 | -1/2 | 15.50 | 121/4 | 25.9 |
| BB- | Mascotch | NY | 4.500 | 12/03 | 5.8 | 8.6 | 7 | 77 | -11/2 | 31.00 | 125/8 | 89.1 |
| BBB | MascCorp | NY | 5.250 | 02/12 | 5.4 | 5.4 | 1 | 98 | ... | 42.28 | 283/8 | 46.0 |
| NR | Maxtor | O | 5.750 | 03/12 | 7.8 | 8.8 | 30 | 74 | -11/2 | 40.00 | 65/8 | 346.8 |
| B- | Maxxim | NY | 6.750 | 03/03 | 6.0 | 4.7 | 50 | 112 | -2 | 18.00 | 183/8 | 9.7 |
| CCC+ | Mediq | Am | 7.500 | 07/03 | 8.8 | 10.4 | 17 | 851/2 | +1/2 | 15.30 | 93/4 | 34.2 |
| NR | MensWrhs | O | 5.250 | 02/03 | 5.2 | 5.1 | 100 | 101 | -1 | ... | ... | ... |
| NR | Mercury | Am | 7.750 | 02/06 | 7.3 | 6.8 | 6 | 1061/2 | -1/2 | ... | ... | ... |
| CCC | Micropolis | O | 6.000 | 03/12 | 12.9 | 14.8 | 35 | 461/2 | -1/2 | 48.50 | 2.10 | 875.2 |

in Figure 4–3. It lists the Standard & Poor's bond rating, the specific issue, the exchange on which the issue is traded, the coupon rate, the date the bond matures, the current yield, the yield to maturity, the sales volume for that day, the closing price, the net change from the previous day, the conversion price, the closing price for the company's underlying stock, and the percentage premium or discount. (i.e., conversion premium).

Convertible preferred stocks are also listed in the financial press. Unlike the bond listings, there is no way to distinguish between convertible preferreds and straight preferreds. All preferreds are identified by the dividend rate. If there are multiple issues by a company, a letter designation is used. In Figure 4–4, The Travelers Inc. has three preferreds listed: preferred A with a $2.03 dividend, preferred B with a $2.75 dividend, and preferred D with a $2.31 dividend. There is nothing to indicate that the preferred B is a convertible preferred.

Volume is indicated in the financial press along with the current quotation. These statistics are based on bonds traded on the floor of the New York Stock Exchange. Although this is a mean-

## F I G U R E  4-4

*The Wall Street Journal,* Listings of Preferred Stocks—Monday, March 11, 1996

| NEW YORK STOCK EXCHANGE COMPOSITE TRANSACTIONS | | | | | | | | | | | |
|---|---|---|---|---|---|---|---|---|---|---|---|
| **52 Weeks** | | | | | **Yld** | | **Vol** | | | | **Net** |
| **Hi** | **Lo** | **Stock** | **Sym** | **Div** | **%** | **PE** | **100s** | **Hi** | **Lo** | **Close** | **Chg** |
| 151/8 | 103/4 | TansTech | TT | 0.26 | 1.9 | 14 | 270 | 14 | 133/4 | 133/4 | - 1/4 |
| 701/2 | 365/8 | **Travelers** | TRV | .90f | 1.4 | 11 | 20164 | 651/4 | 611/8 | 631/4 | - 4 |
| 263/8 | 243/8 | Travelers pfA | | 2.03 | 8 | ... | 119 | 251/2 | 251/4 | 251/2 | - 1/8 |
| 951/4 | 56 | **Travelers pfB** | | 2.75 | 3.2 | ... | 464 | 887/8 | 86 | 86 | - 55/8 |
| 267/8 | 251/2 | Travelers pfD | | 2.31 | 9 | ... | 101 | 257/8 | 253/4 | 253/4 | - 1/4 |
| **33** | 83/8 | **Travelers wt** | | | ... | ... | 1809 | 291/2 | 245/8 | 271/4 | - 31/2 |
| s  261/8 | 123/4 | Tredegarlnd | TG | 0.24 | 1 | 13 | 63 | 233/4 | 231/4 | 231/4 | - 3/8 |
| 263/4 | 111/4 | Tremont | TRE | | ... | 33 | 27 | 243/4 | 241/4 | 241/4 | - 3/8 |
| 25 | 201/2 | TriContl | TY | 2.74e | 11.7 | ... | 1279 | 237/8 | 233/8 | 231/2 | - 1/2 |
| 36 | 311/4 | TriContl pf | | 2.50 | 7.1 | ... | 15 | 351/4 | 35 | 35 | - 5/8 |
| 163/4 | 91/2 | Triarc A | TRY | | ... | dd | 395 | 123/4 | 121/4 | 123/8 | - 1/2 |
| 69 | 533/4 | Tribune | TRB | 1.20f | 1.8 | 16 | 2280 | 671/4 | 655/8 | 655/8 | - 2 |

ingful indication of the volume of securities traded in that specific issue, the volume given in the bond pages does not necessarily reflect the actual volume of bonds traded in the larger institutional market. Furthermore, the NYSE's nine-bond rule requires that orders for nine bonds or fewer be sent to the floor for one hour to seek a market. This is the bond market's equivalent of odd-lot trading. It means that a certain percentage of bonds traded on the floor will be in very small quantities, and the trading statistics (price and commission) will not necessarily reflect the much larger institutional trading.

Thus, bond trading, which is largely an institutional activity, tends to be inactive on the NYSE, so most bond trades are handled in the over-the-counter market. Convertible bonds follow this trend, and most convertible bond trading is done away from the exchange in a very active dealer market. Investors trading convertibles must deal with brokers who are knowledgeable and have access to this dealer network.

For this reason and others, price quotes in the financial press do not always accurately reflect the actual market for a particular convertible security. This is an important fact not only when buying or selling convertibles, but also in determining current market prices for portfolio evaluation. The professional services that sell prices to consultants for portfolio evaluation often misprice convertibles. Convertibles need to be priced carefully because their value can change without a bond being traded. The price of a convertible security is partially determined by changes in the underlying common stock. If the stock has made a significant change, the convertible's true value has changed, whether or not bonds have traded.

## COMMISSIONS

Commissions for convertible bonds are competitive and negotiable, and vary from firm to firm. Most bonds are sold on a principal basis, meaning that convertible dealers are making markets and trading from their own account. It is irrelevant to the investor whether the dealer is making a profit. What matters is that the price of the security being traded reflects its current market price. The actual commissions on principal trades are not easily determined. In an agency trade, a firm acts only as a broker and has arranged the transaction between buyer and seller (a broker never owns the security; in a principal trade, on the other hand, the dealer first buys and then sells the bond). Commissions on an agency trade are indicated on the confirmations of sale or purchase and vary with the number of bonds being traded. Convertible bond commissions usually fall under the corporate bond commission schedule.

Convertible trades usually have commissions that are far lower as a percentage of assets than those for similar common stock strategies. Since the convertible is technically a fixed-income instrument, it will trade with fixed-income commissions, which are typically much lower than stock commissions. Yet the convertible has an equity value. Each convertible bond represents a certain quantity of stock. If the investor were to buy a quantity of stock equal to that represented by the convertible, it would cost him or her significantly more. Therefore, investors employing convertibles as an alternative to common stock will substantially reduce their trading costs. With convertibles, it is especially important to have knowledgeable brokers executing trades. Proper execution, a feel for the market, and knowledge of the inventory flows in the dealer network are more important factors in successful trading than discounted commissions.

## MARGIN REQUIREMENTS

Convertible securities can be purchased on margin. A margin account at a brokerage firm allows customers to buy securities with money borrowed from the broker. Margin accounts are governed by Regulation T of the Federal Reserve Board, by the National Association of Securities Dealers (NASD), by the New York Stock Exchange, and by individual brokerage house rules. The required margin on convertible securities is currently 50 percent. However, there are special convertible arbitrage circumstances where the margin requirement can be reduced to as little as 10 percent.

## TAX TREATMENT OF CONVERTIBLES

The current tax treatment for convertibles is a result of the Taxpayer Relief Act of 1997. In the past, convertible strategies have been used effectively to make the most of the tax code. For those seeking capital gains or income, convertibles are a suitable investment from a tax treatment point of view. However, there are certain factors investors need to be aware of.

### Capital Gains

Convertibles are like other securities in that increases in their principal value are taxed as capital gains. Long-term capital gains are subject to a maximum 28 percent rate. Whether or not there is a distinction between short- or long-term gains, the investor must keep records showing the holding period. Any trade closed within one year or less is considered a short-term capital gain. The Taxpayer Relief Act of 1997 allows a taxpayer with a net capital gain to separate it into three groups:

- *28% group:* includes capital gains and losses, for assets held for more than one year, taken into account before May 7, 1997, or after July 28, 1997. This category also includes long-term capital-loss carryovers.

- *25% group:* includes long-term capital gains attributable to prior depreciation on realty; does not apply to securities.

- *20% group:* encompasses net capital gain from capital assets held more than one year (if taken into account after May 6 but before July 29) or, if taken into account after July 28, more than 18 months.

The new rules regarding net capital allow taxpayers to reduce net gains in each group in descending order against net short-term losses. Therefore, gains in the highest-rate group are offset before gains in the lower rate groups. A similar pattern applies to net losses from each of the long-term categories.[1]

Converting a convertible security to the underlying common stock is considered a nontaxable exchange and therefore not a taxable event. Investors are often confused by this. In this case, the holding period of the stock begins when the convertible security is purchased, and the cost basis is the purchase price of the convertible security. Upon conversion to stock, any accrued interest will be lost. This presents a very simplified view of this issue, and an investor who wishes to know more should consult his or her tax advisor.

One way to capture the accrued interest on the convertible bond and still affect a sale of the bond prior to the payment date is to sell an equivalent amount of stock short against the convertible bond. Much like being short against the box, this technique has the advantage of locking in the profit and obtaining the accrued interest. It is used when the convertible's market price is slightly below its conversion price, which often happens when convertibles trade in ranges above 150. Most bond specialists feel they're entitled to a risk-free profit for handling the entire transaction. A bondholder can prevent this by simply selling the stock short (no uptick is required because conversion will be made) and holding the short sale until the interest payment date. At that time he would convert the bond into stock and deliver that stock against the short sale. For tax purposes, the short sale constitutes the actual selling date and determines the holding period.

Tax issues are complex, and again, we recommend that an investor consult with a tax advisor.

## Interest

Convertible bond coupon interest is taxable income to individual and corporate investors. Like all corporate bonds, convertibles trade with accrued interest. Domestic convertible bonds typically pay interest twice a year, while Euroconvertible bonds pay interest once a year. Individual investors must be careful in determining the amount of interest paid at the end of the year for tax purposes. A problem often arises in computing the amount of interest received and the amount reported. For example, if an investor buys a bond with coupon payment dates of June 30 and December 30, and the settlement date for the trade is December 28, the investor would have to pay accrued interest from June 30 until December 28. On December 30, the investor would receive the full six month's interest. The investor earns interest only for the length of time he or she owned the bond, which is three days. However, either the company or the stockbroker will send the investor a 1099 tax statement showing he received a full six months of interest, which is also reported to the Internal Revenue Service. To prevent paying taxes on the unearned interest portion, the accrued interest paid must be shown as a deduction from the total interest received.

## DIVIDEND RECEIVED DEDUCTION

Under current federal tax law, C corporations that invest in the stock of other corporations can exclude from their federal taxes 70 percent of the dividends received from those stock investments. This favorable treatment of intercompany dividends is commonly referred to as the dividend received deduction, or DRD. Investments such as convertible preferred stock and preferred stock are generally considered "DRD eligible." For a company in the 35 percent corporate tax bracket, the tax advantage of the DRD allows approximately 90 cents of every dividend dollar to flow to its after-tax income, compared to only 65 cents of every interest-income dollar. In other words, due to the DRD, the effective tax rate on intercompany dividends is only 10.6 percent. As a result, to calculate a pre-tax-equivalent rate for a corporate bond, an investor can multiply the preferred stock (or convertible) yield by 1.3769, assuming a 35 percent corporate tax bracket. Therefore, a 7 percent yield on a tax-advantaged preferred stock equates to a 9.63 percent yield on a fully taxable corporate bond. Figure 4–5 shows a sample calculation for a DRD security. A company can invest in common stocks, preferred stocks, or convertible preferred stocks and receive the DRD. A corporation typically issues preferred stocks to maximize the tax-advantaged yield, and convertible preferreds can provide a balance between yield and equity participation for total return.

The favorable after-tax returns from the DRD have led to a practice of "dividend stripping." A corporation purchases the stock of another company just prior to the ex-dividend date and then, after qualifying for the dividend, sells the stock. The Taxpayer Relief Act of 1997 now requires a 45-day rule to be applied

**F I G U R E  4–5**

Sample Calculation for a Dividend Received Deduction

---

**Dividend Received Deduction:**
**Sample Preferred Security**

**After-tax Yield Calculation**
    7.00%  Current yield*
−  4.90%  Tax-excluded portion (70%)
    2.10%  Taxable portion
×    35%  Corporate tax rate**
    0.74%  Actual tax portion

    7.00%  Current yield*
−  0.74%  Actual tax portion
    6.26%  After-tax yield

**Equivalent Pre-tax Yield = 9.63%**
    6.26% / 65% = 9.63%
    (65% represents the net earnings after deduction of the
    35% corporate tax rate.)  In addition, this pre-tax
    equivalent can be obtained by multiplying the security's
    current yield by 1.3769.

**Assumptions:**
    *Current yield of the hypothetical preferred security:  7.00%
    **Corporate tax rate:  35%

on a dividend-by-dividend basis. Prior to the new law, after a 45-day holding period was established, the corporation could fully hedge the security and still receive the benefit of DRD.

## WITHHOLDING FOR NONRESIDENT ALIENS

Convertible bonds can represent a significant investment opportunity for nonresident aliens of the United States. IRS Code Section 871(h) states that all nonresident aliens purchasing fixed-income securities issued after July 18, 1984, are exempt from the 30 percent withholding requirement on earnings. The interest from convertible securities is therefore not subject to withholding requirements, and yet the convertible has the upside potential of an equity investment. This represents a significant opportunity for nonresident aliens to earn above-average total returns compared to other fixed-income instruments.

## COMMENTS ON COMMISSIONS, TAXES, AND MARGIN

Frequent changes in the tax code, margin requirements, and commission rates among brokers cause these factors to remain in a constant state of flux. Investors can obtain current information on commissions and margin requirements from their brokers, but they should seek expert advice in handling complex tax calculations.

We will ignore the effect of taxes and commissions in the remainder of this book. In sections on convertible strategies, we will disregard the expense of commissions for executing transactions because an all-inclusive statement as to their amount cannot be made. However, investors must take these factors into account when evaluating an opportunity.

### Investment Returns and Taxes

Managing an investment program for specific tax purposes is often difficult. Choosing securities that qualify for a taxpayer-specific purpose often results in securities that are chosen solely to satisfy those requirements rather than because of investment merit. It is not a simple manner to satisfy both tax issues and investment criteria. For example, the advantage of obtaining a long-term capital gain may result in holding on to an inferior position while awaiting the time to elapse to take advantage of the favorable tax treatment on long-term capital gains. Considering the vagaries of the financial markets, a potential long-term gain may become a long-term loss.

Corporations seeking the DRD have a limited universe from which to select convertible preferreds. They often forego excellent opportunities in convertible bonds with high potential for total return in an effort to save some tax dollars.

Individual investors with a myopic focus on taxes may view the interest income from convertibles as less attractive than a stock that pays no dividend. Their erroneous conclusion is that the stock will have the potential for all of the gain to be taxed as long-term capital gain rates. A benefit of convertible investing is the downside protection afforded in volatile markets by the convertible's fixed-income characteristics. Interest income and principal protection go hand-in-hand in providing the basis of wealth creation in volatile markets. Our view is that markets will continue to be as volatile in the future as they have been in the past. An investor making an assumption that a security, if held long enough, will result in a long-term capital gain is making a tremendous leap of faith.

For convertible investors, the investment objective should be to seek the highest total return without regard to the tax consequences. Some tax planning near the end of the year can be accomplished without disturbing the investment merits of the portfolio. However, managing risk is the foundation of wealth creation in volatile markets.

# E N D N O T E S

1. Robert Willens, CPA, Lehman Brothers; *Tax and Accounting*, October 27, 1997, Volume 10, Issue 107 (October 27, 1997).

# 5

CHAPTER

# New Convertibles:
# Equity-Linked Securities

The innovative financial engineering of Wall Street has created securities with names such as DECS, ELKS, MIPS, PERCS, and PRIDES, among others.[1] As investment bankers anxiously coin acronyms, they add more confusion to what are already complex securities. These new securities fall into the general category called equity-linked securities. LYONs do not belong grouped in with these securities because they are a traditional convertible bond in a zero-coupon structure. (LYONs are discussed in Chapter 3.)

This large and growing market has brought to market more than 64 public equity-linked security deals, with a market value of $19.5 billion at end of 1996. Equity-linked securities are not a fad. The increasing sophistication of investors and their greater capacity to understand and accept complex securities means that the use of these securities should continue to expand. These instruments have certain risk characteristics as stand-alone investments. When added to a portfolio, they may alter the risk characteristics of the portfolio as a whole. It is therefore important for the investor to understand how they are used and when they may be appropriate for inclusion in a portfolio.

Each type of equity-linked security has its own legal structure and unique risk and reward characteristics. They have all essentially been derived from the classic convertible bond. Equity-linked securities trade off the various characteristics of a convertible in order to satisfy a particular need of an issuer or a specific class of investors. Sometimes higher yield is achieved by capping the upside potential. In other cases, the security will offer good upside potential and a handsome yield but will also include almost all of the downside of the stock, making it inherently less conservative. Many paths of innovation have grown from the traditional convertible structure.

The investor must analyze each trade-off in the equity-linked security's design. The basic premise of the analysis is that there is no free lunch. To get a higher yield, the investor gives up some of the upside potential and accepts downside risk greater than that of a traditional convertible. The investor must decide whether the trade-off results in a security that is fairly priced and attractive, given the investor's portfolio objective.

Before reviewing the investment characteristics of these securities in more detail, consider the simplified payoff profiles shown in Figures 5–1a and 5–1b. These graphs are simplified versions of the graphs introduced in Chapter 2. Almost all convertible hybrids can be understood by referring back to the basic underlying structure of a convertible security. The foundation begins with the payoff graph of common stock and a traditional bond, as shown.

The risk/reward of common stock is one for one. An increase in the price of the stock results in a return on investment in direct relationship to the increase in the stock price. As Figure 5–1a illustrates, a gain of 50 percent in the stock price provides a return on investment of 50 percent. A decrease of 50 percent in the stock price would result in a negative return of 50 percent.

In this simplified example, the change in stock price relative to that of a straight corporate bond is shown in Figure 5–1b. As stock prices change, the corporate bond price remains the same and is influenced by fixed-income factors like creditworthiness and interest rates rather than changes in stock prices.

An equity-linked security or derivative security alters the basic payoff relationship. As we have discussed in previous chapters,

**F I G U R E  5–1a**

Simplified Payoff Profile of Common Stock

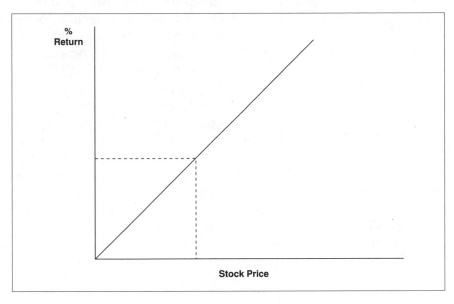

**F I G U R E  5–1b**

Simplified Payoff Profile of a Traditional Bond

combining a stock with a corporate bond creates the convertible bond payoff graph, which is shown in Figure 5–2. Notice that as the stock increases in price, the convertible bond price also rises. However, a decreasing stock price will result in a decline in the value of the convertible bond only to its investment value, as shown by the horizontal line. When confronted with complex equity-linked securities, it is useful to keep the payoff graph relationships in mind to determine the risk/reward.

At this point, the risk/reward of the common stock is one for one. An increase in risk causes an equivalent increase in price. For the bond, an increase in risk has essentially no effect on the value of the bond.

A convertible bond's payoff profile is a combination of the stock and the bond profiles, as shown in Figure 5–2. As we begin to look at the various hybrid financial securities that have been derived from the traditional convertible, keep in mind what the profile of the traditional convertible looks like. The convertible's risk/reward profile is favorable; it possesses the capital appreciation potential of the stock, with limited downside.

Mandatory convertibles (ACES, DECS, MARCS, PEPS, PRIDES, SAILS, and STRYPES) have an enhanced equity character (Figure 5–3). Notice that risk and return are similar to those of common stock, although the investor gives up some potential for capital appreciation in exchange for a higher current yield. There is also no downside protection.

Other modifications were preferred equity redemption cumulative stock (PERCS) and equity-linked notes (CHIPS, ELKS, PERQS, YEELDS). The payoff graph for these securities is shown in Figure 5–4. In exchange for a higher dividend, a portion of the capital appreciation is capped and there is no downside protection. There is no downside protection due to the mandatory conversion to stock.

## MANDATORY CONVERTIBLES

Mandatory convertibles have demonstrated steady growth within the overall convertible market since the first securities of this kind were issued in 1991. As of December 31, 1996, they represented 19.5 percent of total convertible market value, up from 9.8 percent

## F I G U R E 5–2

### Simplified Payoff Profile for a Convertible Bond (Combination of Stock and Bond)

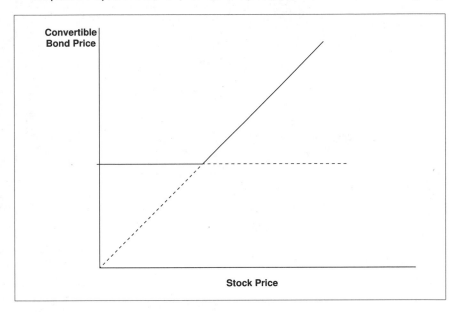

## F I G U R E 5–3

### Simplified Payoff Profile for Mandatory Convertible

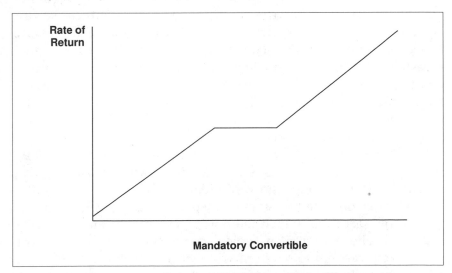

In an exchange for a higher dividend, a portion of the potential capital appreciation is sacrificed.

**F I G U R E  5–4**

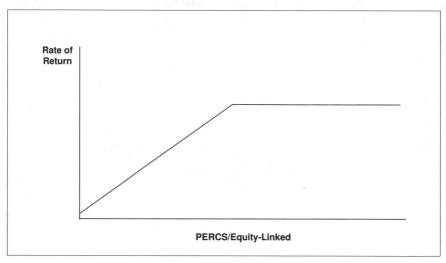

In exchange for a higher dividend, a portion of the capital appreciation is capped, and there is no downside protection.

in 1992. (The trend is shown in Figure 5–5.) In Figure 5–6, the convertible market is segmented by the various types of convertibles issued. Equity-linked securities were initially marketed to equity-income funds and individual investors who want a higher yield than that offered by the underlying stock. Often these securities are held by institutional investors because the securities are issued as 144A securities. However, they also attract individual investors who are seeking income. Depending on who underwrites and issues it and the name recognition of the equity, the target market may be one or the other type of investor. The largest buyers today are probably equity-income, growth and income, and balanced mutual funds.

A company can issue mandatory convertibles with voting rights; they can also be issued by a third party as a derivative security with no voting rights. Mandatory convertibles will automatically be converted to stock at a specified time, unlike normal convertible securities, which the holder has the right to convert at any time. The holder of a typical convertible may also choose never to convert but to retain the fixed-income vehicle, whether as a bond or preferred stock. This provides downside protection for the investor if the stock does not perform as expected. Securities

## F I G U R E 5–5

### Growth of Mandatory Convertible Securities

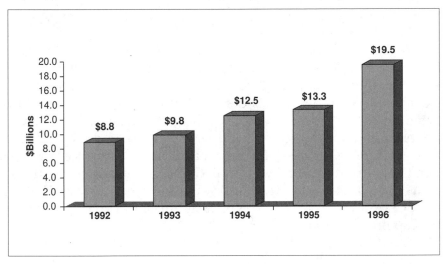

Source: Merrill Lynch Convertible Research.

## F I G U R E 5–6

### Growth of Convertible Market by Type

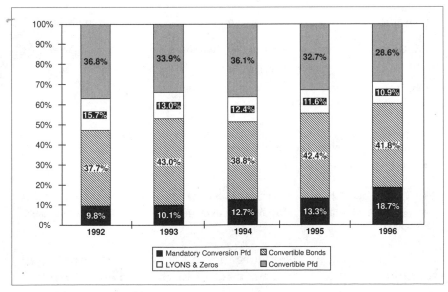

Source: Merrill Lynch Convertible Research.

with a mandatory conversion do not have this important feature and therefore have the same downside risk as the underlying common stock except for the yield advantage. Therefore, the yield advantage could in itself be an important reason for the investor to purchase the security.

Mandatory convertibles have a variety of names. Morgan Stanley issues PERCS—preferred equity redemption cumulative stock; Goldman Sachs underwrites YES—yield enhanced stock; Donaldson Lufkin Jenrette issues PACERS—preferred adjusted to common equity redeemable stock. These dividend-paying securities offer investors a higher yield than the common stock and participate in price increases for the stock up to a cap price. At that point, the upside potential is capped and has been sacrificed for greater yield. However, if the stock price reaches the cap, the investor possibly will have received a significant price gain, despite the cap on further gains

PERCS can be called at any time, but the call price is usually at a premium to the cap price. The earlier the call, the higher the premium and the annualized return. Therefore, an early call may not be a negative event for the investor.

## PERCS: Issuers and Features

| Symbol | Instrument | Underwriter |
| --- | --- | --- |
| PERCS | Preferred Equity Redemption Cumulative Stock | Morgan Stanley |
| YES | Yield Enhanced Securities | Goldman Sachs |
| PACERS | Preferred Adjusted to Common Equity Redeemable Stock | DLJ |

◆ Investors participate 1:1 below the cap price but forego any capital appreciation above the cap price. The security is issued by the company.

◆ Equivalent synthetic position:
  Long common stock.

◆ Short an out-of-the-money call between 30 and 45 percent above issue price.

◆ Conversion is mandatory, payable in cash or shares of common stock, at issuer's option.

For example, in 1995, Morgan Stanley issued preferred equity redemption cumulative securities (PERCS) for Time Warner Financing Trust (a subsidiary of Time Warner Inc.). Time Warner brought this issue to market so it could convert its remaining stake in Hasbro into cash and use the proceeds to reduce debt.

In the Time Warner issue, the price of the PERCS was based on the market price of shares of common stock of Hasbro at the time of the offering. The issue was subject to mandatory redemption in December 1997. The payout will be equal to an amount per PERCS of the lesser of $54.41 and the current market value of a share of Hasbro common stock, payable in cash or shares of Hasbro common stock, at Time Warner's option.

The PERCS structure is designed to complement the LYONs issued by Time Warner in 1992, which are also exchangeable into Hasbro common stock. Through its conversion option, the LYONs issue provides LYONs holders the value of Hasbro stock above $54.41. The two securities' issues together eliminate Time Warner's exposure to movement in the Hasbro stock price.

The relationship of the RJR Nabisco 9.25 percent PERC due 1997 to its common stock is outlined in Figure 5–7. The shaded area shows the excess value of the PERC over the common stock, which is accounted for by the PERC's higher dividend payment. The PERC increases in value as the stock increases until it reaches its cap value of $9.425, at which point it has no further upside potential.

The risk/reward profile is shown by the percentage move of the PERC relative to the movement in the RJR common stock. Based on historical stock volatility, if the stock were to increase 37.1 percent, the PERC would participate in 52 percent of the upside move. If the stock were to decline by 27.1 percent, the PERC would participate in 49 percent of the downside move. The risk/reward is not favorable—about half the upside potential and about half the downside risk as well.

There are still other variations of mandatory convertibles: DECS—dividend enhanced common stock, underwritten by Salomon; ACES—automatically convertible equity Securities, underwritten by Goldman Sachs; and PRIDES—preferred redemption increased dividend equity securities, underwritten by Merrill Lynch. Companies issue these securities to provide investors with a higher yield than that available on common stock. They have no price appreciation up to the conversion price, usually 20 to 25

# F I G U R E  5–7

RJR Nabisco Holdings 9.25% Due 1997
PERCS (Preferred Equity Redemption Cumulative Stock)

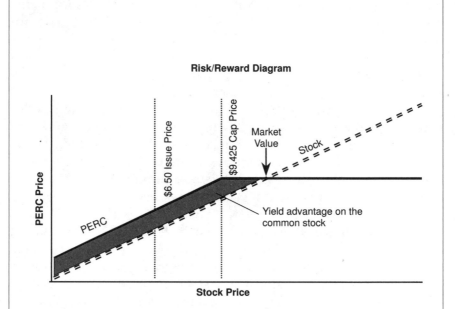

RJR Nabisco Hldgs 9.25% Due 1997 (PERCS) Risk/Reward Table

|  | Time | Stock Px % Change | PERC Px % Change | PERCS Participation |
|---|---|---|---|---|
| **DOWNSIDE** | 1.00 yr | −27.1 | −13.2 | *49%* |
|  | .50 yr | −20.0 | −10.0 | *50%* |
|  | .50 yr | 25.0 | 18.5 | *74%* |
| **UPSIDE** | 1.00 yr | 37.1 | 19.2 | *52%* |

percent above the issue price. Beyond the conversion price, the investor retains a portion of the appreciation, usually 80 percent, which is accomplished by changing the conversion ratio above the conversion price. The terms are set at the time of issuance.

These securities are similar to the other mandatory convertibles in that they give investors a one-for-one participation with the common stock on the downside. Like the other mandatory convertibles, these securities allow an investor to have some equity participation in a company, but with a yield advantage to the common stock.

It is difficult to generalize on the terms of these securities. Each unique structure must be reviewed carefully. An example is the Microsoft 2¾ percent convertible exchangeable principal-protected preferred shares issued by the company in December 1996 and brought to the market by Goldman Sachs in a structure called ACES. This issue is similar to PERCS; it has a cap of 28 percent above the issuing price of $79.875 per share, for a cap price of $102.24. The common stock price and the issue price of the preferred were identical at $79.875 per share. The holder receives $2.196 per annum per share, paid quarterly, for a current yield of 2.75 percent. The issue provides that the original issue price will have principal protection. If the stock has averaged below $79.875 for 20 days prior to December 15, 1999, the company will adjust the ratio through a mandatory conversion so that the value of $79.875 is guaranteed. The company retains the option of a cash settlement. The income stream is considered to be interest, which means that the dividend-received deduction is not available for corporate investors. Additionally, there are no voting rights with this preferred stock, and the company can exchange the preferred stocks for convertible notes.

An interest-conscious, conservative investor would not normally be attracted to the volatile common stock of Microsoft, which pays no dividend. The dividend-paying preferred stock, with principal protection and some upside capital gain potential, provides an attractive vehicle for these investors.

Mandatory convertibles can be issued by a third party. Because the issuer and the underlying credit are different, mandatories are considered derivative securities. Investment banking firms create these securities when they sense a demand for them. Salomon Brothers issues ELKS—equity linked securities; Lehman Brothers issues YEELDS—yield enhanced equity-linked debt securities; and Bear Stearns issues CHIPS—common-linked higher income participation securities. They are like the PERCS previously described but are structured as debt securities of the issuing firm with a link to the common stock of another company. Interest is paid quarterly. The securities are noncallable and retain no voting rights. Additionally, the settlement at mandatory conversion is for cash, not for common stock. With this type of issue, the cap price is usually 30 to 55 percent above the issue price. The underlying credit of this debt security is that of the third-party issuer, not that of the parent company of the common stock.

## ELKS: Issuers and Features

| Symbol | Instrument | Underwriter |
| --- | --- | --- |
| ELKS | Equity-Linked Securities | Salomon |
| YEELDS | Yield Enhanced Equity-Linked Debt Securities | Lehman |
| CHIPS | Common-linked Higher Income Participation Securities | DLJ |

◆ Investors participate 1:1 below the cap price but forego any capital appreciation above the cap price. They are structured as nonvoting debt securities of the issuing firm linked to the common stock of another company. They pay quarterly interest instead of dividends.

◆ Equivalent synthetic position:
  Long common stock.

◆ Short an out-of-the-money call between 30 and 55 percent above issue price.

◆ Conversion is mandatory, payable in cash. Security is noncallable.

ELKS are considered total return vehicles that pay high quarterly cash income and participate in some of the upside potential of the common stock. They can be issued either as a debt instrument or equity. If issued as a debt instrument, the structure resembles a short-term corporate bond. If issued as a preferred stock, they have attributes like other preferred stock, including the dividend received deduction for corporate investors.

For example, in August 1994, Salomon Brothers issued an ELK linked to the performance of Digital Equipment Corporation, a computer systems and components producer. In return for accepting the limitation on upside potential, the investor receives a yield premium of 6.75 percent over the common stock. This is very similar to the covered call strategies popular with many stockholders, where the owner of a certain stock sells out-of-the-money call options against the stock to collect an upfront premium. The investor's upside potential on the stock is limited to the strike price of the option; however, until the stock price reaches this level, the investor can continue to collect premiums by writing call options.

The Digital Equipment ELK possesses the same characteristics as the covered call strategy. The owner of the ELK receives the security's yield the same way the call writer receives the premium income. Both give up some of the upside potential of the stock in return. ELKS and similar instruments are essentially options programs investors could construct for themselves, but since these have been packaged by Wall Street, investors save on transaction costs.

The risk profile on these third-party mandatories is like that of the others discussed. The security provides a yield advantage over the common stock as well as some upside potential from the stock. In return, the investor trades away the downside protection offered by a traditional convertible. The issue's credit may or may not be better than that of the underlying stock. Since the mandatory conversion is for cash, the investor can participate in the upside of a particular stock without ever owning it.

In summary, ELKS provide high current income and should be considered a total return vehicle. In return for maximum income, they trade away the stock's upside potential by capping the maximum price increase. They are designed to attract income-oriented investors to stocks with high volatility and low or no dividends. At maturity, the value is settled in cash rather through conversion to the common stock. If the stock has reached the cap price or above, the settlement is the value of the cap price. If the stock is below the cap price, settlement value is the value of the common stock at maturity. Of course, the high income stream, along with some capital appreciation potential, provides the incentive for investors to purchase these securities.

## DECS: Issuers and Features

| Symbol | Instrument | Underwriter |
|--------|------------|-------------|
| DECS | Debt Exchangeable for Common Stock | Salomon Brothers |
| DECS | Dividend Enhanced Convertible Stock | Salomon Brothers |
| PRIDES | Preferred Redeemable Increased Dividend Securities | Merrill Lynch |

◆ Investors participate 1:1 below the cap price but forego any capital appreciation until the conversion price has been attained and then receive 80 to 90 percent of the upside. The security is issued with voting rights, and most have three-year call protection. After three years, the company can call the issue at prespecified premiums to the issue price plus accrued dividends.

◆ Equivalent synthetic position:
   Long common stock.

◆ Long an out-of-the-money call option with a strike price at the conversion price times the conversion ratio.

◆ Short an at-the-money call option on the stock

◆ Present value of income advantage over common stock dividend.

◆ Conversion is mandatory, payable in cash or shares of common stock, at issuer's option. Prides automatically convert into one share of common stock upon maturity, usually in four years.

Another variation is the DECS security, with a different risk and return profile. The typical DEC is often issued by a company to facilitate deleveraging of the balance sheet. The DEC uses a convertible preferred structure that provides the investor with high income and participation in common stock appreciation. The rating agencies view these securities as equity on a company's books. When used as an alternative to debt, a DECS issue has the effect of strengthening the company's balance sheet. For tax purposes DECS are treated as preferred stock, and corporate investors are entitled to the dividend received deduction. Like other convertibles, conversion to stock is a tax-free exchange for investors.

American Express used this structure to convert book assets to cash, issuing a DEC on its stake in First Data Corp. (FDC). This allowed American Express to sell its stake at a potential premium to the current market price and yet also defer the capital gain. The assets remained on the books while the company was able use the cash. This particular security was issued as a three-year mandatory convertible exchangeable security at a conversion premium of 22 percent. Investors were to receive between 0.82 and 1.0 shares of common stock at redemption. At the end of year three, if the stock were above the conversion price of $44.875 per share, the investor would receive 0.819 shares of common stock; if the stock were below the conversion price of $44.875 per share, the investor would receive one share of common stock. Unlike a PERCS structure, the investor's upside was not capped, so the upside potential was 82 percent of the upside above the conversion price. The premium varied when the security traded between the issue price of $36.75 and the conversion price of $44.875. Upon redemption, it was the issuer's option whether to redeem in stock or cash. This uncertainty as to what the investor will receive can cause a DEC to trade at a slight discount to the stock price.

This issued worked out well for both investors and American Express. On the maturity date, October 15, 1996, with FDC trading near $78 per share, the maturity value could have been paid in either stock or cash at the option of American Express. As long as the average price of FDC for the trading days from September 16 through October 11 was at least $44.875, which it was, then each DECS would be exchanged for 0.819 shares of FDC, valued at about $64 per share. For the investor that purchased the original issue at $44.875, the capital gain was 42.6 percent plus interest income.

Figure 5–8 illustrates the risk/reward diagram of the James River Corp. 9.00 percent DECS, due 1998. Hatched area 1 shows the value of the DEC below the issue price. At this stage, the DECS' price appreciation is 1:1 with stock price appreciation. The higher value of the DEC is due to the higher level of dividends paid out at this point in the structure. Hatched area 2 shows the DECS continued price appreciation at a lower rate once the DECS has achieved the conversion price. At this stage, price appreciation is 85 percent of that of the stock.

Preferred redeemable increase dividend securities, PRIDES, brought to the market by Merrill Lynch, have characteristics similar to those of DECS. They automatically convert into common stock upon maturity, which is usually four years. If PRIDES are redeemed prior to maturity, the holder is paid in common shares. The issuing company may call all or part of the issue with 15 days notice after the call date. Like DECS, if the common stock price is

## F I G U R E  5–8

James River Corp. 9.00% Due 1998
DECS (Dividend Enhanced Common Stock)

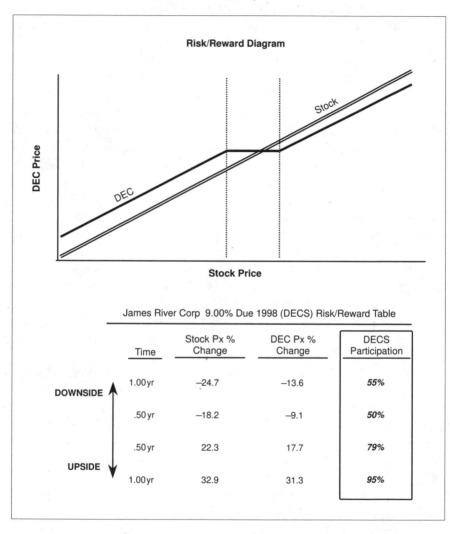

**Risk/Reward Diagram**

James River Corp  9.00% Due 1998 (DECS) Risk/Reward Table

|  | Time | Stock Px % Change | DEC Px % Change | DECS Participation |
|---|---|---|---|---|
| DOWNSIDE | 1.00 yr | −24.7 | −13.6 | *55%* |
|  | .50 yr | −18.2 | −9.1 | *50%* |
|  | .50 yr | 22.3 | 17.7 | *79%* |
| UPSIDE | 1.00 yr | 32.9 | 31.3 | *95%* |

higher than the call price, the holder will receive less than one
share, usually .80 to .90 shares. If the common stock at redemption
is equal to or below the call price, the holder will receive one full
share. Both PRIDES and DECS are convertible preferred stock and
rank ahead of common stock for dividend payment and distribu-

tion of assets upon liquidation. The investor has an incentive to purchase these securities because the dividend yield is higher than that of the common stock and because the securities offer some opportunity for stock appreciation as well.

## CONVERTIBLE MIPS

There is also a debt variation of equity-linked securities called convertible MIPS—monthly income preferred stock, underwritten by Goldman Sachs; or SAILS—stock appreciation income-linked securities, underwritten by First Boston. This security approximates a convertible preferred, but with an important difference: MIPS are issued by a special-purpose entity, often referred to as a special purpose subsidiary (SPS), set up by the parent company. This entity most often takes the form of a limited partnership, but could also be a limited liability corporation or a trust. The dividends paid by the MIPS are tax-deductible to the corporation—an advantage to both the issuer and the investor. The special-purpose entity issues the MIPS, which are a form of corporate preferred stock, and then lends the proceeds of the stock sale to its corporate parent. With the proceeds of the sale, the SPS buys a convertible subordinated debenture from the primary issuer, with terms identical to those of the convertible MIPS. The primary issuer becomes the general partner in the SPS.

The intermediation of the partnership or trust is what makes this structure unique. The parent pays interest on the loan to the special-purpose entity. The special-purpose entity, however, pays out income to the shareholders. From the investor's point of view, the income is a dividend like that on any corporate preferred stock. However, the corporate parent can deduct the interest payments on the debt, which significantly reduces the company's overall borrowing cost. Thus, although MIPS resemble convertible preferred stock, they are tax-deductible (like a bond) for the issuer. However, the dividend payments of MIPS are not eligible for the dividend received deduction.

The MIPS structure gives the holder the right to convert to a fixed number of shares of common stock at any time before the bond is called, and call terms are fixed at the time of issue. Similar to a bond, MIPS offer call protection—usually up to 5 years—and mature in 30 years at par value with possible extensions.

## The New Preferreds: Issuers and Features

| Symbol | Instrument | Underwriter |
|--------|-----------|-------------|
| MIPS | Monthly Income Preferred | Goldman Sachs |
| SAILS | Yield Enhanced Equity-Linked Debt Securities | First Boston |
| TOPRs | Trust-Originated Preferred Securities | Merrill Lynch |

+ Structured as a debt instrument that matures in 30 years with creditor rights and monthly income. No cap price, with a risk/return profile similar to that of a convertible preferred. Typically noncallable for three years.

+ Equivalent synthetic position:
Long straight 30-year bond with three-year call protection.
Long an out-of-the-money three-year call between 20 and 55 percent above stock price at time of issue.

+ Conversion to common stock is at option of the holder at any time prior to conversion expiration date. Redemption at par value at the issuer's option and upon maturity.

Companies have been issuing the new preferreds in large quantities because of the benefits for both issuers and investors. In this section, we use the term "MIPS" generically, to refer to all the new preferreds; MIPS were the first. As of June 30, 1996, total MIPS issuance since the first issue in October 1993 was 102 issues, with a total market value at issuance of $25.3 billion. Of this amount, 20 issues with a value of $6.3 billion were convertible MIPS.

The MIPS structure allows a lower cost of financing than traditional preferred stock. Since MIPS are viewed as equities by the rating agencies, the issuing company reduces the level of debt carried on its balance sheet and gains additional flexibility in its financing needs. To obtain this advantage, companies such as AMR Corp., Equitable Companies Inc., and UAL Corp. have issued convertible MIPS. An additional advantage for the issuer is that the legal structure of the MIPS allows issuers to defer dividends for up to 60 months, although it is unlikely that many issuers will choose to do so. This is similar to the structure of preferred stock, where dividends accumulate in arrears when they are not paid currently.

MIPS offer advantages for the investor as well. Companies entice investors to accept the exchange of debt for MIPS by offering them a higher yield on the MIPS—as much as three-quarters of a percentage point over regular preferred stock, and up to one and one-half percentage points over the yield on long-term corporate debt. MIPS allow a yield-conscious investor to participate in the potential growth of a company with some reduction in volatility. Furthermore, MIPS dividends are paid monthly, rather than semi-annually like traditional bonds or corporate preferred stock, a feature that appeals to many investors.

In addition, because many companies have issued MIPS rather than other kinds of debt or equity, these equity-linked securities often provide investment opportunities in certain companies that would otherwise be unavailable. Convertible MIPS have been issued by Texaco Inc., Transamerica Corp., Aetna Life and Casualty Co., GTE Corp., and other well-known companies. If certain companies continue to buy back their stock and issue equity-linked securities, investors may find that these securities represent their only investment access to such companies.

When an originally issued MIPS involves a limited partnership, dividends for the issue are reported on a partnership tax form called a K-1, rather than on the more familiar 1099. This could represent a higher tax-preparation expense for taxpayers and has annoyed some investors, although others find the income from a K-1 an advantage. When a MIPS uses a trust instead of a partnership, the trust pays a dividend, eliminating the K-1s. The appropriate structure is a function of demand for the security and regulations in place at the time of issuance. St. Paul Companies, Inc., issued convertible MIPS using a limited liability corporation called St. Paul Capital L.L.C., a wholly owned subsidiary. This company existed exclusively for the purpose of issuing the MIPS security. This structure eliminated the problems of having to issue K-1s for the limited partnership and accomplished the same result.

The added protection provided by the MIPS structure over preferred stock is that, under certain conditions, the holder has the right to exchange the MIPS for the convertible subordinated debentures held by the special purpose subsidiary. These are new securities, and therefore the possibility exists that the tax treatment might not pass the scrutiny of the IRS. Additionally, if dividends on the convertible MIPS fall 15 months or more into arrears, this would trigger an exchange to the convertible subordinated debt.

This unpleasant situation might arise where the issuer does not make the payment to the SPS for the dividends on the MIPS to be paid. If this occurs, the dividends will continue to accrue and the issuer would be prohibited from paying dividends on its own common or preferred stock. Therefore, the MIPS are similar to cumulative preferreds in both investor benefits and protection.

The issuer has another, tax-related reason to issue MIPS. A convertible preferred trading well below the conversion price is called a "busted" or "hung" convertible, and it is difficult to force investors to convert this security into stock. In such a situation, the issuer can offer to exchange the convertible preferred for a convertible MIPS with identical terms. The issuer benefits as follows:

1. The dividends that were nondeductible now become deductible as interest expense.
2. Rating agencies may give the issuer slightly more equity treatment on the new security since the possibility of five-year dividend deferral gives the issuer more financial flexibility.

AMC Corp. was the first issuer to take advantage of the above arrangement. They offered the holders of the convertible preferreds an exchange to the underlying convertible subordinated debentures. It was probably management's hope that the rating agencies would look through the details of the structure to the underlying economics of the debt.[2]

## VALUATION OF EQUITY-LINKED SECURITIES

The analytical process for PERCS, MIPS, or other equity-linked securities must take into account many factors. The prevailing method used is a profit-and-loss analysis for the underlying common stock, performed over a wide range of prices and time horizons, to determine the return on investment relative to buying the common stock. Once the investor has determined that an equity-linked security is an appropriate investment, the evaluation process is essentially the same as that for other convertible securities, including a thorough analysis of the fundamentals and creditworthiness of the company. In addition, the convertible aspect is analyzed to determine the risk/reward of each issue within the context of the trade-off inherent to equity-linked securities. The application of option price theory or Black–Scholes option modeling is extremely helpful in determining whether the trade-off between increased yield and loss of potential appreciation is fairly priced.

The investor must take an additional step with equity-linked securities to determine if the security is fairly priced: the investor needs to analyze how to replicate the payoff of the hybrid security in the marketplace with other investment vehicles or with a synthetic instrument. To do this, the cost of the replicated position is calculated and compared to the cost of the hybrid security. The differential between this theoretical fair price and the current market price becomes part of the decision-making process for purchase or sell recommendations. This is necessary because the cap price and other additional risk factors must be considered.

For example, the analysis of the popular Microsoft 2.75 percent Convertible Exchangeable Preferred provides a good illustration of the analytical methodology. A summary of the issue terms is outlined in Figure 5–9. (The symbol for Microsoft stock is MSFT and for the convertible preferred issue is MSFTP.)

One could analyze this issue at the maturity date. Such an analysis would be straightforward; the stock price at the maturity date on December 15, 1999, would determine the value of the preferred. The annualized minimum return on investment would be 2.75 percent if, in three years, the stock were worth $79.875 or less. The maximum annualized return on investment over three years would be 11.4 percent if the stock were $102.24 or greater.

However, analysis in the interim is more difficult because the value of the options will depend on volatility assumptions and time remaining to expiration. The theoretical fair price for the Microsoft exchangeable preferred issue is best determined using the methodology of a synthetic position. The equivalent synthetic is :

Long common stock at 79.875.

Long put on common stock at a strike price of 79.875, expiration December 15, 1999.

Short call option with a strike price of 102.24, expiration December 15, 1999.

Yield advantage over common stock 2.75 percent.

At the time of issue, the convertible preferred was undervalued by 2.2 percent, as shown by the arbitrage pricing approach.

## F I G U R E  5–9

### Key Terms and Structure—MSFT 2.5% Convertible Exchangeable Preferred

◆  MSFT 2.75% has the following features worth highlighting: (1) upside participation is capped
   at $102.24 (28.0%), (2) principal protection at par ($79.875), (3) combination of investment-
   grade credit (A1/AA–) and DRD eligibility, (4) exchangeable into a like debt instrument, (5)
   optional cash and/or stock-settle redemption feature, (6) slightly short first quarterly dividend
   ($0.5369 versus $0.5491 regularly), and (7) 3.0-year term maturity (noncall life).

**Summary Term Sheet/Structure—Microsoft 2.75% Convertible Exchangeable Preferred**

| | |
|---|---|
| Denomination: | $79.875 par |
| Dividend: | 2.75% ($2.196 annual/$0.5491 quarterly) |
| Dividend Settlement: | Cash |
| Dividend Dates: | 3/15, 6/15, 9/15, 12/15 (record date declared by board) |
| First Dividend: | 3/15 (short dividend of $0.5063 based on 12/23–3/15 day count period) |
| DRD Eligible: | Yes |
| DRD Adjusted Yield: | 4.025% ($3.215 effective dividend) |
| Conversion Prices: | High Strike = $102.24 (Cap Price). Low Strike = $79.875 (Floor Price). |
| Conversion Premium: | 28.0% ($102.24 Cap Price vs. $79.875 common price at issuance) |
| Convertibility: | Not before maturity (European style option) |
| Hard Call: | Non call life = 3.0 years (12/15/1999) |
| Maturity: | 12/15/1999 |
| Maturity Settlement: | Paid in stock and/or cash based on 20-trading day MSFT average close ending 2-trading days prior to maturity date. |
| | If $79.875 >= MSFT <= $102.24, Investor gets 1.0 share of MSFT or the cash equivalent. |
| | If MSFT <= $79.875, Investor gets the number of MSFT shares equivalent in value to $79.875 or the cash equivalent. |
| | If MSFT >= $102.24, Investor gets the number of MSFT shares equivalent in value to $102.24 or the cash equivalent. |
| Exchangeability: | Into MSFT 2.75% Convertible Notes due 1999 beginning 3/15/97 on any dividend date. Terms essentially are identical to MSFT 2.75% Cvt. Pfd. except for certain maturity settlement features (see below). |
| Maturity Settlement (bond): | Differs from MSFT 2.75% Cvt. Pfd. in three respects: |
| | 1. Investors must elect conversion option or bond automatically will be redeemed for $79.875. |
| | 2. Investors receive an additional $0.40/share if they elect to convert at maturity. |
| | 3. If settled in stock, investors get the number of shares equal to 99.5% of the maturity settlement value (as defined above). |
| Credit Rating: | A1/AA– |
| Issue Size: | $1.0 Billion (12,519,562 shares) |
| Voting Rights: | None |
| Registration: | NASDAQ listed |
| Convertible Ticker: | MSFTP |
| Underlying Ticker: | MSFT |

Source: Lehman Brothers and prospectus.

## F I G U R E  5–10

Microsoft 2.75%—Theoretical Payoff Pattern

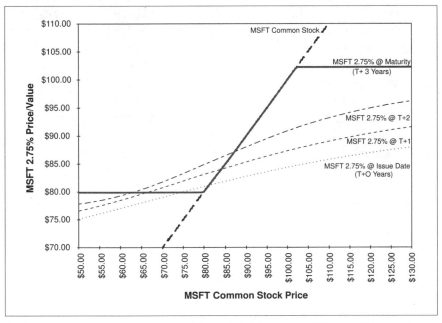

Source: Lehman Brothers, Inc. research paper, *Everything You Wanted to Know about Microsoft 2.75% Convertible Preferred*, January 27, 1997, p. 5. Used with permission.

Figure 5–10 uses a payoff graph to show the relationship of the Microsoft preferred to the underlying common stock. Notice that if the stock declines, the value of the put increases, offsetting the loss from the long stock position and protecting the principal investment of $79.875. Proceeds from the sale of the call option becomes an income distribution to the preferred holders and caps the maximum gain at $102.24 per share. The value of the preferred will depend on the Microsoft stock price on December 15, 1999. This structure has to use a European-style option since the holder cannot exercise the option until expiration.

The payoff profile chart compares the common stock to the preferred issue over a wide range of stock prices and values of the preferreds at one-year intervals—T+1, T+2, and T+3 maturity. Notice that, at all prices below a stock price of $102.24, the preferred outperforms the common stock when considering the position at maturity. However, the preferred can lag the stock significantly before maturity because the embedded options retain their value.

The trading of the preferred relative to the common stock occurred as expected. The common stock rallied significantly in late 1996, reaching a high in January 1997 of $103.125 and exceeding the cap price of $102.75. However, the preferred did not have a significant price gain. Figure 5–11 shows the price action over those months for MSFT, MSFTP, and the theoretical fair value price track. Notice how accurately the track reflected the actually trading experience. The preferred lagged the increasing common stock price because the long put declined in value as the stock increased, while the short call increased in value as the stock approached the strike price. Since this figure reflects only a few months of trading, it does not show time decay taking much of a toll on option premiums. This demonstration of the use of option

## F I G U R E  5–11

Microsoft 2.75%—Price and Fair Value History, 21 Nov 96–24 Jan 97

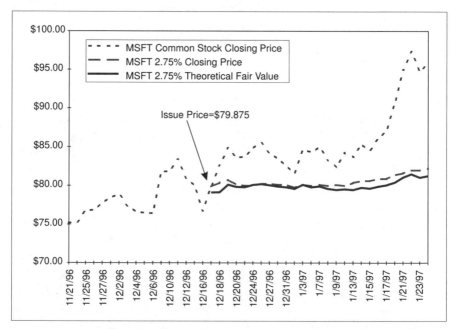

Source: Lehman Brothers, Inc. research paper, *Everything You Wanted to Know about Microsoft 2.75% Convertible Preferred,* January 27, 1997, p. 5. Used with permission.

theory shows how tracking theoretical fair prices over time can allow an investor to find securities that may be undervalued.

## CONCLUSION

Securities customized to particular legal structures and risk parameters can potentially provide significantly increased flexibility to both issuers and investors. Corporations can optimize debt and capital issuance, and investors can truly fine-tune their portfolios to reach the most advantageous point on their efficient frontiers. Issuers attain low cost and investors achieve maximum return for a given level of risk.

Financial engineering using derivative technology will lead to the creation of even more convertible structures. The analytical tools now available for the valuation and trading of convertibles will likely allow underwriters to create unlimited hybrid products, which investors will find useful in achieving their investment objectives.

## E N D N O T E S

1. Much of this material on equity-linked securities was originally published in an article in *Personal Financial Planning*: John P. Calamos, "Investment Risk Management: Innovative Risk Management Using Equity-Linked Securities," Volume 7, No. 6 (September/October 1995): 52–56. Used with permission.
2. Convertible Special Report, "Convert Structures: A Spectrum of Alternatives," Merrill Lynch, February 26, 1997, pp. 20–21.

# 6

## C H A P T E R

# Related Securities: Warrants, LEAPS, and Synthetics

## INTRODUCTION

It is important to the analytics of convertible bonds to describe a number of other types of convertibles and closely related instruments, such as warrants. The convertible market has been expanded by the introduction of these various, derivative types of convertibles, which are still analyzed using the underlying principles of traditional convertible securities.

The convertible's bond or investment value is its value as a straight bond. Its equity component is an implied warrant giving the holder the right to buy the underlying common stock at a specified price over a specified time. For most convertibles, the two parts cannot be separated.

Convertible securities are attractive to investors because they provide the safety of fixed income with the equity potential of common stock. The bondholder can retain the bond and collect coupon interest as long as it is profitable to do so. Or the bondholder can make the conversion to common stock when that is the more profitable option. When the equity underlying the convertible increases in value, the convertible security also increases in value, and the bondholder does not necessarily have to convert the bond to profit from an increase in its equity value.

Convertibles are universally described as the combination of a bond and a warrant. It is important to first understand the characteristics of warrants and options in order to understand convertibles because of the similarities between the two securities.

## WARRANTS

A warrant (sometimes called an equity warrant) is an option to buy a specific common stock at a specific price over a specific time. Warrants are similar to call options on stocks except for two important differences: Warrants are issued by the corporation itself, and their time to expiration is much longer than that of a call option. The listed option market has the benefit of offering a standardized option contract, while each company issuing warrants sets terms that are unique to the specific issue. Warrants are often, but not always, issued as part of a corporate bond offering but are detachable after a short time. The warrant is used as an inducement to purchase the bonds and is detachable immediately after the offering date. In the after market, both the bond and warrant trade separately, with each finding its own market price. The value of the warrant depends on its terms, notably its exercise price and the time to expiration.

A warrant may offer the right to buy either more or less than one share of common stock. The *exercise price* of the warrant is determined at the time of issue. The investor exercising the warrant has the right to purchase the underlying common stock at the stated exercise price. Since most warrants are issued as part of a unit consisting of a bond plus a warrant, the investor may use the straight corporate bond that was part of the unit in lieu of cash to exercise the warrant. The bond is called a *usable bond,* and its value is important in determining the *effective exercise price* of the warrant. Since the bond can be used in lieu of cash, any purchase of the bond below par would effectively reduce the exercise price of the warrant. For example, if the usable bond is trading at 80, representing a 20 percent discount to par, the warrant exercise price is also effectively reduced by 20 percent. The effective exercise price is an important consideration in evaluating the warrant.

Speculators like warrants because, like stock options, they offer a high degree of leverage on each investment dollar. The investor can control large quantities of the underlying common stock with a relatively small investment. Using warrants successfully depends on the evaluation process and strategy employed by the investor. Conservative investors may combine warrants with fixed-income securities to create synthetic convertibles.

There are two main types of warrants: American style and European style. The American style warrant allows the holder to exercise the option at any time during its life. The European style allows the option to be exercised only on the option's maturity date. The difference sways the valuation of equity warrants. The American style is more attractive than the European style because it allows the investor to take advantage of stock volatility; the option can be exercised any time the stock increases in value over a set period of time. The European style of exercise only at maturity reduces the value of the option to the holder.

Exercise terms for warrants vary from issue to issue and from country to country. Issues in the Euro and Swiss markets are mostly American style, while the terms of exercise vary in the United Kingdom. Some terms allow the warrant to be exercised anytime over its life; others specify exercise for a set period—for example, it is tied to the date of the annual general meeting, or can be exercised only if certain financial conditions are met. Equity warrants are typically protected against dilution from rights issues, stock splits, or the issue of equity-linked securities. However, the exercise of warrants forces the company to issue new shares of stock, causing a certain amount of dilution.

Equity warrants are evaluated according to the same process used to evaluate the equity portion of the convertible bond. Equity warrants are similar to listed options and are evaluated as such.

## Covered Warrants

Covered warrants are typically issued by a commercial or investment bank and are exercisable into the shares of another company. The risk is covered by the issuer (the bank) and is its financial obligation to the company. Since no new shares are being issued, there is no dilution with covered warrants. The terms must be carefully reviewed to determine whether shares or the cash equivalent will be delivered upon exercise. Use of covered warrants has increased with the sophistication of the equity derivative market. Unlike convertibles or company-issued warrants, most covered warrants are not backed by the shares to be delivered upon exercise. Therefore, the credit strength of the issuer becomes critically important. This tends to restrict covered warrant issuance to large, highly rated institutions. For example, Bankers Trust issued call warrants convertible into Hong Kong Shanghai Banking Corp. common stock on September 11, 1996. The warrants expire on February 16, 1998.

The basic structure is similar to that used for most equity warrants and specifies the assets into which the warrant can be exercised as well as the currency. At issue, the prospectus will state the number of warrants issued along with the minimum or maximum number that can be issued. The prospectus will state the warrant holders' rights concerning expiration date, exercise period, exercise price, and the number of warrants required to obtain a unit of assets. It also states whether the warrants will be listed, which laws apply, and if there is any residual value should the exercise price not be met.

The covered warrant market emerged in the late 1980s and grew dramatically in the 1990s. First issued in the Swiss market, they quickly spread to other markets around the world. The Japanese covered warrant market has been very successful and has expanded to include a variety of issues. Figure 6–1 provides some examples of larger European covered warrants.

Most covered warrants are not accessible to U.S. investors due to a difference in underwriting syndicate procedures. Most securities issued outside the United States are available to be purchased by U.S. investors once the issue has seasoned, which typically occurs 40 to 90 days after the closing of the underwriting syndicate. However, most issuers of covered warrants leave the syndicate open to supply any additional warrant demand that may arise after the first issuance. Therefore, since the syndicate doesn't close until close to the expiration of the warrant, the warrants do not season until very close to, or even after, expiration.

**F I G U R E 6–1**

Sample of Larger European Covered Warrants

| Underlying Equity | Issuer | Expiration | Warrant Market Cap (U.S. millions) |
|---|---|---|---|
| Glaxo | Swiss Bank | 11/10/97 | 305.5 |
| Roche | UBS | 12/18/98 | 283.4 |
| British Petroleum | Swiss Bank | 11/10/97 | 238.2 |
| Bayer | Commerzbank | 09/17/97 | 175.4 |
| Royal Dutch Shell | Merrill Lynch | 10/15/97 | 160.8 |
| British Aerospace | Merrill Lynch | 07/09/98 | 157.7 |
| BASF | Salomon Bros. | 06/26/97 | 156.9 |
| Volkswagen | Commerzbank | 03/18/98 | 142.0 |
| Daimier-Benz | Robert Fleming | 01/23/98 | 140.8 |
| BMW | Commerzbank | 06/18/97 | 117.2 |
| Asea Brown Boveri | Morgan Stanley | 05/01/97 | 107.0 |
| Hoechst | Commerzbank | 07/15/00 | 103.1 |

## LEAPS

Long-term equity anticipation securities, or LEAPS®, are long-term options on individual stocks. They are created by the stock or options exchanges (the Chicago Board Options Exchange, the New York Stock Exchange, etc.) where they are listed and traded. Like other options, there are two types of LEAPS: a call and a put. Note how the definition of LEAPS already differs from that of warrants: LEAPS are exchange-issued and available as either a put or a call; warrants are issued only by individual companies and are available only as a call—they provide the right to convert into stock, but have no corresponding put form. Warrants are also traded on the stock exchanges.

LEAPS give the owner the right to buy or sell the underlying stock at a specified price on or before a stated date that is up to two years in the future—the major way LEAPS differ from normal exchange-listed equity options, for which the longest strike date is no more than nine months in the future. Warrants may be created with end dates up to three to five years in the future.

Since transactions involving either LEAPS or standard options are external to the company itself, when either type of option is exercised, it will involve only stock that has already been issued (and is held by one of the parties to the transaction). This does not create the kind of stock dilution that may be caused by warrants.

The company whose stock underlies a LEAPS issue will not necessarily receive its introduction enthusiastically since LEAPS represent a derivative of the underlying stock and are outside the company's area of control. The exchanges create the LEAPS they think will be actively traded. Institutional investors participating in the LEAPS market can influence the creation of LEAPS by informing the exchanges of the demand they see for them.

LEAPS brought an exciting new element into the market. Listed call options are too short in maturity for the purposes of creating synthetic securities; synthetics are most effective when used for somewhat longer-term investing. Warrants are ideal, but of course the investor's choices are limited to those companies that choose to issue warrants. LEAPS brought another significant source of supply into the market.

As with standard call options, LEAPS purchasers (whether of puts or calls) are limited to the loss of the premium they paid and are not exposed to the potentially infinite loss of the LEAPS seller.

Figure 6–2 illustrates the risk/reward structure of LEAPS versus that of shorter options and stocks.

## CONVERTIBLE UNITS

Although the unit form has not been used in the public convertible market of the United States in recent years, it is still in widespread use in the international markets and demonstrates the main principles of a synthetic convertible. It is widely used in the U.S. private-placement convertible market. A company issues a convertible unit that consists of a straight bond and warrant. The bond has a coupon and maturity date and can be used at par instead of cash to exercise the warrant. The warrant gives the holder the right to buy the stock at a specific price for a specific time period. The value of the warrant will induce investors to accept a lower coupon rate on the debt issue because the investor hopes to profit from the rising equity value. The unit is sold to the public as a

## F I G U R E  6–2

LEAPS and Options

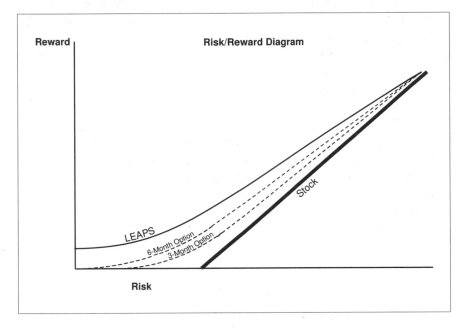

convertible security, and the original purchasers of the issue may buy it only in unit form—both parts together.

However, since the terms of the offering allow the bond and warrant components to be detached and sold separately, an after-market develops where three separate securities trade: the unit, the straight bond, and the warrant. The unit looks and feels like a straight convertible bond and is evaluated as one. The straight bond portion is valuable for its fixed-income attributes. The warrant may be listed and trades like an option to purchase stock. The warrant has a specific exercise price and expiration date.

Since the bond portion of the convertible unit can be used to exercise the warrant, the valuation process becomes more complex. For all practical purposes, the bond is a straight bond and will trade off its credit quality and yield to maturity. However, since it can be used at par in lieu of cash to exercise a warrant, this can affect its market value. The straight bond of the unit may have an additional value above its value as a straight bond since it may be usable in lieu of cash at par. Thus if it appeared that the warrant were close to being exercised, the bond would approach par as investors purchased the bonds and exercised the warrants. If the warrant is in-the-money and the stock price is above the exercise price, then the bond will be at par value regardless of its coupon. If the bond is trading below par, investors would purchase it to use to exercise the warrant because the company has to redeem the bond at par, regardless of its market price.

The warrant value is thus affected by the value of the straight bond. If the bond is trading at a discount from par due to its coupon and credit standing, then the exercise price of the warrant should reflect this discount. If the bond's discount were 20 percent, for example, the investor reflects this by adjusting the exercise price of the warrant. The adjusted exercise price of the warrant is as follows:

$$\begin{matrix} \text{Adjusted} \\ \text{exercise} \\ \text{price*} \end{matrix} = \begin{matrix} \text{Warrant} \\ \text{exercise} \\ \text{price} \end{matrix} \times \left( \frac{\text{Market price of bond}}{\text{Par value}} \right)$$

* Not to exceed warrant exercise price.

Investors using convertible units and adjusting the warrant exercise price should realize that if many investors attempt to exercise a particular warrant, the demand for its bonds will increase—thereby driving up the bond price and reducing the effective exercise price.

## SYNTHETIC SECURITIES[1]

Not every company has issued a convertible, but there are nearly a thousand of them for investors to choose from. It is possible that characteristics slightly different from those chosen by the issuer would do a better job of maximizing value for the potential investor. The convertible market has been expanded by the increasing sophistication of investors and the increasing use of financial engineering; investors can create the convertibles of their choice by combining two or more securities. Synthetic convertibles are one of the most important innovations produced by Wall Street, and they offer investors both additional profit opportunity and the ability to control risk.

Synthetic convertibles are similar to the unit form of a convertible bond. However, a synthetic is not issued; it is created, usually by a third party other than the corporation whose underlying stock performance ultimately determines its value. There are, in general, two main types of synthetic securities. A *convertible principal-protected note* (sometimes called a convertible structured note) is arranged by an investment banker and has the credit risk of a third party. It is a form of structured note and is sold as a complete package. A *synthetic convertible unit* (SCU) is created by an investment manager, who purchases the separate parts to construct the unit.

## Convertible Principal-Protected Notes

Convertible principal-protected notes are derivative securities created by investment bankers. They have the attributes of a convertible security, with one important difference: The credit risk is not that of the company whose common stock underlies the convertible security and provides the convertibility feature but, instead, that of a third party. For example, the convertible principal-protected note may have the equity potential of Microsoft common stock and the credit backing of the Wall Street firm that issued it. The principal-protected notes trade as a security and are often issued with little fanfare as a private placement to a limited number of institutional investors. Because these securities are private placements, liquidity can become an issue. Investment managers will often negotiate the terms of these principal-protected notes on behalf of their institutional clients.

Convertible principal-protected notes are part of the structured note market and are fixed-income debentures linked to equity. They can be issued by corporations, banks, financial institutions, municipalities, agencies of the U.S. government, sovereigns, and supranationals, but are typically issued by financial institutions. Maturities range from as short as three months to as long as 10 years.

Convertible principal-protected notes can take many different formats, such as the Morgan Stanley Technology Basket, 0 percent coupon, due May 1, 2001. The 144A structure is based on five different technology stocks, shown in Figure 6–3 along with the

## F I G U R E  6–3

Morgan Stanley Technology Exchangeable Note Trust Certificates—
0 percent 5/1/2001, callable 5/1/99

At maturity, the units will redeem for the greater of par (1,000) or the cash value of the technology basket.

| Technology Basket | Exchange Ratios |
|---|---|
| 1. Cisco Systems | 2.03875 |
| 2. Electronic Data Systems | 2.67055 |
| 3. Hewlett-Packard | 2.77160 |
| 4. Intel Corp. | 1.17199 |
| 5. Microsoft | 0.95306 (presplit) |
| 6. Oracle | 3.02505 |

exchange ratio (in shares) for each of the stocks. The issue is call-protected until May 1, 1999. At maturity, the units will redeem for the greater of par or the cash value of the technology basket, meaning that the investor will never own actual stock in these companies. The unit carries a higher yield than that of the stocks in the basket of 0.34 percent. The issue carries the credit rating of Morgan Stanley senior debt, A1/A+ and an NAIC rating of 1. The conversion premium at issue was 18.875 percent.

Bundling technology stocks into a zero coupon convertible provides the investor with exposure to the risky technology sector in a format that provides downside protection and the ability to dampen that sector's high volatility.

A Microsoft issue from 1994 provides another interesting example of a principal-protected note. Merrill Lynch brought the Exchangeable Structured Liquid Yield Option[sm] Notes due June 30, 1999, to market as a 144A issue; in other words, these securities were exchangeable LYONs. As such, they were issued at a discount, which in this case was 99.3 percent of par, with a premium redemption at maturity at 113.992, to yield 2.76 percent over the life of the bond. The issue was call-protected for its entire life. At any time during the life of the maturity, the bondholder could exchange the LYON for shares of Microsoft common stock.

This might seem like an interesting way to invest in Microsoft stock because it would allow the investor the opportunity to participate in a significant amount of Microsoft price appreciation while receiving a certain level of guaranteed return from the zero coupon bond, compared to Microsoft stock itself, which has a very low dividend yield. Furthermore, if Microsoft were to experience significant volatility over the period, the LYON's fixed-income characteristics would provide a floor. Although the 2.76 percent yield is quite low for a convertible, the issue is a five-year maturity and compares to short-term paper.

The issue is collateralized by Merrill Lynch equity participation securities due June 30, 1999. These securities, previously issued by Merrill Lynch, are not interest-bearing and their holders will be entitled to receive the principal amount plus an interest payment (supplemental redemption amount) based on the percentage increase, if any, in the S&P 500 Composite Stock Price Index since June 16, 1993, multiplied by 128 percent. The minimum value for the supplemental redemption amounts will not be less than $200 per $1,000 principal amount of Merrill Lynch EPS.

Most principal-protected notes are created by a swap transaction; this is one of their key characteristics. The issuer typically has hedged away—at some appropriate profit—the risks embedded in the principal-protected note. This allows issuers such as large investment banks to produce notes tailor-made to the specifications of the institutional market. For the investor who buys the principal-protected note, the swap transactions are transparent, and the only credit risk is that of the issuer.[2]

New issuance of corporate principal-protected notes increased dramatically from 1990 through 1994. Although principal-protected notes can be considered derivative securities, they are quite different from the derivatives involved in the highly publicized Orange County case. Because principal-protected notes are not leveraged, those who hold them do not have the unknown (and possibly unlimited) risk caused by leverage. Potential loss is limited to the original investment amount. The risk of loss of principal on a principal-protected note is like that of any corporate bond and is based on the creditworthiness of the issuer. Rating agencies can help the investor determine the level of risk involved in any given security.

Interestingly, although the security has the credit of a third party (a structure that might in itself entail risk), the corporate principal-protected note ratings tend to be quite high. Over 97 percent of all principal-protected notes issued are rated A or higher.[3] Often the credit of the third-party issuer is higher than that of the company from which the equity participation is derived.

## Synthetic Convertible Unit

The synthetic convertible unit is a convertible created by combining securities. A typical synthetic convertible combines a separate, fixed-income security, such as a highly liquid U.S. government Treasury note, with a long-term equity warrant or LEAPS. As mentioned above, synthetics typically use warrants or LEAPS for the equity component because of their relatively longer time to expiration. The short life span of regular call options would incur significant market risk.

The investor holds both securities. The Treasury note yields income and repays principal at maturity like the bond portion of a convertible security. The warrant or LEAPS offers the potential to own the underlying equity, like the convertible feature of the straight convertible security.

This technique of combining these two securities is limited by the number of warrants and longer-term options available. Opportunities were once limited, although in recent years the CBOE has expanded LEAPS issuance, allowing this technique to be used more widely. Each component of the synthetic trades independently of the other.

To create a successful synthetic convertible, bond market, conditions must be favorable. Yields on straight convertibles tend to be parallel to the longer end of the market, whereas the synthetic convertible uses a shorter-term government note. The ideal scenario for synthetics is thus a flat or inverted yield curve, when the spread between short-term and long-term rates is narrow. In this situation, synthetic and straight convertible debt will have similar yields, and synthetic convertibles can be created without sacrificing current yield. When the yield curve is steep, the synthetic convertibles will have an interest rate like that of the shorter end of the market and the straight convertible will be priced like longer instruments. In this case, the synthetic will sacrifice current yield for equity participation. Market conditions in 1995 provided a good balance between attractive current yield, equity participation, and downside safety. Figure 6–4 illustrates graphically how

Traditional and Synthetic Convertibles—Opportunities in Different Yield-Curve Environments

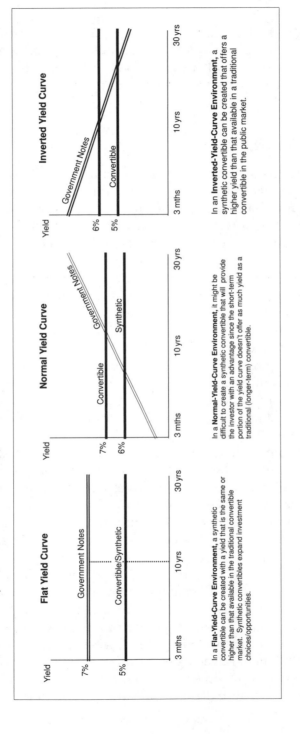

In a **Flat-Yield-Curve Environment**, a synthetic convertible can be created with a yield that is the same or higher than that available in the traditional convertible market. Synthetic convertibles expand investment choices/opportunities.

In a **Normal-Yield-Curve Environment**, it might be difficult to create a synthetic convertible that will provide the investor with an advantage since the short-term portion of the yield curve doesn't offer as much yield as a traditional (longer-term) convertible.

In an **Inverted-Yield-Curve Environment**, a synthetic convertible can be created that offers a higher yield than that available in a traditional convertible in the public market.

different yield curve environment affect the construction of synthetic convertibles. Notice that the most favorable environment is a flat to inverted yield curve. In those cases, short- to intermediate-term current yields are comparable to those of long-term governments.

## BENEFITS AND RISKS

Creating the synthetic convertible unit allows flexibility in developing the risk/reward attributes of the security. Three of the most important characteristics of any debenture are duration, credit risk, and liquidity. For a straight convertible, these three factors, along with every other aspect of the bond, come "prepackaged." The synthetic allows these characteristics to be chosen separately.

When the fixed-income portion of a convertible is a government note, the investor has the widest possible choice of duration in an instrument that is considered to have no credit risk and no liquidity issues. The bond of course remains a bond and is subject to interest-rate risk, although interest-rate risk can be minimized by choosing a note from the short end of the market. Government notes are available in every duration, including many possible permutations of coupon rate, discount or premium, maturity date, and so on. Liquidity would be a consideration only in exceptional circumstances.

During periods when the yield curve is inverted, combining a Treasury bill with a warrant results in a synthetic convertible with a yield higher than that of convertible bond alternatives, which would typically have a longer term. The unit has no credit risk and very little interest-rate risk. When the yield curve reverts to its normal shape, the fixed-income component is not subject to rapidly declining principal value.

The investor can then focus on providing the appropriate equity exposure for the synthetic. A synthetic can make profitable use of even the riskiest warrant or LEAPS and is limited only by what is available. Even if the warrant expires worthless, the government security providing the fixed-income exposure remains. One of the main advantages of straight convertibles is providing a less risky way to invest in a risky company, and synthetics are even better because the fixed-income portion of the convertible is a government note. In fact, one could construct an investment-grade synthetic which has equity exposure for a company whose credit was well below investment grade. Liquidity issues would affect only the equity portion of the synthetic.

Corporate bonds may also be used to create a synthetic, but a corporate bond presents more variables because it has its own credit risk. Furthermore, it may be more difficult to find the corporate bond with exactly the desired credit quality, yield, liquidity, and duration that must be combined precisely with the warrant or LEAPS.

Time premium decay is an additional risk factor that must be evaluated properly. Warrants and LEAPS are more affected by premium decay than a convertible bond trading at a discount from par or even convertibles above par because a convertible will typically have a longer term. The equity component of synthetic convertibles is more likely to be short-term. This is most noticeable when using listed options, given their short life span. The longer life of LEAPS and warrants provides an obvious advantage.

The investor can further reduce risk by diversifying the expiration dates of the equity components of the SCUs held in a portfolio. An additional advantage is flexibility in determining the level of the SCU's equity participation by varying the number of warrants attached to each fixed-income security. For example, a higher level of equity participation would be more desirable in a strong bull market than in a more uncertain market.

Finally, although the straight convertible market continues to grow, it remains limited to those companies that understand the advantages of convertibles. Synthetic convertibles can dramatically expand the universe of convertible securities by adding all those companies that issue warrants or LEAPS and offering more opportunities to tailor a portfolio precisely to the needs of the investor.

## DISADVANTAGES

Although the hybrid nature of convertibles provides them with unique advantages, the benefits do come with a cost. For example, although LEAPS have made an important contribution to the world of convertible securities, unfortunately they are not yet widely issued. Constructing a synthetic depends largely on having appropriate LEAPS or warrants available.

We have discussed the interest-rate environments in which synthetics are particularly effective and mentioned that convertibles don't work as well when the yield curve is steep, for two reasons. First, in that environment, there will be a relatively large difference between the longer-term rates on convertibles and the shorter-term rates on the Treasury notes typically used for synthetics. Using a synthetic would sacrifice yield. Second, when shorter-term rates are quite low, such as 3 percent, as seen in 1993, the yield on the Treasury notes is barely higher than the dividend yield available on the underlying common stock and would not offer the yield advantage over stock that is typical for the security. At 3 percent, a synthetic does not offer much of an income stream. Therefore, synthetics might not be an appropriate investment over the entire market cycle.

Synthetic convertibles are quite complicated to use and are not a likely choice for an individual investor who might not have the financial background necessary to construct a synthetic and, more importantly, monitor it closely. They are more appropriate for professional money managers who use them within a portfolio. They are most effectively used as risk-control adjuncts to a larger portfolio rather than as single investments.

## AN EXAMPLE

Let us consider an example to illustrate the composition and analysis of a Johnson & Johnson synthetic convertible unit. Consider a hypothetical example that might have been established in April 1994, when the underlying common stock traded at around $40 and did not have a convertible bond. The SCU combined a 6 percent Treasury note with LEAPS.

To construct the SCU, three LEAPS were allocated to each Treasury bond; the bonds are priced at 100 percent each. The LEAPS cost $6.47 each, for a total value of 119.41 percent. This means that the JNJ Synthetic Convertible Unit is priced at $1,194.10 per unit. The fixed-income component provides downside protection by establishing a minimum value, which will be $1,000 (par) plus the interest accumulation, as long as interest rates remain stable.

## F I G U R E  6-5

Risk/Reward—JNJ Synthetic Convertible Unit A

|  | Downside Risk | | Current* | Upside Potential | |
|---|---|---|---|---|---|
|  | 1 year | 6 months | Current* | 6 months | 1 year |
| A Percent change in stock price | −23.5% | −17.2% | 0.0% | 20.9% | 30.8% |
| B Stock price | $30.70 | $33.22 | $40.13 | $48.51 | $52.48 |
| C Bond price | 100.00 | 100.00 | 100.00 | 100.00 | 100.00 |
| D Warrant or option price | 0.57 | 1.84 | 6.47 | 11.24 | 13.61 |
| E Equity unit value = 3 = D X 3 | 1.71 | 5.52 | 19.41 | 33.72 | 40.83 |
| F Synthetic convertible unit price = C + E | 101.71 | 105.52 | 119.41 | 133.72 | 140.83 |
| G Unit Change (not including interest) | −14.8% | −11.6% | 0.0% | 12.0% | 17.9% |
| H Total Return on Investment | −8.9% | −8.6% | 5.9% | 15.0% | 23.8% |
| I Participation relative to Stock = I / A | 38% | 50% | | 72% | 77% |

*April 25, 1994

Note: This figure assumes that interest rates remain constant.

Source: Calamos Asset Management, Inc.

As Figure 6–5 illustrates, if the stock price dropped 23.5 percent over the next year (equivalent to 22 percent if dividends are taken into consideration), the JNJ synthetic convertible unit A would be expected to drop only 8.9 percent. On the upside, if the stock price increased 30.8 percent (equivalent to 32.3 percent with dividends), the convertible value (including income) would be expected to increase 23.4 percent

This synthetic convertible had no credit risk because the equity component was provided by a call. The call could drop to zero in value, but no further amount is at risk and the convertible would still have provided downside protection. The warrant portion of this security is particularly attractive because it is noncallable for 1.67 years. The synthetic also has minimal interest-rate risk due to the relatively short term of the Treasury note.

Figure 6–6 illustrates the risk/reward structure of a synthetic. Panel a shows that the U.S. Treasury note is not affected by changes in the stock's price. Panel b shows the stock price as the diagonal line, and the value of the J&J LEAPS is shown by the dashed line. The upside potential of the LEAPS depends completely on the behavior of the stock price. Panel c shows the risk/reward of the synthetic convertible, which has been constructed by adding the two parts together. The value of the Treasury note remains constant, no matter what happens to the stock price, and acts as a floor even if the stock price goes to zero. If the stock price rises, the value of the synthetic convertible rises with it.

The risk/reward analysis indicates the changes in stock price over a 12-month period based on the stock's historical trading range. The Johnson & Johnson SCU demonstrates a risk/reward relationship that is more favorable than that of the common stock. Notice that the risk/reward of the SCU has a two-to-one advantage, providing 79 percent of the upside of the common for only 39 percent of the downside.

The position was established on April 15, 1994, with the risk/reward as indicated. If the stock had declined, the LEAPS would have expired worthless, and the bond's value would have been unaffected. However, the JNJ stock made a dramatic upward move. In April 1995, the position was reevaluated. The JNJ synthetic convertible unit A had increased from $1216.90 to $1626.10— nearly a 41 percent increase, including interest income received.

A benefit of the synthetic convertible's unique structure is that the equity component can be adjusted without changing the fixed-income portion. To lock in the profit, the equity position (40-strike LEAPS) was sold and a new position of LEAPS was established with a higher strike price. This reestablished a favorable risk/reward similar to that of the original position. The new position, the JNJ synthetic convertible unit B priced at $1238.40, continued to progress well. On November 15, 1995, the JNJ synthetic convertible unit B had increased from $1,238.40 to $1,825.90, an increase of nearly 50 percent, with interest included.

In this example, the SCU was profitable due to the increasing stock price. However, SCUs are important not only for their ability to generate profits when the stock increases but also for their ability to limit capital losses when the stock decreases. These defensive

Johnson & Johnson SCU (Synthetic Convertible Unit)—8% Treasury Note + J&J LEAPS = SCU

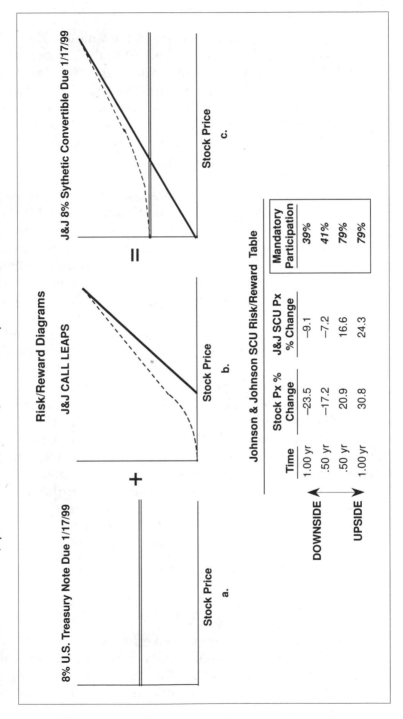

### Risk/Reward Diagrams

**8% U.S. Treasury Note Due 1/17/99**

Stock Price

a.

**J&J CALL LEAPS**

Stock Price

b.

**J&J 8% Sythetic Convertible Due 1/17/99**

Stock Price

c.

### Johnson & Johnson SCU Risk/Reward Table

|  | Time | Stock Px % Change | J&J SCU Px % Change | Mandatory Participation |
|---|---|---|---|---|
| DOWNSIDE | 1.00 yr | −23.5 | −9.1 | 39% |
|  | .50 yr | −17.2 | −7.2 | 41% |
| UPSIDE | .50 yr | 20.9 | 16.6 | 79% |
|  | 1.00 yr | 30.8 | 24.3 | 79% |

115

characteristics were very important, for example, when this JNJ position was established. Throughout 1994, the consensus view of the market was not predominantly bullish, given increasing interest rates. This position provided a means to participate defensively in the increasing stock price that could result if the consensus proved incorrect. Of course the consensus was wrong, and the market reached new highs by late 1995. The consensus at the end of 1995 was again skeptical that the market could continue to achieve new highs.

However, occasionally the consensus is correct. What if the market does not perform well? In our example, what if the stock decreased and remained below the exercise price of the option over the life of the synthetic convertible unit? What would the performance of the SCU have been, and would the synthetic convertible have accomplished its objective of preserving capital under poor market conditions? At maturity, the bond would have been worth par plus accumulated interest, with the warrant cost of $194.10 completely lost. The loss on the total position would have been 6.6 percent-versus providing 79 percent of the stock's upside potential.

The analysis above demonstrates that the fixed-income portion of the synthetic would preserve principal under the test of declining market conditions. In a volatile market climate, equity prices can decline quickly for a number of reasons. Often the mere prospect of higher inflation and higher interest rates, a recession, or other unforeseen events can send the stock market into a tailspin. But this would have had minimal effect on the principal of the maturing government security that constituted the fixed-income portion of the SCU. Thus, the SCU accomplishes its objective of preserving capital in face of declining financial markets.

## SUMMARY

Synthetic convertibles have a number of advantages, including:

1. *Customization:* Synthetic convertibles can be customized to fit the unique requirements of individual investors. The financial planner's ability to use this security to design specific solutions is unique among fixed-income

products and is a driving force in the continued growth of this area.

2. *Yield enhancement:* Financial planners may obtain higher-than-market yields by using synthetic convertibles designed for a specific investment outlook.

3. *Exotic payoff:* Synthetics present opportunities that are not typically otherwise available in the fixed-income area.

4. *Diversification:* Synthetic units permit investors to diversify their portfolios and help control risk. They allow investment exposure to market sectors where traditional convertibles are not well represented.

5. *Liquidity:* Since the synthetic convertible units trade individual components separately, and the components are accounted for separately on the portfolio accounting statements, the liquidity for the separate components can differ. In the typical synthetic convertible unit, the government note that makes up the fixed-income portion of the security and constitutes a significant portion of the total investment is highly liquid. The liquidity of LEAPS and warrants depends on the size and volume of both the individual security and the amount needed for the particular synthetic security and does not present unusual constraints.[4]

It's clear that synthetic convertibles offer additional flexibility and opportunity in managing convertible portfolios. The main advantage of synthetic convertibles is to enhance and further diversify convertible portfolios by expanding investment opportunities; they are used more often to supplement rather than replace convertible bonds. Synthetic convertibles increase the potential size of the convertible market and the investor's ability to control risk and achieve above-average returns.

# E N D N O T E S

1. The material on synthetic securities was originally published in an article in *Personal Financial Planning*: John P. Calamos, "Investment Risk Management: Synthetic Convertibles," Vol. 8, No. 5 (July/August 1996): 45-50. Used with permission.

2. Peng, Scott Y., and Dattatreya, Ravi E., *The Structured Note Market* (Chicago: Probus Publishing, 1995), p. 2.
3. *Ibid.*, a Federal Reserve report, p. 4.
4. *Ibid.*, pp. 3–4.

# 7

## CHAPTER

# The Global
# Convertible Market

The capital markets' growth over the years has produced a convertible market that is now significant in size and global in breadth. Like the patterns seen in the stock and bond markets, this growth has been sporadic. There are highly developed convertible markets in the United States and Japan. There are also advanced convertible markets in England, France, Australia, Canada, Sweden, and Switzerland. The convertible markets in many other countries are developing rapidly, with the emerging markets showing notable growth. The global market includes convertibles from companies in 38 different countries, with over 2,300 issues outstanding and a combined issue size of over $400 billion.

The convertible market continues to expand with additional types of convertibles and variations of the traditional convertible bond. Companies and third-party investment bankers alike have added equity-linked securities to the global convertible universe, which has further expanded and altered the convertible universe.

For international investors, the Eurobond market, with its depth and diversity, is the most significant. That market is open to both international investors and issuers. In addition to the United States, the major domestic convertible markets are Japan, Switzerland, France, and the United Kingdom.

In this chapter we review the characteristics of the global market and those of the major markets as well. Our emphasis will be on the Eurobond market as the most significant international market and on the United States as the primary market for U.S.-dollar-based investors.

## GLOBAL CONVERTIBLE UNIVERSE

The increased interest in convertibles worldwide is evidenced by the growing number of investment firms now devoting resources to researching convertible markets, data, and trends. It wasn't very long ago that most convertible research basically focused on domestic markets and their corresponding issues only. Today, firms around the globe create indexes to track the market and devote resources to trade and research convertibles.

Many factors have contributed to this increased interest in convertibles, one of the most important being the enormous growth of the capital markets. This growth phenomenon has been driven by the acceptance of free markets that has occurred globally since the end of the Cold War. In turn, this has created an investment atmosphere with significant longer-term implications. Privatization and infrastructure rebuilding in both emerging and developed markets have been fostered by the increased recognition that the discipline of investors' capital can allocate resources better than public funding. Multinational companies are enjoying increased market expansions. Many rely on convertible debt financing as a source of capital that provides investors with debt instruments having capital appreciation potential.

The total global convertible universe on December 31, 1997, was approximately $400 billion, of which the U.S. market represented approximately 43 percent and the Japan convertible market approximately 40 percent. Figure 7–1 shows the percentage of market capitalization accounted for by each country represented. Figure 7–2 shows total dollar value of market capitalization in the convertible market by region or country.

Emerging markets represent a growing segment of the international convertible market. Since 1990, countries in the Far East, Africa, and Latin America have issued many convertibles. Privatizing their telecommunication industry resulted in a number of convertible debt issues: Philippine Long Distance Telephone Com-

## F I G U R E 7–1

Global Convertible Market Capitalization as of December 31, 1997

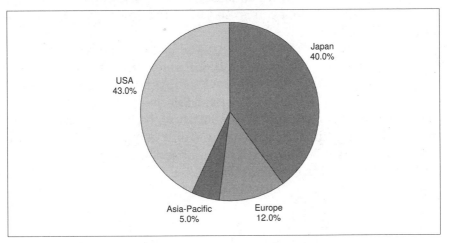

Source: Morgan Stanley Convertible Research.

## F I G U R E 7–2

Market Capitalization of the Global Convertible Market
as of December 31, 1997

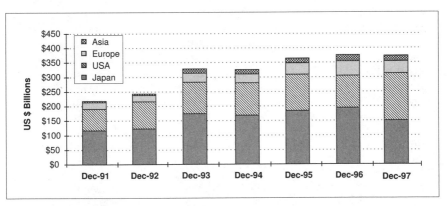

Source: Morgan Stanley Convertible Research.

pany, Telefonica de Argentina S.A. and Telecom Argentina Stet, Telefonos de Mexico S.A., Compania de Telefonos de Chile S.A., and others issued convertible debt. Infrastructure financing, as done by Renong of Malaysia, Cemex, and New World Infrastructure, also used convertibles. Pacific Rim countries have used convertibles extensively in financing their growth, and the trend has been increasing: There were 30 issues in 1993 and more than 81 in 1995. Convertibles have been issued in China, Russia, South Korea, India, and Pakistan.

The developed markets of Europe have used convertible debt financing for many years. Large companies such as British Aerospace, L. M. Ericsson, Grand Met, Phillips, and Aegon all issued convertible bonds. The global convertible market is as diverse as the global financial markets in general; both include representation from different industries and various size companies throughout the world. Figure 7–3 shows the 20 largest non-U.S. convertibles outstanding as of December 31, 1997.

**F I G U R E  7–3**

Largest Non-U.S. Convertibles as of December 31, 1997

| | US$Millions | |
|---|---|---|
| Sony #4 | 3,249 | Japan |
| Bell/NA Telecom 5.75% 2003 | 2,611 | New Zealand |
| Mitsubishi Bank 3% 2002 | 2,058 | Japan |
| Italy/INA 6.5% 2001 | 1,984 | Italy |
| Italy/INA 5.0% 2001 | 1,752 | Italy |
| Hitachi #7 | 1,619 | Japan |
| Roche I 0.0% 2008 | 1,574 | Switzerland |
| Sanofi 4.0% 2000 | 1,551 | France |
| Matsushita Electric #4 | 1,548 | Japan |
| Roche III 0.0% 2012 | 1,464 | Switzerland |
| Alcatel Alsthom 6.5% 2002 | 1,455 | France |
| Sony #5 | 1,432 | Japan |
| NEC 1.9% 2004 | 1,157 | Japan |
| Sandoz 1.25% 2002 | 1,339 | Switzerland |
| Tokyo Elec. Power #1 | 1,327 | Japan |
| Kansai Elec. Power #3 | 1,289 | Japan |
| Roche II 0.0% 2010 | 1,245 | Switzerland |
| Sandoz 2.0% 2002 | 1,243 | Switzerland |
| Allianz / Duetsche Bank 3.0% 2003 | 1,239 | Gemany |
| Toshiba #7 | 1,130 | Japan |
| Alcatel Alsthom 2.5% 2004 | 1,127 | France |

Source: Merrill Lynch Convertible Research.

## The United States Convertible Market

The U.S. domestic convertible market is one of the most important in the world, although it is not the largest. The size of the convertible market has kept pace with the growth of capital markets worldwide. It is a diverse market representing a broad spectrum of industries and companies within the United States. It is primarily an institutional market where many plan sponsors and consultants consider convertibles a separate asset class. Some pension funds—both public and corporate—make specific convertible allocations with dedicated convertible portfolios. In the United States, growth and income mutual funds often use convertibles. According to Morningstar, Inc., there were 47 convertible funds devoted specifically to convertible investing and representing total assets of $6.4 billion as of June 30, 1997. The convertible market has ample liquidity, provided by a highly developed network of market makers and hedge funds.

There are many different types of convertible securities outstanding in the U.S. market, including:

- Convertible bonds.
- Convertible preferred stock.
- Convertibles with put features.
- Zero-coupon convertible bonds.
- Third-party convertible notes.
- Mandatory convertibles.

The primary types are convertible bonds, convertible preferred stocks, zero-coupon convertibles, and mandatory convertibles. Figure 7–4 indicates the breakdown by convertible type as of December 31, 1997, when the total U.S. convertible market was $157.61 billion.

The dollar amounts of convertibles issued over the years effectively demonstrates the growth of the convertible market in the United States. Before 1980, the convertible new-issue market was relatively inactive, after a growth phase in the late 1950s and 1960s. A small number of new issues replaced those that had been called by companies or converted to stock by investors. For the most part, it was a special situation market. However, the new-issue market grew dramatically during the 1980s, reflecting the expan-

## F I G U R E  7–4

Convertible Domestic Market
935 Issues—$157.61 Billion—December 31, 1997

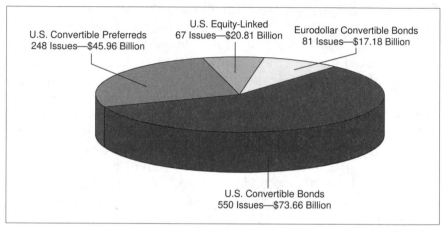

Source: Morgan Stanley & Company Convertible Research.

sion of the capital markets and rising interest in convertible securities. New issuance hit record levels in 1991, 1992, and 1993, but there was a pullback in issuance during 1994 due to that year's difficult bond market. Convertible investing over this period became a serious area of institutional interest.

The number of new issues coming to the market since 1982 is shown in Figure 7–5. Eurobonds were strong in the period 1986 through 1987, while the issuance of traditional convertible bonds has been relatively stable throughout the years. Convertible preferred securities issued by cyclical companies increased dramatically during 1991–93. The banking crises of that period brought many convertible preferreds to the market, as banks were required to increase balance-sheet equity. Convertible preferreds were the primary financial instrument used to raise the necessary new capital. Other cyclical industries characterized by companies with stretched debt equity ratios, such as the automotive, airline, and paper industries, used the convertible preferred market to provide additional capital.

Financial engineering by Wall Street investment bankers brought equity-linked securities to the market beginning in 1988 with an Avon issue. The equity-linkeds are still classified as con-

**F I G U R E  7–5**

Convertible New Issue Volume—January 1, 1982, to December 31, 1997

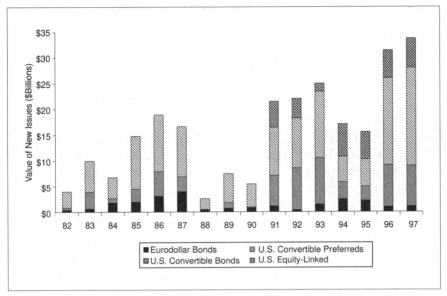

Source: Morgan Stanley & Company Convertible Research.

vertible securities and have now become a significant component of the convertible market. The increasing ability of investment bankers to create securities with specific investment characteristics for specific investment groups is a trend that will continue to expand the convertible market.

Eurodollar convertibles are issued by U.S. companies and are convertible into U.S. domestic common stocks, but are initially sold outside the United States to non-U.S. residents. U.S. investors can purchase these securities after they have been seasoned, usually 45 to 90 days after issuance. This too has expanded the universe of U.S. convertibles, with 81 Eurodollar issues worth $17.18 billion outstanding as of December 31, 1997. As the globalization of the financial markets continues, the issuance of convertibles worldwide will continue to expand the market even further.

The U.S. new issue market has been very active in recent years; 1997's issuance of $31 billion of new convertibles surpassed the previous record of $23 billion issued in 1993. New issues during 1997 were predominantly below investment grade. This below-

investment-grade issuance, combined with redemptions and calls
of investment-grade issues, is once again changing the nature of
the convertible market.

The composition of the U.S. market continues to reflect the
dynamic nature of the U.S. economy. In 1996 and 1997, convertible
market representation shifted from predominantly large-cap, cyclical companies to growth companies. The economy-wide emphasis
on increasing productivity in a low-inflation environment is causing capital flows to technology and similar industries to increase.
Convertibles are a primary source of financing for these companies—the convertible market saw $11 billion of investment-grade
and $12 billion of intermediate-grade convertible issuance in 1997.

U.S. convertible issues generally have three years of protection before they can be called or redeemed. The large number of
issues being retired alters the convertible market. Figure 7–6 indicates both the dollar amount of new issues and the corresponding
dollar value of issues either redeemed or called. By this definition,
the convertible market actually decreased in size. However, when
using market value, which considers performance over that pe-

**F I G U R E  7–6**

Domestic New Convertible Issues versus Retired Issues
1989 through December 31, 1997—In Billions of Dollars ($)

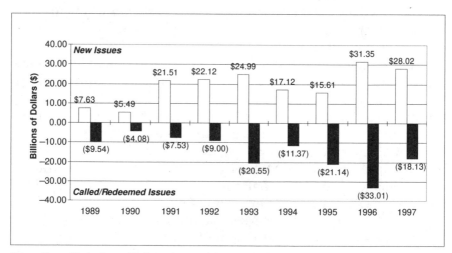

Source: Morgan Stanley Convertible Research.

riod, the U.S. convertible market as of December 31, 1997, had increased to $157.61 billion—more than double the 1989 value.

*Credit Quality* It is also interesting to segment the convertible market by credit quality, as shown in Figures 7–7 and 7–8. Notice that about half the convertible market is investment-grade by dollar amount, and 27 percent is investment-grade by number of issues. The record levels issued in 1992–93 were achieved with both investment-grade and below-investment-grade issuance. From the mid-1980s through 1995, the number of investment-grade issues coming to the domestic market remained relatively stable. In recent years, investment-grade issues from other sources (such as 144A issues) have increased.

There is a significant amount of convertible issuance by companies in the mid-grades—those rated BBB and BB by Standard & Poor's. This is a result of mid-cap growth companies accessing the convertible market. Their ratings are lower than they might otherwise be due a lack of trading history; however, these convertible issues are often the company's only debt outstanding. Some of the premier U.S. growth companies have effectively used convertible

**F I G U R E    7–7**

Convertible Market Credit Quality Sorted by Market Value
as of December 31, 1997

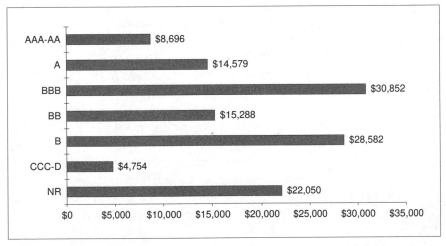

Source: Morgan Stanley Convertible Research.

**F I G U R E  7–8**

Convertible Market Credit Quality Sorted by Number of Issues
as of December 31, 1997

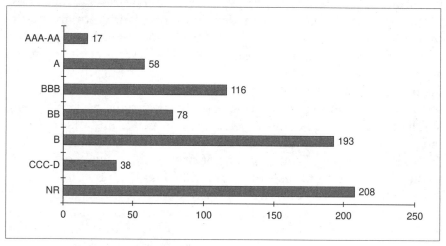

Source: Morgan Stanley Convertible Research.

debt financing as the means to grow their businesses. Many companies issued convertibles securities rated below-investment-grade
in their earlier growth phase, including MCI, Thermo Electron,
and Home Depot. Figure 7–9 shows the breakdown by credit quality over the past six years.

   *Sector Distribution and Types*   As illustrated in Figure 7–10,
convertibles are issued by companies in many different industries. Although the growth of the convertible market in recent
years has allowed convertible portfolios to become more diversified, some industry sectors use convertibles much more than
others. Industry representation in the convertible market is fluid
and dependent on each sector's financing needs. Convertibles
often seem to be issued in bunches when a whole industry ex-
pands. For example, many companies covering the whole quality
spectrum in the hospital care group issued convertibles in large
numbers during the late 1970s. Over the past 20 years, the technology sector has constituted one of the most important sectors
of the convertible market. Investors who purchase convertibles
predominantly in the new-issue market sometimes see their portfolios become heavily weighted in a particular industry group.

## F I G U R E  7–9

Domestic Convertible Market Value Breakdown by Rating—1992 through 1997

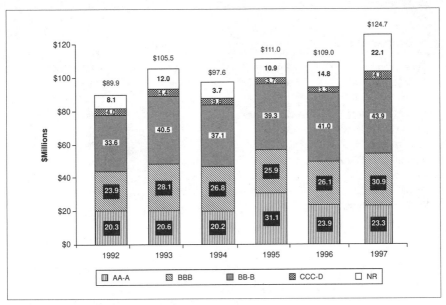

*Excludes 144A and Equity-Linked Securities.

Source: Morgan Stanley Convertible Research.

## F I G U R E  7–10

Convertible Market Sector Distribution as Represented by the First Boston
Convertible Index as of December 31, 1997

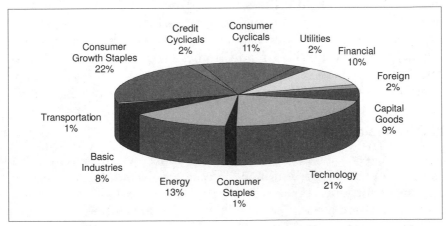

Source: CS First Boston and CAM.

F I G U R E    7–11

Top 10 Largest Domestic Convertible Issues as of 12/31/97 Sorted by Issue Size

| Company Name | Issue Size (Mil) | Coupon | Maturity |
|---|---|---|---|
| Time Warner Inc. | 2,415.00 | 0.00% | 06/22/13 |
| Hewlett Packard | 1,800.00 | 0.00% | 10/14/17 |
| Hasbro Inc. | 1,651.49 | 0.00% | 12/17/12 |
| News Corp. Ltd. | 1,350.00 | 0.00% | 03/11/13 |
| Lowes/Do | 1,150.00 | 3.12% | 09/15/07 |
| K Mart Corp. | 1,000.00 | 7.75% | preferred issue |
| News Corp. (BSkyB) | 1,000.00 | 5.00% | preferred issue |
| Costco Ind. | 900.00 | 0.00% | 08/19/17 |
| Automatic Data | 801.70 | 0.00% | 02/20/12 |
| ADT Ltd. Com. | 776.30 | 0.00% | 07/06/10 |

Growth companies in general make up the largest type of company accessing the convertible market.

The largest outstanding issues give an indication of the character of the convertible market. Figure 7–11 shows these companies and the size of the issues.

## INVESTMENT CHARACTERISTICS OF THE U.S. CONVERTIBLE MARKET

The investment characteristics of the U.S. convertible market reflect the impact of both the stock and bond markets. Generally, new convertibles carry a conversion price that is 15 to 25 percent over the price of the underlying common stock when the convertible is brought to market. In addition, they often carry an interest rate that is two to four percentage points lower than that of a straight corporate bond issued by the same company.

### Yield Characteristics

The average annual income of all convertible new issues has ranged from as low as 4.7 percent in 1993, which reflected the decrease in long-term corporate bond rates, to 9.5 percent in 1982, when bond rates hit historic highs. Convertible coupon rates follow the corporate bond market, and this relationship remained relatively constant throughout the years up to 1990. As interest rates decreased, investment bankers were able to price convertible securities off different parts of the yield curve. For example, zero-coupon convertibles are priced to reflect their yield-to-first-put, which is often 3 to 5 years. The investment value therefore reflects the effective shorter maturity of these vehicles. Overall, the average maturity level has steadily decreased over the years. As of third quarter 1996, the average-years-to-maturity of the convertible universe is 5.08 years (according to the First Boston Convertible Index), while in the mid-1980s the average-years-to-maturity was closer to 20 years. In recent years, 10-year notes have been the typical issuance.

Using the First Boston Convertible Index as a proxy for the convertible market, notice how the yield component of converts has made a significant contribution to total return. Figure 7–12 shows total return of the First Boston Index and the average yield for each 12-month period. In the three negative years—1987, 1990,

## F I G U R E  7–12

Historical Performance Breakdown for the Convertible Market Using the FBCI as a Proxy for the Market—Total Returns versus Returns from Income January 1, 1982, through December 31, 1997

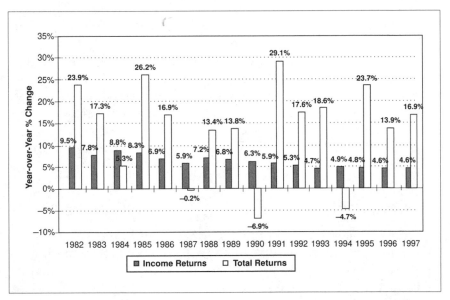

Source: CS First Boston and CAM.

**F I G U R E  7–13**

Historical Current Yield of Convertible Securities Compared to the Dividend Yield on Underlying Stocks Using the FBCI as a Proxy for the Market January 1, 1982, through December 31, 1997

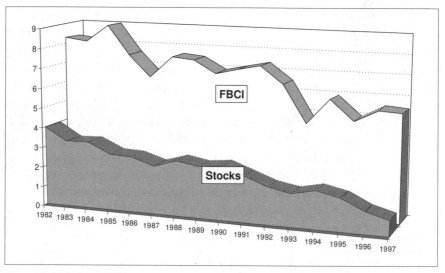

Source: CS First Boston and CAM.

and 1994—the income from convertibles helped offset significant price declines in principal values.

Figure 7–13 shows the current yield of convertibles against the dividend yield of the stocks underlying the convertibles. As of December 31, 1997, the average yield of the underlying stocks was 1 percent, reflecting the lower yields on the broader cross-section of the convertible market as compared to those of narrower indexes like the S&P 500. The yield advantage of convertibles continues to be significant.

## Equity Characteristics

The convertible's level of equity participation is measured by its conversion premium. As one might expect, conversion premiums have not remained constant. Market sentiment clearly influences conversion premium levels. Consider the situation in 1982, when the traditional relationship between conversion premium and coupon rate applied: Lower-quality issues required a higher coupon and carried a higher conversion premium. The conversion premium for an average new-issue investment-grade convertible was 16.5 percent, with a coupon of 9.1 percent. New issues of below-investment-grade convertibles averaged 21.8 percent, with a coupon rate of 10.2 percent. In 1987, the average coupon for an investment-grade convertible was 6.5 percent, with an average conversion premium of 23.4 percent, while below-investment-grade issues had a higher coupon rate but a lower conversion premium. The two years are highlighted in Figure 7–14.

The differences in conversion premiums for 1987 indicate the effect of market sentiment in a volatile environment. During that period, conversion premiums for new issues averaged 23.2 percent, the highest in years. While the average coupon rate decreased, reflecting decreasing rates in the bond market in 1987, conversion premiums increased. This led some analysts to conclude that the new-issue convertible market was overpriced and should be avoided.

In 1987, investors seemed willing to pay more for a higher conversion premium for investment-grade convertibles than for below-investment-grade convertibles. In other words, investors accepted a lower coupon rate (6.5 percent versus 7.2 percent) for a higher conversion premium (23.2 percent versus 22.2 percent). This curious relationship led observers to question whether investors may have been overpaying for those investment-grade issues.

**F I G U R E    7–14**

| | Investment Grade | | Below Investment Grade | |
| --- | --- | --- | --- | --- |
| | Coupon Rate | Conversion Premium | Coupon Rate | Conversion Premium |
| 1982 | 9.1% | 16.5% | 10.2% | 21.8% |
| 1987* | 6.5% | 23.2% | 7.2% | 22.2% |

*Through September 30, 1987.

Source: Investment Dealers Digest.

The relationship that existed in 1982 was more customary—conversion premiums on investment-grade convertibles were well below those of the higher-risk, below-investment-grade issues. Investors expect to receive a higher coupon rate on below-investment-grade convertibles and are usually willing to accept a higher conversion premium because those stocks have more volatility, higher risk, and, therefore, greater price movements. Presumably, common stocks of these smaller companies have greater growth prospects, so the conversion premium of their convertibles could be made up more quickly than with a staid, blue-chip stock.

The conversion premium in the new-issue market trended upward in the bull market phase of the 1980s. This trend is indicated in Figure 7–15.

In 1995 and 1996, high-tech companies issued convertibles with conversion premiums of 50 percent—thereby indicating a strong belief in the upward trend of the underlying stock. A company wanting a higher conversion price for its stock would have to raise the coupon rate. National Semiconductor Corporation brought an issue to the market in September 1995 with a coupon that was relatively high for the time, 6.5 percent, and a conversion premium of 45 percent. The stock has to rise by a large amount before the bondholder will benefit by converting. This works well

**F I G U R E   7–15**

Convertible Debt Offerings Highlights

| Year | Number of Issues | Market Value (millions) | Average Coupon | Average Convertible Premium | % Investment Grade |
|------|------|------|------|------|------|
| 1982 | 67 | 3,172.6 | 10.2 | 21.2 | 23.9 |
| 1983 | 113 | 6,056.6 | 9.2 | 19.1 | 27.4 |
| 1884 | 66 | 4,078.7 | 9.6 | 19.1 | 42.4 |
| 1985 | 137 | 10,283.0 | 8.7 | 19.6 | 27.7 |
| 1986 | 206 | 10,966.6 | 7.4 | 21.3 | 6.8 |
| 1987* | 148 | 9,400.7 | 7.2 | 23.5 | 16.9 |

*Through Sept. 30, 1987.

Source: *Investment Dealers' Digest* (domestic market only).

in a bull market, but wouldn't sell nearly so well in a more bearish market. In any event, National Semiconductor compensates bond-holders with the higher coupon rate while they wait for the stock price to increase. Another example is 3Com Corporation, which brought an issue to market in November 1994 with a 10.25 percent coupon—and a conversion premium of 70 percent!

The convertible market reflects the dynamics of the financial marketplace. Conversion premium levels ebb and flow, depending on market sentiment. In a bullish environment, the enthusiasm of the market boosts premium levels. (Investors will buy a convert-ible with a high premium believing the underlying stock will ap-preciate quickly.) When market sentiment changes, premium levels can decrease very rapidly.

During the 1982–87 period, the blue-chip market was any-thing but staid. The high-quality sector of the stock market contin-ued to outpace the riskier growth areas. Demand for investment-grade convertibles was reflected in higher conversion premiums. The new-issue, investment-grade convertible market may have seemed overpriced by historical standards, so managers should have been wary.

On the other hand, investors' enthusiasm for the aggressive sectors of the market did not match that for the blue-chip sector. Conversion premium levels for below-investment-grade convert-ibles remained relatively stable over those years. These issues were fairly priced, and occasionally mispriced, providing some value for investors.

During the late 1980s and the first half of the 1990s, the accep-tance of theoretical valuations changed the new-issue market. The widespread use of option price theory in valuing new-issue con-vertibles provided a check on overpricing new issues. In 1995, the demand for new issues was extremely high, with many issues oversubscribed by a wide margin. However, if investment bankers tried to take advantage of the demand by overpricing the issue, demand faded fast. Even with the heavy demand for convertibles in 1992, 1993, and 1995, most issues were priced at a discount to fair value.

Figure 7–16 provides an interesting illustration of the mar-ket's tendency to fair value. The first scattergram shows valuation of new convertibles at issuance; the widely scattered trendline is

**F I G U R E  7–16**

1996 Domestic New Convertible Issues Over/Under Valuation Scatter Diagram
Valuation at Issue

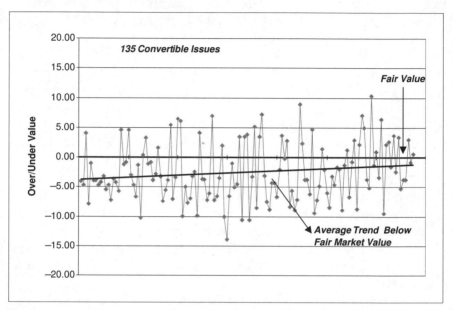

Source: Calamos Asset Management (excludes equity-linked securities and issues under $50 million).

below 0.00, the fair value line. At a later time, after these issues
have traded in the market for some time, the trendline is right on
top of the fair value line, showing how the market tends to fair
value (as illustrated in Figure 7–17).

Investment bankers responded to the market by changing the
terms that affect valuations. For example, decreasing the number
of years until the convertible bond's maturity allowed the coupon
to be lowered. Many bonds were issued with a maturity of 10
years or less. Buyers readily accepted this because shorter maturities have greater downside safety. Many new issues could be
priced off commercial paper rates instead of longer bond yields.

Investors who buy primarily in the new-issue convertible
market may be disappointed over time because the best opportunities often occur in the aftermarket. Because of its ample supply,
it may be easier to use the new-issue market to build a convertible

## F I G U R E  7–17

1996 Domestic New Convertible Issues Over/Under Valuation Scatter Diagram
Valuation as of December 31, 1996

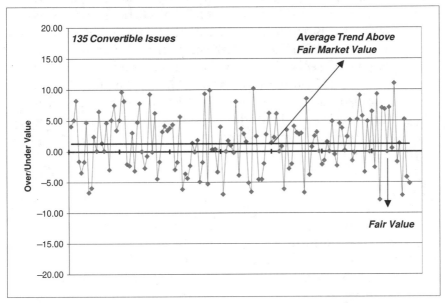

Source: Calamos Asset Management (excludes equity-linked securities and issues under $50 million).

portfolio, but because the new-issue market is often concentrated in a few popular sectors at any one time, the resulting convertible portfolio may lack the proper balance.

The most exciting feature of the new-issue convertible market is its tremendous growth. In the past, many large investors, such as pension funds, were hesitant to participate in the convertible market because of its relatively small size. Today, the burgeoning convertible market provides ample opportunities for even large institutional investors. With the relatively low coupons on straight bonds available in the 1990s (as compared to the 1980s), convertibles have become attractive to straight fixed-income buyers. Insurance companies and other traditional, straight fixed-income buyers are active institutional investors in the convertible market.

Merger activities have added to the U.S. convertible market. The mid-1980s supplied two good examples of changes in investors' perceptions of convertibles. IBM acquired Rolm Corporation, a leading telecommunications company, and in November 1984, IBM's exchange offer for Rolm resulted in a $1.25 billion convertible bond issue, the largest convertible issue of that time. Rolm shareholders received IBM convertible bonds. The merger between Sperry Rand and Burroughs, now called Unisys, resulted in what was at the time (1986) the largest convertible issue ever offered. The exchange of securities between the companies was accomplished by a $1.425 billion offering of a $50 par value, $3.50 convertible preferred. The attention the IBM convertible and Unisys brought to the convertible market helped dispel the misconception that convertibles are issued only by marginal companies in dire financial straits.

## Trading

In the U.S. convertible market, the many market makers and hedge funds provide liquidity. It is primarily an institutional market, wherein many participants use convertible models and hedging techniques. U.S. convertibles can be theoretically undervalued at times, reflecting market sentiment regarding either convertibles in general or companies and industries specifically. However, for individual investors, selecting U.S. convertibles in the aftermarket becomes more complicated. Investors must pay attention not only to the level of the conversion premium but also to the call features, yield-to-maturity, bond value and, of course, growth prospects of the underlying common stock. A major advantage of selecting U.S. convertibles in the aftermarket is the occasional inefficiency that can cause an issue to be underpriced or undervalued.

The U.S. convertible market represents the complete spectrum of the stock market—from New York Stock Exchange blue chips to aggressive, high-technology issues to more speculative OTC stocks and energy sectors on the American Stock Exchange.

## EUROBOND CONVERTIBLE MARKET

The Eurobond market's size and diversity of issuers makes it important to investors throughout the world. The Eurobond market is not a market for Europeans only, but a significant market for any investor desiring to participate in the convertible market of any country, including the United States. Convertibles of U.S. companies issued in the Eurobond market trade as easily as any domestic U.S. convertible bond. Today's Eurobond issues present liquidity and depth equal to any security issued in the U.S. domestic market. There is little need to restrict an investment manager's use of Euroconvertibles due to fear of illiquidity.

*Eurobond* is one of the more loosely defined words in finance. While it originally represented bonds issued outside the United States but denominated in U.S. dollars, it has come to represent any bond issued outside the issuer's local market. In today's convertible market, Eurobonds are issued by U.S., European, Asian, and Latin American companies. While U.S. and European companies typically issue Euroconvertibles in their own currency, cross-currency bonds are issued occasionally. Most Asian and Latin American companies issue bonds denominated in U.S. dollars, with the Swiss franc market being the major exception.

The Eurobond market grew from $8.1 billion in 1990 to $14.0 billion in 1995. The period 1990-93 saw particularly substantial growth. In the Eurobond market, bonds with equity warrants are considered to be part of the total convertible universe since both convertible bonds and bonds with detachable equity warrants have hybrid characteristics. Statistics for the Eurobond market thus usually combine the equity-related issues together as a subset of the total Eurobond market.

The Eurobond market, in general, often sees clusters of issuance in a particular style. One company tries a new structure, and others see how beneficial it might be. Use of premium redemption and put features is higher in markets that tend to have lower stock dividends and lower in markets with higher dividends, such as Hong Kong, where the stock market is dominated by real estate companies that tend to pay out higher yields.

In fact, put features have become quite common in Asia. Prior to 1994, many bonds were issued with low coupons. Issuers could get away with such structures due to the extremely strong equity market performance of the prior years. In other words, it was a seller's market. However, many of these issues performed poorly (although still not as badly as their underlying stock) in the aftermath of the Mexican peso devaluation, which redefined upward the market's interpretation of credit risk in emerging markets. Issuers were faced with a market that demanded much higher bond floors.

To meet this requirement, issuers have tended to follow two paths. The most frequently used approach has been a low coupon coupled with a put at five years (with bonds typically having maturities of 7 to 10 years). This yields a premium to the then-prevailing 5-year U.S. Treasury note rate, gives the investor the protection of a high bond floor, and allows the issuer to pay a much lower coupon than investors would otherwise demand. If the stock performs well the bond gets converted, and the issuer never pays the put. The other option is to shorten the bond's maturity to 5 years. Stronger credits will be able to issue moderate coupons (4 to 5 percent) due to the shorter maturity.

As another example, the French Euroconvertible market sees many premium redemption issues because the French market tends to be a bond-value-driven market—meaning that investors see convertibles as fixed-income instruments with the conversion feature offered as a kicker. The high investment value that results from the premium redemption feature makes that structure popular.

It is interesting to compare Eurobond new issuance for straight convertibles with that for equity-related securities; the comparison highlights fluctuations in popularity among issuing companies. While convertible bond issuance showed steady increases for the period 1990–93, growing from $4.2 billion in 1990 to $17.2 billion in 1993, equity-related issuance has been volatile. In 1990, only 18 percent of total convertible and equity-related issuance was in convertible bonds. By 1993, the convertible-bond portion had grown to 57 percent, and the equity related segment decreased to 43 percent. As of September 30, 1996, convertible bonds accounted for 62 percent of new issuance, and equity-linked securities accounted for 12 percent.

This change was caused by the increased number of Japanese issuers favoring convertible bonds over bonds with equity warrants and was the beginning of an important new group of borrowers from the emerging markets, who continue to constitute a significant segment of the convertible market. The decrease in equity warrant issuance is a result of the poor equity market in Japan. The collapse of the Japanese market caused warrants issued in the past to quickly become substantially out of the money.

## Japan

Japan is the largest convertible market in the world, representing about 40 percent of the global convertible universe (as of December 31, 1997). The Japanese market has some internal peculiarities that cause it to seem larger than it is. Many of the convertibles are illiquid, almost private placements, making them unavailable for investors. Additionally, companies rarely call their convertibles and instead leave many deep-in-the-money convertibles outstanding. This is changing quickly because many of these convertible bonds are reaching maturity. Nineteen percent of the market matures by December 1998, 23 percent by the year 2000, and 33 percent by 2004. Only 25 percent of the convertibles currently outstanding in the Japanese market have a maturity beyond 2004. In other markets, such as the United States, companies call convertibles at the earliest opportunity. However, in Japan, with the underlying common stocks down since 1989, most bonds are trading as fixed-income instruments with an insignificant equity factor. This has affected statistics on the global markets. Those creating indexes must make major decisions on how to represent Japan.

Convertible bonds have been a significant means of financing for Japanese companies for nearly 25 years. Although they were permitted by Japanese authorities in 1938, few were issued until the 1970s. The Japanese commercial code was amended in 1974 to allow companies to issue convertibles by board resolution rather than by shareholder vote. This increased the ease with which convertible bonds could be brought to market. Another factor that increased corporate use of the convertible vehicle was the security industry's 1978 relaxation on constraints on the maximum size of an issue, which had previously been restricted to 30 billion yen. This additional interest in converts also caused an increase in the number of different structures used: The first put bond and the first premium redemption were brought to market that same year. In addition, the use of convertibles was driven by demand: The lack of a corporate, straight-bond market made convertibles the only alternative to Japanese government bonds for fixed-income investors.

Further changes to the Japanese market continued in the 1980s. The Tokyo Stock Exchange expanded order execution to include all convertibles in 1987. In 1988, the Tokyo Stock Exchange book-entry clearing system allowed all convertible bond transactions to be cleared through it and by 1990 began to trade all but 50 issues on the computerized trading system.

Although the Japanese convertible market is a significant part of the total convertible universe, it remains for the most part a domestic market with few foreign listings. In 1988, Peninsular & Oriental Steam Navigation listed the first foreign-currency convertible, and in 1991 Glaxo Holdings was the first yen-denominated foreign issue. The obvious attraction was accessing the large pool of capital available in the Japanese markets, but few followed. The lack of foreign issues can be explained by the potential currency risk and the difference in terms between the low-premium Japanese market and the other international markets.

The Japanese domestic convertible new issue volume followed similar patterns of other markets. During the 1980s, the strong equity markets of Japan led to an increase in convertible new issues. When the equity markets suffered, new issuance in the convertible market also declined significantly. Figure 7–18 shows new issue activity from 1984 through 1996. Consistent with the experience of other major markets when economic activity is high, convertible

**F I G U R E  7–18**

Size of the Japanese Convertible Bond Market

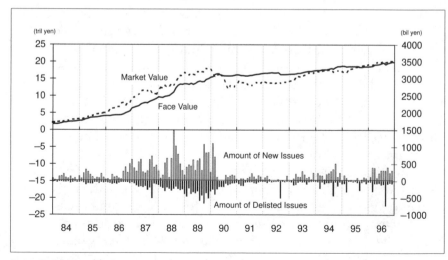

Source: Nomura Securities Co., Ltd. Used with permission.

issuance is increasing, compared to little convertible issuance during the era of depressed economic activity in the 1990s.

Relative to the U.S. market, the Japanese convertible market has higher credit ratings (only 3 percent of convertibles outstanding are below investment grade), lower coupons (82 percent of convertibles outstanding have coupons of 2 percent or below), and larger issue size on average. Figure 7–19 shows the composition of the convertible market.

Liquidity is important in any market, but investors must pay particular attention in the Japanese convertible market, where only 20 percent of the issues are considered liquid. Liquidity is defined as issues with more than yen 9 billion outstanding, more than three

**F I G U R E  7–19**

Characteristics of the Japanese Convertible Market

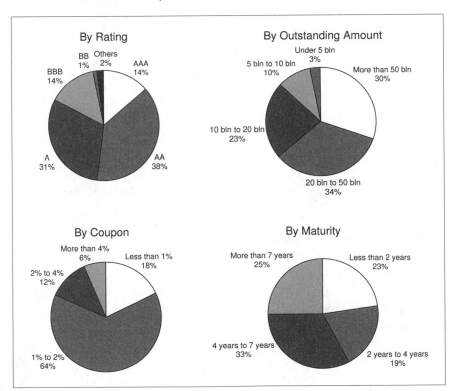

Nomura Securities Co., Ltd.

years to maturity, and daily turnover of more than yen 20 million. Considering the above criteria in light of market value rather than number of issues, only half the market is considered liquid.

In the Japanese market, convertibles are considered a separate asset class by institutional investors. Japanese rules have restricted pension funds in the type of investments they may make. This has come to be known as the 5:3:3:2 rule. The rule limits the maximum amount in the following asset classes:

| | |
|---|---|
| Fixed-income assets | Minimum 50% |
| Equity assets | Maximum 30% |
| Foreign assets | Maximum 30% |
| Other assets (real estate, etc.) | Maximum 20% |

Convertibles are used by some pension funds to increase the equity exposure above the 30 percent limit. Other pension funds use convertibles in their fixed-income allocation to enhance fixed-income returns. And still others consider convertibles a separate asset class. There has been discussion within the regulatory agencies to remove the 5:3:3:2 restrictions for some pension plans. Convertibles have added value to the asset allocation by outperforming equity over the last 10 years, but they have underperformed the bond market. Therefore, it is uncertain how rule changes would affect convertible issuance in the future.

However, the need for capital is driven by the equity market, and unless equity markets improve, convertible issuance will remain small. An improvement in the equity market could bring back individual investors, who in the past have participated extensively in the convertible market.

In October 1995, the Japanese new-issue market perked up with several convertibles from the banking sector designed for the international market. In an effort to boost balance-sheet equity, the banks set up a program to obtain capital for nonperforming loans stemming from Japan's burst real estate bubble. The top Japanese banks issued *resetable mandatory exchangeable convertible securities*. The notable feature was a reset schedule that would increase the conversion ratio should the stock decline over a stated time period. With the decline in the Japanese stock market, and with bank stocks in particular not in favor, the selling point to entice investors to purchase these securities is this reset feature, which has the effect of keeping the value of the bond near par even if the stock declines. Therefore, the bond value is stabilized by the reset and it has capital gains potential if the stock increases above the original conversion price.

The first of these securities was the Mitsubishi Bank $2 billion issue brought by Morgan Stanley, one of the largest convertible issues ever. Desperately in need of capital, Mitsubishi Bank's total capital ratio will increase from 9 to 11 percent when the bonds convert to stock. The banks' objective was to raise capital; therefore, the deal was structured as a mandatory conversion to stock. Since mandatory conversion issues are less attractive to investors, the bank added the reset feature. Over the next five years, Mitsubishi has the right to redeem 20 percent of the issue. The conversion is to ADS with an original conversion price of U.S. $22 and an initial reset of 65 percent of U.S. $13.61. As the prospectus states:

> Repayment in Shares may only be made if the ADS Equivalent Price on the Calculation Day immediately preceding the day notice is given is at least equal to the Notice Threshold Share Price. The notice of repayment in Shares shall specify that repayment in shares will become effective only if the Average ADS Equivalent Price on the date of maturity is not lower than the Minimum Repayment Price (an amount equal to 50 percent of the initial Exchange Price set forth on the cover page of this Prospectus, subject to Antidilution Adjustment). If repayment in Shares is not effective, the Notes will be repaid in cash at their principal amount plus accrued interest.

Each year on the annual reset date of November 30, the conversion price is reset at 65 percent of the original conversion price, stepping down to 50 percent in the final year.[1]

Other Japanese banks quickly followed this issue. Tokai Bank issued a yen 100 billion 2.75 percent NC preferred share in March 1996; Sumitomo issued a yen 100 billion 0.75 percent non-cum; Sakura Bank a yen 150 billion issue; and Fuji Bank a yen 100 billion 0.25 percent. Generally the structure seemed similar, but in reality the slight differences made each issue unique in its valuation and different enough to make valuation difficult. Figure 7–20 outlines the particulars about terms of each issue. Additionally, the Mitsubishi Bank issue is based on the underlying ADS, resulting in its having currency exposure. A weakening yen would adversely affect the security's value.

# FIGURE 7-20

## Fixed Issuance Terms and Current Pricing for the Principal Japanese Bank Resetable Convertibles

| | Daiwa Bank Step Down | BOT-Mitsubishi Bank | Tokai Bank | Sumitomo Bank | Sakura Bank | Fuji Bank | Sumitomo T & B | Toyo T & B |
|---|---|---|---|---|---|---|---|---|
| **Fixed Issuance Terms: (a)** | | | | | | | | |
| Issue Date: | Mar-94 | Sep-95 | Mar-96 | May-96 | Aug-96 | Dec-96 | Jun-1997 | May-1997 |
| Issue Size: | Yen 50 bn | US$2 bn | Yen 100 bn | Yen 100 bn | Yen 150 bn | Yen 210 bn | Yen 100bn | Yen 50bn |
| Lead Manager: | Salomon Bros | Morgan Stanley | Salomon Bros. | Goldman Sachs | Merrill Lynch | SBC Warburg | Salomon | SBC Warb./G.Sachs |
| Coupon: | 2.25% down 1.25% | 3% | 2.75% NC.Pref.Shr. | Non-cum 0.75% | 0.75% | 0.25% | 0.50% | 0.75% |
| Coup.Freq./Dates: | Semi, Mar31/Sep 30 | Semi, Nov30/May31 | Semi, Sep30/Mar31 | Semi, Nov30/May31 | Semi, Oct31/Apr30 | Semi, Mar31/Sep30 | Semi, Apr1/Oct11 | Semi, Mar31/Sep30 |
| Maturity: | March 31, 1998 | November 30, 2002 | October 31, 2004 | May 31, 2001 | October 31, 2001 | February 1, 2002 | October 1, 2007 | Perp. reverts to FRN |
| Conversion Period: | Apr.'94–Mar.'98 | Apr.'96–Nov.'02 | Jul.'01–Sep.'04 | Aug.'96–May'01 | Jul.'97–Sep.'01 | Jul.'97–Jan.'02 | Aug.'97–Sept.'07 | Jul.'97–Sept.'02 |
| Ticker: | 8319.T | 8315.T | 8321.T | 8318.T | 8314.T | 8317.T | 8403.T | 8407.T |
| **Early Mandatory Conversion: (b)** | | | | | | | | |
| Beginning Date: | None | Nov. 30, 1998 | Oct. 5, 2002 | May 31, 2000 | Oct. 1, 1999 | Oct. 1, 1999 | Oct. 1 | 2002 |
| Annually Onwards: | | Nov. 30 | and Oct. 5, 2003 | | Oct. 1 | Oct. 1 | Oct. 1 | Sept. 30 |
| Performance Criteria: | | ADS–US$16.50 | — | Close Pr. on 31/3/00 | 1-47 day close 85% | 1-47 day close 85% | — | — |
| | | | | 85% conv.price | of Init.Conv.Price | of Init.Conv.Price | | |
| %, Carry Forward (Y/N): | | 20%, Yes | 33%, Yes | 50% | 33%, Yes | 30%, 50%, Yes | | Must call full amount/ subj. to MoF approval |
| **Reset' Features: (c)** | | | | | | | | |
| 1st 'Reset' Date: | Mar. 31, 1995 | Nov. 30, 1996 | Oct. 5, 2001 | May 31, 1997 | Dec. 8, 1997 | Oct. 1, 1997 | Oct. 1, 1998 | June 30, 1998 |
| Annual 'Reset' Date thereafter: | Mar. 31 | Nov. 30 | Oct. 5 | May 31 | Oct. 1 | Oct.1 | Oct.1 | June 30 |
| Final 'Reset' Date: | Already at floor | Nov. 30, 2002 | Oct. 2003 | May 2001 | Oct. 2001 | Feb. 2002 | Feb. 2006 | Jun. 2002 |
| Reset Calculation Period: | 15-day period excl. hols. Jap, NY, Lon. ending:1 - 14 days | 20-day period excl. hols. Jap, NY, Lon. sending:1 - 15 days | 30-day period excl. hols. Jap, NY, Lon. starting:1 - 45 days | 20-day period excl. hols. Jap, NY, Lon. ending:1 - 15 days | 30-day period excl. hols. Jap, NY, Lon. starting:1 - 45 days | 30-day period excl. hols. Jap, NY, Lon. starting:1 - 45 days | 20-day period excl. hols. Jap, NY, Lon. starting:1 - 15 days | 30-day period excl. hols. Jap, NY, Lon. to June 15 |
| Calculation Type: | simple average | simple average | simple average | simple average | simple average | simple average | simple average | arithmetic avg. |
| FX(Yen/US$) Benchmark: | | 12 pm NY Fed.Rate | | | | | | |
| Percentage 'Reset' Trigger: | >1% below conv.pr. | >1% below conv.pr. | | | | >1 Yen chg.reqd. | >1% below conv.prm. | > 1 Yen chg. reqd. |
| Original Conversion Price: | Yen 1,097 | US$22 | Yen 1,397 | Yen 2,255 | Yen 1,122 | Yen 2002 | Yen 1,133 | Yen 831 |
| Current Conversion Price: | Yen 549 | US$20.95 | Yen 1,397 | Yen 1,492 | Yen 1,122 | Yen 2002 | Yen 1,133 | Yen 831 |
| Initial 'Reset' Floor (%): | 50% | 65% | 35.80% | 50% | 44.50% | 65% | 44% | 48% |
| Initial 'Reset' Floor (Price): | Yen 549 | US$13.61 | Yen 500 | Yen 1,128 | Yen 500 | Yen 1301 | Yen 500 | Yen 400 |
| Final 'Reset' Floor (%): | 50% | 50% | 35.80% | 37% | 44.50% | 35% | 44% | 48% |
| Final 'Reset' Floor (Price): | Yen 549 | US$10.47 | Yen 500 | Yen 850 | Yen 500 | Yen 700 | Yen 500 | Yen 400 |
| Cash Option: | No | Yes | No | No | No | No | No | Reverts to FRN paying LIBOR +250, semian. |
| **Current Pricing: (data as at Jan. 13, 1997)** | | | | | | | | |
| Current CB Offer Price: | 109.25 | 109.75 | 101.75 | 128 | 100 | 103.5 | 111.75 | 115.5 |
| Current Parity: | 108.37 | 92.9 | 80.88 | 126 | 73.44 | 81.41 | 105.91 | 111.07 |
| Premium to Parity (%): | 0.81% | 18.14% | 25.80% | 1.59% | 36.17% | 27.13% | 5.51% | 3.99% |
| Current Share Price: | 595 | 1130 (ADR 19.75) | 1,130 | 1,880 | 824 | 1,630 | 1,200 | 923 |
| Share price from Floor (%) | 8.38% | 45.11% | 126.00% | 66.67% | 64.80% | 25.29% | 140.00% | 130.75% |
| CB Offer Price, 6-mo. Range | 63.25–112 | 97.25–110.5 | 86.75–103 | 95–129.25 | 87–102.125 | 84.5–104.75 | 100–113.5 | 100–116.75 |

Source: Colum McCoole, "Japanese Bank Resetables—Testing Times," Research Memorandum, Morgan Stanley & Co., International, January 13, 1997, p. 3. Used with permission of Morgan Stanley.

## Continental Europe

The Continental European convertible market is mixed. The French market has been relatively stable, and the Swiss and German markets have been growing rapidly. The most exciting recent development has been increased issuance by German companies. Issues involving Daimler, Bayer, Allianz, and Siemens have been well received by international investors. The issuers in this market tend to be large-cap, blue-chip companies usually denominated in local currency, along with a few that are denominated in U.S. dollars. The structure is often OID with semiannual coupons and a 10-year maturity; in Germany, many of the issues have nondetachable warrants.

*Switzerland*  The Swiss investor's international approach to investing has long encouraged active convertible issuance. Unlike other major markets, the companies issuing convertibles in Swiss francs are not Swiss companies but companies from around the world. Typically 90 percent of corporate bonds issued in Switzerland are issued by non-Swiss companies.

The Swiss franc bond market uses traditional convertible bonds as well as convertible units.[2] Convertible bonds of both types make up a significant portion of the Swiss franc bond market. In recent years they have represented 27 percent of the total bond market.

Since foreign companies are the predominant issuers in the Swiss franc market, currency factors are an important consideration. The Swiss franc has historically been a strong currency, which has made convertible units more attractive than convertible bonds. The convertible unit allows the straight bond with a fixed rate to be separated from the warrant, making it easier to hedge against currency risk. The usable bond trading separately can be used as a swap to eliminate currency risk. The embedded option in a straight convertible makes it more difficult to hedge against currency risk. Since the value of the convertible can be significantly altered by rising equity value, hedging becomes much more complicated and difficult.

The Swiss franc market also has shown a tendency for shorter maturities when compared to the Euromarket. For example, many Japanese companies requiring equity capital are attracted to the Swiss market because convertible bonds can be issued in shorter maturities with low conversion premiums, resulting in early conversion to equity, whereas equity warrants have a tendency to remain outstanding until expiration date.

The number of countries issuing in the Swiss franc market is in direct contrast to issuance in the Euromarket. There are many more Asian issues in the Swiss franc market than in the Euromarket. In recent years, issuers from the Asia-Pacific region accounted for 80 to 90 percent of the total new-issue volume. In past years, a majority of the issuers were Japanese, while in more recent years other emerging Asian countries have accessed this market. The Swiss franc market now includes issues from Hong Kong, Malaysia, Korea, Taiwan, Thailand, and China. Swiss franc bonds issued by Asian companies are typically smaller in size than the average U.S. dollar Euroconvertible, tending to make them significantly less liquid than U.S. dollar Euroconvertibles for the same country.

**Terms.** The terms of the Swiss market reflect the preferences of Swiss investors. The generally lower level of interest rates results in generally lower coupon rates. Swiss investors are typically more equity oriented. Conversion premiums are also low, reflecting the many Japanese issuers that have come to the market with premiums as low as 5 percent, ensuring that the bonds will be converted. Already other Asian issuers have conversion premiums around 10 percent, much lower than those in many other markets. Swiss companies issuing convertibles tend to have conversion premiums around the more typical 20 percent range since there is little concern about currency hedging.

Along with the lower coupon and conversion premium, the maturities of convertibles issued in the Swiss market tend to be much shorter than those of other markets, especially since many convertibles are issued with a put feature with a relatively short period. The put is often less than three years, effectively decreasing the bond's time to maturity. Callability varies from issue to issue, with many issues noncallable for up to half of their life. Provisional calls are used extensively, allowing a bond to be called once a specified price is reached.

The Swiss franc market has added a twist with a very low coupon convertible that can be put back to the issuer at a premium. These premium puts, which are conventional convertibles, are very popular in the Swiss market.

The Swiss franc convertible market has allowed the well-respected Swiss investor to gain equity exposure in many areas of the world. In recent years, Swiss investors have demonstrated their interest in the volatile emerging markets of Asia by buying Swiss-franc-denominated convertibles issued through local banking relationships. This is a convenient and attractive way to obtain equity exposure and is another example of how the convertible vehicle allows an investor to participate in a volatile sector of the market with reduced risk.

*France*  The French market is the largest in Europe and is dominated by large-cap companies with good credits. Although most are denominated in French francs, they are actively traded by global convertible investors. The coupons are payable annually, many at the start of January, with maturity dates of 7 to 10 years. Most of the trading takes place in Paris among French convertible and fixed-income investors.

An interesting French Franc issue was the EuroDisney convertible used to finance the Disneyland in Paris. The issue has had a volatile history, however. In April 1997, it reached its redemption price of FF154 over 3.5 years ahead of schedule. In 1995, the bond was busted, with a 19 percent yield at the time EuroDisney was restructured. Although the bond is still busted, its improved credit quality allows it to trade above its redemption value. Some of the large issues in the French market are Societe Generale, Michelin, Peugeot, Havas, and Generale des Eaux.

## United Kingdom

The Eurosterling market is an important capital market for British companies and foreign companies issuing convertibles in sterling. This market is considered very liquid and is mainly used by British companies.

Domestic convertibles listed on the London Stock Exchange have existed for some time. During the 1960s, many convertibles were issued to finance takeovers. The market has progressed over the years with issues of foreign companies and features other than the conventional ones. Most convertibles are listed on the London Stock Exchange, which regulates both the new issue and the secondary market. Although many issues have both registered and bearer tranches, the registered bonds are listed on the exchange.

The convertible issues in this market are called convertible loan stock, which includes unsecured debt and a variety of preference shares. The sterling market is significant, and like most markets, the new-issue volume has varied from year to year, with record years of over $1.6 billion issued in both 1990 and 1993. Although by tradition British convertible issues pay interest annually, the market has recently seen issuance of bonds that pay interest semiannually.

The British sterling convertible market is dominated by preference shares, which have comprised as much as 80 percent of the new-issue market in recent years. The preference shares are usually perpetual, although some have call features. These issues pay coupons twice a year, similar to dividend payments on most ordinary shares. An additional type of convertible issued in the sterling market is a convertible bond with a premium put.

The U.K. Euroconvertible market has been suffering from a lack of significant new issues since 1993. The market shrank by 1,206 billion in sterling in 1996, with only a few new issues coming to the market.

The U.K. domestic convertible market is not used by international investors due to some negative factors associated with it:

1. *Net-paying dividends:* U.K. tax-exempt investors must claim back ACT from the U.K. Treasury.
2. *Preferreds:* Many issues are convertible preferreds, and many investors are precluded from owning this type of security.
3. *Small issues:* Many issues are very small and liquidity can be almost nonexistent; liquidity on the underlying shares can also be poor.
4. *Annual convertibility:* Many issues allow conversion into the underlying shares of stock only once or twice a year.

However, there are occasionally some interesting issues that trade actively in the U.K. market.[3]

## Emerging Markets

Emerging markets have fostered the growth of many new convertibles for international investors. Convertibles are being issued in

Latin America, India, and even some of the former Eastern Bloc countries. The most exciting growth area in recent years has been the Asia Pacific market. This convertible market has exploded with new issuance in recent years, producing a whole new universe of opportunities for international investors. These markets include Hong Kong, Taiwan, Malaysia, Philippines, Thailand, Indonesia, Korea, and China.

*Asia Pacific* The Asia Pacific market is an interesting market with an array of opportunities. Many of the convertibles in these markets are a result of the privatization of government-owned industries.

There are advantages to investing in convertibles in the emerging markets. One of the most important is that convertibles are often mispriced according to theoretical valuations, sometimes providing very profitable opportunities. This also allows investors to participate in the stocks of highly volatile companies through an investment in the corresponding convertibles, which have reduced volatility. The convertible issues are often as liquid and, in some cases, more liquid than the underlying common stock.

Almost all Euroconvertibles in this market are denominated in U.S. dollars. This attracts interest from U.S. investors and affords some currency protection to other investors who might be nervous about holding emerging market currencies.

There are over 200 U.S.-dollar-denominated issues outstanding from over a dozen countries. Most companies are growing fast but do not have a strong balance sheet. Several are rated by Moody's/S&P, although many are not. Besides the U.S.-dollar-denominated issues, some are Dutch special-purpose vehicles. The issue size ranges from $50 million to $250 million with semi-annual coupons, a maturity of up to 10 years, and a 5-year put structure.

## SUMMARY

The development of the convertible market in the United States was discussed in Chapter 1. A theme throughout that chapter was that in periods of strong economic growth, convertible issuance also increased. That theme is also evidenced in the global convertible market. When economies struggle, as they do in many areas of Europe, the need for capital is subdued and convertible issuance stagnates. In areas of the world where economic growth is on the upswing, convertible issuance is high. The globalization of economies has given rise to convertible issuance in high-growth areas, most notably, the United States and Asia Pacific markets.

## E N D N O T E S

1. Prospectus, The Mitsubishi Bank, Limited, U.S. $2,000,000,000, Morgan Stanley & Company, September 22, 1995, p. 64.
2. Convertible units are straight bonds issued in combination with equity warrants. See Chapter 6.
3. Deutsche Morgan Grenfell, DMG Global Convertible Research, February 1997.

# PART TWO

## CONVERTIBLE EVALUATION

# 8
## CHAPTER

# Anatomy of a Convertible Bond

To determine whether a convertible bond is attractively priced, each separate component must be evaluated carefully. In this chapter, we discuss how to calculate bond value and provide insight into some of the more common mathematical methods used to evaluate convertibles.

## CALCULATING BOND INVESTMENT VALUE

A convertible bond is in fact a corporate bond, which is a contract that entitles the holder to a series of interest payments and the return of principal at maturity. This is an important feature of the convertible bond. It provides the downside safety of the investment. The investment value of a convertible bond is its fixed-income value calculated without the convertibility feature. As we discussed in Chapter 2, the rate used to discount the convertible is not its coupon rate but the estimate of the yield-to-maturity of a nonconvertible bond of similar quality and term to maturity. The investor can estimate this yield-to-maturity by looking at the yield-to-maturity of straight bonds with the same Standard & Poor's or Moody's bond ratings. The bond investment value is equal to the

### F I G U R E 8–1

Bond Investment Value Calculation

| Years | (1)<br>Present<br>Value<br>Payment | (2)<br>Present<br>Value<br>Factor* at 10% | (1) × (2) |
|---|---|---|---|
| 1–20 | $80 | 8.514 | $681.12 |
| 20 | $1,000 | 0.149 | 149.00 |
| Bond investment value (SV(t)): | | | $830.12 |

$$Sv\,(t) = \sum_{t=1}^{n} \frac{c}{(1 + r)^t} + \frac{p}{1 + r^n}$$

P  =  par value

r  =  discount rate

C  =  coupon rate

n  =  number periods to maturity

*Obtained from interest tables.

present value of the interest and principal payments discounted at the straight (nonconvertible) bond interest rate.

Figure 8–1 indicates the calculation for an 8 percent, 20-year bond using standard interest tables.[1] In this case, a discount rate of 10 percent is used to determine the investment value, which is $830.12. Once this discount rate (the yield-to-maturity of a similar, nonconvertible bond) has been chosen, the convertible's investment value can easily be determined. A calculator with financial functions can accomplish this by using the par value at maturity as the future value, coupon rate as the payment, and years to maturity as n time periods, and then solving for bond investment value (present value).

The difficult part of the calculation is estimating the discount rate. The interest rate used to discount the interest and principal payments reflect market rates of interest, which include a risk premium assigned by market forces. It is generally not too difficult to estimate the discount rate for investment-grade issues because bonds of similar quality tend to have similar interest rates. However, below-investment-grade issues with similar rat-ings can vary greatly. The investor must take into consideration the width of the spread on market interest rates for bonds with the same rating because that spread will affect the investment value of a convertible.

In many cases, investors can use bond ratings from Standard & Poor's and Moody's to locate bonds of similar quality in the financial pages and thus find a comparable current yield-to-matur-ity. However, ratings are not very responsive to changing financial fundamentals, and the lag can cause significant errors in estimat-ing the discount rate. Studies indicate that bonds undergo most of their price change relating to a rating change about one year before the rating changes. There have even been occasions when a com-pany has filed Chapter 11 proceedings while the bond rating was still investment grade. When monitoring investment values, it is critical to pay attention to credit-watch news and other fundamen-tal information on the company. The market quickly assesses in-vestment value in response to news items.

The financial difficulties of Orange County, California, pro-vide one of the best examples of how credit rating agencies can lag circumstances. The county's pension obligations, issued in Sep-tember 1994, were rated A1 by Moody's and AA- by Standard and Poor's. By December 1994, Orange County was forced to default on some of its debt obligations, and the pension obligations that were A1/AA- just three months earlier were downgraded to Caa/D.

Since market sentiment plays an important role in assessing a convertible's bond risk, monitoring the prices of the straight debt issues of the underlying company can be helpful in selecting the proper discount rate. Often the apparent deterioration of the creditworthiness of an issue will not be reflected in the convertible price because the common stock may be rising. This might seem like a contradiction at first glance, but think about what a company is likely to do when business is on an upswing: It takes on addi-tional debt to finance expansion.

The stock price reflects the increase in business, while the bond value reflects the increase in the debt/equity ratio. While ratings lag, astute bond traders quickly reappraise the straight debt, reflecting the higher credit risk. By monitoring the straight debt, the investor is able to detect a declining investment value of the convertible long before the rating changes.

In other words, we know that the value of a firm is equal to the value of its debt plus the value of its equity:

value of a firm = debt + equity

The market value of debt can go down while the market value of equity goes up, thus leaving the overall value of the firm unchanged.

Consider two different IBM bonds available in 1987. Both bonds mature in 2004. The straight bond has a 9.375 percent coupon, and the convertible has a 7.875 percent coupon. Using a financial calculator, we find that the 9.375 percent coupon straight bond has a yield-to-maturity of 9.77 percent. Using the 9.77 percent as discount rate, we find that the convertible bond's investment value is $845.00. One can have a great deal of confidence in this estimate of the investment value of a particularly highly liquid convertible bond.

Not all bonds are as easy to estimate as the above example might imply. In general, whether the investment value truly acts as the investment floor of the convertible in a declining market depends on how accurately it has been estimated. Therefore, great care should be exercised in determining this important value.

## MEASURING INVESTMENT VALUE RISK

Every investment needs to be evaluated for its level of risk. Selecting the appropriate way to do so is one of the most difficult decisions facing the convertible investor. Many practitioners ignore this process and simply rely on published bond ratings to evaluate the risk of bond investment values. Others may try to simplify the analytical process by assuming away possible changes in risk. Ignoring deteriorating fundamentals or changing interest rates that reflect changing risk factors may work some of the time, but the investor using that approach should be mentally prepared to accept an inordinate number of decreasing ratings or even bankruptcy situations in the portfolio.

The proper measure of risk will reflect the uncertainty of achieving expected return. Without measuring all known risk factors, the implied assumptions of the analysis can be misleading. For example, convertible bonds have an extra risk factor in that they are generally subordinated debentures. The resulting lower ratings imply that the issuing company's convertible debt has a higher risk than its senior debt, not merely that it has a higher yield.

## DEFAULT RISK OF CONVERTIBLES

A discussion of investment value is not complete without reviewing the most serious consequence that can occur to any convertible bondholder: default. Default losses are rare, but do occur from time to time. It is important for convertible investors to realize that high yield alone cannot compensate for lower quality. It may take years of interest payments to compensate for the loss of principal value that can occur in the event of default. In the classic work *Security Analysis*, Benjamin Graham observed that "deficient safety cannot be compensated by an abnormally high coupon rate alone." The additional reality of the marketplace is that lower-quality bonds are much more susceptible to price breaks on changing company fundamentals. Convertible investors and managers run into trouble if they think a high-grade convertible bond is the same as a lower-grade convertible except for a yield adjustment. Common sense tells us that the same formulas cannot evaluate both a high-quality convertible bond and an unseasoned, lower-quality issue. Since the companies are not readily comparable, neither are their securities. Investment-grade issues must be compared to issues of the same quality.

It is interesting that convertible securities generally have experienced a lower default rate than straight debt issues of comparable quality. In the *Journal of Finance*, Eric S. Rosengren examined the defaults of convertible bonds that were high yield at original issue and concluded that high-yield convertibles have a lower default rate than nonconvertible high-yield bonds. Furthermore, both rated and nonrated convertibles had substantially lower default rates than nonconvertible debt.[2]

Several reasons may account for the favorable default experience of convertibles. First, convertibles seemed to be called at a greater frequency than nonconvertible debt. This makes sense, because convertibles have an additional reason to be called. If the stock price has increased above the conversion price, the company may benefit by calling the convertible, forcing conversion to common stock and thus saving the interest carrying cost while taking debt off the balance sheet. If the company is progressing well and the stock price is increasing, the company would have a reason to call the convertible even if interest rates were increasing. This would not be the case with nonconvertible debt.

The lower default rate on convertibles may also be a function of the lower coupon on convertibles. When company business plans go awry due to an unexpected downturn in business, the lower interest cost on the convertible debt may allow the company to survive the temporary financial crisis. Many defaults occurred in the high-yield market in the recession of 1990; convertibles fared much better. The convertible benefited the bondholder as well as the company, the convertible bondholder getting paid the coupon interest while waiting for the business to resume its upward trend. At that time, the investor expects to receive the equity kicker.

Convertibles provide corporations with additional flexibility. Many firms use the retirement of convertibles to reduce their leverage, thus decreasing the probability of bankruptcy. Convertible debt allows a more orderly control of the debt/equity of firms. As stock prices increase, convertible debt is exchanged for equity, allowing firms the flexibility to add more debt.

When nonconvertible debt goes into default, bondholders are forced to take stock in an effort to allow firms to continue doing business. Those companies may have been better served by initially issuing a lower-coupon convertible instead of a high-coupon, high-yield bond that forced them into bankruptcy. Sharing equity with the bondholders via the convertible could make the difference in surviving difficult times.

Figure 8–2 covers a 16-year period ending in 1986 and highlights the importance of monitoring industry economic factors. It indicates the public defaults of both straight bonds and convertible bonds by industry sector. The concentration of defaults in certain industry sectors (steel and energy issues) reflects the troubled times in these segments of the economy. It also highlights possible consequences of buying mostly in the new-issue market. In the volatile investment environment of 1996 and beyond, some indus-

## F I G U R E  8-2

Public Defaults by Industry Sector: 1970–1986 (millions of dollars)

| | Number of Companies | Straight Debt | Percentage of Total Straight | Convertible Debt | Total in Default | Percentage of Total |
|---|---|---|---|---|---|---|
| **Industrial** | | | | | | |
| Retailers | 15 | $556.74 | 7.14 | $211.87 | $768.61 | 7.7 |
| General Mfg. | 23 | 2,301.49 | 29.53 | 331.64 | 2,563.73 | 25.68 |
| Elec./Computer & Comm. | 22 | 200.79 | 2.58 | 413.58 | 614.37 | 6.15 |
| Oil & Gas | 29 | 1,581.09 | 20.29 | 449.65 | 2,030.74 | 120.34 |
| Real Estate-Const., Supplies | 13 | 103.93 | 1.33 | 126.55 | 230.48 | 2.3 |
| Misc. Industries | 18 | 570.3 | 7.32 | 177.68 | 747.98 | 7.49 |
| TOTAL | 120 | $5,314.34 | 68.19 | $1,710.97 | $6,955.91 | 69.66 |
| **Transportation** | | | | | | |
| Railroads | 9 | $1,260.22 | 16.17 | $31.10 | $1,291.32 | 12.93 |
| Airlines/Cargo | 7 | 211.81 | 2.72 | 122.81 | 334.62 | 3.35 |
| Sea Lines | 4 | 243 | 3.12 | 123.1 | 366.1 | 3.67 |
| Trucks/Motor Carriers | 3 | 48.31 | 0.62 | $9.75 | $58.06 | 0.58 |
| TOTAL | 23 | $1,763.34 | 22.63 | 268.76 | $2,050.10 | 20.53 |
| **Finance** | | | | | | |
| Financial Services | 11 | $436.09 | 5.6 | 164.04 | $600.13 | 6.01 |
| REITs | 12 | 279.71 | 3.58 | 99.46 | 379.17 | 3.8 |
| TOTAL | 23 | $715.80 | 9.18 | $263.50 | $979.30 | 9.81 |
| **TOTAL** | 166 | $7,793.48 | 100.00 | $2,261.23 | $10,054.71 | 100.00 |

Source: Edward I. Altman, *Financial Analysts Journal*, vol. 43, no. 4 (July/August 1987):21.
Reprinted, with permission, from *Financial Analysts Journal*, July/August 1987.

tries will do well while others experience severe problems; monitoring industry and sector trends is very important.

Although Figure 8–3 includes both nonconvertible and convertible debt, it is useful to review the rating distribution of defaulting issues prior to default. Notice the jump in the default rate from the medium-grade BB to B ratings. It is also interesting to note the original rating of bond issues that eventually defaulted. These fallen angels can be troublesome to investors who rely on rating alone to determine the investment value of convertibles.

Being aware of the probability of default and monitoring the financial condition of the company are necessary procedures in updating investment values. Investors who are surprised by a default clearly have not done their homework. We reiterate that relying on rating services alone to calculate investment values is not sufficient to prevent investment errors.

If an investor is holding a convertible issue and a default is announced, is it better to sell immediately or try to ride it out? Although most issues drop in price prior to the actual announcement, reflecting ongoing financial deterioration of the company, there is still a significant drop in price around the announcement date. For example, at one time, Interstate Department Stores' convertible issue had the dubious distinction of registering the largest one-month decline after the default announcement, dropping 89.4 percent. In 18 of the 195 cases of defaulting bonds, bond prices actually rose in the month the default was announced. In fact, the three that increased most were convertible issues, and in 10 cases there was no price change.[3]

However, the answer to the question, "Is it better to sell or ride out a defaulted convertible issue?" is "Sell," although investing in defaulted convertible issues can be extremely profitable. Interstate Department Stores' bankruptcy had a happy ending in that the company became tremendously successful as Toys "R" Us. The Anacomp defaulted convertible issue rallied from 50 to nearly 200 in two years as the company came out of bankruptcy. Finding convertible issues after the terms have been negotiated is a much better strategy than holding and hoping for favorable treatment throughout the bankruptcy proceedings.

The good news in the lower-grade market is that the actual instances of default on convertible bonds are comparatively rare.

Rating Distribution of Defaulting Issues at Various Points Prior to Default: 1970–1986

| Original Rating | AAA | AA | A | BBB | BB | B | CCC | CC | Total |
|---|---|---|---|---|---|---|---|---|---|
| Number | 0 | 3 | 11 | 29 | 26 | 79 | 33 | 1 | 182 |
| Percentage | 0.00% | 1.65% | 6.04% | 15.93% | 14.29% | 43.41% | 18.13% | 0.55% | 100.00% |
| **Rating One Year Prior** | AAA | AA | A | BBB | BB | B | CCC | CC | Total |
| Number | 0 | 0 | 2 | 11 | 29 | 81 | 67 | 9 | 199 |
| Percentage | 0.00% | 0.00% | 1.01% | 5.53% | 14.57% | 40.70% | 33.67% | 4.52% | 100% |
| **Rating Six Months Prior** | AAA | AA | A | BBB | BB | B | CCC | CC | Total |
| Number | 0 | 0 | 2 | 3 | 11 | 77 | 95 | 15 | 203 |
| Percentage | 0.00% | 0.00% | 0.99% | 1.48% | 5.42% | 37.93% | 46.80% | 7.39% | 100.00% |

Source: Edward I. Altman, *Financial Analysts Journal*, vol. 43, no.4 (July/August 1987): 22.
Reprinted, with permission, from *Financial Analysts Journal*, July/August 1987.

The convertible investor can prevent such disasters from occurring by assuming an active role in managing the portfolio. Since most defaults are issuer- and industry-related, proper diversification can reduce risk. Poor economic conditions can heighten the threat of default, so investors tend to avoid lower-quality issues in a weak economy, thereby widening the yield spread between high- and low-quality issues. The market generally announces its concern over pending default by sharp price breaks and a continual stream of bad news. To ignore these warnings is poor portfolio management, whether one is investing in convertibles, stocks, or straight fixed-income securities.

Controlling default risk in convertible bonds begins with ranking convertibles in quality levels. For investment-grade convertible securities, the bond ratings usually accomplish just that. Extra care must be taken in estimating investment value of below-investment-grade convertible securities.

## INVESTMENT VALUE FOR
## BELOW-INVESTMENT-GRADE SECURITIES

As we have mentioned, estimating investment value in the high-risk sector of the convertible market is much more difficult than the same task for investment-grade securities. The returns of lower-quality bonds are more closely correlated to returns on common stocks because the level of concern about default varies with the same factors that drive the stock market. For example, during the stock market crash of 1987, investment-grade and below-investment-grade securities behaved very differently. Even though interest rates declined slightly during those hectic weeks, the investment values of below-investment-grade issues plummeted as a flight to quality occurred. In the very poor bond market of 1994, below-investment-grade issues suffered much greater losses than investment-grade issues. In periods of uncertainty and volatility, spreads between higher-quality and lower-quality securities generally widen, and there is often a flight to quality. The convertible investor needs a method by which to categorize convertibles into various risk classes. Only then can convertibles be matched appropriately to the investor's own investment objectives.

Many investors believe the extra return paid by below-investment-grade securities is an acceptable reward for incurring greater default risk, but the fact is that they need clearer guidelines that correlate risk tolerance levels with investment objectives. A company's investment policy statement should address this very important issue. For example, the convertible bond issued by a high-risk stock will always have less risk than the underlying common stock. Therefore, if the investment guidelines called for participation in the high-risk sector of the stock market, a convertible bond with a CCC S&P rating might be appropriate.

## CREDIT ANALYSIS OF CONVERTIBLE SECURITIES

Credit quality is most important in the down phases of the market. In Figure 8–4, notice the differences in relative performance between investment-grade and speculative-grade. In the recession year 1990, investment-grade convertibles significantly outper-

**F I G U R E  8–4**

Year-by-Year Comparison of Investment-Grade Convertibles versus Speculative-Grade Convertibles, 1990–1997

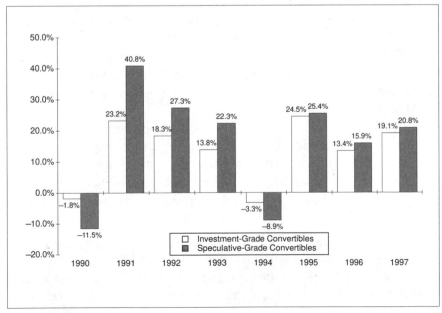

Source: Merrill Lynch Convertible Research.

formed speculative-grade convertibles, –1.8 percent versus –11.5 percent. In weak equity markets, it is very common to see valuations on below-investment-grade convertibles sinking below their investment floor. In 1994, speculative-grade convertibles again performed poorly compared to investment-grade securities.

Credit analysis plays a significant role in evaluating convertible securities. As discussed earlier, the investor must determine the appropriate discount rate to use in calculating the convertible security's straight bond value, which provides the cushion for the convertible when equity prices fall.

The convertible analyst puts on the bond-analyst hat and looks only at the convertible's fixed-income attributes. The key factors that determine the credit risk of a convertible security are outlined below. These are the same factors a bond analyst would use to determine the risk of straight fixed-income instruments.

*Industry risk:* competitiveness, growth, government regulations, cost factors, operating coverage, cyclical nature of the business, and the issuer's position within the industry.

*Financial considerations:* how conservative are the accounting practices, financial goals, and policies of the company?

*Profitability ratios:* return on equity, profit margins, earnings growth, coefficient of variation for return on earnings, and coefficient of variation for earnings per share.

*Financial ratios:* debt to equity, interest coverage, operating income to sales, equity turnover, net income to total assets, working capital to total debt, debt in payback period, and total debt as percent of capital.

*Management considerations:* operating track record, change in key personnel, depth of management, cost-control effectiveness, labor relations, and capacity for innovation.

*Other considerations:* issue size, issue subordination, firm size, financial flexibility, future capital needs, and product diversification.

It is always important to compare the factors and ratios mentioned above with industry averages. The trend and variation in ratios may be as important as the ratio itself. The company's future capital needs and goals also must be considered. However, it is beyond the scope of this book to go into fixed-income analysis in further detail. Our purpose is not to discuss fixed-income credit analysis in depth, but to alert the investor to the importance of these factors when analyzing investment value.

## INTEREST-RATE SENSITIVITY

Using yield-to-maturity equalizes various coupons and maturity dates. Changes in yield-to-maturity values can then be easily related to changes in bond investment value. There is, of course, an inverse relationship between the level of interest rates and the convertible's investment value.

Figure 8–5 indicates how changes in interest rates cause changes in investment value. For example, if a convertible bond with a 6 percent coupon and a 10-year maturity were issued when long-term interest rates were 8 percent, its investment value would be $866. If long-term interest rates declined to 6 percent, the investment value would be at par.

## F I G U R E  8–5

Bond Valuations Depend on Yield-to-Maturity

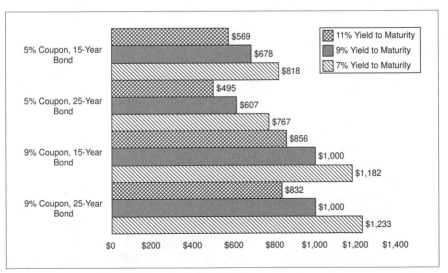

## DURATION ANALYSIS

Fixed-income analysts use duration analysis to provide a very accurate measure of how bond values (including the investment values of convertible securities) change with changing interest rates. Duration analysis is valuable because it not only takes into account the bond's coupon rate and maturity date but also weights the cash flows for their time value. Bond-price volatility is related to the length of time over which the instrument is outstanding, but the series of payments over the life of the bond are a much more important factor than the final maturity date, when the principal comes due.

The volatility of interest rates over the past two decades has brought about a renewed interest in the concept of duration. Adjusted duration formulas have been used to provide a time-based measure, which can be matched against the same time measure of liabilities, thereby reducing investment risk. Financial analysts use these immunization techniques in managing fixed-income portfolios. We use duration analysis to estimate the sensitivity of interest-rate changes on the convertible security's embedded investment value and its market price.

*Duration*[4] is the weighted average time to full recovery of principal and interest payments. Each payment is time-weighted by its present value, with the largest payment occurring at the time the bond matures.

Duration analysis:

$$
D = \frac{\sum_{t=1}^{n} C_t(t)/(1 + i)^t}{\sum_{t=1}^{n} C_t/(1 + t)^t}
$$

where:

$t$ = time period
$C_t$ = coupon and/or principal payment
$i$ = market yield

Holding all other variables equal, higher-yielding bonds will have a lower duration than lower-yielding bonds because more of the cash flows will occur earlier in the life of the bond. (For a bond with a lower coupon rate, the principal repayment at maturity assumes relatively more importance in the cash flows than would be the case for a bond with a higher coupon rate.) A bond with a longer term to maturity will have a higher duration than one that will mature in a shorter period. For coupon-paying bonds, the duration number will always be less than the number of years to maturity. For zero coupon bonds, the duration number will equal the number of years to maturity. Duration of a perpetual bond approaches a number equal to one divided by the coupon. This can be used as the duration of a preferred stock.

Duration can be adjusted to determine how sensitive investment value is to a change in interest rates. The adjusted duration (D adj) number for the investment value will indicate how much the investment value will change for a one percentage point change (100 basis points) in interest rates. If the duration is 10 and interest rates fall by one percentage point, the investment value would rise by 10 percent:

$$\text{Adjusted duration (D adj)} = \text{duration (D)}/(1+Y)$$

where:

Y = yield

To determine the duration of the convertible's investment value, present value calculations are accomplished as indicated in Figure 8–6. The discount rate of 9.5 percent is used because a non-convertible bond of similar quality would have a yield-to-maturity of 9.5 percent. The duration is the time-weighted present value of the series of payments and is equal to 9.4 years. To determine interest-rate sensitivity, duration value is adjusted by dividing it by one plus the yield. In this example, the adjusted duration is 8.59 years, indicating that if long-term interest rates were to increase by 100 basis points, this bond would decrease in value by 8.59 percent.

## Duration Analysis Applied to Convertibles

Up to now we have been estimating the effect of interest rates on the investment value of the convertible bond and ignoring the convertible's equity component. We have analyzed the convertible as though it were nonconvertible. However, the convertible's equity component has an important influence on the bond's invest-

## F I G U R E  8–6

Computation of Convertible's Interest-Rate Sensitivity

**Security data:** IBM 7.875% due November 21, 2004

Market price (Cv(t) = 104
Stock = $118.00 per share
Current yield (CY) = 7.57%
Conversion premium = 35.43%
Investment value yield-to-maturity (Y) = 9.5%

| Year | Payments | PV at 9.5% | PV of Payments | PV as % of Price | PV of Payment Time Weighted |
|------|----------|------------|----------------|------------------|------------------------------|
| 1988 | 78.7500 | 0.9133 | 71.9224 | 0.0830 | 0.0830 |
| 1989 | 78.7500 | 0.8341 | 65.6854 | 0.0758 | 0.1516 |
| 1990 | 78.7500 | 0.7618 | 59.9918 | 0.0692 | 0.2076 |
| 1991 | 78.7500 | 0.6957 | 54.7864 | 0.0632 | 0.2528 |
| 1992 | 78.7500 | 0.6354 | 50.0377 | 0.0577 | 0.2886 |
| 1993 | 78.7500 | 0.5804 | 45.7065 | 0.0527 | 0.3164 |
| 1994 | 78.7500 | 0.5301 | 41.7454 | 0.0482 | 0.3371 |
| 1995 | 78.7500 | 0.4842 | 38.1308 | 0.0440 | 0.3519 |
| 1996 | 78.7500 | 0.4423 | 34.8311 | 0.0402 | 0.3617 |
| 1997 | 78.7500 | 0.4040 | 31.8150 | 0.0367 | 0.3670 |
| 1998 | 78.7500 | 0.3690 | 29.0588 | 0.0335 | 0.3688 |
| 1999 | 78.7500 | 0.3371 | 26.5466 | 0.0306 | 0.3675 |
| 2000 | 78.7500 | 0.3080 | 24.2550 | 0.0280 | 0.3638 |
| 2001 | 78.7500 | 0.2813 | 22.1524 | 0.0256 | 0.3578 |
| 2002 | 78.7500 | 0.2570 | 20.2388 | 0.0233 | 0.3502 |
| 2003 | 78.7500 | 0.2348 | 18.4905 | 0.0213 | 0.3413 |
| 2004 | 1,078.7500 | 0.2145 | 231.3919 | 0.2670 | 4.5382 |
|      |          |        | 866.7863 | 1.0000 | 9.4054 |

Investment value (Sv(t)) = 886.79
Duration (D) = 9.41 years

**Investment Value**
**Interest Rate Sensitivity: Adjusted Duration (D adj.):**

$$D\ adj = \frac{D}{1 + Y} \qquad\qquad 8.5894 = \frac{9.4054}{1.095}$$

**Convertibles Interest Rate Sensitivity (Dcv):**

$$Dcv = D\ adj.\left(1 - \frac{C/I}{2}\right) \qquad\qquad 4.7844 = 8.5894\left(\frac{1 - \frac{767.9440}{866.7863}}{2}\right)$$

Notes:  1.  Duration calculated assuming annual interest payments.
         2.  Present value (PV) factors obtained from interest-rate tables.

ment value. The equity component of the convertible bond may dampen the convertible's interest-rate sensitivity, depending on the bond's equity participation. Convertible bonds trading high above their investment value will be less sensitive to interest rates than bonds that are trading close to their investment value.

To fully understand a convertible's valuation, it is best to determine both the interest rate sensitivity of a convertible bond price and its investment value. As we have shown, this can be accomplished by applying duration analysis to convertibles. The mathematics and the methodology of duration analysis are detailed in the appendix to this chapter. We have developed a short-cut that allows investors to quickly determine the interest-rate sensitivity of a convertible bond. The formula for the convertible bond's interest rate sensitivity (Dcv) is:

$$D^{cv} = (D \text{ adj})\left(1 - \frac{C/I}{2}\right)$$

where:

$C$ = conversion value

$I$ = investment value

Figure 8–6 indicates the use of the formula for the adjusted duration of the convertible, given as 4.78 in this example. Notice that the convertible's interest-rate sensitivity is lower than that of its investment value considered alone; this reflects the influence of the equity component.

For convertible investors, $(D^{cv})$ becomes a valuable tool to measure the convertible's vulnerability to changing interest rates. It can also be used by investors who want to use interest-rate forecasting as part of the investment management process.

The value of a warrant actually increases in price as interest rates rise, providing an offset to the decline in investment value.

## DETERMINING INVESTMENT VALUE FOR ZERO-COUPON BONDS

In Chapter 3, we introduced liquid yield option notes (LYONs), created by Merrill Lynch in 1985. A LYON takes a zero-coupon security and adds both convertibility and a put feature. Each factor must be considered in determining the convertible's investment value. LYONs are interesting instruments because their short maturity means they trade in the shorter-term market alongside commercial paper. They can be issued at short-term rates.

The National Medical Enterprises, Inc. LYON was a zero-coupon bond with an 18-year maturity, issued with a yield-to-maturity of 7.5 percent per annum (computed on a semiannual bond equivalent basis), calculated from the date of issue. This issue is particularly interesting because it was the first LYON ever offered.

The bond's investment value would be the present value of the par value discounted at an appropriate equivalent bond rate. An appropriate discount rate as determined by bond ratings at the time would have been 10 percent. Therefore the investment value at the time of issue was estimated to be $245.25.

The bond also had a put feature. The prospectus stated that ". . . each LYON will be repurchased by the company at the option of the holder on December 31, 1988, and on each December 31 thereafter prior to maturity at repurchase prices as set forth in this prospectus." The holder of the bond could put the bonds back to the company as early as December 31, 1988. The investment value had to be adjusted to take the repurchase price into account.

Figure 8–7 lists the schedule of the repurchase prices as stated in the prospectus. Figure 8–8 indicates the LYON's repurchase price graphically over time and shows the relationship of the purchase price to the investment value. Investment value in this case is estimated by the present value over two years, the length of time the holder can put the bond back to the company, at a discount rate of 10 percent. The rate used to discount the bond should be adjusted as interest rates change over time.

Since the holder can receive $296.75 on December 31, 1988, the investment value becomes the present value of that amount discounted at an appropriate short-term rate, which in this case we determined was 10 percent. Thus the investment value of the National Medical Enterprises, Inc. LYON at the time of issue is $245.25.

In October 1987, the investment firm of Morgan Stanley offered a LYONs issue with a crucial difference: Morgan Stanley eliminated the put feature. The trade-off was a maturity reduced to seven years.

## F I G U R E 8–7

National Medical Enterprises, Inc.

LYONs—Repurchase Price
The repurchase price payable to the holder of a LYON demanding repurchase
thereof shall be as follows:

| Repurchase Date | Repurchase Price | Yield to Holder[1] | Investment Value[2] |
|---|---|---|---|
| 12/31/88 | $296.75 | 6.00% | $245.25 |
| 12/31/89 | 320.84 | 6.50 | 265.16 |
| 12/31/90 | 350.23 | 7.00 | 289.45 |
| 12/31/91 | 386.01 | 7.50 | 319.02 |
| 12/31/92 | 415.50 | 7.50 | 343.39 |
| 12/31/93 | 447.25 | 7/50 | 369.63 |
| 12/31/94 | 481.42 | 7.50 | 397.87 |
| 12/31/95 | 518.21 | 7.50 | 428.27 |
| 12/31/96 | 557.80 | 7.50 | 460.99 |
| 12/31/97 | 600.42 | 7.50 | 496.21 |
| 12/31/98 | 646.30 | 7.50 | 534.13 |
| 12/31/99 | 695.68 | 7.50 | 574.94 |
| 12/31/00 | 748.83 | 7.50 | 618.87 |
| 12/31/01 | 806.05 | 7.50 | 666.16 |
| 12/31/02 | 867.64 | 7.50 | 717.06 |
| 12/31/03 | 933.93 | 7.50 | 771.84 |
| 12/31/04 | 1,000.00 | 7.50 | 826.45 |

Notes: 1. Yield to holder is per annum as computed on a semiannual bond equivalent basis.
2. Discount rate 10 percent; two years to each put.

LYONs continue to be a popular means of financing for quality companies such as Disney (EuroDisney issued a LYON), Motorola, USF&G, Automatic Data Processing, News Corp., and Whirlpool, to name some well-known examples. LYONs now make up about 25 percent of the convertible market.

## CALL PROTECTION FOR CONVERTIBLES

As we mentioned in Chapter 4, a convertible's call features are critical to its value and structure. A convertible's yield-to-call is usually more important than yield-to-maturity.

## F I G U R E  8–8

National Medical Enterprises, Inc.

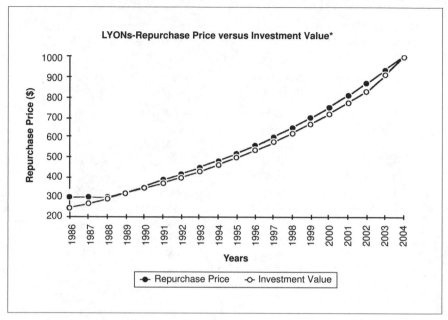

*Investment Value assumes a 10 percent discount rate, two years to next put.

## Yield Advantage of Convertible Securities

Convertibles generally offer more income than the underlying common stock. The difference between the current yield of the convertible and the dividend yield of the common stock is the convertible's yield advantage. The direct yield comparison is important since owning a convertible can be viewed as an alternative to the purchase of common stock. Break-even analysis can be used to compare both the yield advantage and conversion premium.

## Review of Convertible Formulas

Before proceeding to the break-even calculations, let's review the following formulas, using the example below.

| | |
|---|---|
| Stock price | $30.00 per share |
| Stock dividend | $0.50 per share |
| Convertible market price | $100 or $1,000 |
| Coupon rate | 7.00% |
| Maturity date | 20 years |
| Conversion price | $36.37 |

*Stock dividend yield* = the annual dividend rate divided by the current stock price:

$$\frac{\text{stock dividend}}{\text{stock price}}$$

$$1.67\% = \frac{\$0.50}{\$30.00}$$

*Convertible current yield* = coupon rate divided by current market price of the convertible:

$$\frac{\text{coupon rate}}{\text{convertible market price (expressed as a percent of par)}}$$

$$7.00\% = \frac{7.00}{100}$$

*Conversion price* = the price stated in the prospectus at which each convertible security may be exchanged into the underlying common stock.

*Conversion ratio* = the number of shares for which one bond may be exchanged:

$$\frac{\text{par value}}{\text{conversion price}}$$

$$27.50 \text{ shares} = \frac{1000}{\$36.37}$$

*Conversion value* = the equity value or stock value of the convertible security:

conversion value = stock price × conversion ratio
$825.00 per bond or 82.50 = ($30.00)(27.50)

*Conversion premium* = the difference between the market price and the conversion value, usually expressed as a percentage:

$$\text{conversion premium \%} = \frac{\text{convertible price} - \text{conversion value}}{\text{conversion value}}$$

$$21.21\% = \frac{100 - 82.50}{82.50}$$

*Dollar premium* = the difference between the market price and the conversion value, expressed in dollars or points:

$$\text{convertible price} - \text{conversion value}$$

$$17.50 \text{ points} = 100 - 82.50$$

## Break-Even Calculations

Break-even calculations have long been used to analyze convertible bonds. At one time, break-even was particularly widely used by trading desks because it provided a method for making a quick decision on a security. In general, break-even is more helpful in generating a rough estimate of whether the conversion premium is justified rather than in helping an investor decide whether or not to convert the bond into stock. Usually stated in years, break-even is simply the conversion premium divided by the convertible's yield advantage over the underlying common stock yield. The calculations are accomplished using data from above.

$$\text{break-even (years)} = \frac{\text{conversion premium}}{\text{convertible yield} - \text{stock yield}}$$

$$3.98 \text{ years} = \frac{21.21}{(7.00 - 1.67)}$$

In other words, break-even represents the number of years necessary for the stock investor to recover the conversion premium (the extra cost of buying the convertible rather than the stock) from the convertible's higher income relative to an investment of an equivalent amount in the stock. In this case, the convertible costs 21.21 percent more than an equivalent amount of stock. The difference between the yield on the convertible (7.00) and the yield on the stock (1.67) is 5.33 percentage points. Using this method, after 3.98 years, the convertible has made up, in income alone, the amount of the conversion premium. Using break-even, without regard to other valuation methods, if this bond has four years of call protection, then the conversion premium is probably fairly priced; if call protection is only three years, then the bond is probably overpriced.

The two most common break-even methods are dollar maintenance and equity maintenance.

The *dollar maintenance* method of break-even measures the time it takes for the convertible yield advantage to pay for its premium compared to an equivalent dollar amount purchased of the underlying stock.

$$\frac{\text{Dollar}}{\text{maintenance}} = \frac{\text{convertible market price} - \text{conversion value}}{\text{Cvt. coupon} - \left(\dfrac{\text{Cvt mkt. price}}{\text{stock price}}\right)\text{stock dividend}}$$

$$3.98 \text{ years} = \frac{100 - 82.50}{7.00 - \left(\dfrac{100}{30.0}\right)0.50}$$

The *equity maintenance* method of break-even compares the premium paid (conversion premium) to the yield advantage of owning the same number of shares of stock as the convertible bond converts into. If an investor bought the convertible below, which converts into 27.5 shares of stock, it would take 3.11 years to recover the premium compared to an outright purchase of 27.5 shares of stock:

$$\frac{\text{Equity}}{\text{maintenance}} = \frac{\text{convertible market price} - \text{conversion value}}{\text{cvt. coupon} - [(\text{stock dividend})(\text{conversion ratio})]}$$

$$3.11 \text{ years} = \frac{1000 - 825}{70 - [(0.50)(27.50)]}$$

These methods provide a way of evaluating the conversion premium, but they focus solely on the income aspect of a convertible, versus the dividend yield of the common stock. A complete evaluation of a convertible security must take many other factors into account. Break-even analysis is based on the theory that there would be little incentive for an investor to hold the convertible bond if it did not offer a yield advantage over the common stock, and convertibles with a small yield advantage would command very little conversion premium. The theory would also dictate that the investor convert to the common stock if the yield premium of the bond over the stock is below a certain stipulated amount.

In the marketplace many bonds are converted that probably would not be if a more sophisticated method of evaluation were used. Although it is extremely rare for a convertible to yield less than its underlying stock, it is interesting to examine such a case for what we can learn about the break-even analysis mechanism. Consider a convertible bond that yields less than its underlying common stock, is trading at a discount from par, offers no conversion premium, and is due to mature in the very near future. Theoretical break-even analysis would suggest that the bond be converted into the stock immediately, due to the stock's higher yield.

However, the investor who stops to consider the risk/reward basis can see that this bond is a better buy than the common stock. If the stock price goes up, the convertible also goes up by the same amount, less the small difference in yield. On the other hand, if the stock declines, the bond value will be par at maturity, rather than tumbling with the stock. The investor would be foolish to convert to the stock when the bond has such a favorable risk/reward relationship. In other words, the bond gets almost all of the upside potential of the stock and almost none of its downside.

For example, Chase Manhattan's 6 percent convertible bond had a negative yield advantage to its common stock (that is, the common stock had a higher yield than the convertible) but had a favorable risk/reward relationship. Consider the situation as it was on June 11, 1984. The common stock of Chase Manhattan was trading at $41.125, and the convertible bond was trading at 74. The bond was convertible into 17.391 shares of common stock. Thus the conversion value for the bond was $71.520 (17.391 × $41.125), representing a slight conversion premium of 3.47 percent. Although the current yield of the convertible bond was slightly less than that of the common stock and thus would be unattractive according to straight break-even analysis, the convertible offered a tremendous risk/reward advantage. This is shown in Figure 8–9, which compares the risk/reward of holding the common stock to

## F I G U R E  8–9

Chase Manhattan Risk/Reward Analysis—June 11, 1984

|  | Price | Yield |
|---|---|---|
| Common stock price | $41.13 | 8.9% |
| Convertible bond price | $74.00 | 8.8% |

**Profit/loss estimates over next 12 months:**

| Change in stock price | −50% | −25% | 0 | +25% | +50% |
|---|---|---|---|---|---|
| Return on stock investment | −41.1% | −16.1% | +8.9% | +33.9% | +58.9% |
| Return on convertible investment | −6.0% | −2.0% | +8.8% | +30.0% | +53.0% |

Conversion ratio: 17.391 shares of stock per each bond.

Chase Manhattan Corporation convertible bond: 6.5 percent due July 1, 1996.

Chase Manhattan Corporation convertible bond yield-to-maturity: 10.7 percent

that of the convertible bond. Please note that the "Stock investment" and "Convertible investment" lines show profit/loss estimates (in percentage terms) rather than prices or yields.

The risk/reward analysis is based on upside potential versus downside risk. In this case the common stock investment has slightly more potential, as shown in Figure 8–9. For an increase of 50 percent in price, the stock's total return would be 58.9 percent, compared to 53.0 percent for the convertible investment. But if the stock decreased by 50 percent, the convertible return would be −6.0 percent, compared to a −41.1 percent from the stock investment. The slight yield advantage that the common stock enjoys would mean very little in a declining market. Notice that if the stock declines, the investment value of the discounted bond cushions the loss and preserves capital. The convertible bondholder achieves a significant reduction in risk. Based on the risk/reward analysis, the convertible is a better investment than the common stock, regardless of the conclusion drawn from the break-even analysis.

This example illustrates the main drawback of the break-even method: Although it considers conversion premium and yield advantage, it can be misleading and does not provide an adequate way to compare alternative opportunities in the market. Unfortunately, many convertible research reports published by brokerage firms rely on break-even analysis as the basis for selecting one convertible over another. Break-even analysis also ignores the convertible's main advantage: the upside potential on the underlying equity. In most cases, the most important determinant of convertible profitability is what happens to its underlying stock.

It also ignores the significant margin of safety offered by the convertible with the repayment of principal at maturity. A refined break-even analysis would consider the payment at par at maturity as a put received by the convertible investor. The calculation would subtract this dollar value (calculated as a percentage of par) from the conversion premium dollar value in the equation's numerator. The improved example would work as follows:

Years to maturity: 5
Bond price: 100
Coupon: 7 percent
Stock yield: 1.67 percent
Conversion premium: 21.21 percent
Break-even as previously calculated: 3.98 years.
Value of a put at par five years out: $75, or 7.5 percent of par

$$\frac{(21.21 - 7.5)}{(7.0 - 1.67)} = \frac{13.7}{4.19} = 3.27 \text{ years}$$

This method offers a fairer comparison of the equity to the convertible because the convertible debt feature includes the coupon rate as well as the put value calculation.

## From the Trader's Perspective

Professional traders use some general rules of thumb based on break-even analysis. For example, in the new-issue market, break-even for investment grade issues should not exceed five years. For BB– to strong B-rated bonds, break-even should not exceed one year past call date. For B and below, call protection should be at least equal to break-even.

Traders also use another version of break-even to decide between a straight bond and a convertible bond. The 200-basis-point rule says to swap into the convertible if the yield advantage of the straight bond over the convertible is less than 200 basis points.

This is truly a simplistic rule because many other factors enter into the analysis.

Professional traders have a great interest in tracking the arbitrage potential between various issues of convertibles and among convertibles, straight bonds, and common stock. Swaps are often initiated based on break-even analysis. A swap, when executed, maintains the exact call on common in the purchased security as in the one sold. If the equity maintenance formula (as described above) is used, additional dollars will be required. (A convertible security that converts into 27.5 shares of common stock will generally cost less than a purchase of the 27.5 shares of stock themselves.) Dealers in the convertible market often do swaps to derive arbitrage profits and facilitate trades for their clients. Swaps are also done by investors who are committed to a long equity position in the company and, therefore, will be long either the common or the convertible, depending on premium levels and break-even analysis.

The advantage of rule-of-thumb trading is that decisions can be made very quickly, which can be a great help in an active market. The disadvantage is that such decisions are based on limited information and may cause investment errors. As we have often discussed, the investment decisions for convertibles require a more thorough evaluation process, especially for long-term, fundamental investors.

## EQUITY RISK MEASURES

A convertible must be evaluated for its equity component in addition to its fixed-income characteristics. A significant part of the appeal of a convertible security depends on its potential for capital gains as the underlying stock increases in value. Fundamental analysis is helpful in selecting the best prospects for growth but is often very subjective. Our discussion will be limited to the more objective statistical risk measures used to evaluate the equity component of the convertible security: beta and total variance.

### Beta

The common stock beta coefficient (b) is a measure of a stock's systematic (market-related) risk. It is the portion of a stock's variance or volatility that can be explained by general market movements. A beta of 1.0 indicates the stock is expected to move up or down equally with the market. A stock with a beta 1.50 is expected to be 50 percent more sensitive to market gyrations than the market. Thus a high-beta stock is expected to move up more quickly than the market averages in rising markets and decline more quickly in periods of declining market averages. Beta is often considered the only relevant risk of a stock in a well-diversified portfolio because any unsystematic risk (non-market-related) can theoretically be eliminated through proper diversification.

Stock beta measures can be found by regressing stock price changes (usually weekly) against the market average-price changes. Five years of data points are generally used. The beta coefficient on average explains about 50 percent of a stock's total volatility. However, the beta of individual stocks does not adequately explain the riskiness of the stock. Throughout its dying years, PanAmerican Airlines had a beta of 0.6, which is well below market average. The troubled airline, trying to keep out of bankruptcy, was surely risky, but statistically it did not correlate well with market averages, as indicated by its low beta. Beta's usefulness to an investor can be significantly increased by computing the weighted portfolio beta for a well-diversified portfolio. This can account for as much as 98 percent of the portfolio volatility and is a good measure of market risk.

## Beta of a Convertible

When applying beta to convertible analysis, the unique advantage of the convertible becomes apparent. The risk/reward relationship of the stock is linear because beta measures the change in the stock over various time periods and market cycles. The theory of increased risk leading to increased returns is at the heart of beta.

However, due to the conversion premium, as the stock goes up the convertible increases at a rate that is different from the stock's rate of increase. On the downside, the investment value causes the convertible to decline at a rate that is lower than that of the common stock. The convertible's relationship to the value of the common stock, as prices change, is not linear, and the beta of a convertible is therefore different from that of its underlying common stock. Unlike a stock's beta, the convertible's beta changes as stock prices or interest rates change. In fact, the convertible has both an upside beta (bcu) and a downside beta (bcd).

To determine the convertible's betas, the investor must calculate its sensitivity to changes in general market moves. Figure 8–10 uses the convertible security of a common stock with a beta of 1.2 to determine the convertible's betas. The common stock arbitrary percentage moves, expressed as a ratio, are compared to corresponding moves in the convertible, also expressed as a ratio. For example, the downside of the common stock is assumed to be 50 percent. That being the case, it is estimated that the convertible would decrease by 30 percent. Since the convertible decreases only 60 percent (30/50) of the amount the common stock decreases, the convertible's beta will be 60 percent of the stock's beta of 1.2, or .72. The convertible upside beta of .93 is calculated by the same procedure.

The convertible's beta will approach the stock's beta as it rises above its investment value and becomes more equity-sensitive. This makes sense because the convertible trades increasingly like the stock as it rises in value. Unlike a stock's beta, the convertible beta changes as stock prices change. It will decrease as the price declines and the convertible becomes less equity-sensitive. In effect, in rising

## F I G U R E    8–10

Calculating Convertible Beta

| | | | | |
|---|---|---|---|---|
| Stock beta = 1.2 | | | | |
| Stock price move % | −50 | −25 | +25 | +50 |
| Expected convertible price move % | −30 | −15 | +18 | +40 |

$$\text{Downside ratio} = \frac{(-30) + (-15)}{(-50) + (-25)} = .600$$

$$\text{Upside ratio} \quad = \frac{18 + 40}{25 + 50} = .773$$

Downside beta = .600 × 1.2 = .72

Upside beta    = .773 × 1.2 = .93

markets the convertible's stock market exposure increases; in falling markets, it decreases and bond market sensitivity becomes more important. A well-constructed portfolio of convertibles should have a low downside beta and a higher upside beta. This satisfies our requirement for a convertible portfolio that has most of the upside potential of stock but limited downside potential.

## Total Variance

The variability of a stock's return is the measure of its total risk. The higher the variability of returns, the more likely the stock's actual return will vary from its average or expected return. Thus, the higher the variance, the higher the risk. The stock's historical standard deviation (variance of returns) measures both systematic and unsystematic risk and is therefore known as the total risk measure. The PanAmerican common stock mentioned above had a low beta but a high stock variance. Its total risk was high, reflecting the high risk of the stock.

Calculating the stock's total risk measure is quite simple if a large database of stock returns is available. The majority of academic studies indicate that the most relevant price return information resides in the most recent time period. Investors can estimate the stock's variance and standard deviation for the past year, as shown in Figure 8–11.

Stock variance is an important input variable for the convertible pricing model and other analytical models that assess risk. Some analysts make such predictions directly without using statistical measures; nevertheless, statistical measures allow for a better comparison of opportunities without the interference of subjective factors. However, the investor must realize that stock variance is the most difficult variable to estimate. Stock models and convertible models assume that variance remains stationary, which may or may not be true. Although estimates are easily obtainable by many stock research services, considerable thought should be given to this input variable because past variance is an important guide to future volatility. Profitability depends on the accuracy of the estimates in input variables. Volatility estimates are readily available from investment research sources. For example, Bloomberg allows the user to select effortlessly the time frame and market index needed to calculate the volatility of a stock.

**F I G U R E   8–11**

Estimating Stock Variance

| Month | Closing Price(s) | Price Relative (S+1/S) | Log of Price Relative ($X^1$) | Difference $(X^1 - \overline{X})^2$ |
|-------|------------------|------------------------|-------------------------------|-------------------------------------|
| 01 | 20.00 | | | |
| 02 | 22.00 | 1.1000 | 0.0953 | 0.0035 |
| 03 | 27.00 | 1.2273 | 0.2048 | 0.0283 |
| 04 | 23.00 | 0.8519 | −0.1603 | 0.0387 |
| 05 | 24.00 | 1.0435 | 0.0426 | 0.0001 |
| 06 | 28.00 | 1.1667 | 0.1542 | 0.0139 |
| 07 | 31.00 | 1.1071 | 0.1018 | 0.0043 |
| 08 | 30.00 | 0.9677 | −0.0328 | 0.0048 |
| 09 | 27.00 | 0.9000 | −0.1054 | 0.0201 |
| 10 | 33.00 | 1.2222 | 0.2007 | 0.0270 |
| 11 | 29.00 | 0.8788 | −0.1292 | 0.0275 |
| 12 | 32.00 | 1.1034 | 0.0984 | 0.0038 |
| 13 | 31.00 | 0.9688 | −0.0317 | 0.0047 |

Average return $(\overline{X}) = 0.0365$

$$Monthly\ Variance = \frac{\sum_{n=1}^{12} (x^1 - \overline{x})^2}{N - 1} = \frac{0.1766}{11.0000} = 0.0161$$

Monthly standard deviation = $\sqrt{0.0161} = 0.1269$

Annualized variance = $0.0161 \times 12 = 0.1932$

Annualized standard deviation = $\sqrt{0.1932} = 0.4395$

## SUMMARY

We have considered both the fixed-income and equity characteristics of convertible securities. Each factor in the analysis of convertible securities is influenced by many variables—putting these factors together into a comprehensive model that properly evaluates the convertible security has yet to be done. It's apparent that these individual elements and how they are calculated are as important as the model itself.

**A P P E N D I X**

# INTEREST-RATE SENSITIVITY IN CONVERTIBLE SECURITIES

The effects of interest-rate changes become complex when evaluating a convertible as a combination of bond value Sv(t) and equity or warrant value Wv(t). Increasing the risk-free rate or short-term interest rate will increase the warrant value of the convertible, holding all other variables constant. This is explained at greater length in Chapter 10.

The value of the convertible bond is also sensitive to changes in long-term bond yields. If long-term interest rates increase, then the debt value of the convertible will decrease, causing a decline in the convertible's value. The adjusted exercise price (the price at which the conversion option is struck) for the convertible will also decrease. As we have mentioned, convertibles with smaller investment value premiums trade more closely to their bond value than to their stock value and will therefore be more responsive to changes in interest rates and less responsive to changes in stock prices. Thus, the duration of a convertible bond is strongly affected by the conversion and investment value premiums. In general, the larger the spread between conversion value and investment value, the lower the duration.

Under certain conditions, an upward shift in the yield curve would not change the value of the convertible. For example, if the short-term rate increases, the value of the option portion of the convertible also increases. But the increase in the long-term rate would lower the convertible's investment value. It is possible to have the increase in the equity value offset any loss in the debt value with a net result of no change in the convertible value.

The duration (Dcv) of a convertible security can be explained as a function of the following:

$$Dcv = \frac{\partial Cv(t)}{\partial i} = f\left[\frac{\partial Sv(t)}{\partial i} , \frac{\partial K}{\partial Sv(t)} , \frac{\partial Wv(t)}{\partial K} , \frac{\partial Wv(t)}{\partial i}\right]$$

where:

    $i$ = long-term interest rates

The following algorithms can be used to measure the duration of a convertible bond.

The dollar change is Sv(t) with respect to a percent change in interest rates:

$$\frac{\partial Sv(t)}{\partial i} = Sv(t)1 + 0.1\left((ti_t/1 + ym)^t )/Sv(t)\right) - Sv(t)$$

The dollar change in the adjusted exercise price with respect to the dollar change in Sv(t):

$$\frac{\partial K}{\partial Sv(t)} = (\partial Sv(t)/\partial i/Cr(t))$$

The dollar change in the Wv(t) with respect to the dollar change in the adjusted exercise price:

$$\frac{\partial Wv(t)}{\partial K} = Cr(t) - e^{-rT} N(H - \sigma\sqrt{T})$$

The dollar change in Wv(t) with respect to a percent change in interest rates:

$$\frac{\partial Wv(t)}{\partial i} = Cr(t)TKe^{-rT} N(h - \sigma\sqrt{T})$$

These equations determine the interest-rate sensitivity of a convertible bond. Almost every variable is affected by changing interest rates, the debt being inversely related and the warrant portion positively related. Also, the duration of Sv(t) may be found to equal the duration of the adjusted exercise price. Also, the duration of a convertible cannot exceed the duration of Sv(t):

$$\text{Dur } Sv(t) = \text{Dur } K$$

$$\text{Dur } Cv(t) < = \text{Dur } Sv(t)$$

where:
  Cv(t) = convertible value
  Sv(t) = straight bond value
    i = long-term interest rate
    k = exercise price (adjusted)
  Wv(t) = warrant value

t = time period (current)

Ym = straight bond value discount rate

Cr(t) = number of shares the convertible is exchangeable into

T = time period remaining for convertibility

e = exponential functions

$\partial$ = derivative notation

$\sigma$ = stock's variance

N = univariate cumulative normal

h = upper limit of integration

## E N D N O T E S

1. Interest tables are found in most investment textbooks. Computer spread sheets and financial calculators also provide a convenient means to access present value formulas and determine investment value.

2. As reported by Eric Rosengren, "Defaults of Original Issue High-Yield Convertible Bonds," *The Journal of Finance*, March 1993.

3. Edward I. Altman, *Financial Analysts Journal 43*, July/August 1987, p. 23.

4. Frederick R. Macaulay, "Some Theoretical Problems Suggested by Movements of Interest Rates, Bond Yields and Stock Prices in the United States Since 1856" (New York: National Bureau of Economic Research, 1938).

# 9

## CHAPTER

# Convertible Bond Pricing

## DETERMINING THEORETICAL FAIR MARKET VALUE

So far we have defined and discussed the various components of a convertible security when considered as a debt instrument with an implied warrant or embedded option. How those factors interrelate in the marketplace determines the value or market price of a convertible security. Since the marketplace is generally an efficient mechanism for determining value, the convertible security's market price should tend towards its theoretical fair value. To gain an edge in the marketplace, an astute investor should seek out convertibles trading below theoretical fair value and avoid those above the theoretical fair value. Unfortunately, determining theoretical fair value is a complicated problem involving a number of assumptions.

In the fast-paced financial arena, some traders base their trading decisions on simple rules of thumb and ignore the more complicated theoretical fair value calculation. In convertible trading, this typically takes the form of rules based simply on break-even analysis or on a maximum number based on conversion premium. These guidelines are used to simplify a complex problem. A thorough analysis of a convertible security involves identifying key variables such as conversion premium and yield advantage. This chapter describes the evolution of the mathematical evaluation process and the underlying assumptions on which theoretical fair value formulas are based. The discussion should provide some valuable insight as to how these variables combine to determine the theoretical fair value of a convertible, especially when considered in light of its relationship to the market price.

The mathematical valuation of convertible securities has been pursued vigorously in recent years. However, Benjamin Graham applied little mathematical analysis to convertible securities in his classic investment book, *The Intelligent Investor*.[1] His analysis was based on the underlying fundamentals of the issuing company and a subjective feeling as to whether conversion premium was high or low. Without the benefit of mathematical models in use today, his comments on convertibles indicate both his mastery of investing and the limitations of that era's technology. The formulas in use today attempt to quantify what investment masters like Graham took years to assimilate.

The evolution of the mathematical process used to evaluate convertible securities parallels the growth of modern portfolio theory. Some have attempted mathematical evaluation of convertible securities by analyzing the latent warrant embedded in the security[2] or by presenting convertibles as a present value problem. In the past, others have used the naive approach of a French curve and graph paper to indicate the relationship between the straight bond value, current market price, and an assumed point where conversion price and market price would be equal.

Four main approaches predominated before option theory began to be applied to pricing convertibles: stock-picker, current price track, historical price track, and theoretical price. All except the stock picker seek to estimate the value of the convertible security by evaluating changes in the underlying stock price. Properly estimating the various prices at which the convertible may trade allows the investor to make important risk/reward estimates.

## The Stock Picker

Many convertible investors are stock pickers. They purchase a convertible in the hope that the underlying stock will increase in value. Investors who use fundamental analysis of the common stock as the primary reason to purchase the convertible will have to be extraordinarily successful in their stock selection. They may often find that they were correct on the stock, but the convertible did not follow. This method largely ignores the investment characteristics of the convertible and relies on stock fundamentals, often negating the basic advantages of convertible investing. Convertible investment managers using this method have a tendency not to sell convertibles as the underlying common stock advances, meaning they do not take profits when the convertible's risk/reward profile is no longer attractive.

One such manager held Westinghouse convertible bonds in his client's account prior to the stock market crash of 1987. Figure 9–1 compares the risk/reward of the convertible bond and the common stock. Notice that in this case the convertible had little advantage over the common stock.

Because the manager was hired to invest in convertibles, he might have maintained the convertible in the account even though it was inferior to the common stock. The Westinghouse convertible bond lost 100 points in the stock market crash of 1987, falling from 240 to 140 on October 19. The convertible had increased so much in

**F I G U R E  9–1**

Risk/Reward Analysis, Westinghouse 9% of 8/15/2009

September 4, 1987

|  | Price | Yield |
|---|---|---|
| Common stock price | 68.63 | 2.51% |
| Convertible bond price | 225.00 | 4.00% |

| Profit/Loss Estimates over Next 12 Months | | | | | |
|---|---|---|---|---|---|
| Stock change | –50.0% | –25.0% | 0 | +25.0% | +50.0% |
| Stock ROI%* | –47.5 | –22.5 | +2.5 | +27.0 | +53.0 |
| Convertible ROI%* | –41.0 | –20.0 | +4.0 | +30.0 | +54.0 |

*Includes income.

Note:    October 19, 1987:
        Stock price: 40.25           Drop since 9/04/87 –41.35%
        Bond price: 140.25       Drop since 9/04/87 –37.67%

value that it provided no cushion on the downside and had the same risk/reward as the common stock.

Some advisory services recommend convertibles that have little risk/reward advantage over the underlying stock simply because they like the common stock. Investors basing their selection process on fundamentals alone may often choose convertibles that act like common stock, thus resulting in higher risk portfolios that will likely negate any of the convertible's risk-control advantage. Furthermore, by ignoring the convertible's premium they may purchase overpriced convertibles that do not respond to increases in stock prices, possibly affecting performance.

How might the investor improve on this strategy? Selecting convertibles by picking stocks and without regard to the risk-control attributes of the convertible security can eventually lead to high-risk portfolios and disappointing overall results. Performance probably will be erratic and will follow the roller-coaster ride of the stock market.

Researching company fundamentals is essential to successful convertible investing. Convertible investors cannot perform an accurate mathematical analysis of the convertible security without analyzing the underlying common stock fundamentals. On the other hand, convertible investors who believe that diversification replaces the fundamental analysis of individual securities are often disappointed when they rely on leverage estimates alone; ignoring fundamentals will result in more defaults and overall poor performance. Therefore, investors must blend fundamental analysis with the proper analytical methods to determine the theoretical fair value of the convertible security.

## Current Price Track—Naive Approach

The most simplistic method used to estimate the price track of a convertible security is called the naive approach. It assumes that all convertibles are basically the same and has the least number of assumptions. It begins with a graph showing the convertible price on the vertical axis and the stock price on the horizontal axis. The investment value becomes a minimum value below which the convertible price cannot fall. The conversion value becomes a diagonal line beginning at zero and determined by the conversion ratio, as discussed in Chapter 3.

Earlier books on convertibles spent a great deal of time describing how to draw the price curve, based on some minimum and maximum values and basic curve fitting. The minimum value is the investment value of the convertible. The maximum value is the point where conversion value and market price converge; the analyst makes an assumption as to where this would occur (typically at 40 percent above par). With the current market price of the convertible security known, a curve is fitted through those three points, as indicated in Figure 9–2. The main problem becomes finding the correct curve-fitting technique once the three points have been determined.

The advantage of this method is that it is quickly obtainable; one needs only graph paper and a French curve—or a computer program. These programs are curve-fitting mathematical formulas that will draw a smooth curve through the three points. The curve will probably approximate how the convertible trades for small price moves over relatively short periods of time.

**F I G U R E  9–2**

Convertible Bond Price Track

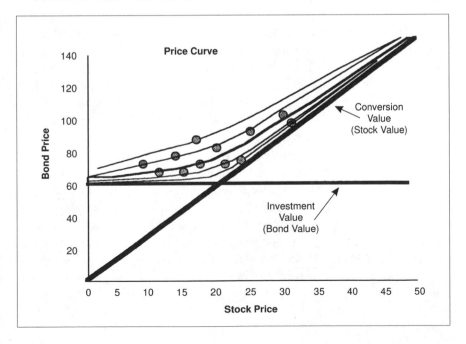

The naive approach has many disadvantages. To begin with, this method does not determine theoretical fair value. It assumes the current market price to be theoretical fair value and simply determines a track that the convertible may take if that assumption is correct. This method does not adjust for convertibles that may be called. Furthermore, as we will see later, for many convertibles the actual price track is not a smooth curve between three points.

During rising markets, the estimated curve holds fairly well because a convertible will advance towards conversion value as the underlying stock increases. There will be many occasions when investors will be disappointed because the convertible seems to lag the upside and not follow a smooth, upward-sloping curve. This occurs because under this method it is impossible to take into account other variables such as the bond's call features. A number of other factors also might cause the convertible price to not follow the smooth curve, thus creating errors. Such factors include dramatic changes in interest rates, overvaluation, a provisional call feature that kicks in, time decay, and so on. These errors may be masked in rising markets because the result is forsaken gains rather than losses.

A larger problem with using this method occurs at the most critical juncture in the investment cycle: the declining phase. An investor purchases convertibles to provide a downside cushion in declining markets. If the investor has miscalculated how much the convertible's price will drop in response to a given price decrease in the underlying stock, then the convertible will not provide the protection which motivated its purchase in the first place.

In declining markets, this method can lead to severe estimate errors. Market decreases are often accompanied by changing market sentiment, which is beyond the scope of this method. This changing sentiment can cause the convertible price curve to shift, causing a greater loss than had been originally forecast. At such times, the conversion premium is increasing as the underlying common stock price is decreasing, resulting in the greatest possibility for error: The greater the conversion premium, the more accurate the convertible bond price track must be to avoid serious losses.

Although this method has been surpassed with more accurate methods for estimating convertible valuations, it did at least attempt to predict the risk/reward ratio of convertible securities and was better than making no estimate at all. It served investors as a first step in understanding convertibles.

## Historical Price Track—Logarithmic Regression

This method attempts to solve the main drawback of the naive approach by analyzing historical price relationships. The investor uses regression analysis to analyze the relationship between the prices of common stock and those of convertible securities to determine the most accurate track based upon these historical relationships. Figure 9–3 indicates how a scattergram imposed on a track can indicate whether or not the convertible is priced on track.

We can see that this method may be sufficient over small price moves and small time periods. It is easily accomplished by computing a logarithmic regression analysis on past prices using

**F I G U R E 9–3**

Convertible Bond Price Track (Regression)

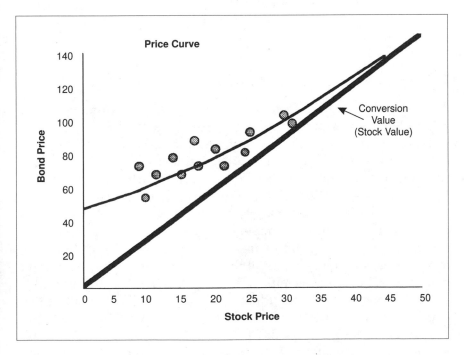

computer software and is widely used by convertible trading desks. This method seems to be a favorite among convertible market makers who, over short periods of time, can make markets based on movements of the convertible along its regression line.

This method is definitely an improvement over the naive approach, but still has some serious drawbacks. Any changes in interest rates would quickly move a convertible off its recent track. This method does not provide a means to determine how the convertible price track may change as interest rates change. The track can also be changed when the bond becomes callable or when the underlying stock volatility changes. Changes in overall market sentiment often influence conversion premium levels, which could cause the bond to trade on another price track.

Despite its shortcomings, however, this method is useful because it allows an investor to view the historical trading pattern of an unfamiliar convertible issue. Past trading patterns give the convertible investor a feel for how the supply and demand forces have interacted in the past. This method may also be preferred in foreign markets. The basic theoretical models often do not hold in foreign markets because some do not allow stocks to be sold short. This violates the neutral hedge argument built into the option models.

## Models Based on Theoretical Formulas

Applying option pricing models to convertible valuation was a significant step in determining theoretical fair value for convertibles. Formulas that include many variables can overcome most of the drawbacks of the naive and historical methods. These formulas can quickly determine theoretical fair value for the convertible under various assumptions. They adapt quickly to changes in interest rates, stock volatility, and bond callability. Since each theoretical fair value is determined independently of the others, adjustments for call features and bond values can be predetermined. Applying option theory to many financial instruments has created a superior means by which to determine a theoretical fair value of convertible securities and is further evidence of the versatility of option theory. Figure 9–4 indicates how the actual convertible price track would look over a wide range of prices for a callable bond. Notice the flat portion of the price track, caused by the fact that this par-

**F I G U R E  9–4**

Historical Prices versus Theoretical Price Track

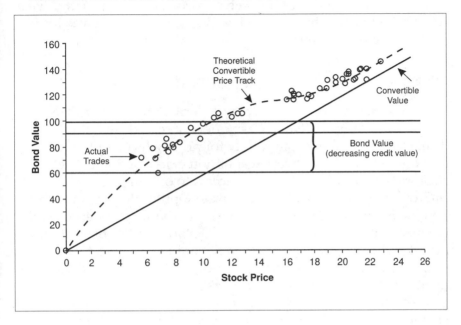

ticular convertible is callable. None of the other methods adequately adjusts for callable versus noncallable securities.

Figure 9–4 shows the history of a convertible bond's actual prices with the theoretical convertible price track overlaid. As the stock declined in value, investment value also declined, due to credit deterioration. It indicates the importance of credit and fundamental analysis as well as validating the theoretical methodology. Properly calculating the input variable at investment value gives the investor the most probable risk/reward estimate.

Figures 9–2 through 9–4 illustrate the evolution of convertible bond pricing. It is apparent that option theory provides a means to evaluate convertibles in a way that is similar to that used for listed options. The application of option theory to convertible pricing is compounded by the complexity of convertibles and by the intricacies of the option pricing formula. For example, the call feature varies from issue to issue; interest rate changes affect the assumptions used to determine the value of both the straight bond and the latent warrant; and stock volatility caused by changing company fundamentals also affects the value of both the straight bond and the latent warrant.

Before applying option theory to convertible pricing, we'll review the Black–Scholes model, which serves as the basis for understanding option theory.

## OVERVIEW OF THE BLACK–SCHOLES OPTION MODEL

The Black–Scholes option model was derived by Fischer Black and Myron Scholes in 1973 and was widely accepted by both the academic and investment community for pricing listed options. Many services provide both theoretical option prices and hand-held calculators that allow instantaneous access to option prices. However, as Professor Bookstaber pointed out in Option Pricing and Strategies in Investing, "The number who use the formula exceeds the number who understand it."[3] The popularity of the Black–Scholes model is due in part to the ease in obtaining variables that are not subject to investors' preferences or attitudes towards risk. The only highly subjective variable is the stock's variance of returns.

The Black–Scholes option formula determines the value of an option for a given stock price and a given time to maturity. It does not depend on the investor's expectations for the direction of the stock price move. The value of the formula is that it determines a theoretical fair value for the option without regard to investor preference. An investor who expected a particular stock to go down would not buy the stock or the call regardless of their prices. The simplest version of the option formula assumes that the short-term interest rate and the volatility of the stock do not change, that the stock pays no dividend, and that there are no transaction costs. There are five variables needed in the formula: (1) stock price, (2) time to maturity, (3) exercise price, (4) interest rate, and (5) stock volatility.

If one assumes that the formula produces the correct value, appropriate action becomes clear. If the market price of the option is below the theoretical fair value that has been determined, the buyer would have an advantage; if it is above the theoretical fair value, the seller would have the advantage. The seller's gains are the buyer's losses, and vice versa. Because it is a theoretical fair value, the assumption is that market prices will revert to it in the long run. Any deviation from theoretical fair value will be temporary and regarded as inefficiency in the marketplace.

   This model is based on the neutral option hedge argument and states that individual stock risk (unsystematic risk) can be completely eliminated through the use of option hedging. A neutral hedge is one that is low in risk for small moves in the stock price and is constructed so that any change in stock price causes an instantaneous offset in the option position. The model determines the hedge ratio, which is the ratio of stock to options needed for a neutral hedge. It is based on the input variables for a particular security, and the value of the long position need not equal the value of the short position. The gains and losses of the long position will offset the gains and losses of the short position. Since the risk-free interest rate remains constant over the short term, the option's theoretical fair value can be determined.

   The Black–Scholes model uses complicated but logical mathematics. Conceptually, the model calculates the present value of the stock price at expiration of the option. This takes into consideration the cost of money (or carrying cost) and shows how the interest rate influences the price. The present value is multiplied by the probability that the stock price will exceed the exercise price, and this probability is based on historical volatility. From this, we subtract the present value of the payment of the exercise price, multiplied by the probability of payment. The formula is shown in the appendix to this chapter.

   The Black–Scholes model has a number of shortcomings, which are apparent when reviewing the underlying assumptions. For example, it assumes the following:

- Option exercised only at maturity(European style option).
- Transaction costs ignored.
- No dividends on stocks.
- Interest rates assumed constant.
- Volatility assumed constant.
- Stock price changes are assumed to be lognormal.
- Dilution impact ignored.

The model assumes a lognormal distribution of stock prices so that calculations can be made easily within the formula.[4] However, studies have indicated that the actual distribution of stock price changes does not necessarily follow a lognormal curve. Still, the main benefit of the Black–Scholes model is that it has five variables, of which four are known. Therefore, from a practical viewpoint, it is relatively easy for investors to apply in determining the theoretical fair value of options. When applying the Black–Scholes model to convertible analysis, its shortcomings can be modified, as we will explain later in this chapter.

The academic and investment communities attempted to match option pricing theory formulas with marketplace realities. Serious studies have been undertaken to adjust the formulas for more realistic price distributions and to explain differences between theoretical fair value computations and observed market anomalies. Other academic studies have used the Black–Scholes model to price various financial instruments. In addition, most reviews of actual option pricing indicate wide acceptance of the model. All of this has made the Black–Scholes model the starting point for understanding the development of a theoretical fair value model for convertible securities.

To apply the Black–Scholes model to options, the analyst must input current stock price, exercise price of the option, time to expiration, and an estimate of the underlying common stock variance. Floor traders on the Chicago Board Options Exchange use calculators with the formula already set up so that trades can be made quickly on the basis of over- and undervaluation.

The basic form of the Black–Scholes option model cannot be used to value convertibles, due to the complexity of convertibles. The exercise price can vary depending upon conditions. The time to expiration of the conversion feature also can vary, depending on whether or not the bond is callable. A model for convertibles must adjust for these factors and others to determine accurate theoretical fair value for convertibles in all cases. The following pages discuss the variables that apply in this case and the logic behind using a modified Black–Scholes option model to better understand the application of option theory to convertible valuation.

## CONVERTIBLE THEORETICAL FAIR VALUE MODEL

Through the application of option pricing theory, this model for theoretical pricing of convertible securities considers all factors and does not depend on investors' subjective attitudes. It encompasses both callable and noncallable bonds, synthetic convertibles, and warrants. This section discusses the model as an extension of the basic convertible factors outlined in previous chapters.

This evaluation process is complicated by the fact that a convertible security actually incorporates a "dual option." The bondholder has the option to convert to the underlying common stock of the issuing firm with certain restraints, and the issuing company has the option to call the bonds for redemption within certain restraints. Both options must be clearly identified and quantified within the model.

In each convertible security there is an investment value, Sv(t), and an option or warrant portion, Wv(t). The warrant is embedded in the security and is nondetachable in most cases. Each portion of the security is evaluated separately and then combined to determine the theoretical value of the convertible security as a whole, Cv(t).

Thus:　　Theoretical　　=　　Investment　　+　　Warrant
　　　　convertible value　　　　value　　　　value
　　　　　　Cv(t)　　　　=　　　Sv(t)　　　+　　Wv(t)

where:
　　t = current time period and Cv(t) and Sv(t) is greater than zero.

To determine the theoretical fair value price of a convertible, the formula must be modified to reflect the individual investment characteristics of a particular convertible issue. In the next section we discuss the basis to use to modify the formula to determine the theoretical fair value. The specific mathematical adjustments to the formula are not given, but the appendix to this chapter provides a version to determine the theoretical fair value of a convertible security.

## Convertible Security's Investment Value, Sv(t)

At first glance, the straight fixed-income portion, Sv(t), of the convertible security is a relatively straightforward calculation based on the yield-to-maturity calculation. That calculation is accurate for noncallable securities and for those with a low probability of being called. However, upon closer examination, some adjustments need to be made to reflect the fixed-income value and determine a theoretical convertible value that would apply in all cases. Depending on whether the security is callable or noncallable, as well as its coupon rate relative to current rates and other factors, the analyst must determine the probability of its being called. A convertible security that is likely to be called tends to trade on a yield-to-first-call basis rather than a yield to maturity. The investor must then make that determination and adjust the investment value accordingly.

## Adjustment for High Probability of Call

The investment value of the convertible is sensitive to the probability of being called for redemption. For example, during periods of declining interest rates, many convertible bonds are considered to have a high probability of call. During such periods, making this adjustment is particularly important to determine theoretical fair value prices. Companies will call bonds to refinance their debt at the then-current lower interest rate. Convertible bonds are very likely to be called at their next call date. Thus, the bonds trade as short-term paper, maturing at the first call date, and the bond's duration is significantly reduced. This becomes apparent when a bond is subject to call and carries a significantly higher coupon rate than a similar bond in the new issue market. Since most bond indentures require 30-day notice of call, the minimum value becomes its present value, plus a 30-day option on the underlying stock.

## Adjustment for Forced Conversion

Convertible securities are often called prior to the interest payment date. This is usually done to force conversion because the conversion value at the time is well above that of the call price. By forcing conversion at that point, the company saves the six-month interest payment. (This has been described in previous sections as the screw clause.) The bondholder is forced to convert to the underlying stock and foregoes the interest that has accrued from the previous payment date. In most cases the marketplace has anticipated the call, so the bond will already be trading at a discount from conversion value. That discount is typically the amount of accrued interest due at the time. Unless this is taken into account in a pricing model, the convertibles trading at slight discounts from conversion value will seem to be mathematically undervalued as compared to noncallable bonds.

## Boundary Conditions

In developing a convertible pricing model, boundary conditions must be established that hold true for all convertibles under normal conditions. Special boundary conditions must also be established that distinguish between callable and noncallable convertibles.

Boundary conditions can be described as the minimum and maximum values of the convertible. A number of minimum and maximum values must be included as boundary conditions. The market value should not fall below conversion value because that would present a no-risk profit opportunity that the floor specialists or arbitrageurs would quickly seize upon. They would only have to short stock in the amount equal to the conversion ratio of the bond, then purchase the bond and convert it to stock; transaction costs are minimal for such professional arbitrageurs.

For this professional arbitrage strategy to work, the convertible's market value must be below the conversion value. If this condition is met, bond market traders will avail themselves of this potential arbitrage profit, and the excess demand for the convertible will push the bond back to equilibrium.

Similarly, when a convertible's investment value exceeds its market price, a trader might find an arbitrage opportunity by shorting a straight bond against a convertible bond of the same coupon, quality, and maturity date, but this is less likely to occur. Nevertheless, fixed-income and convertible traders are quick to take advantage of convertible bonds that are trading below the market's perception of their straight bond value.

The result is the second arbitrage condition, which states that the convertible price must always be greater than its straight bond value. This holds true no matter how unlikely it is that the stock price will reach its conversion price. For most purposes, investors should consider that the convertible price will always be greater than or equal to investment value.

The remainder of the boundary conditions result from the call provisions of the bond or the investor's determination of the probability of call. In the interest of maximizing profits for a bond that has been called, the bondholder will always choose the greater of conversion value or the call price.

## Adjusting for Callable Bonds

Bonds that are currently callable but seem unlikely to be called due to the current interest-rate level and the coupon rate on the bond must be evaluated differently by investors. Although no call protection remains, if the bonds are not be likely to be called, then the convertibility option should command some premium.

The first step in evaluating bonds with conversion value above or very near the call price (after hard call protection has expired) is to determine at what level the issuing corporation is likely to call the bonds. Although the optimal call strategy would be for the firm to call the bonds when the conversion value equals the call price, this is rarely the case. Studies have determined that firms typically call convertibles when the conversion value exceeds the call price by an average of 43.9 percent.[5] Firms do not call at the theoretically optimal point (when the conversion value reaches its call price) because slight market fluctuations in the underlying common stock between the time the call is made and its value date could cause a redemption of the bond at the call price, rather than forcing conversion.

Companies typically call bonds to force conversion and usually wait until the conversion value is well above call price. For example, in September 1987, IBM called the IBM Eurobond, convertible into Intel common stock. Although the conversion value was well above the redemption price of the bond at the time of the announcement, by the final redemption date some 30 days later, it was to the investor's advantage to redeem rather than convert. The stock market crash of 1987 caused Intel common stock to decline dramatically over that 30-day period. Companies can protect against this risk by entering into an agreement with an investment firm that guarantees conversion. An investment banker has fewer regulatory restrictions on certain strategies (such as shorting the stock) and can lock in a price more effectively than the company can—for a fee, of course.

Considering these actual call policies of convertible issuers, the investor must estimate the expected time remaining on the warrant portion of the convertible. The company's or industry's past call patterns should be examined carefully, along with the company's financial ability to call the bonds. In addition, the bond indenture should be checked for provisions that could initiate a call. For example, the bond may not be callable until a specified date or until the common stock trades at or above 150 percent of the conversion price for 30 days. This is commonly called the 150 percent provisional call. It may be an indication of the target price the company has set before forcing conversion even after the call date. If information is not readily attainable, the average of 43 percent above the call price may be used as an estimate.

## Time to Expiration

The final step is to estimate the most likely stock price movement over a specified time period. This is an extremely important step because it determines the range of stock prices used in the risk/reward analysis. Many convertible advisory services use an arbitrary percentage move in the common stock to determine leverage estimates—the amount the convertible price will change in response to a given change in the stock price. This analysis allows a determination of the implied time premium; the conversion premium at that point then can be more accurately determined. By applying the stock's historical return pattern and the investor judgment of the future volatility, the expected time premium can be estimated. The expected time to likely call is based on the stock moving above the provisional target or a price likely to trigger a call.

The convertible embedded option is valued by the time remaining during which the option can be exercised. When there is a small time premium, little time remains until expiration of the option, which means it has low value. There will be a larger time premium when a longer time period remains in which to exercise the option. The longer time period results in a higher value because there is a much greater probability that the underlying stock will gain in value.

Consideration of the time premium remaining on the convertible bond assumes that the bond's buyer and seller reach an equilibrium position in order to facilitate a trade. In this process, the buyer attempts to minimize the value of the bond and the seller attempts to maximize it. Specifically, the formula considers the time premium for a callable bond with a low probability of call. The buyer of a convertible bond should be willing to pay the premium for the time that remains, or a price lower than this, because this represents a fair evaluation for the value of the implied warrant based on the stock's historical volatility. Any price higher than that would be to the seller's advantage.

## Evaluating the Conversion Feature, Wv(t)

It should be clear that the underlying stock volatility influences both the investment-value and the warrant components of the convertible security. How the various factors interact with each other must be considered in order to accurately determine theoretical fair value under many different circumstances.

The conversion feature or warrant portion of the convertible bond is complicated by a number of conditions. Two variables need to be input into the option formula to use the model for evaluating the conversion portion of our model: the time to expiration and the exercise price. The time premium that remains on the conversion feature must be considered carefully. Clearly, if it is known that the convertible security will be called on a specific date, the input variable would simply be the time period. However, convertibles may or may not be called for a number of different reasons. In addition, the exercise price varies with changes in interest rates that affect the straight bond value, analogous to the way the value of a usable bond changes. The adjustments to the convertible theoretical fair value model for these various conditions are discussed below.

*Estimating the Time Premium to Conversion* Investors realize that the longer the time available in which to convert the convertible security to common stock, the more valuable the implied warrant of the convertible. Many convertible securities have long maturities, implying that the opportunity to convert persists for a long time. However, most convertibles can be called by the issuer years prior to the maturity date of the bond. The time at which the warrant ceases to be exercisable becomes an important consideration and affects the value of the convertible security.

The simplest case is a noncallable bond: The maturity date of the bond coincides with expiration of convertibility. For callable bonds, the investor must estimate the minimum time that the convertible bond will likely be outstanding and adjust the time to expiration. That becomes the worst-case scenario and is based on the assumption that the issuer will call the bond at the time that is most beneficial for the company. The factors to consider in estimating this are:

- The date the security becomes callable.
- The likelihood of bond call based on stock price.

This time period then becomes one of the factors used to determine the value of the warrant portion.

*Determining Exercise Price*  When pricing a convertible bond as a straight nonconvertible debt instrument with a warrant attached, the conversion price or exercise price of the warrant portion must be adjusted. The convertible bondholder must give up the bond portion in order to exercise the convertibility feature. Therefore, the exercise price continually changes as the value of the straight bond portion changes. This becomes apparent in situations where the warrant is actually detachable from the bond. These kinds of convertible (called units) are issued much like typical convertible bonds but soon after being offered can be traded separately. The warrant retains a specific exercise price that does not change. However, the bond portion, which now trades independently of the warrant, can be used at par value in lieu of cash when exercising the warrant. Obviously, if the straight bond is trading at a discount to par due to the current interest rate structure, it could be purchased and submitted to the company along with the warrant to obtain the stock; the exercise price of the warrant is effectively reduced by the amount of the bond's discount. Furthermore, as the straight bond value changes, the effective exercise price of the warrant also changes. The formula used must therefore take these changes into consideration.

This adjustment should be made in any evaluation of warrants where usable bonds apply. For example, Tiger International had a warrant outstanding with an exercise price of $12.50 per share. Since the straight bond could be used in lieu of cash upon the exercise of the warrant, the effective exercise price was reduced by any discount from par for which the bond could be purchased. In this case, with the bond trading at 85 in November 1987, the exercise price was reduced by 15 percent to $10.63.

Thus we can see that our model can evaluate the theoretical price of warrants by simply removing the fixed-income portion of our formula. It should also be clear that the exercise price of the convertible is now inversely related to interest rates and subject to further adjustments due to the creditworthiness of the issuing company and the call probability of the bond.

*Adjusting for Dividends* The convertible model must take stock dividends into account. The assumption that the stocks pay no dividends is a serious drawback of the Black–Scholes formula. In those cases where convertibles have little or no yield advantage over the underlying common stock dividend, they will command little or no conversion premium. Conversely, when the yield advantage is high, investors expect to pay a higher conversion premium. Of course, this is the essence of the commonly used "break-even analysis" calculation for evaluating convertibles. Therefore, the amount of the underlying stock dividend cannot be ignored, and an allowance for dividends is necessary to determine the theoretical fair value price.

Dividends affect the options model due to the fact that the stock price will decline on the ex-dividend date by the amount of the dividend. For ease of calculation, the dividend adjustment is assumed to be at a continuous rate. This modification is accomplished by reducing the stock price by the present value of the dividend pay-out and reducing the risk-free yield by the amount of the dividend to re-establish a no-risk hedge. The growth rate of the dividend could be included to reflect that factor.

Several important variables have been determined thus far:

- Straight bond value with its adjustments for callable and noncallable bonds.
- Time to expiration with its adjustment for callable bonds.
- Exercise price and its relationship to interest rates.

◆ Adjustment to the model for the underlying common stock dividend, including a growth assumption for the dividend rate.

*Dilution* Dilution results when holders of convertible bonds eventually convert to the underlying common stock. Since dilution affects valuation, calculating the fully diluted number of shares outstanding must be based on the assumption that all the securities that may have conversion rights will be converted. Other issues that may be converted into stock could include privately held convertible preferred stocks, privately held bonds, or options. Dilution does not result from exchangeable convertibles or other third-party securities that do not create additional shares.

## BINOMIAL MODEL

This chapter would not be complete without mentioning one of the newer models used to evaluate options, the binomial model. The increased complexity of convertibles and equity-linked issues in the marketplace of the 1990s has called for a more flexible pricing model. Derivations of the Black–Scholes model for convertible pricing may become very cumbersome in this new age of financial engineering. The binomial pricing model offers additional flexibility and a greater ease in making adjustments to the model as new wrinkles in the convertible market appear.

The binomial option model uses a lattice, or tree, approach to value an option, thereby providing a more flexible methodology for making the mathematical adjustments needed to improve the Black–Scholes model. The assumptions that need to be relaxed include constant stock volatility, constant interest rates, and stock-price distribution changes (Black–Scholes assumes a Brownian motion for stock price changes). These changes are usually necessary for a convertible model. Furthermore, the increasing complexity of new issues requires ever-increasing new adjustments for such complexities as step-up coupon payments, dual or triple options on the same security, and dual securities that a single issue converts into.

The binomial model can be best understood from Figure 9–5, a binomial tree diagram. Each branch represents a different stock

## F I G U R E 9–5

Stock Price Volatility

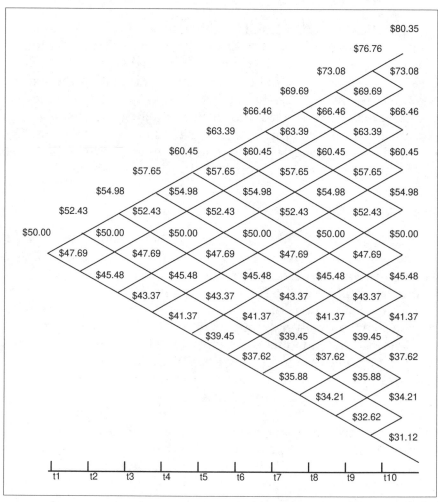

Source: Calamos Asset Management, Inc.

price and the corresponding probability of obtaining that price. The tree begins with the initial date (today) and ends at the expiration of the option. At each node of the tree, the stock price can either move up or down from the current time period to the next. The probability of the move up or down is also assigned at each node. For the sake of simplicity, we will describe a two-

## F I G U R E  9–6

Minimum Convertible Price Valuation

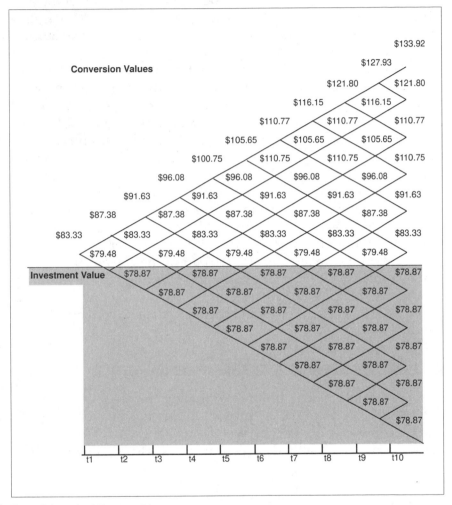

Source: Calamos Asset Management, Inc.

period binomial model. The current period stock price is represented by $S_o$. During the first period, the stock price can either
go up to $S_u$ or down to $S_d$. We will assume that each occurrence
has an equal probability. If the stock price goes up in the first
period, then during the second period, the stock can either move
up to $S_{u2}$ or down to $S_{d2}$. This process continues over the entire

valuation period. The model determines all possible stock price movements up to and including the time of expiration. It then computes the terminal option value relative to the range of possible stock prices at expiration. The model then moves back step-by-step along each branch from the expiration time to determine the current option price.

The convertible model starts with the maturity date of the bond. At each node, the security at maturity is worth the maximum of the conversion value or par value. The process then moves to one period from maturity; at this point, the expected present value of the convertible (if not converted) is assigned to each node. This process continues for each time period until the current period is reached. All boundary conditions initially required with the derivation of the Black–Scholes model for convertible pricing are still necessary.

The binomial approach to convertible pricing allows the user to make adjustments more easily to the more complex features we see in the convertible market today. It is also suitable for the early call events and conversions that are part of the convertible market. The binomial stock-price tree can also be combined with an interest-rate tree to allow for changes in the yield curve over the valuation period. Figure 9–6 indicates how such a convertible tree would look.

## ALTERNATIVE APPROACH—STOCK-PLUS VALUATION

The most intuitive method for determining the value of a convertible bond is to separate the option or warrant portion from the fixed-income component, as we discussed earlier. There is another appropriate method, which involves adding together three parts:

1. The convertible's stock value (or parity).
2. The value of the convertible's yield advantage over the estimated life of the security.
3. A put.

We will break down the rationale for this approach and work through an example.

As a convertible owner, you have the right to receive the conversion value or parity value of the convertible at any time. The first step in this analysis is to determine the parity value of the security, which is equal to the stock price multiplied by the conversion ratio. The convertible owner also has a right to receive the interest payments on the bond over the expected life of the security. The value of this stream of cash flows is discounted at a rate appropriate to the credit risk and expected life of the security. But since the convertible owner is giving up the dividend stream on the underlying stock, the present value of the dividend stream should be subtracted from the present value of the interest-payment stream.

The last component of this model is the put feature. Since we are looking at the convertible as a stock plus the yield advantage the convertible offers, we must also evaluate the fact that the convertible matures at par value and the investor's principal is protected to the extent that the issuer remains solvent. In this valuation approach, the bond feature or discounted par value is represented by a put (see Figure 9–7). This makes sense because even if the stock price declines well below the exercise price on the convertible (par/conversion ratio), the convertible investor will still receive par value at maturity, not parity. In effect, the convertible provides a put feature to the investor.

**F I G U R E  9–7**

Two Convertible Valuation Approaches

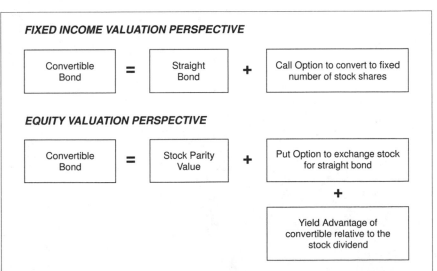

## THE CALAMOS THEORETICAL FAIR VALUE MODEL FORMULA

In this chapter we have presented a discussion of how option theory can be applied to the pricing of convertible securities. We discussed the many factors that must be taken into account to accurately arrive at the theoretical fair value of a convertible security. The appendix to the chapter explains the mathematical derivation of such an application.

The Calamos Theoretical fair Value Model (CFP) considers many variables in determining the theoretical fair value of a convertible security and is, in our opinion, an accurate determination of the theoretical fair-value value. Other analysts may make different assumptions as to callability, the underlying stock's price distribution, and other important factors that are critical to the analysis. Our purpose here is to show that the application of option theory can provide the basis for determining the theoretical fair value price of a convertible security. This is clearly a complex problem. We have confidence that the CFP model considers the many variables and accounts for their influence to the theoretical fair-value price. Whether investors accept our model or derive their own, similar model, it is clear that this is the most accurate means currently available to determine the theoretical fair value price. This methodology has replaced the simplistic methods used in the past. Throughout the remainder of the book, the CFP model will be used as the method for determining the theoretical fair price of a convertible.

# A CONVERTIBLE PRICING MODEL

The convertible pricing model used is derived from the Black–Scholes model; we will explain it in its simplest form. The convertible theoretical fair value model of a convertible security includes part latent warrant and part straight bond, with each component priced separately. The model combines the two parts to determine the theoretical fair value of the convertible security.

The convertible pricing model is subject to many more variables than the option pricing model. It also includes many variables that are dependent upon estimates (i.e., time to expiration, call probability, and bond discount factor). For explanatory purposes, we will assume we know all variables with certainty. The value of XYZ Company's convertible bond, 7.00 percent of 11/15/2004, can be determined given the following values:

| | | |
|---|---|---|
| (1) | Stock price = | $30.00 |
| (2) | Conversion price = | $25.00 |
| (3) | Stock volatility = | 35.00% |
| (4) | Risk-free rate (two-year) = | 8.50% |
| (5) | Time to known expiration = | 2.00 years |
| (6) | Call features of bond = | 2.00 years of absolute call protection |
| (7) | Bond discount factor = | 8.50% |
| (8) | Debt spread = | 4.00% |
| (9) | Adjusted conversion price = | $24.30 |
| (10) | Bond coupon rate = | 7.00% |
| (11) | Stock dividend yield = | 0.0% |
| (12) | Bond call price = | $1,000.00 |
| (13) | Conversion ratio = | 40.00 shares |
| (14) | Call in two years is known to be certain | Y/N |
| (15) | Market value convertible = | 130.00 |

## Straight Bond Value Sv(t)

$$\sum_{t+1}^{n} \frac{C}{(1+Ym)^n} + \frac{P}{(1+Ym)^n} = \text{Straight bond value}$$

$$\sum_{t=1}^{2} \frac{70}{(1.085)^2} + \frac{100}{(1.085)^2} = 972.9$$

## Black–Scholes Warrant Value

$$d_1 = \frac{1n\frac{1}{2} + \left(r + \left(\frac{s}{k}\right)\sigma 2\right)T}{\sqrt{T}}$$

$$d^1 = \frac{1n(1/2) + (.085 + \frac{30}{24.3} \times 0.123)(2)}{0.35\sqrt{2.0}} = -0.443$$

$$(N)\,d1 = 0.4801$$

$$d2 = -0.443 - .495 = -0.938 \quad d2=d1-\sigma\sqrt{t}$$

$$(N)\,d2 = 0.1711$$

Warrant Value = Wv(t) = SN(d1) - Ke$^{-rT}$ N(d$^2$)

$$30(.4801) - 24.3(.844)(.1711) = 10.89$$

Convertible's Equity Portion - Wv(t) × Cr(t)

$$(10.89)(40.00) = Cv(t)$$

$$\$972.90 + \$435.60 = \$1,408.50$$

## Over-/Undervaluation

The theoretical convertible value is then compared to the current market value to determine over-/undervaluation.

$$\frac{\text{Actual} - Cv(t)}{Cv(t)} = \text{Over/Under}$$

$$\frac{137.0 - 140.85}{140.85} \times 100 = -2.73\%$$

Applying the option theory to a security as complex as a convertible requires many estimates. To determine the theoretical fair value of an option, there are six variables, all of which are known except one—volatility. For convertibles, there are seven variables, of which five must be estimated. Because analysts may arrive at different conclusions as to the value of the estimates, the convertible market will most likely continue to exhibit pockets of inefficiencies.

## E N D N O T E S

1. Benjamin Graham, *The Intelligent Investor* (New York: Harper, 1965), pp. 120–122.
2. Edward O. Thorpe, *Beat the Market* (New York: Random House, 1967), pp. 141–161.
3. Richard M. Bookstaber, *Option Pricing and Strategies in Investing* (Reading, Mass: Addison-Wesley, 1985), p. 40.
4. Gary Gastineau, *The Stock Options Manual* (New York: McGraw-Hill, 1979), pp. 249–251
5. Jonathan E. Ingersoll, "An Examination of Corporate Call Policies on Convertible Securities," *The Journal of Finance, No. 2* (May, 1977): pp. 289–321.

# 10 CHAPTER

# Applying the Calamos Theoretical Fair Price Model for Convertibles

**D**eveloping a theoretical formula in investment analysis is an important first step, but the financial journals are littered with impractical formulas. A formula must meet the test of real-world investing to be valuable to investors. The investor must be able to apply it and produce accurate, profitable results. Any given formula has been derived under a set of conditions that the investor must evaluate when applying it. As with any financial formula, the importance of accepting the underlying assumptions cannot be overemphasized. If the assumptions do not apply, then they must be revised to produce meaningful results.

Applying the *Calamos Theoretical Fair Price (CTFP)* model to the pricing of convertible securities introduces a series of changes in the variables that are, in part, subject to the investor's best estimates. How different investors arrive at these estimates may well be the deciding factor in how accurately the model portrays reality. Experience in the marketplace is important in adjusting the model. For example, the probability of call not only affects the adjusted exercise price but also the term to expiration of the option portion of the convertible. These variables would be static under normal option pricing conditions. The exercise price also becomes sensitive to changes in interest rates and the credit rating of the issuing companies' debt securities. For these reasons and others, the convertible market will almost always display a degree of inefficiency. This is, of course, good news for the investor able to seek out such opportunities.

It is also important to distinguish between the meaning of a short-term inefficiency to traders or arbitrageurs, who may be able to exploit it, and its different meaning for the long-term investor in the convertible market. Marketplace efficiency contributes to the long-term trading process by assuring that the long-term investor in convertibles receives a price that approximates fair value. Swaps from one convertible to another may be accomplished more readily in an efficient marketplace. Investors who can consistently exploit the undervaluation of the convertible market should gain a significant advantage in relative performance.

A number of inputs are required to use the formula: stock price, exercise price, time to maturity, interest rate, and stock volatility. Of these, only the stock price and the interest rate are easily obtainable. By investigating the sensitivity of these variables to our formula, the investor will gain a greater understanding of the model's application.

In addition to understanding how the model reacts to changes in the variables, we will review the effect of various factors on convertibles, including changing interest rates, an increase in stock dividends, and the difference between callable and noncallable bonds. The real effect of these changes on convertibles has often confused investors; therefore, we simultaneously test our model against the way we intuitively expect the convertible price to respond to a given factor and also provide the reader with a greater understanding of how those changes influence the price of convertibles in general.

## INVESTIGATING THE SENSITIVITY OF THE VARIABLES

Combining the investment value and the implied warrant to determine a fair value convertible price causes the sensitivity of the variables to react quite differently than an option calculated by the Black–Scholes model. Using the CTFP formula, the interactions between the variables give the net effect of the change in the convertible price. Throughout this analysis, we change one variable at a time, holding all other variables constant, so that the effect of the single variable can be illustrated.

## Volatility

**Vega** indicates the convertible's sensitivity to changes in stock price volatility. It expresses the change in the convertible's price with respect to the change in the volatility of the underlying stock.

Changes in the volatility of the underlying stock complicate the evaluation of a convertible. Under normal option-pricing conditions, increasing the volatility would increase the value of an option because stock with higher volatility has a higher possibility of increasing (as well as decreasing) in value. However, the bond portion of a convertible security would be expected to decrease in value with increased stock volatility, due to increased risk to the firm which may cause revisions to estimated earnings, financial ratios, interest-coverage analysis, and other measures of the firm's financial stability. If the increase in volatility causes the firm's beta, or risk factor, to increase, then it may be assumed that both equity and debt holders will expect a higher return to compensate for the higher risk factor. The effect of an increase in the stock's volatility on the convertible bond is illustrated in Figure 10–1. Increased volatility leads to an increase in the value of a convertible bond, holding all other variables constant, due to the important increase in the value of the convertible's option component. At this point, it is the option component that determines the convertible's market value.

Figure 10–1 also shows the effect of time remaining before which the bond may be called. If the time of absolute call protection increases from one year to three years, the impact of the change in volatility increases. Notice that the value of the convertible bond increases with the increase in volatility; furthermore, the longer the time to absolute call, the greater the in the convertible bond price.[1]

Figure 10–1 ignores the impact of the change in the debt value of the convertible bond due to changes in the underlying stock's volatility. This could be measured by applying a Merton debt valuation model that prices the debt of a firm as a function of the

**F I G U R E  10-1**

Convertible Bond Sensitivity Analysis Relative to Underlying Stock Volatility

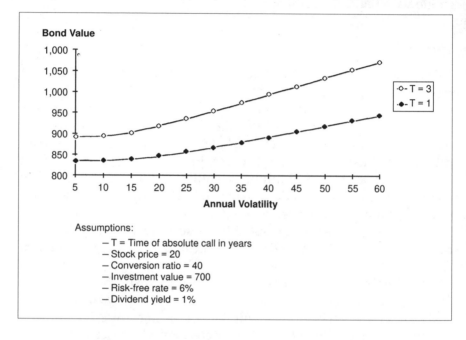

Assumptions:

  — T = Time of absolute call in years
  — Stock price = 20
  — Conversion ratio = 40
  — Investment value = 700
  — Risk-free rate = 6%
  — Dividend yield = 1%

value of the firm, maturity value of the debt, time to maturity of the debt, risk-free rate of return, and volatility of the equity.[2]

The application of Merton's model[3] implies that as the volatility of the firm increases,the value of the debt will decrease in order to produce a higher return to bondholders. In other words, a company with a volatile common stock must pay higher interest rates for debt. Investors realize that, as the stock goes down (demonstrating high volatility), their debt is in jeopardy. The results of increasing volatility can lead convertible investors into a trap: The convertible holder who has evaluated the increase in volatility from the equity side of the convertible will ignore the decreasing debt value and greatly underestimate the downside risk of the convertible. This is why some convertible securities decline in value as much as their common stock counterparts. Investors who evaluate convertibles on the basis of a constant bond value are, to their chagrin, usually quite surprised to see the price of their convertibles fall below the bond value that they have estimated poorly. This is particularly common with convertibles issued by secondary or low-capitalization companies.

High-capitalization companies are not immune to this phenomenon, either. Union Carbide's Bhopal, India, disaster in 1986 caused the volatility of that stock to increase substantially due to the uncertain financial liability the company could incur from the accident. The convertible bond value and its accompanying straight bond value also decreased substantially. Usually such cases are not signaled by so dramatic an event, but by something much more subtle. Accurately estimating the stock's future volatility becomes an extremely important part of accurately determining the convertible bond's value. Historical volatility and the fundamental data of the company become important inputs to this process as a guide to estimating future volatility.

## Interest-Rate Sensitivity

**Rho** is used for the convertible's sensitivity to changes in interest rates. The convertible will have one Rho for short-term rates and one for long-term rates that will differ in some instances. Rho is used to indicate the change in a convertible's price with respect to changes in interest rates.

Using the CTFP allows the investor to see the effects of changing interest rates on convertible securities. If the short-term risk-free rate increases, the equity value of the convertible should also increase, assuming all other variables are held constant. It may be an unlikely situation that would find short-term rates changing without a corresponding change in long-term rates; however, this isolates and illustrates the influence of changes in short-term rates alone. This is demonstrated graphically in Figure 10–2.

A convertible bond trading at $872 when one-year Treasuries are at 7 percent would increase to $890 if one-year Treasuries increased four percentage points to an annual rate of 11 percent. This is consistent with how stock options react to changes in short-term interest rates. The option premium increases in value as short-term rates rise; similarly, the embedded warrant in the convertible also increases with rising short-term interest rates.

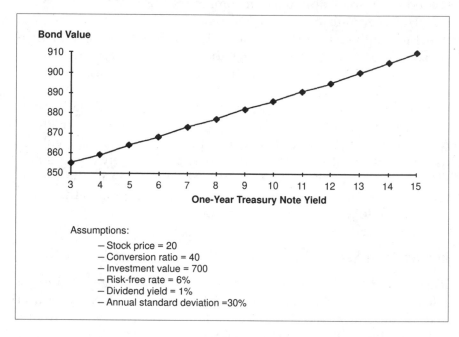

F I G U R E  10-2

Convertible Bond Sensitivity to Short-Term Interest Rates

## Convertible Sensitivity to Long-Term Interest Rates

The value of the convertible bond is also subject to changes in long-term bond yields. The effect of changes in long-term interest rates on bond value was discussed in Chapter 8. If long-term interest rates increase, then the debt value of the convertible will decrease, causing a decline in value. The adjusted exercise price for the convertible will also decrease for the reasons given in Chapter 9.

Figure 10–3 indicates the net effect changes in long-term rates have on convertible-bond and straight bond values. This is the measure of duration for a convertible bond. Figure 9–4 demonstrated duration for a convertible bond with a large premium over investment value. The result shows that as the convertible's premium over its investment value increases, the likelihood of the convertible's sensitivity to changes in long-term interest rates decreases. Figure 10–3 indicates that the long-term straight bond is

**F I G U R E  10–3**

Convertible Bond Duration (Interest-Rate Sensitivity)—7% Coupon, 20 Years

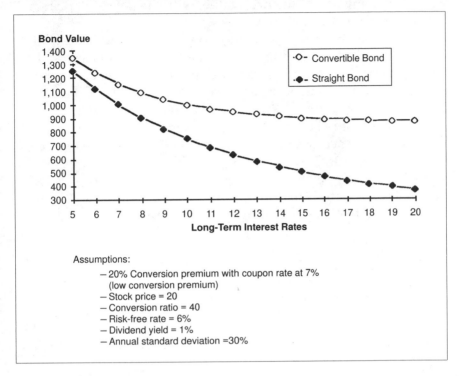

Assumptions:
- 20% Conversion premium with coupon rate at 7% (low conversion premium)
- Stock price = 20
- Conversion ratio = 40
- Risk-free rate = 6%
- Dividend yield = 1%
- Annual standard deviation =30%

much more sensitive to interest rates than a convertible bond trading high above its investment value. As we have discussed, when a bond trades well above its investment value, it trades on and is protected by its equity value. Duration analysis of a convertible bond becomes an excellent method for determining the sensitivity of interest rates.

In general, the higher the investment premium (meaning the more a convertible's price is determined by its equity value), the greater its tendency not to be influenced by changing interest rates. The dominant influence becomes the stock price rather than its bond attributes. If both long-term and short-term interest rates increase, there may be no change in the convertible's price. For example, when the short-term rate increases, the option portion of the convertible increases in value. But the increase in the long-term rate results in a decrease in the value of the bond portion of the convertible. It may be possible to have the increase in the equity value offset any loss in the debt value, with the net result being no change in the convertible value.

Figure 10–4 illustrates how a convertible bond with a high conversion premium and low investment premium is affected by interest rates. Unlike the previous example, the convertible bond and the straight bond are affected nearly equally. Convertible bonds that are trading close to their investment value become more sensitive to changes in long-term interest rates because, at that point, they act more like bonds than like stocks. Nearly every variable is affected by changing interest rates; the investment value is inversely related to changes in long-term rates or to rates that match the bond's maturity, while the warrant portion is positively related to changes in short-term interest rates.

**F I G U R E  10–4**

Convertible Bond Duration, High Conversion Premium

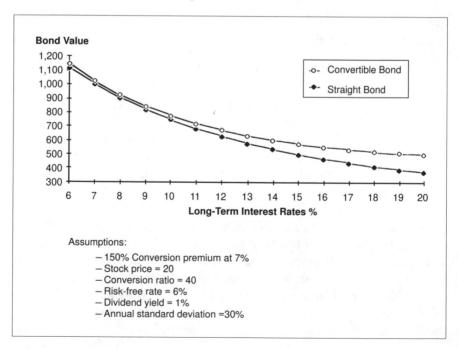

Assumptions:
— 150% Conversion premium at 7%
— Stock price = 20
— Conversion ratio = 40
— Risk-free rate = 6%
— Dividend yield = 1%
— Annual standard deviation =30%

## Convertible Sensitivity to Stock Dividend Yield

**Psi** is used to denote the convertible's sensitivity to changes in the dividends of the underlying stocks. It indicates the change in the convertible's price with respect to a change in the dividends of the underlying stocks.

The convertible bond value will also be inversely related to the dividend yield of the underlying stock, due primarily to the decrease in the warrant value. Figure 10–5 illustrates the sensitivity of a convertible to changes in the stock's dividend yield. The figure shows that, as dividends are increased, the conversion premium would be less valuable, all other factors being equal, because the stock would be paying out some of its increased value in dividends rather than retaining all increased value. The CTFP model accounts for this by reducing the warrant value of the con-

**F I G U R E  10–5**

Convertible Bond Price Sensitivity to Stock Dividend Yield

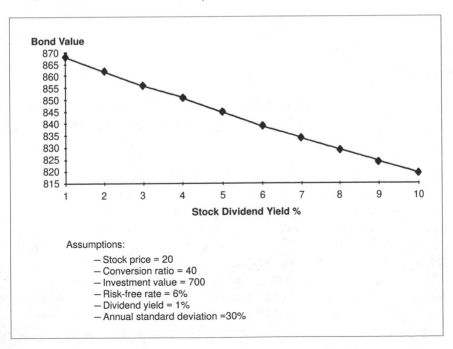

Assumptions:
- Stock price = 20
- Conversion ratio = 40
- Investment value = 700
- Risk-free rate = 6%
- Dividend yield = 1%
- Annual standard deviation =30%

vertible by the present value of the expected dividend stream over the expected remaining life of the convertible.

## Convertible Sensitivity to Time to Expiration

**Theta** is used to express the convertible's sensitivity to time premium decay. It indicates the change in the convertible's price with respect to a change in call protection or remaining estimated life of the security.

The more time an investor has to exercise the convertibility feature, the more premium that investor should expect a convertible to command, in much the same way a longer-term option is more valuable than a short-term option. The amount of time remaining to expiration is affected by the maturity date of the bond or the amount of the call protection. The investor must assume that the convertible may be called at the earliest possible time by the company and should pay only the value of premium to the first call. Figure 10–6 indicates that as the years of absolute call protection decrease, the convertible bond price will also decrease. It's interesting to note that, under the same assumption, the straight bond value also increases to its call price. Again, the CTFP model matches convertible holders' intuitive expectations.

## Convertible Sensitivity to Common Stock Price Changes

**Delta** expresses the convertible's sensitivity to changes in the stock price. It expresses the change in the convertible price per unit of change in the underlying stock price.

**Gamma** is the second derivative with respect to the price change in the underlying stock. It is expressed as a change in delta per unit change in stock price. The delta measure is nonlinear. Gamma's relationship to delta is similar to the relationship that convexity has to duration in the fixed-income security analysis.

Finally, with all other variables considered, the common stock price is input into the formula, and a theoretical convertible bond price results. The model now can estimate convertible bond prices for various changes in the common stock price. The resulting changes in the convertible bond price can be used to develop the expected price track of the convertible security. Holding all other

## F I G U R E 10–6

Convertible Bond Time Premium Decay

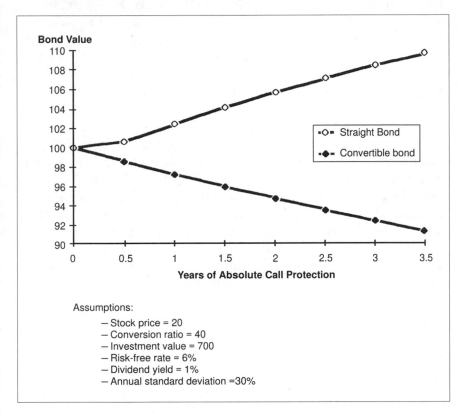

Assumptions:

- Stock price = 20
- Conversion ratio = 40
- Investment value = 700
- Risk-free rate = 6%
- Dividend yield = 1%
- Annual standard deviation =30%

variables constant, an increase in the stock price will result in an increase in the convertible price.

## SUMMARY

Throughout this chapter we have tested the CTFP model by changing only one variable at a time while holding all the others constant. As we have seen, the model accounts for the variables and matches what experienced convertible investors would expect, given changes in the many variables. Any model that attempts to encompass all situations must be continually scrutinized for subtle errors.

The option-pricing model is vulnerable to some of the same criticisms when applied to convertible pricing. For example, many analysts feel that deep-in-the-money options are evaluated incorrectly and tend to be underpriced to their true value, whereas out-of-the-money options are usually overpriced relative to their true value. Since the CTFP model applies the option-price formula, the same errors may occur. Yet as we test and work with the CTFP model, its usefulness in evaluating a convertible security becomes apparent. As we learn more about the intricacies of these complex securities, the model also changes.

It is clear that the CTFP model fills a void in convertible evaluation. It determines more accurately than past models the fair value price of a convertible security. Its application to "what-if" scenarios replaces the guesses and hunches of the past. Investors can determine how changes in interest rates, dividends, volatility, and other factors will influence their convertible portfolios.

The most direct benefit of the CTFP model is that it can be used to estimate the price track and thereby derive the important risk/reward analysis of the convertible security.

# E N D N O T E S

**1.** This relationship can be explained by the following equation:

$$\frac{\$ \text{ change in Cv(t)}}{1\% \text{ change in } \sigma} = \frac{\partial Cv(t)}{\partial \sigma} = Cr(t)\, S\, \sqrt{T}\, N'(h)$$

where:

$$N'(h) = 1/\sqrt{2}\pi\, e^{\frac{-h^2}{2}}$$

and

$$H = \log(S/Ke\text{-}rT)/\sigma\sqrt{T} + 1/2\sigma\sqrt{T}$$

**2.** $D = f(V, T, B, r, o)$, Merton
**3.** Merton, R.C. "On the Pricing of Corporate Debt: The Risk Structure of Interest Rates," *Journal of Finance* 29 (May 1974): 449–470.

# Estimating Risk and Reward of Convertibles

## EVALUATION PROCESS

In prior chapters we have seen how a convertible's price track can be estimated using option theory. In this chapter, we compare how convertible leverage has been used in the past and how our application of the CFP model can be used to improve on traditional analysis. Accurately estimating the convertible price track is important because it is part of the risk/reward analysis and shows the potential profit and loss of a position. If the price track is incorrect, the risk/reward analysis that follows will also be incorrect. The investor should also be concerned with whether the convertible security is mathematically under- or overvalued since the convertible, over time, should tend toward its fair value price track.

The following process ascertains whether a convertible security has favorable leverage. Leverage refers to the portion of the stock's upside performance captured by the convertible bond in relationship to the amount of downside performance captured by the convertible. Risk/reward (upside versus downside) is another way of referring to leverage. The ideal convertible, of course, captures a large percentage of any upside moves in the underlying stock and only a small portion of any downside moves. Since convertible performance is being compared directly to that of its underlying common stock, the range over which the stock price might move becomes an integral factor in the profit-and-loss estimate. Generally, a relatively large move is required to determine a meaningful risk/reward relationship.

The traditional method used by many popular convertible advisory services typically uses an arbitrary large movement in the underlying stock and then estimates the corresponding price of the convertible security. Comparing many different convertible issues under this method often becomes meaningless because each common stock has its own particular range of movement. We will use this method as a frame of reference and then show how it can be improved upon.

## RISK/REWARD ANALYSIS: TRADITIONAL METHOD

Under the traditional method, the common stock is assumed to either advance or decline by 50 percent; then the corresponding convertible security price is estimated. To complete the evaluation, the investor must then try to determine the risk/reward analysis and the advantage the convertible enjoys over the underlying common stock. Figure 11–1 is an example of a typical risk/reward analysis for a utility company whose stock has exhibited low volatility.

There are several problems with using this method. First, as discussed in the previous chapter, the price track that determines

---

**F I G U R E  11–1**

Risk/Reward Analysis: Traditional Method

| XYZ Company Risk/Reward Analysis | | | | | |
|---|---|---|---|---|---|
| Stock change | –50% | –25% | 0 | +25% | +50% |
| Stock price | 8.50 | 12.75 | 17.00 | 21.25 | 25.50 |
| Convertible price | 93.50 | 97.90 | 110.00 | 125.40 | 143.00 |
| Convertible % move | –15.00 | –11.00 | 0 | +14.00 | +30.00 |

convertible prices should take into account all variables. Second, the arbitrarily designated price moves in the stock have no relationship to the most probable movement of the underlying common stock. It becomes extremely difficult to compare the relative attractiveness of convertible securities using this method. For example, variance and beta on utility stocks are typically lower than those of the average common stock. Applying the risk/reward analysis to such a security may result in the utility convertible seeming relatively more attractive than the alternatives.

Figure 11–1 compares the risk/reward of XYZ company stock to that of its convertible security. An investor using this information would probably decide to buy. However, a more complete analysis will demonstrate why this would be an incorrect choice (see Figure 11–5 later in the chapter.)

We will now develop a worksheet that takes into account more completely the multitude of factors that should be considered before investing in a convertible security.

## CALAMOS CONVERTIBLE EVALUATION WORKSHEET

### Company and Common Stock Information

Figure 11–2 shows that the analysis must begin by considering both the fundamentals of the company and some statistical risk measures.

The common stock section takes both beta and total risk factors into account. The common stock's rating is considered along with capitalization and the important debt/equity ratio. The analyst can add both the fundamental opinion of the stock and technical price action; both are subjective.

The convertible security section gives the details of the particular convertible. These include coupon, maturity date, interest payment dates, call terms, issue size, rating, and conversion ratio. This section also lists the current market prices of both the common stock and convertible, with their corresponding yields. The investment value yield is determined by the analyst's evaluation, as discussed in Chapter 8, and corresponds to the Calamos Convertible Evaluation Grade. These grades allow the analyst to fine-tune the investment value yield and override the security bond

**F I G U R E  11–2**

Convertible Security Worksheet

Company: XYZ Company    Sector: Capital Goods Technology
                        Industry: (14) F-Computers and Peripherals

|  | Symbol | Market | Current Yield |
|---|---|---|---|
| Common Stock | XYZ | 33.000 | 2.12 |
| Convertible | XYZ-R | 94.000 | 7.97 |

**Common Stock**

| Beta: | 1.45 | Fund. Rating: | 8 | Debt/Equity: | 0.32 |
|---|---|---|---|---|---|
| Stnd Risk: | 43.71 | Opin Rank: | 2 | Tech Rank: | 3 |
| Cap (mill$): | 660.00 | Stock Div.: | 0.70 | RX Agency: | Internal |

**Convertible Security**

| Desc: 7.500-06/15/2010 | Pymts: JUN–DEC-15 | Call Feature: 12/90 *150 |
|---|---|---|
| Risk Level: AGG | Inv. Val YTM: 12.90 | Credit Rating: BBB |
| Issue Size (mill$): 175.000 | CCES Grade: 10 | Conv. Ratio: 24.0000 |
| Next Call Price: 105.075 | Underwriter: Drexel | Bnd Hld Rts: None |

**Convertible Analysis**

| Conversion Value | Conversion Premium | Investment Value | Investment Value Premium |
|---|---|---|---|
| 79.20 | 18.68% | 60.88 | 54.38% |

| BARA | Yield to Maturity | Fair Value Over/Under | Interest Rate Sensitivity |
|---|---|---|---|
| 1.35 | 8.00% | −0.56% | 4.47 |

| EROI | Upside Beta | Downside Beta | Break Even |
|---|---|---|---|
| 17.44% | 1.04 | 0.63 | 3.19 |

Source: Calamos Convertible Evaluation System.

rating. Investment value grades are assigned according to the Calamos Convertible Evaluation System (CCES) and vary from 1 to 20. The risk level of the convertible is determined by the investment value grade and the underlying risk factors of the common stock. The following sections describe the individual items included in the worksheet analysis.

*Sector*  Indicates the economic/industry sector to which the company belongs. The investor needs to analyze the economy and financial markets in light or his or her own forecast of economic conditions to determine which sectors might be expected to perform best. The main sectors include:

- Credit cyclicals.
- Financial.
- Consumer growth staples.
- Consumer staples.
- Consumer cyclicals.
- Capital goods—technology.
- Capital goods—industrial.
- Energy.
- Basic industrial.
- Transportation.
- Utilities.

*Industry Group*  Refers to the industry group (within the sector) to which a particular convertible's issuing company belongs. After selecting the economic sectors most likely to perform best, the investor should analyze those industry groups within the sector that are expected to perform best. Industry diversification is an important consideration.

Many research organizations provide a breakdown of industry groups. SIC codes list over 100 industry groups, from aerospace to utilities.

*Beta*  The beta coefficient presented here is the beta of the underlying common stock. It measures the stock's historical systematic risk or the portion of a stock's volatility that can be explained by the volatility of broad stock market movements. The investor needs to use a beta weighted by portfolio components to evaluate a portfolio's total exposure to systematic risk. By selecting convertibles carefully, the investor may reduce the systematic risk for a given company during declining phases of the market while allowing for a significant portion of the company's systematic risk in rising phases of the market.

Merrill Lynch, Value Line, Standard & Poor's, and other research departments publish beta coefficients. Investors should be consistent in their choice of beta measures because they are re-gressed against various indices and over different time frames.

*Standard Risk or Volatility* The stock's volatility (total risk) measures the standard deviation of the stock returns over a speci-fied time period. It is based on the stock's historical volatility of returns and is used as an estimate for the future expected stock distribution of returns and total risk. This becomes the relevant risk measure for a nondiversified portfolio.

Standard deviation may be calculated from stock returns for as little as the past 30 days to as long as the previous five years of weekly returns. The most meaningful time frame probably falls somewhere in between. Before using past volatility measures for companies that have been reorganized or have been involved in merger activities, the investor should scrutinize the data very closely. The objective is to estimate the most likely future stock volatility. Focusing on historical numbers can trap the investor. For example, if a company had not been leveraged (meaning the capital structure included a low level of debt) but then leveraged its balance sheet, future stock volatility would be much higher than the historical numbers would predict The reverse is also true.

Value Line provides this risk measure for 1,700 stocks on a relative basis. They calculate it using five years of weekly price changes comparing each stock's volatility with the other 1,699 in their universe. Value Line's relative volatility values range from approximately 50 to 230. The stocks that exhibit average volatility are assessed a value of 100, while stocks that are 50 percent more volatile than the average are assessed a value of 150. Similarly, stocks that have a less-than-average volatility will have a value less than 100.

*Financial Rating* This measure, provided by the Standard & Poor's stock guide, is helpful in establishing a stock's risk class. Please note that this financial rating applies to the company itself, not to the specific security. (Each security issued by a given com-pany will have a separate credit rating.) The financial rating indi-cates the company's consistency of dividend payments and stability in earnings. A+ is the highest rating is reserved for com-panies that have shown a history of paying dividends and stable earnings. Stock ratings range from A+ to D.

*Debt/Equity Ratio* The debt-to-equity ratio is an indication of a firm's leverage (as stated in the standard terms of corporate finance; this is different than the leverage on a convertible security). Although the beta coefficient is, to some degree, a measure of the company's leverage, it is usually calculated over a long time and may not be a clear indication of the company's sensitivity to changing market conditions. Firms with higher debt-to-equity ratios are generally more sensitive to changing market environments than those with lower debt-to-equity ratios.

It is important to compare the debt-to-equity ratio with the average within the company's industry group.

*Capitalization* Capitalization is a measure of a firm's equity market value. It is calculated by multiplying the total common shares outstanding by the market price of the common stock. Smaller-cap companies are generally  considered to have relatively more risk than larger-cap companies.

### Convertible Security Information

*Description*: Provides the convertible's coupon rate, maturity date of the bond, and other pertinent information.

*Payments*: Indicates the dates the bond pays interest, typically semiannually for domestic bonds and annually for Eurodollar issues.

*Call features*: The call features of the convertible security are extremely important. The convertible's provisional or absolute call protection, and the date the call protection expires, are noted here. This information can be obtained from various research sources or the bond's prospectus.

*Risk level*: This is an indication of the broad overall risk level of the convertible, including both equity and bond risk measures. It is a means to distinguish between the various opportunities available on the basis of relative risk. Three levels of risk are recommended: Investment-low, medium-grade, and speculative.

*Investment value yield*: The investment value yield is the estimated yield to maturity used to calculate the straight bond portion of the convertible. This can be determined by evaluating any straight debt the company may have outstanding or debt of similar quality found in the marketplace. This was discussed in detail in Chapter 8.

*Conversion ratio*: The conversion ratio determines the number of shares of common stock into which each convertible can be exchanged. The conversion ratio is determined upon original issuance of the security and is provided for in the indenture.

*Issue size*: Indicates the size of the convertible issue in millions of dollars for bonds and millions of shares for preferreds. An issue's liquidity depends partly on its size.

*Credit rating:* The credit rating provides an indication of the creditworthiness of the security itself. Due to the variation in the structure of different securities, an individual company might have different securities with different credit ratings. Ratings range from the highest, AAA+, to the lowest, D. This may be a good place to begin the credit analysis.

*CCES grade*: The CCES grade classifies the convertible risk. Grades range from 1 for the highest quality to 20 for the lowest grades. This allows for a wider classification of grades than can be obtained through the rating services.

*Next call price*: Determined at or prior to issuance, this is the price at which the issuer may redeem the bond or preferred stock prior to maturity. The call price is usually above the par value of the security in order to compensate the holder for the loss of income prior to maturity. The earliest call dates are specified in the prospectus for a callable bond.

*Underwriter*: This specifies the security's lead underwriter, who should be able to provide information on the security and company.

*Bondholders' rights*: Investors should review their protection against the elimination of conversion rights due to takeovers. Convertibles without adequate protection are less valuable than those with protection. Avoid new issues whose trust indentures lack protective clauses against takeovers, whether friendly or hostile.

### Convertible Analysis
*Conversion value*: This can be determined by multiplying the common stock price by the conversion ratio. The conversion value is the equity value of the convertible security.

*Conversion premium*: As explained in Chapter 8, this measure determines the convertible's additional premium above the equity value of the security.

*Investment value*: This is the convertible security's straight bond value, as discussed in Chapter 8. It becomes significant in determining the downside risk of the convertible.

*Investment premium*: This measures how much additional premium the convertible commands above the straight bond value. In essence, it is the difference between the market value and the investment value as a percentage of the convertible's investment value.

*Balanced approach relative advantage (BARA)*: The balanced approach's advantage is a measure of the convertible's attractiveness relative to a 50/50 combination of bonds and stocks. The performance of a convertible security does not duplicate the performance of a combination of stocks and bonds, and this is one way to measure that difference. Because of their hybrid characteristics, convertible securities can be compared to the balanced approach, but for investment purposes it would preferably offer an advantage to it.

In the 1960s, an investor would buy bonds, including long-term bonds, for safety. Investors saw Treasury securities as important, stabilizing instruments. The highly volatility interest-rate environment of the late 1970s and 1980s brought about a change in balanced-approach investing because high and highly volatile interest rates resulted in long-term bond performance that was more volatile than that of stocks. At this time, investors began to view the 10-year Treasury note as a long-term bond with most of the return and only a fraction of the volatility of a 30-year bond. The following algorithm indicates the relative advantage offered by the convertible:

$$\frac{\dfrac{CV_G + Y}{(0.5)(ST_G + DY) + (0.5)YTM} + \dfrac{(0.5)(ST_L + DY) + (0.5)YTM}{CV_L + Y}}{2.0} = BARA$$

where:

$CV_G$ = Convertible percent gain
$CF_L$ = Convertible percent loss
$ST_G$ = Stock percent gain
$ST_L$ = Stock percent loss
$Y$ = Convertible yield
$DY$ = Dividend yield
$YTM$ = Investment value

If the BARA is equal to one, then the convertible offers approximately the same performance (meaning the same upside and the same downside) as this hypothetical 50/50 combination of stocks and bonds. If, for example, the BARA is 1.4, the convertible offers 40 percent more upside potential than the 50/50 combination of stocks and bonds.

*Over/Undervaluation* This measures the percentage value by which the convertible is mispriced when compared to theoretical fair value. Positive numbers indicate the convertible is currently underpriced. It is determined by the CFP model discussed in Chapter 9.

*Interest-Rate Sensitivity* This is a measure of the convertible security's sensitivity to changes in interest rate(s), as discussed in Chapter 8.

*Upside and Downside Betas* This measure indicates the convertible's price sensitivity to changes in the overall stock market (not including the income portion of the convertible). Upside and downside betas are outlined in Chapter 8.

*Break-Even* The break-even determines the time necessary for the convertible's yield advantage to make up the conversion premium paid; also discussed in Chapter 8.

## RISK/REWARD ANALYSIS

With these factors in mind, the analyst has determined that this convertible has an attractive yield relative to both stock and bond markets. The investor has considered the risk factors of both the common stock and the convertible; the next step is to consider the advantage the convertible has over its common stock. This is determined by the risk/reward analysis shown in Figure 11–3.

Notice how the price range in this analysis differs from the arbitrary change in stock prices assigned by the traditional method. Investors should use a range of stock prices that suits the volatility of the security under consideration. This is a major change in how convertible leverage estimates have been made in the past and significantly increases the investor's ability to select convertibles properly. We will next describe this process.

### Estimating Stock Price Range

To estimate the common stock's most likely price range over the near term, the investor should consider its past volatility. A stock's volatility is measured by its standard deviation and is widely used

**F I G U R E   11–3**

Risk/Reward Analysis

|                              | 12 mo.  | 6 mo.   | Current | 6 mo.   | 12 mo.   |
|------------------------------|---------|---------|---------|---------|----------|
| Percent change in stock price | −35.3%  | 26.5%   | Current | +36.2%  | +54.8%   |
| Stock price                  | 21.31   | 24.22   | 33.00   | 44.95   | +51.09   |
| CFP convertible track        | 79.39   | 82.22   | 94.53   | 124.86  | +131.20  |
| Convertible percent change   | −15.54  | −12.53  | 0.56    | +32.83  | +39.57   |
| Convertible total return percentage | −7.56 | −8.54 | 8.54 | 36.82 | +47.53 |

in modern portfolio theory. Standard deviation is a statistical tool that measures the degree to which an individual stock in a probability distribution tends to vary from the mean of the distribution. The greater the degree of dispersion, the greater the risk. Since standard deviation includes both general market risk (systematic risk) and individual company risk (unsystematic risk), it is an excellent measure of total risk and can give the investor the means to estimate the probable range of stock prices for the risk/reward analysis. Fortunately, there are many services that provide these statistical measures

The variance is based on the historical trading pattern of the stock and is used as an estimate of future volatility. The investor can and should make a judgment as to whether past volatility is an accurate guide to the future. In Figure 11–3, we present a lognormal distribution based on the underlying stock volatility factor at a one standard deviation move for both 6 and 12 months.

After determining the price range, the investor can calculate the actual stock and convertible prices and their percent changes. Notice how using this kind of range for the stock prices provides a clearer reflection of the potential of the underlying stock than simply using an arbitrary 50 percent, up or down. The analysis provides investors with an estimate of future performance as well as downside risk, based on the stock's underlying trading habits. Should the investor decide that recent events might increase the stock's future volatility, the model can quickly incorporate this subjective judgment into the decision-making process by estimating the effect of the increased volatility on the convertible price.

The current yield can also be incorporated to analyze the convertible security on a total-return basis. Total return is an important consideration in convertible investing because a large portion of the convertible's return is from the coupon interest or dividends received from the convertible. Investors often shun convertibles with little or no yield advantage. The main drawback of break-even analysis is that it ignores total return in favor of relative return.

Total return, then, as indicated above, puts yield in proper perspective. Investors who continually use yield advantage as the major determinant in selecting a convertible will find that they unwittingly construct a high-risk portfolio whose underlying common stocks pay few dividends but do represent a cross-section of the market. That selection process narrows their universe to the more risky segments of the financial markets.

The total return in our example in Figure 11–3 shows that this convertible demonstrates a favorable risk/reward relationship relative to the common stock. Its upside potential is a 46.7 percent return, for a 54.8 percent move in the common stock. The convertible retains 87 percent of the upside potential of the common stock. On the other hand, if the stock was to decline 35.3 percent, the convertible would show a decrease of only –7.6 percent. Obviously, the convertible preserves capital on the downside while retaining the upside potential of the common stock. In addition, its current yield of 8.5 percent is attractive if the stock doesn't increase in price.

It's important to keep in mind the underlying assumptions upon which the worksheet is based. The investment value assumes that interest rates remain stable throughout the period of time under consideration. However, since we have determined the interest-rate sensitivity, the investor can estimate how any change in interest rates would influence the convertible. Furthermore, the worksheet assumes a holding period of either 6 or 12 months. The interest received over that period of time constitutes an important component of total return. If the stock moves dramatically in shorter periods of time, then the estimates of return may not hold. The advantage of the worksheet is that it considers all factors and provides the most probable risk/reward relationship of a particular convertible in light of uncertain markets. Figure 11–4 shows the completed worksheet.

**F I G U R E  11–4**

## Convertible Security Worksheet

Company: XYZ Company                Sector: Capital Goods-Technology
                                    Industry: (14) F-Computers & Peripherals

|               | Symbol | Market | Current Yield |
|---------------|--------|--------|---------------|
| Common Stock  | XYZ    | 33.000 | 2.12          |
| Convertible   | XYZ-R  | 94.000 | 7.97          |

**Common Stock**

| Beta:         | 1.45   | Fund. Rating: | 8    | Debt/Equity: | 0.32     |
|---------------|--------|---------------|------|--------------|----------|
| Stnd Risk:    | 43.71  | Opin Rank:    | 2    | Tech Rank:   | 3        |
| Cap (mill$):  | 660.00 | Stock Div.:   | 0.70 | RX Agency:   | Internal |

**Convertible Security**

| Desc: 7.500-06/15/2010      | Pymts: JUN-DEC-15   | Call Feature: 12/90 *150 |
|-----------------------------|---------------------|--------------------------|
| Risk Level: AGG             | Inv. Val YTM: 12.90 | Credit Rating: BBB       |
| Issue Size (mill$): 175.000 | CCES Grade: 10      | Conv. Ratio: 24.0000     |
| Next Call Price: 105.075    | Underwriter: Drexel | Bnd Hld Rts: None        |

**Convertible Analysis**

| Conversion Value | Conversion Premium | Investment Value | Invest Value Premium |
|------------------|--------------------|------------------|----------------------|
| 79.20            | 18.68%             | 60.88            | 54.38%               |

| BARA | Yield to Maturity | Fair Value Over/Under | Interest Rate Sensitivity |
|------|-------------------|-----------------------|---------------------------|
| 1.35 | 8.00%             | –0.56%                | 4.47                      |

| EROI   | Upside Beta | Downside Beta | Break Even |
|--------|-------------|---------------|------------|
| 17.44% | 1.04        | 0.63          | 3.19       |

**Risk/Reward Analysis**

| Estimated Stock Move     | 12 mo.  | 6 mo.   |         |          | 6 mo.   | 12 mo.  |
|--------------------------|---------|---------|---------|----------|---------|---------|
| Percent Change 1 in      | **–35.3%** | **–26.5%** | **CURRENT** | **+36.2%** | **+54.8%** |         |
| Stock Price              | 21.313  | 24.224  | 33.000  | 44.953   | 51.094  |         |
| CFP Convertible Track    | 79.390  | 82.220  | 94.530  | 124.860  | 131.200 |         |
| Convertible Percent Change | –15.543 | –12.532 | 0.564   | 32.830   | 39.574  |         |
| Conv. Total Return %     | **–7.564** | **–8.542** | **8.543** | **36.819** | **47.553** |         |

Source: Calamos Convertible Evaluation System.

## F I G U R E 11–5

Comparison of Risk/Reward Analysis Methods:
Traditional versus Volatility-Adjusted

| | | | | | |
|---|---|---|---|---|---|
| **Traditional Method** | | | | | |
| Percent change in stock price | −50% | −25% | -0- | +25% | +50% |
| Stock price | 8.50 | 12.75 | 17.00 | 21.25 | 25.50 |
| Convertible price | 93.50 | 97.90 | 110.00 | 125.40 | 143.00 |
| Convertible % move | −15.00 | −11.00 | -0- | +14.00 | +30.00 |
| **Volatility-Adjusted Method** | | | | | |
| Standard Deviation | −17.6% | −12.7% | -0- | +14.7% | +21.4% |
| Stock price | 14.00 | 14.84 | 17.00 | 19.50 | 20.64 |
| Convertible price | 100.10 | 104.50 | 110.00 | 115.50 | 121.00 |
| Convertible % move | −9.00 | −5.00 | -0- | +5.00 | +10.00 |

Note: Does not include income. Based on 12-month holding period.

When applied to the example using the traditional method, the worksheet shows the value of more complete evaluation. Figure 11–5 indicates a more likely risk/reward analysis for the convertible under consideration. Because it uses a more probable price range for the stock, it reaches the opposite investment conclusion. XYZ Company, in this case, was a low-volatility stock. Experienced investors do not need statistical analysis to know that this particular convertible's price range is grossly inaccurate. But every stock has its own price range based on its total risk. If the traditional method can present an investment trap when comparing a utility stock to an industrial stock, won't it also present a trap when comparing one industrial stock to another with more subtle changes? The value of the convertible risk/reward analysis is that it can account for even the most subtle changes in risk factors.

## APPLICATION TO THE NEW ISSUE MARKET

The CFP model for the new-issue market allows new convertible securities to be analyzed easily. Its flexibility enables the investor to evaluate risk factors of the issuing company in order to determine whether the convertible is priced fairly. This evaluation may also benefit issuers. More convertibles could be issued at higher conversion premiums and higher coupons if investors felt the trade-off were equitable. This has historically been difficult to evaluate, for investors and issuers alike. The CFP model can show how the trade-off between higher coupon and conversion premium affects fair value. As long as the convertible is issued at a fair-value price, new-issue buyers will be adequately compensated for the difference between conversion premium and yield.

The Calamos convertible evaluation worksheet can be applied to the new-issue market. Figure 11–6 shows an analysis of the General Instrument convertible bond issued on May 28, 1987. The preliminary term of the offering indicated that this convertible was priced below its fair value price as determined by the model (and was, therefore, a good buy). The subsequent trading after the offering confirmed the advantage of using the model to determine whether to buy a new issue. Immediately after the offering, the common stock price dropped from 33.27 to 32. The convertible bond price actually increased to 103 from 100 as it tended toward its fair price value.

Reviewing the new-issue market can give investors a means to evaluate the level of conversion premium over time.

## CONVERTIBLE OFFERINGS AND THEORETICAL FAIR PRICE VALUES

Convertible investors often debate whether the new offerings of convertibles are priced fairly. Subjective fundamental factors that will affect the supply and demand for convertibles enter into the decision process. Future prospects of the company, the industry group, and other fundamental elements, along with persuasive security salespeople, all play an important role in the pricing of new offerings. Our studies indicate that general market sentiment is also a critical item causing convertible new offerings to be either under- or overpriced, depending on the market environment.

We have calculated Figure 11–7 using the CFP model to price new issues and determine an under/overvaluation. Notice that from 1985 until 1990 there is a wide divergence in pricing, and many issues are overpriced. Increased volume resulted in overval-

## F I G U R E  11–6

### Convertible Security Worksheet

Company: Hilton Hotels

Sector: Consumer Cyclical
Industry: (49) Hotel/Gaming

| | Symbol | Market | Current Yield |
|---|---|---|---|
| Common Stock | HLT | 102.125 | 1.17% |
| Convertible | HLT-RC | 100.000 | 5.00% |

**Common Stock**

| | | | |
|---|---|---|---|
| Beta: | 1.42 | S&P Stk Rank: | FBCI Wght: 0.000 |
| Stnd Risk: | 35.22 | VL/CAM/Lev/Univ: 2/4/0/0 | |
| Cap (mill $): | 4,932.63 | Stock Div.: 1.20 | RX Agency: |

**Convertible Security**

Desc: 5.000-05/15/06      Pymts: Jun-Dec 15          Call Feature: 05/99 *ABS
Put Feature:                   Inv. Val Yld: 7.65          S&P/Moody: BBB/Baa2
Issue Size (mill$): 500.000  CCES Grade: 7            Conv. Ratio: 7.7444
Next Call Price: 102.857     Underwriter: DLJ          Iss. Dt.: 05/09/96

**Convertible Analysis**

| Conversion Value | Conversion Premium | Investment Value | Premium Over |
|---|---|---|---|
| 79.08 | 26.43% | 81.58 | 22.57% |

| BARA | Yield to Maturity | Fair Value Over/Under | Duration |
|---|---|---|---|
| 1.47 | 5.00% | −3.64% | 5.78 |

| EROI | Upside Beta | Downside Beta | Break-Even |
|---|---|---|---|
| 11.58% | 0.87 | 0.54 | 6.91 |

| Adjusted Exercise | Call Probability | Risk Free Rate | Debt Spread |
|---|---|---|---|
| 105.342 | Low | 6.31 | 2.65 |

| Warranty/Share | Time Value | SC Time | CD Time |
|---|---|---|---|
| 28.488 | 3.016 | 1.3136 | 3.0164 |

**Risk/Reward Analysis**

| | 12 mo. | 6 mo. | | 6 mo. | 12 mo. |
|---|---|---|---|---|---|
| Estimated Stock Move | | | | | |
| Percent Change 1 In | **−29.7%** | **−22.0%** | **CURRENT** | **+28.3%** | **+42.2%** |
| Stock Price | 71.802 | 79.606 | 102.125 | 131.012 | 145.252 |
| CFP Convertible Track | 89.122 | 91.138 | 103.644 | 118.228 | 124.926 |
| Convertible Percent Change | −10.877 | −8.861 | 3.644 | 18.228 | 24.926 |
| Conv. Total Return % | **−5.877** | **−6.361** | **8.644** | **20.728** | **29.926** |
| Conversion Premium | 60.271 | 47.829 | 31.046 | 16.525 | 11.055 |
| Convertible % Participation | 19.8% | 28.9% | | 73.3% | 70.9% |

Source: Calamos Convertible Evaluation System.

Convertible Under-/Overvaluation Chart

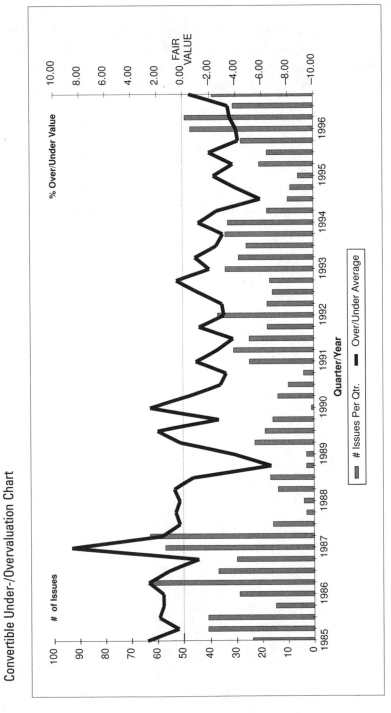

Source: Calamos Asset Management, Inc.

247

ued issues. As the use of theoretical fair pricing models has become more widespread in the market, overpricing has declined significantly. Even high volume does not produce overvaluation, and, on the whole, issues tend to be priced at fair value or below.

## SUMMARY

In this chapter we discussed using the CFP model to analyze individual securities. It is a relatively easy transition to move from a discussion of individual securities to a portfolio of convertibles. In the next chapter the CFP model is used to evaluate a convertible portfolio.

# PART THREE

# CONVERTIBLE
# STRATEGIES

# 12 CHAPTER

# Convertible Bond Strategies

Convertible investing continues to attract interest among a variety of investors. In September 1996, 38 mutual funds used convertible securities as their primary vehicle, and many more used them in their portfolios. Institutional pension funds currently make an asset allocation to convertible investing specifically, and many institutional consultants recommend that specific assets be devoted to convertibles. Individual investors now can access a professionally managed convertible portfolio through programs sponsored by many of the major brokerage firms.

Fueling this interest has been the continual growth of the new issue market, which had volume exceeding $20 billion in 1992, 1993, and a record $31 billion in 1997. The combination of attractive yield and excellent performance throughout the volatile 1970s and 1980s has generated enthusiasm for these issues among many investors. Convertible interest fluctuates depending largely on how the stock and bond markets are impacting the convertible market in the short term.

The strength of convertible investing is their hybrid nature—the fact that they are part bond and part stock. Certain market conditions cause one factor to have a greater influence on convertible prices than the other. For example, in 1994, considered by many to be the worst bond market of the century, convertible prices were pulled down by rising interest rates. Since stock prices remained relatively stable, they provided some support for convertible prices. Convertibles had negative returns similar to those of intermediate government bonds but less than those provided by the stock market. However, as interest rates rose again in early 1996 and again produced negative returns for most bond indexes, convertible performance kept pace with the strong stock market and outperformed the bond market by a wide margin.

Where do convertible securities fit into the allocation of investors' assets? Of course, an investor's choice of convertible strategy depends on his or her investment objectives and risk tolerance. Convertibles are versatile instruments, and portfolios can be designed to accommodate both conservative and aggressive investors. In our experience, convertibles are not easily categorized. We have used them for insurance companies that view them as part of their fixed-income allocation. Other investors consider convertibles a lower risk alternative to the stock market. Still others consider them as a separate asset class. Each category has its merits; the decision depends on the investor's objective and view of future secular trends.

## CONVERTIBLES AS A LOW-RISK EQUITY ALTERNATIVE

A traditional role for convertible investing is as a low-risk equity alternative. Since convertibles are part bond and part stock, they represent the best of both worlds, offering a way to remain invested in equities in a defensive fashion.

Convertibles selected to play this role in a portfolio balance the upside potential of the stock and the downside safety provided by the bond's fixed-income characteristics. Such convertibles generally have two-thirds of the upside potential of the common stock and one-third of the downside risk. Part of the reason for the non-parallel risk is the fact that the convertible continues to pay income, no matter how the stock price moves, and they also repay principal at maturity unless the company goes bankrupt. Furthermore, not only do convertibles provide downside protection, but since they are structured as subordinated debt they also maintain priority over common stock.

The convertible increases in value along with its underlying stock, but the increased value of a convertible results in a change in its risk/reward profile, reducing the advantage the convertible enjoyed near par. When the risk/reward of a convertible is no longer favorable, it should be sold and replaced with one that does have a favorable risk/reward relationship. This protects the profit taken in rising markets while continually upgrading the portfolio's risk/reward ratio.

Portfolio adjustments must also be made in declining markets. As a common stock declines in value, the convertible's income attributes work to preserve value. However, the risk/reward is no longer favorable, even though the convertible has accomplished its purpose. The investor should again make swaps to upgrade that relationship.

This can be an attractive strategy for investors who feel that markets will continue to experience a high degree of volatility. Because of their hybrid nature, convertibles offer investors the ability to remain invested in the markets at a lower risk posture and with dampened volatility. This is important because many investors with a shorter-term focus are frequently set up for a classic whipsaw situation: sell now and hope to buy in when the market is cheap. This violates the one important rule of wealth building: It's not timing the market that's important, but time in the market. Convertibles offer investors *time in the market at a comfort level* that neither stocks nor bonds can duplicate.

Yield-conscious investors will also find the convertible strategy attractive. In 1996, convertible yields of around 5 to 6 percent were higher than those of the typical common stock and competitive with those of fixed-income investments, including utility stocks. In fact, with the deregulation of utilities, convertibles could offer the traditional, yield-conscious investor a much better alternative than dividend-paying utility stocks, because the average convertible yielded over 6 percent, and a higher quality convertible portfolio yielded around 5 percent. For the risk-averse, convertible bonds offer both higher yields and capital gains potential.

When considering convertibles as a low-risk equity alternative, it will be helpful to review types of companies active in the convertible market. Convertible issuers represent the broad market rather than the large-company weighting of the narrower S&P 500.

**F I G U R E   12–1**

Convertible Styles—S&P 500 Index

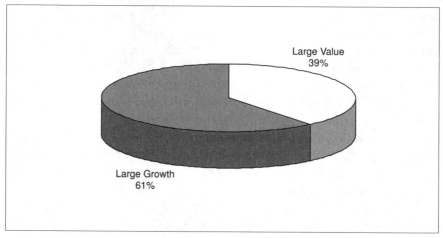

Source: FAF Letter.

Within the S&P 500, 61 percent of the companies are considered large-growth companies and 39 percent large-value, as shown in Figure 12–1. When viewing the convertible market with the First Boston Index as a proxy, 27 percent of the convertible market is considered large-growth and 23 percent is large-value, as shown in Figure 12–2. The remaining segments are 37 percent in small-growth and 13 percent in small-value.

We believe convertible securities represent an attractive alternative for investors who wish to increase their exposure to small-cap equities while reducing volatility. Since small-cap growth is vulnerable to severe spikes in volatility, the reduction of risk is a valuable contribution to the asset allocation equation.

Notice in Figure 12–3 that convertible performance has responded well in the up phases of the investment cycle. However, their value added is considerable during the down phases. Notice also that in each of the troughs of the Russell 2000, convertibles declined significantly less than the stock index. The small- to mid-cap market has a history of spikes both up and down. The value of a well-managed convertible portfolio is that it cushions the downside and provides returns through income while waiting for the next up spike.

## F I G U R E 12–2

Convertible Styles—Convertible Securities Index

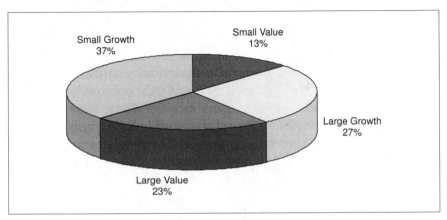

Source: FAF Letter.

## F I G U R E 12–3

First Boston Convertible Index versus Russell 2000
January 1, 1982, through December 31, 1997

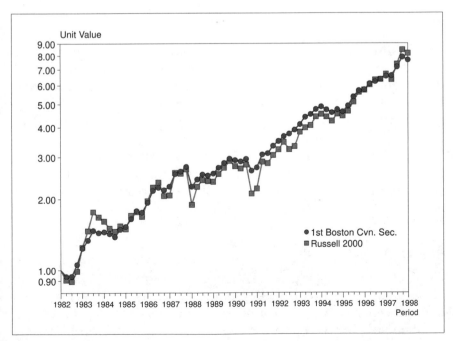

Source: © Frank Russell Company.

Convertible Performance versus S&P 500 Stock Index
October 1, 1979, through December 31, 1997

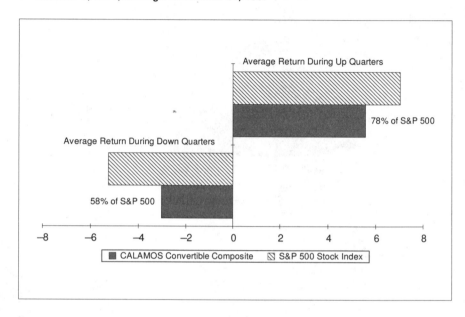

To illustrate the performance of convertibles as compared to the S&P 500, we analyzed the relative performance of up and down quarters (see Figure 12–4).[1] Over this period, notice that convertibles were able to participate in 78 percent of the S&P 500's returns in positive quarters and only 58 percent in the negative quarters. When using the broader market as identified by the Russell 2000, the performance is even more striking, providing 71 percent of the upside and only 35 percent of the downside Figure 12–5. We have also included the bond market relative performance for illustrative purposes, in Figure 12–6.

## Aggressive Convertibles

Using the more aggressive segment of the convertible market can be seen as a variation on using convertibles as an equity alternative. However, investors cannot rely on the bond component to dampen volatility on speculative-grade convertibles. Typically this

**F I G U R E   12–5**

Calamos Convertible Performance versus Russell 2000
October 1, 1979, through December 31, 1997

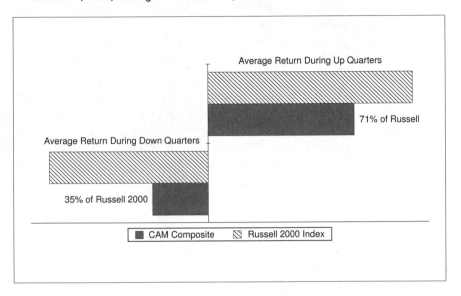

**F I G U R E   12–6**

Convertible Performance versus Salomon Brothers Corporate High-Grade
Stock Index—October 1, 1979, through December 31, 1997

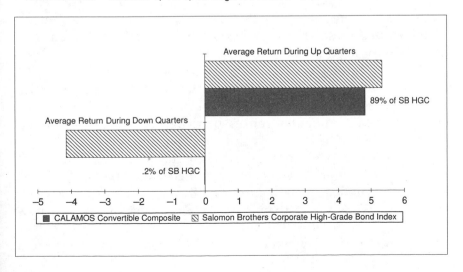

segment of the convertible market is called "growth convertibles" in up markets and "junk converts" in down markets. The bond floors on speculative convertibles are very soft and tend to be much more highly correlated to the underlying stock price than the investment values of straight bonds.

"Aggressive convertibles" is a more reassuring term than "high-risk" or "speculative-grade convertibles." In fact, these convertibles are generally issued by smaller companies or companies whose underlying stocks are much more volatile than those of more seasoned companies. Many investors believe that this sector of the financial market and over-the-counter stocks presents good opportunities, and with good reason. Many academic studies have shown that small-company stocks have outperformed those of larger companies over many years. Unfortunately, this was not the case in the bull market of the 80s. Small company stocks disappointed those who were relying on that trend to continue.

Investing in these smaller companies has always been a risky proposition. Using their convertibles provides an excellent means to reduce risk and participate in the low-cap sector of the market. The current yields are generally very attractive, sometimes averaging as much as 500 basis points greater than the investment-grade issues. Like most convertibles, if the risky stock increases in value, the convertible will also increase in value. If, however, the stock does not do well, then the bond's investment value and coupon interest are in jeopardy for many such issues. This is illustrated in Figure 12–7. Note that in 1990–3, 1992–2, and 1994–3, the Russell 2000 declined quite sharply while the convertibles declined less, displaying protection on the downside.

Thus, aggressive convertibles may offer investors less risk than their underlying common stock, despite the risky companies they represented. As a subset of the low-cap sector, the convertibles on these companies represent firms that have substantial long-term debt. The investor can help reduce the risk of this type of investing by performing thorough fundamental and credit analysis, a process not easily accomplished with small companies. Investors should also be aware that this group exhibits spikes, either up or down, and therefore measures of stock risk, such as beta, are not as helpful. The preferred-risk measure is stock variance (standard risk), which calculates total risk. It is an important

Russell 2000 versus Speculative-Grade Convertibles
Growth of a $1 Investment, 1990–1997

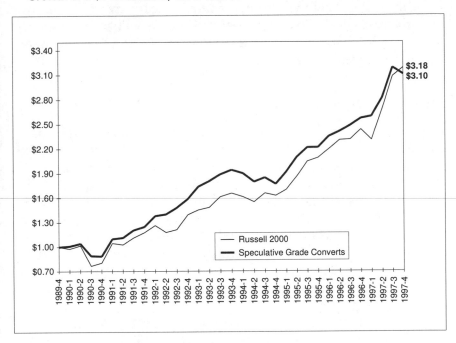

ingredient in estimating the price range of the convertible in risk/reward analysis.

## DIVERSIFYING FIXED-INCOME WITH CONVERTIBLE BONDS

The second opportunity offered by convertibles is diversifying a portfolio's fixed-income allocation. We believe strongly that the successful management of fixed-income assets depends on proper diversification and an accurate understanding of future inflation trends. Early in 1996, the bond market was nervous about the prospect of growing inflation caused by economic growth. In this scenario, convertible bonds are well suited to adding significant value to a portfolio's fixed-income allocation. In light of where interest rates were in 1996 and where they may be in the intermediate term, we believe this trend will continue.

We recommend that investors diversify their fixed-income investments with convertibles. The debt spread between 10-year bonds and the average convertible is only 50 basis points. We find that this is a compelling argument in favor of convertibles. However, the case for diversifying the fixed-income allocation does not rest on yield characteristics but on the investor's view of longer-term secular trends in inflation.

## Secular Trends in Inflation

There has been nothing more devastating to bond market investors than incorrectly gauging longer-term inflationary trends. Inflation has been a permanent part of the financial landscape since World War II. Sometimes inflation has been subdued, as in the 1950s and early 1960s, and other times it has been rampant, as in the late 1970s and early 1980s. Even with the decreasing inflation rate during the late 1980s and 1990s, the bond market's long-term memory of inflation fears required a premium on interest rates above the risk-free rate. It is not easy for bond investors to make inflation calls. The perceptions of longer-term secular trends seem to change frequently.

The 1994 bond market was a good example. During 1993, it looked like inflation was under control and declining. The conventional wisdom believed that the inflation premium priced into bonds should decline, bringing down interest rates. However, the opposite happened. A brief fear of inflation caused a selling stampede when highly leveraged derivative positions began to unravel. The five-year Treasury note showed a negative return, down 4 percent for the year—one of the largest declines since Treasury notes were first issued in 1927. The fear of inflation, coupled with the high leverage in the market, caused one of history's worst years in bond performance, although in hindsight it was an aberration. The inflation rate did not increase, and the economy was not on the verge of another inflationary spiral, but the ebb and flow of investors' expectations about inflationary trends continued to cause high bond market volatility.

In Figure 12–8 (which appeared earlier as Figure 1–3), notice the relative performance of bonds versus convertibles for the period 1979–81. With inflation raging, interest rates increasing, and

F I G U R E  12–8

Convertibles Outperformed Other Asset Classes 1979–1984

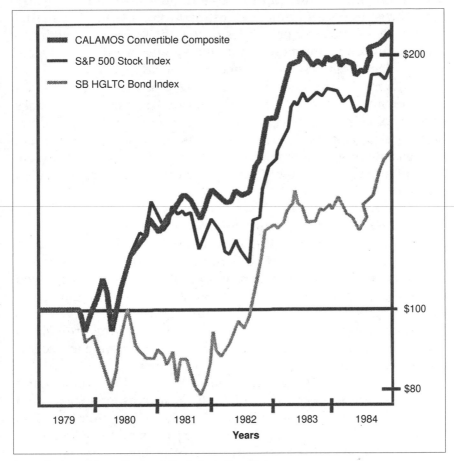

Source: The Carmack Group, Alhambra, California. Used with permission.

stocks locked into a wide trading range, investors not anticipating these volatile conditions suffered greatly. That is why it is so important to understand and evaluate longer-term secular trends. For long-term investors trying to plan for coming decades, the impact can be severe.

An important aspect of the money manager's job is to perform the research necessary to help identify the trends that impact portfolios. We have identified the secular trend as a low-inflation, high-growth environment that should continue throughout this decade and into the next. The secular trend of low inflation will make it much more difficult for straight bond investors to realize the returns necessary to meet investment objectives and actuarial assumptions. Our work persuades us that the forces that will influence these trends are monetary policy, government policy, technology, demographics, and the end of the cold war.

*Monetary policy* is generally recognized as the most important cause of low inflation. In recent years, the global central banks have emphasized price stability as a key objective. The Federal Reserve Board of the United States has now joined the German Bundesbank in risking recession to achieve price stability. Even the high-inflation economies of Canada and others have implemented tight money policies.

*Government policy* also has a enormous influence on inflation. There is tremendous pressure to reduce the government deficit because of its effect on long-term inflation. Balancing the budget was a major issue in the 1996 U.S. presidential elections. But this is more than an issue for politicians to run on; voters have demanded this change in poll after poll. Politicians are merely trying to get in front of a grassroots parade that is already underway. Even with the rhetoric and inaction on this issue, we expect the pressure to cause the deficit/GDP and debt/GDP ratios to continue to decline, helping to sustain the low-inflation environment.

*Technology* is also playing a role in keeping inflation low and expanding the economy. Productivity is increasing for the first time in decades, and this will allow the economy to grow at a faster rate without bumping into capacity constraints, which have caused inflation in the past. The pace of technological improvements has grown, too, keeping labor on the offensive as jobs are eliminated. Downsizing by Fortune 500 companies is headline news, yet jobs are created with little fanfare in other economic areas; the media focus keeps job insecurity high. Ed Yardeni, a well-known economist, said that we now have four economic factors of production instead of three: land, labor, capital, and technology. Technological innovation puts pressure on wages and lowers unit labor costs, thus skewing investments away from people and towards capital investments like equipment and computers.

Other factors are putting pressure on commodity inflation, including changing *demographics*. The baby boomers that bid up housing on increased leverage in the 1970s are paying down debts and buying stocks in the 1990s. Knowledgeable, price-conscious consumers, along with lower wage growth, also contribute to lower inflation.

In the *post-cold-war era*, further pressure is put on inflation by the creation of vast markets with millions of new consumers and cheap labor. Observers often fail to notice the growth potential inherent in this dramatic, unheralded change. Financial markets are playing a key role in economic, political, social, and legal policies. In the cold-war period, many countries could obtain capital only by stating allegiance to West or the East. Today, international markets oversee government policies, in essence dictating to markets and becoming both judge and jury of the economic validity of those policies. Countries recognize that staying competitive is the means to higher living standards, which depend on capital flows. For capital flows to continue, international markets require stability and confidence. A prime example of what can happen when there is a loss of confidence occurred in Mexico in late 1994. The subsequent exodus of capital was a severe punishment for Mexico for its fiscal mismanagement.

The factors stated briefly above are some of the reasons that we believe inflation will continue to remain low in the coming years, with interest rates appropriate to a low-inflation environment. The question for bond investors, then, is how bonds will perform in such an environment. Bond investors accustomed to double-digit returns may have to find means to generate additional capital gains. The convertible market is a natural extension of the bond market and provides the capital gains potential.

## Bond Performance in a Low-Inflation Environment

The U.S. economy is in the late stages of a disinflationary trend that has persisted since the 1982 peak in interest rates. This has provided a backdrop for the bull market of the century for fixed-income investors. Bond performance is of course mainly a result of interest rates declining from double digits in the 1980s to the current level of approximately 6 percent. That environment produced both high coupons and capital gains, which translated into excellent bond performance over that time period.

Over the past 15 years, financial market participants have become very accustomed to high rates of return on investments. But these high returns are unique in the history of our financial markets. If, over the next 15 years, fixed-income investors were to achieve returns equal to those achieved over the past 15 years, the long bond at the end of the coming 15-year period would have a coupon rate of 2.0 percent.

Even in a low-inflation environment, the possibility of a 2 percent 30-year bond seems remote. The current level of interest rates and the unlikelihood that they can decline significantly from these levels materially alter the risk/reward level for bond investors. In fact, in a low-inflation, growth environment, pressure on interest rates at periods within the economic cycle may resurface because of higher demand for money. Thus higher rates are more probable than a further decline that takes the long bond to 2 percent. This leaves bond investors facing a risk/reward profile offering limited upside potential with unlimited downside risk.

## Asset Allocation with Bonds

Using the most recent past experience as the basis for future asset allocation may lead to investment errors. The process is often a function of past correlation between different asset types, classes, or styles. When there is a shift in secular trends, as is now occurring, the asset allocation decision becomes much more difficult. Correlation analysis going back 5 or 10 years may now suggest a high allocation to bonds because of their strong performance during that time as interest rates declined. However, it ignores the fact that there is a level of interest rates below which it would be very unrealistic to expect further declines. By definition, correlation analysis expects the relationship of the past to continue into the future. The decline in interest rates from a double-digit high to a 30-year bond below 6 percent in 1993 created dramatic bond market performance—in fact, the best bond market in history. In our view, that trend is now changing.

The same factors that are creating a low-inflation environment are also creating tremendous opportunities for investment.

Globalization has increased capital flows, and emerging markets, plus the acceptance of free markets, bode well for increased opportunities for growth. However, we expect bond market performance in a low-inflation, growth environment will exhibit continued volatility, albeit within a trading range, as bond investors attempt to gauge inflation expectations in an effort to profit from changes in the yield curve. We believe that the volatility experienced in the 1994–96 bond markets will continue.

Asset allocation must take the shift in secular trends into account. As discussed above, we expect the low-inflation trends that have begun to occur in recent years will continue and that excellent bond performance will not be sustainable in the future. However, bonds will continue to protect against principal loss and provide a safe haven for investments. Adjusting to the new reality will not be easy. Fixed-income investors will have to look carefully at the various bond types, especially convertibles, to maintain performance at acceptable levels.

## Diversifying Fixed-Income Investments: Convertible Bonds

Investors can benefit by adding convertible bonds to their fixed-income allocation. Ibbotson Associates has compared bonds by type for the period July 1, 1976, through December 31, 1997. As Figure 12–9 illustrates, convertibles outperformed the rest. A dollar invested in convertible bonds on July 1, 1976, grew to $12.88 by the end of 1997, outpacing the other bond types considered. Although this period covers the best bond market in history, it also includes the disastrous bond market of the late 1970s and early 1980s.

The data suggests that diversifying the fixed-income portion of a portfolio would have increased returns over this period. During the period of high inflation in the late 1970s and early 1980s, convertibles actually increased in value as other bond types decreased. Even if the above scenario of low inflation were to prove incorrect, using convertibles in a fixed-income allocation makes sense from a diversification point of view.

A main benefit of convertible bonds is that the equity component both provides potential capital gains and offers protection against interest-rate volatility. Convertible bonds are generally issued with a coupon rate that is slightly lower than that on the

Bond Performance by Type of Bond—July 1, 1979, through December 31, 1996

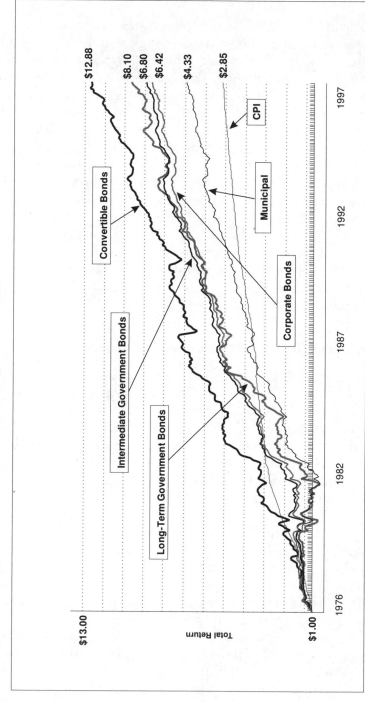

Source: Ibbotson Associates, Chicago, Illinois. Used with permission.

company's straight debt. Since the issuing firm benefits from a lower nominal cost of debt, issuing convertible debt may in fact increase the firm's probability of executing its business plan successfully. This would translate into a higher stock price that also raises the value of the convertible debt—which means that the convertible bond increases in value regardless of fluctuations in interest rates. The studies reveal this by showing that the performance of convertible securities does not correlate directly to that of the bond or stock market. Therefore, a plan sponsor or portfolio manager can add value by diversifying with convertible bonds.

Figure 12–10 demonstrates how blending convertible bonds into a portfolio's fixed-income allocation affects both risk and return. Applying the use of efficient market methodology indicates that, for a given level of risk, blending convertibles with straight bonds increases returns while decreasing risk. Notice that a blend

**F I G U R E   12–10**

Risk versus Return for Combination of Straight and Convertible Bonds
October 1, 1979, through December 31, 1997

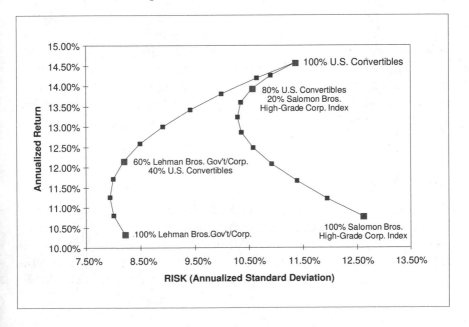

of 80 percent convertibles and 20 percent Salomon Brothers High-Grade Corporate Bond Index (used to represent the performance of long-term bonds) minimizes the risk level at approximately 10.7 percent, as measured by annualized standard deviation. The return is substantially higher than that of 100 percent bonds. When applying the analysis to the Lehman Brothers Government/Corporate Index (which represents an investment in intermediate bonds), a 40 percent allocation to convertibles increases returns while maintaining a risk level that is approximately the same as 100 percent intermediate bonds. In both cases, adding convertible securities increases returns while decreasing risk.

This data suggests that diversifying a fixed-income asset allocation with convertibles makes sense over the longer term. Convertibles increase total returns and decrease their variability when examined over an extended period of time including both rising and falling interest rates.

The possibility of a scenario combining low inflation with growth has caused some analysts to suggest that the bond and stock markets are decoupling. Decoupling occurs when the returns of two or more asset classes diverge. Decoupling of the bond and stock markets would be a departure from the normal historical relationship between stock and bond returns.[2] The change in inflation expectations as discussed above may be the cause of this decoupling. This further strengthens the case to include convertibles as a significant portion of the fixed-income allocation.

Evidence that changes are taking place and that convertible bonds can add value is provided by the relative performance of bond types since December 31, 1994. In 1996 and 1997, convertible securities outperformed all other fixed-income types as shown in Figure 12–11.

## The Equity Component

Convertibles have upside potential due to their equity component. Nevertheless, convertibles are corporate bonds, with typical bond-like characteristics; they are classified as corporate bonds and rated as bonds by the rating agencies. Convertible bonds are typically issued as subordinated debt and have default risk similar to

## F I G U R E  12–11

Convertibles Outperformed Most Other Bond Types

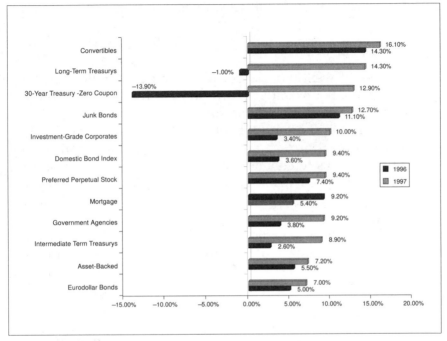

Source: *The Wall Street Journal.*

that of straight corporate bonds, although convertible bonds tend to have a lower default rate. The lower default rate may be a function of the lower coupon on convertibles. When company business plans go awry due to an unexpected downturn in business, the lower interest cost on the convertible debt may allow the company to survive the temporary financial crisis. In return for accepting the lower coupon, the bondholder receives the equity kicker when business improves.

Convertible holders have the right but not the obligation to convert to the underlying common stock. They can convert when it is advantageous to convert and retain the bond when it is not. Convertible holders are therefore protected against stock price declines while benefiting from price increases. The convertible manager performs the analysis that translates these characteristics into a quantifiable risk/reward profile, measuring the upside potential versus the downside protection. Optimal performance is obtained by focusing on managing this risk/reward structure.

## The Pension Liability Trap

Convertibles fit well into the portfolios of many typical fixed-income investors. For example, plan sponsors for pension and other long-term liability plans have assumed an 8 percent rate of return on their overall investment portfolio. With bond rates below their assumed 8 percent growth and return targets, plan sponsors are searching for ways to enhance returns. The drop in interest rates over the past few years has caused the liabilities of those plans to increase, thereby lowering both the rate at which a plan's assets are expected to grow and the discount rate used to determine the future value of the assets. Plan sponsors may need to significantly enhance returns to cover the shortfall. Convertibles can provide diversification as well as increase returns.

## Insurance Companies

Regulations and legal constraints require insurance companies and certain other investors to invest in fixed-income securities. The insurance company must adhere to the guidelines of the National Association of Insurance Commissioners (NAIC) for investing reserve assets. The convertible bonds meeting NAIC ratings are essentially investment grade. The breadth and diversity of the convertible market provides ample opportunity for an insurance company to build a highly diversified, investment-grade portfolio meeting the NAIC guidelines.

In a recent survey of over 800 U.S. insurance executives by Insurance Advisory Services (IAS), 44 percent of those who did not invest in stocks cited RBC and AVR requirements as the reason. Investment-grade convertibles can be carried at cost and have risk-based capital factors of 0.3 to 1.0 percent, versus 30 percent for equities. Therefore, investment-grade convertible bonds offer insurance portfolios equity upside potential at bond RBC requirements. As of December 31, 1997, 36 percent of the U.S. convertible

**F I G U R E   12–12**[3]

| | 1973–1995 | |
| --- | --- | --- |
| Asset Class | Compound Annual Return | Standard Deviation |
| Convertible bonds | 11.70% | 12.47% |
| S&P 500 | 11.84% | 17.27% |
| Long-term corporates | 9.66% | 12.44% |
| Intermediate-term corporates | 9.91% | 8.93% |

Source: Goldman Sachs, 1996.

market was NAIC level 1 and 2. Figure 12–12 shows how convertibles have dramatically outperformed bonds over the last 24 years with the same volatility. According to the same IAS survey, of those insurance executives investing in equities, 84 percent cited growth as their objective. Referring again to the Ibbotson Associates study, convertible securities captured nearly all the upside of the S&P 500 with substantially less risk.

Due to their hybrid nature, convertibles will require more detailed analysis than nonconvertible debt, including the implementation of an option-pricing model. Many insurance companies benefit from hiring a specialized outside manager for this portion of their portfolio.

## Summary

In this section, we have outlined our view of the secular trend in inflation and its impact on the fixed-income investor. We have endeavored to identify the investment environment so as to optimize returns. We realize the factors discussed above are dynamic in nature and that changes in financial markets can occur swiftly, so we constantly monitor events to determine shifts in these longer-term trends.

Successful management of fixed-income assets depends on proper diversification and an accurate understanding of future inflation trends. Our view—that we are in a low-inflation, growth environment for the foreseeable future—profoundly affects our activity in the bond market. Bond performance in this environment will not match that of the recent past, which was higher than normal due to a decade of declining interest rates. Diversification into convertible bonds will increase returns within an expanded fixed-income asset class. Convertible bonds are unique in the fixed-income universe in not depending on falling interest rates to achieve returns. Unlike straight bonds, convertibles do not require an economy to fall into recession to perform well. In short, adding convertible bonds to fixed-income allocations can achieve above-average returns in what looks to be a difficult period for bond performance.

## CONVERTIBLES AS A SEPARATE ASSET CLASS

### Using Asset Allocation

Asset allocation has become a very popular topic of discussion in financial circles over the past few years, with good reason. The volatile, uncertain markets of 1994 left all investors searching for ways to attain investment goals and still manage risk; asset allocation is a way to address those concerns. It is an investment discipline based on the work of Harry Markowitz, who developed modern portfolio theory, and refers to the process of deciding how much a portfolio should invest in different asset classes. In popular usage, it refers to both financial theory as well as sales technique. The decision rests upon determining the client's risk level and then allocating among the various asset classes accordingly.

A portfolio's overall expected returns and volatility depend on the long-term performance characteristics of the asset classes that constitute it. True asset allocation consists of much more than simply buying different mutual funds or owning separate securities within an asset class; it means combining different asset classes that have different risk/reward characteristics and low correlations to each other. An appropriate asset allocation strategy acts to reduce risk while not adversely affecting returns since one market sector will always outperform others at any given point in time. Another Ibbotson study suggests that investing a portfolio randomly in eight asset classes reduces risk by one-third over investing randomly in only one asset class.

This implies that devising the most effective asset allocation mix possible for each client can create financial success. That means finding the place on the efficient frontier that brings the greatest return for a given risk or, correspondingly, that has the lowest risk for a given level of return. Essential to finding this point is matching the portfolio and its efficient frontier to investor characteristics such as long-term objectives, time horizon, risk tolerance, income needs, investment experience, tax status, and liquidity needs. A portfolio can be optimal only in relationship to the customer needs it satisfies.

This is important for convertible investing because investors realize that the purpose of asset allocation is to protect funds against unforeseen events. Unfortunately, this is often accomplished looking backwards. Consider the period 1968–70, which followed two decades of stable bond values, relatively low inflation, and generally rising stock prices. Using past return correlation analysis, an investor could easily have developed a plan that called for bonds for safety and income and stocks for growth. The reality was unforeseen by most participants: The stock market peaked at 1000, a new high for the Dow Jones Industrial Average, and then dropped in 1974 to nearly 500. The broader market did even worse. Bonds were no safe haven either; as inflation began to increase and then accelerate, the bond market plummeted and experienced unprecedented volatility. Refer back to Figure 12–8 to see the relative performance of bonds versus convertibles for the period 1979–81. When inflation raged, interest rates increased, and stocks locked into a wide trading range, unprepared investors suffered greatly. For long-term investors trying to plan for coming decades, the impact can be severe.

Using only the most recent past experience as the basis for future asset allocation may lead to investment errors. The process is often a function of the past correlation between different asset types, classes, or styles. When there is a shift in secular trends the asset allocation decision becomes much more difficult. This takes investment planning and asset selection considerably beyond the "60 percent stocks, 30 percent bonds, and 10 percent cash" formulas that used to be the building blocks of investment strategy. True asset allocation will select among the following, which is not meant to be an all-inclusive list: large-cap stocks, small-cap stocks, corporate bonds, long-term government bonds, international stocks and bonds, real estate, precious metals, convertible bonds, and cash.

One of the advantages of asset allocation in general, and of the use of convertible bonds in particular, is that it replaces the need for market timing. One practices market timing not to enhance returns but to reduce risk, which means staying out of the market during the downswings and getting back in only in bull markets. If an investor could find a market timing technique or system that produced equity-like returns with 25 percent less risk over a 20-year time horizon, he or she would adopt it immediately. Adding convertibles to an asset allocation mix provides like results but without the headaches of actually trying to figure out exactly when to be in and when to be out of the market.

## Convertibles as a Separate Asset Class

Convertibles are frequently assumed to be a subset of the fixed-income or equity markets and therefore not a separate asset class. However, by definition a security is considered a separate asset class if the inclusion of that security improves the risk/reward profile in the efficient frontier optimal portfolio context. Convertible securities offer a unique risk/reward profile because theoretically they have unlimited upside return through their equity component but limited downside risk due to their fixed-income features. In other words, convertibles have a nonlinear relationship to their underlying common stock. Over a complete market cycle period, this unique risk/reward balance places the convertible asset class above the capital market line.

The time horizon is an important factor when assessing asset class performance. Many consultants use a 5- or 10-year interval when evaluating the performance of a particular asset class instead of basing the analysis on a complete market cycle. The problem with this approach is that the true risk/reward nature of a security cannot be accurately evaluated unless at least one full market cycle is considered.

For example, an Ibbotson study[4] demonstrates the benefits of convertibles over a long time horizon. The study concludes that convertibles have performed extremely well over the past 20 years

## F I G U R E  12-13

Risk versus Reward
Convertible Bonds as a Separate Asset Class—1973–1995

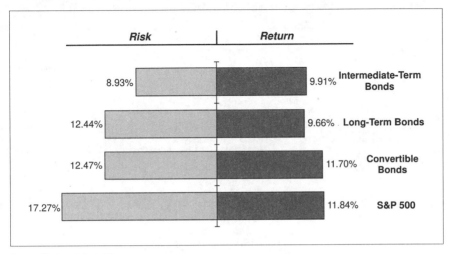

Source: Ibbotson & Associates.

when compared to both the equity and fixed-income markets and that convertibles achieve returns competitive with those of stocks but with lower volatility. This is illustrated in Figure 12–13. Risk, as measured by standard deviation, is 28 percent lower on convertibles than on the S&P 500 (standard deviation of 12.47 percent on convertibles versus 17.27 percent for the S&P), while returns are comparable (11.70 percent compounded annual return for the convertibles and 11.84 percent for the S&P). In other words, convertibles achieve equity-like returns with less risk.

Our own actual experience with managing convertibles confirms the Ibbotson conclusions. Line 1 of Figure 12–14 illustrates a typical efficient frontier for a portfolio that combines the S&P 500 with the Salomon Brothers High-Grade Bond Index. *Notice that the most efficient point on the curve combines 70 percent bonds with 30 percent S&P 500.* Line 2 demonstrates the value added by convertible securities.[5] Adding convertibles to either bonds or stocks moves the efficient frontier lower in terms of risk and higher in terms of reward. *The most efficient point on the curve combines 55*

**F I G U R E  12–14**

Calamos U.S. Convertible Composite Compared to the S&P 500 and Salomon
High-Grade Corporate Bond Index
October 1, 1979, through December 31, 1996

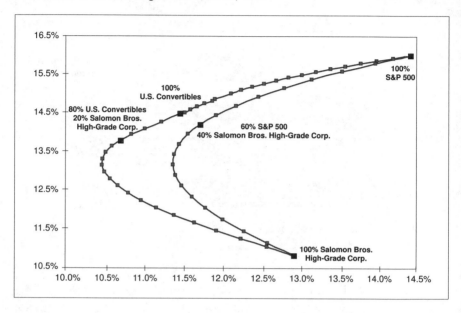

*percent bonds and 45 percent convertibles. Blending convertibles gives
about 13 percent less risk for the same level of return, or about 10 percent
more return for a given level of risk.* Adding convertibles to a portfolio mix generated a significant addition of value, as the figure
illustrates.

The addition of convertibles moves the efficient frontier up
(indicating higher return) and to the left (indicating lower risk).
The performance of convertible securities does not correlate directly to that of the stock or bond markets. In fact, no combination
of stocks and bonds can provide the same risk/reward profile as
convertibles. Convertibles therefore qualify as a separate asset
class.

# E N D   N O T E S

1. We have used the Calamos Convertible Composite as a proxy for the convertible market. The composite is audited and conforms to the performance presentation standards set by the Association for Investment Management and Research (AIMR).

2. *Normal* is defined as the historical relationship over longer time periods. At turning points, what is considered normal begins to be redefined.

3. Scott L. Lummer and Mark W. Riepe, "Convertible Bonds as an Asset Class: 1957–1992," *The Journal of Fixed Income,* Vol. 3, No. 2 (September 1993). With updated data completed by Ibbotson and Associates, as published by Goldman Sachs Global Convertible Research, 1996, "Convertibles as an Asset Class." The dates represented in this particular chart are 1973 through 1995.

4. *Ibid.*

5. We have used the Calamos Convertible Composite as a proxy for the convertible market. The composite is audited and conforms to the performance presentation standards set by the Association for Investment Management and Research (AIMR).

# 13

## CHAPTER

# Convertible Preferreds for Corporate Investors

**H**aving a large amount of cash on hand may seem like a nice problem for a corporate treasurer to have, but placing those corporate funds so as to obtain favorable returns has become an increasingly difficult task in volatile markets. In broad terms, a treasurer has only two alternatives available: the traditional cash management approach using money market instruments, or dividend capture programs, which entail more risk.

When short-term interest rates fell from the double-digit range in the early 1980s to the 5 to 7 percent range in 1986–87, the treasurer's cash management problem became much more challenging. When interest rates were higher, the no-risk money market instruments were the obvious choice of many treasurers. The short-term money instruments provided lucrative returns with little risk and not much effort. However, as these rates declined, after-tax yields in many cases fell below an annualized rate of 4 percent.

The treasurer's other alternative is a dividend-capture program, which invests in dividend-paying stocks. The tax law currently allows corporations a 70 percent deduction for dividends received by another corporation. This substantially increases the after-tax yield on stock portfolios held by the corporation. Since the law requires the stock to be held for a minimum of 46 days, fluctuating stock prices increase the risk. Once the treasurer has decided to increase risk to obtain higher returns, there are different ways to take advantage of the dividend exclusion rule. The purchase of straight preferred stocks or utility stocks with high dividend yields and relatively stable market prices is an obvious choice, but one that is vulnerable to changing interest rates and difficult to hedge.

Adjustable-rate preferreds (ARPs) and the "Dutch-auction" preferreds are a lower-risk variation on preferred stocks. The main benefit of these programs is that they provide money market rates and a dividend exclusion to increase the after-tax yield from, for example, 4 percent to 5.5 percent. These adjustable-rate and "Dutch-auction" preferreds offer a bidding procedure that sets a new dividend rate every 49 days. They both pay a variable-rate dividend, usually on a quarterly basis. The issuer sets the rate within upper and lower limits, called collars, which are based on the highest of three Treasury rates: the three-month Treasury bill; the 10-year Treasury note; and the 30-year Treasury bond. Adjustable-rate preferreds were designed to minimize price fluctuations due to interest-rate movements. This product attempts to protect the investor from nonparallel shifts in the yield curve and provide a short-duration instrument with an option on the entire yield curve.

## CONVERTIBLE-PREFERRED DIVIDEND-CAPTURE PROGRAM

The explosive growth of the convertible securities market provides yet another way to take advantage of the dividend-exclusion rule. The main benefit of a convertible preferred portfolio is that it can provide much higher returns, due to the upside potential provided by the convertibility feature, and accommodate hedging strategies to reduce risk. Because convertible preferred portfolios might be used in a number of different ways, the analysis can become complex. However, the benefits of higher after-tax returns and controlled portfolio risk are well worth the effort.

Convertible preferred programs for corporations have not always been available to the degree that they are now. The convert-

U.S. Convertible Preferred Stock New Issuance through December 31, 1997

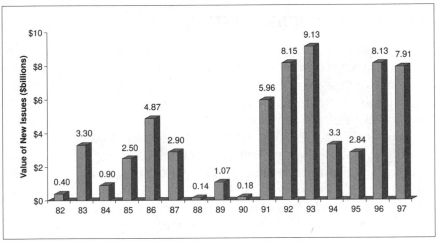

Source: Calamos Asset Management, Inc.

ible preferred market, like the convertible bond market, has expanded greatly over the last few years. Figure 13–1 indicates the growth of the new issue market.

Convertible preferreds seem like an ideal candidate for the dividend capture strategy because this hybrid security has a hedge already built in. Convertible preferreds pay a fixed dividend, typically quarterly, like straight preferreds. Also like straight preferreds, they vary in quality, depending on the issuing corporation, and are rated by Standard & Poor's and Moody's. Dividend rates of convertible preferreds are usually less than those of straight preferreds.

The convertible holder has the right to convert to the underlying common stock of the issuing corporation and in exchange receives less current income. The ability to convert dramatically changes the investment characteristics of this security. The fixed dividend and its status as a senior security give the convertible preferred the safety of a fixed-income vehicle. On the other hand, because conversion to common stock is at the holder's option, any changes in stock price can be reflected in the market price of the convertible preferred, presenting the opportunity for capital gains.

The combination of dividend recapture and capital appreciation is the main reason to use a convertible preferred program.

## EVALUATING CONVERTIBLE PREFERREDS

The evaluation process for convertible preferreds is the same as that for any convertible security. Chapter 11 reviewed in detail the worksheet analysis of a typical convertible security. Notice that it considers both the fundamentals of the company and the risk/reward analysis of the convertible security. It also includes the interest rate sensitivity and the important ex-dividend dates. The same thorough analysis is applied to convertible preferreds. The worksheet again becomes the main tool in the decision-making process.

Figure 13–2 shows a worksheet for a convertible preferred. Like all worksheets, it considers both company fundamentals and the risk/reward analysis of the convertible security. Convertible preferreds differ from traditional convertible bonds in having dividend payment disclosures, adjustment for the perpetual nature of preferreds, and issue size. Under convertible security, description, notice that the convertible preferred has no maturity date listed. The worksheet for the preferred issue lists issue size in number of shares, while the convertible bond worksheet discloses the issue size in dollars. The convertible preferred and convertible bond worksheets treat risk/reward and convertible valuation in fundamentally the same way.

Convertible preferreds provide the corporate treasurer with the flexibility to choose among several variations of a convertible strategy. Which program the treasurer wishes to implement depends on the time horizon and the desired risk tolerance level. The longer the time horizon, the higher the probability that the strategy will achieve its investment objective. It should be emphasized from the onset that the treasurer should not view a convertible strategy, or for that matter, any straight preferred or common stock program, as a corporate checking account. There are costs involved in setting up any program that need to be amortized over time. There are also commission costs for executing trades, and the important bid-ask spread of a marketable security. Even treasurers using adjustable rates have found that bid-ask spreads can be very significant and negate months of dividend income. Over short pe-

## F I G U R E  13–2

### Convertible Security Worksheet

Company: Ford Motor Company        Sector: Consumer Cyclical
                                   Industry: (56) E-Auto Parts-OEM

|                | Symbol | Market | Current Yield |
|----------------|--------|--------|---------------|
| Common Stock   | F      | 25.750 | 6.27          |
| Convertible    | FPR    | 50.000 | 8.40          |

**Common Stock**

| | | | | | |
|---|---|---|---|---|---|
| Beta: | 1.24 | Fund. Rating: | B+ | Debt/Equity: | 7.72 |
| Stnd Risk: | 29.71 | VL/CAM Rank: | 5/4 | Tech Rank: | 3 |
| Cap (mill shr): | 12,260.40 | Stock Div.: | 1.60 | RX Agency: | |

**Convertible Security**

| | | |
|---|---|---|
| Desc: 4.200-Preferred | Ex Dt: May-Aug-Nov-Feb 1 | Call Feature: 12/97 *ABS |
| Risk Level: MED | Inv. Val YTM: 9.25 | Credit Rating: A- |
| Issue Size (mill$): 40.000 | CCES Grade: 8 | Conv. Ratio: 1.6327 |
| Next Call Price: 51.680 | Underwriter: | Bnd Hld Rts: |

**Convertible Analysis**

| Conversion Value | Conversion Premium | Investment Value | Invest Value Premium |
|------------------|--------------------|------------------|----------------------|
| 41.64 | 20.05% | 45.40 | 10.11% |

| BARA | Yield to Maturity | Fair Value Over/Under | Interest Rate Sensitivity |
|------|-------------------|-----------------------|---------------------------|
| 1.64 | N/A | −5.60% | 5.35 |

| EROI | Upside Beta | Downside Beta | Break-Even |
|------|-------------|---------------|------------|
| 21.55% | 0.90 | 0.19 | 9.43 |

**Risk/Reward Analysis**

| | 12 mo. | 6 mo. | | 6 mo. | 12 mo. |
|---|--------|-------|---------|-------|--------|
| Estimated Stock Move | | | | | |
| Percent Change 1 in | −25.6% | −18.9% | CURRENT | +23.4% | +34.6% |
| Stock Price | 18.944 | 20.667 | 25.500 | 31.462 | 34.323 |
| CFP Convertible Track | 47.600 | 48.800 | 52.800 | 59.000 | 61.900 |
| Convertible Percent Change | −4.800 | −2.400 | 5.600 | 18.000 | 23.800 |
| Conv. Total Return % | −3.600 | −1.800 | 14.000 | 22.200 | 32.200 |

Source: Calamos Convertible Evaluation System.

riods of time, day-to-day market fluctuations add an unknown, additional cost factor. The longer the time period, the greater the likelihood that overall cost factors will be minimized.

Although a convertible preferred program has liquidity similar to that of other securities in the public financial markets, the treasurer should determine a minimum time horizon for these funds. If funds are needed for other corporate purposes in less than six months, then a preferred or stock program is not recommended. Assuming that the time horizon is sufficient for using convertible preferreds (although a minimum of six months to a year is a good rule of thumb, a longer period of time allows for dividend maximization), the risk/reward parameters of the strategy should be the next consideration. The risk/reward analysis, which considers the volatility of returns, is the most useful tool in selecting the proper program for the corporation.

## BASIC CONVERTIBLE PREFERRED PROGRAM

The most straightforward investment strategy would be to establish a portfolio of convertible preferreds. This basic program offers the corporation a combination of tax-advantaged yield and capital gains. The dividend yield of convertible preferreds is typically less than that of straight preferreds. In the market environment of December 1987, the yield for straight preferreds was 9.02 percent, while the average yield for convertible preferreds was 7.8 percent. (See Figure 4–5 for the calculation of the pre-tax yield equivalent.) This difference of 122 basis points, or 1.22 percentage points, was less than it had been in many years. In 1996, the yield on the average straight convertible preferred was 7.8 percent, while the average yield on straight convertibles was 5.99 percent. The difference was 190 basis points, or 1.90 percent. As with other convertible strategies, holders received the opportunity for capital gains in return for lower current yield. This important aspect of a convertible preferred program can significantly increase the total return of the program.

Convertible preferreds have outperformed money market instruments and certificates of deposit by a wide margin. Figure 13–3 indicates the performance of the convertible preferred market

## F I G U R E  13–3

Merrill Lynch Convertible Preferred Index versus Money Market Instruments
January 1, 1988, through December 31, 1997

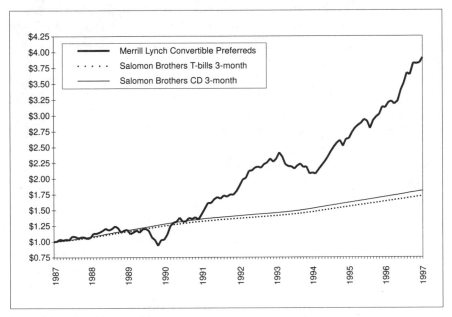

Source: Calamos Asset Management, Inc.

on a total return basis. Introduced in 1988, the Merrill Lynch Convertible Preferred Index has been trading over a period of generally rising stock prices. This favorable stock market environment has created capital gains opportunities, which are an important aspect of the convertible preferred program. Some analysts associate rising stock prices with inflation. The same forces that make common stocks an inflation hedge over time also work to make convertible securities an inflation hedge.

The Merrill Lynch Convertible Preferred Index indicates how convertible preferreds performed, in general, without regard to any selection process. Using the techniques discussed in previous chapters, one would choose convertible preferreds that had superior risk/reward characteristics, which should improve performance and decrease volatility.

## TAX IMPLICATIONS OF CONVERTIBLE PREFERRED PROGRAM

Any discussion of returns is not complete until it addresses the issue of risk. The treasurer's most difficult task is assessing the corporation's tolerance for risk. Figure 13–3 compares convertible preferreds to the minimum-risk investments of money markets and certificates of deposit. The expected return increases with convertible preferreds, but so does the degree of risk. Figure 13–3 shows that there were a number of quarters with negative returns over this period. Quarters such as the third quarter of 1986, which saw the S&P 500 Stock Index drop nearly 7 percent for the quarter, caused negative returns for convertible preferreds for the quarter.

As another example, in March and April 1987, short-term interest rates rose and stock prices fell due to the U.S.-Japan trade restrictions and the falling value of the dollar. Figure 13–4 shows how these events affected the various asset classes during this period. Note that convertible preferreds sustained only a minor loss compared to straight preferreds, utility company stocks, or blue-chip stocks. In advancing stock markets, convertible preferreds are not as directly affected by rising interest rates as other securities are.

In 1995, the Clinton administration proposed reducing the Dividend Received Deduction from 70 percent to 50 percent. At the same time, Wall Street began to issue non-DRD preferred stock such as MIPs, QUIDs, and the like. There was significant volatility in the preferred market as a result. However, preferred stocks stabilized once the market disseminated the information. Supply shortages—as witnessed by the issuance of non-DRD paper—helped offset legislative changes. Market pricing indicated that this proposal is not expected to become law in the near future.

### F I G U R E  13–4

Relative Market Performance, March 31, 1987, through April 15, 1987

| | |
|---|---|
| Lipper Convertible Preferreds | −1.1 percent |
| S&P 40 Utilities Index | −7.9 percent |
| S&P 500 Stock Index | − 4.1 percent |

A company's tolerance for risk should be based on the treasurer's assessment of interest-rate risk, inflation risk, and stock-market risk. A convertible preferred program might well be less risky than a straight preferred program once interest-rate risk and inflation have been considered. The importance of the time horizon becomes apparent when reviewing the figures in this chapter. The longer the time horizon, the higher the probability that the return objective can be met without having to close out the program in unfavorable market conditions. In addition, the volatility of returns can be controlled by hedging techniques, which may allow the treasurer to further reduce the inherent portfolio risk of fluctuating market prices.

## HEDGING CONVERTIBLE PREFERREDS

The flexibility of convertible preferreds is that they can be used with two hedging techniques: a covered call writing program and/or the purchase of index put options. These techniques do not eliminate risk, but they can substantially reduce it. As with any risk-reduction technique, there is a trade-off. With convertible preferreds, returns are reduced during the up quarters, but protection is increased in the down quarters. The net effect should be an overall reduction in quarter-to-quarter fluctuations, which means less volatility and hence less risk.

### Covered Call Writing with Convertible Preferreds

Hedging convertible preferreds is similar to hedging convertible bonds, which will be discussed in Chapter 14. The main difference is that care must be exercised not to jeopardize the tax advantage of the preferred dividend. The tax law has made this distinction to assure that a position is at risk and is not merely being maneuvered to capture dividends at no risk. The same tax law also states that the use of the convertible stock hedge (shorting stock against a convertible preferred) eliminates the tax deduction status, thereby effectively preventing the use of the technique. When options are sold against the convertible preferred, they are either qualified or unqualified. A *qualified option* is one that does not jeopardize the tax deductibility of the preferred dividend; an *unqualified option* is one that does.

A thorough knowledge of the tax rules is helpful in managing a convertible preferred program. The following is a brief discussion of those rules.

1. The convertible preferred stock must be held for at least 46 days. This holding period is important because it establishes the time period necessary to qualify for the dividend.

2. If the preferred stock is cumulative, with an arrearage of more than a year in dividends, the stock must be held for at least 91 days.

3. The dividend deduction is not allowable if a short sale of common stock (substantially identical security) is made against a convertible preferred.

4. The holding period is reduced for any period during which the taxpayer's risk of loss with respect to the stock is diminished because the taxpayer has:

   A. An option to sell, is under an obligation to sell, or has made (and not closed) a short sale of substantially identical stock or securities.

   B. Granted an option to purchase substantially identical stock or securities.

   C. Reduced the risk by virtue of holding one or more other positions with respect to substantially similar or related property.[1]

The writing of qualified covered call options against convertible preferreds *does not* reduce the holding period, and they are not considered to be substantially identical securities. A covered call option is qualified if:

- The option is listed and trading on national exchanges.
- The option has more than 30 days until expiration.
- The option is not deep-in-the-money.
- The option is not granted by an options dealer in connection with his activity of dealing in options.
- Gain or loss with respect to the option is not ordinary income or loss.

The thrust of the rules is to prevent a no-risk hedge position being established to capture the tax-favored dividends, which is why short sales and deep-in-the-money options are prohibited. The tax rules define a deep-in-the-money option as an option with a strike price that is lower than the lowest qualified benchmark.

The *Commerce Clearing House Tax Guide* explains qualified benchmark in the following manner:

> Generally, the lowest qualified benchmark is the highest available strike (exercise) price that is less than the "applicable stock price" (the closing price of the optioned stock on the most recent day on which it was traded before the option was granted or, if more than 110 percent greater than the most-recent-day price, the opening price on the date of grant). However, there are exceptions to the general definition of the lowest qualified benchmark. (The lower the strike price is in relation to the market value of the underlying stock, the more likely it is that the market value of the call will parallel that of the stock.)
>
> A. If an option is granted more than 90 days before it expires and if the strike price is more than $50, the lowest qualified benchmark is the second highest strike price that is less than the applicable stock price.
> B. If the applicable stock price is $25 or less and if, but for this exception, the lowest qualified benchmark would be less than 85 percent of the applicable stock price, the lowest qualified benchmark is equal to 85 percent of the applicable stock price.
> C. If the applicable stock price is $150 or less and if, but for this exception, the lowest qualified benchmark would be less than the applicable stock price reduced by $10, the lowest qualified benchmark is equal to the applicable stock price reduced by $10.

For purposes of the loss deferral rule, a covered call option is not treated as qualified if gain from the disposition of stock to be purchased under the option is included in gross income in a taxable year, after the taxable year in which the option is closed. It is also not treated as qualified if the stock is not held for more than 30 days following the date on which the option is closed. The covered call exception also does not apply in cases where stock is disposed of at a loss in one year, the gain on the option is not included in gross income until the following year, and the option is not held for at least 30 days after the related stock is disposed of at a loss (.25). In determining whether this holding period requirement is satisfied, rules similar to those applicable in determining whether a taxpayer is eligible for the dividend received deduction under Code Sec. 246(c)(3) and (4) will apply (without regard to the exception to those rules for a qualified covered call option).

Effective for positions established after June 30, 1984, in taxable years ending after that date, any loss realized from a qualified covered call option granted by the taxpayer, which has a strike price that is less than the applicable stock price, will be treated as a long-term capital loss if gain from the sale of the stock when the loss is realized would be long-term capital gain. Also, the holding period for stock subject to the option will not include any period during which the taxpayer is the grantor of the option.[2]

As a general guide, options that are in-the-money by more than 12 percent should be avoided because of the possibility of losing the deduction. The use of margin (debt financing) reduces the amount of the deduction received for dividends to the extent of the interest paid to purchase the stock.

Tax rules change frequently and are interpreted differently by professionals. When utilizing a convertible preferred program, it is advisable to seek tax counsel to assure that the deductions are secure and meet all requirements.

## Hedging with Index Put Options

The second way to hedge a convertible preferred portfolio is to use index put options. This helps control market risk. Since not all convertible preferreds have options or are attractive candidates for option writing, investors can use index put options to further reduce portfolio risk. Index options are becoming increasingly popular as a means to provide portfolio insurance against declining markets. Index puts are options that are tied to broad-based indexes, like the S&P 500 or Value Line, or to narrow indexes that are tied to specific industry groups. The specific hedging strategy is covered in detail in Chapter 15.

The principle behind using index puts for risk-reduction purposes is that the put gains in value as the index declines in value. Like all options, the index puts have specified strike prices and time periods. Index puts are purchased at premiums that can vary in response to market sentiment, which can make it difficult to estimate the cost of this insurance. The valuation of the premium levels is an important consideration for the convertible strategist utilizing index puts. The advantage to using index options rather than index futures is that the cost is fixed and the potential loss is limited to the premium price. With options, once the index rises above the strike price, the option may become worthless. With futures, as the index increases, the future contract that was sold increases in value and becomes an extremely costly item.

The use of index puts is a cost-effective means to protect portfolio value and is most useful when there is a high correlation between the index and the portfolio. Figure 13–5 illustrates how an index-put strategy can reduce volatility over a given time period. During the up phases, the puts expired worthless, reducing the

**F I G U R E  13–5**

Convertible Preferred Index—Unhedged versus Hedged

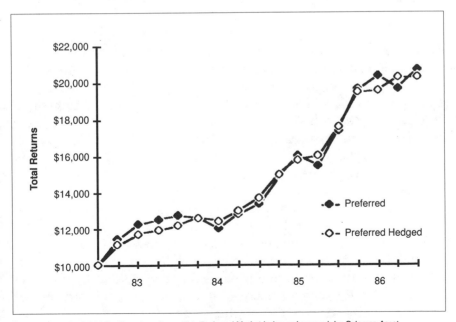

Source: Lipper Analytical Services, Inc.: Convertible Preferred Market Index and research by Calamos Asset Management, Inc.

**F I G U R E  13–6**

Convertible Preferred Quarterly Returns

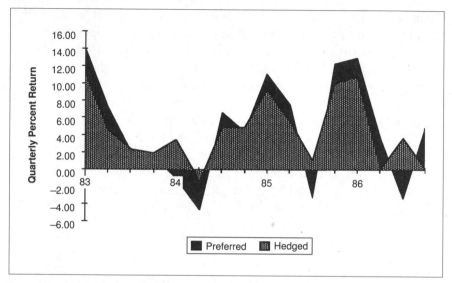

Source: Lipper Analytical Services, Inc.: Convertible Preferred Market Index and research by Calamos Asset
Management, Inc.

return by the cost of the put premium. During down phases, the
puts gained in value, offsetting the decline in the portfolio asset
value. Figure 13–6 illustrates how this strategy affects quarter-to-
quarter fluctuations. Notice the negative quarters of the unhedged
index and how the hedging reduced the return in the up quarters
but increased the returns in the down quarters. During this period
all but one of the negative quarters would have been eliminated by
the hedging technique.

Although we have not illustrated the results from combining
writing call options and buying index puts, this combination gives
the treasurer maximum flexibility in controlling risk. The strategy
is complicated to execute and should be managed by either a specialist in convertible hedging or a treasurer well-versed in the intricacies of that market. Convertible hedging can affect the holding
period and the dividend exclusion rule, so tax consequences of
each position need to be thoroughly reviewed.

## SUMMARY

In recent years, the availability of convertible preferreds has diminished because so many have been called. The new-issue market for convertible preferreds has not kept pace with calls and redemptions. Furthermore, MIPs probably provide a better alternative for corporations than traditional convertible preferreds. The main advantage of MIPs to the issuing corporation is the deductibility of the dividend.

Still, the flexibility of convertible preferreds in a corporate cash management program gives the corporate treasurer the ability to increase returns while adjusting risk to the tolerance level of the individual corporation. Whether convertible preferreds are used alone or in conjunction with hedging techniques to increase after-tax returns, their contribution to the corporate cash as a profit center of the corporation is assured. This important but complicated sector of the financial markets will continue to attract more corporate treasurers.

## E N D N O T E S

1. Commerce Clearing House, Inc., *Federal Tax Guide Reports*, 1987, pp. 1165.
2. *Ibid.*, p. 2101.

# 14

## CHAPTER

# Convertible Hedging

The purpose of hedging is to reduce and control risk. A perfect hedge is one that has eliminated any possible future profit or loss—which is rarely an investor's goal. In convertible hedging the objective is not to achieve perfection but to control risk while retaining acceptable profit opportunities. In a sense, unhedged convertible securities provide a hedge against the volatility of the underlying common stock. As has been demonstrated, convertible securities can be evaluated to ascertain their particular risk/reward parameters. A convertible hedge adds other instruments to the convertible and adjusts the risk/reward relationship to a different profit profile. Because that profit profile can be predetermined and designed by investors, convertible hedging allows them additional flexibility to control risk.

A number of hedging techniques can be applied to convertibles; each has its own advantages and disadvantages. In this chapter, we will cover the convertible stock hedge and convertible option hedging.

## CONVERTIBLE STOCK HEDGE

The convertible stock hedge is a well-known technique applied largely by convertible arbitrageurs, convertible market makers, and convertible hedge funds. Due to its complexity, it is used to a lesser degree by individual investors. The convertible stock hedge is accomplished by selling the underlying stock short against the convertible security. To determine how investors may be able to use this technique, we will consider each of its ingredients.

### The Long Position: Convertible Security

In simple terms, this is the part of the hedge the investor buys and owns. The convertible security for this hedge can be any convertible security, convertible bond, convertible preferred stock, or warrant. Not all convertibles work well in a stock hedge. The most likely candidates have the following attributes:

- *Low conversion premium.* The amount of the convertible's conversion premium is an important consideration. As the underlying common stock increases in value, the conversion premium gradually declines. In a convertible stock hedge, the convertible bond increases in value as the stock increases, but the short sale of stock is offsetting these gains. Therefore, the best candidates are convertibles with low conversion premiums, where changes in the value of the stock have a relatively direct influence on the value of the convertible.

- *Positive yield advantage.* The convertible should enjoy a yield advantage over its underlying common stock. The short sale of stock requires the seller to pay the dividend.

- *Low premium over investment value.* The convertible should be trading close to its investment value for the convertible price to be cushioned if the stock declines in value.

- *Avoid overvalued convertibles.* Since they tend to trade on a fair value price track, convertibles should be avoided if they are overvalued as determined by the convertible pricing model. Overvalued convertibles may decrease to their normal valuation without any change in the underlying stock price.

The above attributes are similar to those that should be used in the selection process for convertibles, as described in earlier chapters. The convertibles that are most suitable for hedging are often those that possess the most favorable unhedged characteristics.

## Short Position: Underlying Common Stock

Each convertible converts into a specific number of shares of common stock. The convertible stock hedge is set up by selling the underlying stock short against the convertible security. The Securities and Exchange Commission's rule on short sales states that they can be executed only in a rising market. Therefore, the following conditions need to be met to execute a short sale on stock exchanges:

- *Uptick or plus tick rule.* The last sale of the stock must be at a higher price than the preceding sale.
- *Zero plus tick rule.* The last sale is unchanged, but higher than the preceding different sale.
- *Short exempt.* Short sales can be made without meeting the above rules if the short sale is made with the anticipation of covering the sale by the conversion of the convertible within a short period of time. This is used frequently when closing out a convertible position by selling the stock first and then converting the bond, which allows the investor to be assured of a stock price without falling victim to administrative delays in the conversion process of the convertible.

Before a short sale of stock can be transacted, the broker must borrow the shares from another investor in order to deliver and complete the sale of securities. The administration is handled in brokerage firms by the stock loan department, whose function is to find the stock, usually from other margin customers or institutions, to accommodate the trading activity. Even large firms have active stock loan operations to facilitate short-sale trading activity. Once the stock has been borrowed, it can remain outstanding indefinitely. However, the institution that has loaned the stock can recall it at any time. Occasionally, this may result in a buy-in to cover the short sale. The broker pays the institutions, based on a percentage of market value, for the stocks they have loaned.

The short sale can be done only in a margin account, which means that any investor using the convertible stock hedge technique must employ a margin account. Margin accounts are governed by Regulation T of the Federal Reserve Board. Under those rules, a short sale of stock against a convertible bond does not require any additional margin. The short sale is considered a *covered short sale.*

Many investors find the concept of *marking-to-market* very confusing. When the short sale is made, the broker must segregate the proceeds of the sale into a subaccount, the short account. That subaccount must always contain the exact amount of funds necessary to buy back the short sale. As the stock changes in price, funds are transferred within the margin account, from one subaccount to another, to maintain the proper balance. If the stock has increased in value, money is transferred from the general account to the short account to bring the account in balance. If the stock has moved down in price, funds are transferred from the short account to the general account. These transfers are made for stock price moves of as little as an eighth of a point. The short account credit balance is a frozen credit that the investor cannot use even to offset debits in other subaccounts. As with all credit balances in the account, the broker does receive the use of the funds. From the investor's point of view, the net effect of this movement of funds back and forth between subaccounts is zero, but it must be done to conform to margin rules.

## Convertible Stock Hedge Profit Profiles

Thus far, we have discussed the mechanics of a convertible stock hedge. We will now cover in more detail how it can be applied under various conditions. Figure 14–1 is an abbreviated version of the now-familiar convertible worksheet analysis. The convertible stock hedge adjusts the risk/reward of the convertible, so the beginning point is to determine the risk/reward and the price track of the convertible security. Other factors discussed at length in previous chapters and detailed in the convertible evaluation worksheet should be considered. For illustrative purposes, we will ig-

## F I G U R E 14–1

### Convertible Stock Hedge Example

XYZ Company 7.75—03/01/1996
  Common Stock Market Price  = $59.25
  Convertible Market Price    = 112.00%
  Conversion Ratio            = 16.44 shares

**Investment:**
Long Position:  100 bonds at $1,120.00 = $112,000
                (remains same for each hedge)

**Short Position:**
Bullish Hedge   300 shares at $59.25 = $17,750
Neutral Hedge   900 shares at $59.25 = $53,325
Bearish Hedge   1,500 shares at $59.25 = $88,875

|                        | –50%     | –25%     | -0-   | +25%     | +50%     |
|------------------------|----------|----------|-------|----------|----------|
| Assumed Stock Price    | 29.63    | 44.44    | 59.25 | 74.06    | 88.88    |
| Est. Conv. Price       | 90.43    | 99.65    | 112.00| 127.48   | 146.08   |
| *Bullish Hedge:*       |          |          |       |          |          |
| Profit/Loss on Conv.   | (21,571) | (12,350) | 0     | 15,477   | 34,082   |
| Profit/Loss on Stock   | 8,886    | 4,443    | 0     | (4,443)  | (8,886)  |
| Bond Interest          | 7,750    | 7,750    | 7750  | 7,750    | 7,750    |
| Stock Dividends Paid   | 0        | 0        | 0     | 0        | 0        |
| Total Profit or Loss   | (4,935)  | (157)    | 7750  | 18,784   | 32,946   |
| Return on Investment   | (4)      | 0        | +7    | +17      | +29      |
| *Neutral Hedge:*       |          |          |       |          |          |
| Profit/Loss on Conv.   | (21,571) | (12,350) | 0     | 15,477   | 34,082   |
| Prof./Loss on Stock    | 26,663   | 13,331   | 0     | (13,331) | (26,663) |
| Bond Interest          | 7,750    | 7,750    | 7750  | 7,750    | 7,750    |
| Stock Dividends Paid   | 0        | 0        | 0     | 0        | 0        |
| Total Profit or Loss   | 12,842   | 8,731    | 7750  | 9,896    | 15,169   |
| Return on Investment   | +11      | +8       | +7    | +9       | +14      |
| *Bearish Hedge:*       |          |          |       |          |          |
| Profit/Loss on Conv.   | (21,571) | (12,350) | 0     | 15,477   | 34,082   |
| Profit/Loss on Stock   | 44,438   | 22,219   | 0     | (22,219) | (44,438) |
| Bond Interest          | 7,750    | 7,750    | 7750  | 7,750    | 7,750    |
| Stock Dividends Paid   | 0        | 0        | 0     | 0        | 0        |
| Total Profit or Loss   | 30,617   | 17,619   | 7750  | 1,008    | (2,606)  |
| Return on Investment   | +27      | +16      | +7    | +0       | (2)      |

Source: Calamos Convertible Evaluation System.

nore those fundamental segments and concentrate on the hedge profile. We will also assume that the most probable price range is an arbitrary plus or minus 50 percent move. When applying this to actual examples, the most accurate price distribution should be used, as discussed in previous chapters.

The convertible in Figure 14–1 has a favorable risk/reward relationship to the underlying common stock. On a total return basis, assuming a one-year holding period, the convertible enjoys 70 percent of the upside potential of the common stock for only 27 percent of its downside loss. Each convertible can be exchanged for 16.44 shares of common stock. Three profit profiles will be reviewed to show the flexibility of this technique.

## Bullish Hedge

An initial position of 100 convertible bonds is purchased at $1,120 for an investment of $112,000, with the simultaneous short sale of 300 shares of common stock at a price of $59.25 per share. Figure 14–1 calculates the profit and loss of the position. Notice that if the stock were to advance dramatically over a 12-month period, the convertible would increase in value for a gain of $34,082 that is determined by the then stock price of $88⅞. Since a short sale was made at $59¼, a loss of $8,886 has also been registered. In addition, interest has been earned on the convertible, and any stock dividends must be paid for to arrive at the total profit of $32,946 on the hedge position. It is estimated that this investment would realize a 29 percent return on investment.

A bullish hedge is set up to prevent losses if the stock declines in value rather than increases as the investor had hoped. With the stock showing a sizable loss of 50 percent, the benefit of stock hedging becomes evident. The convertible decreases in value as the stock declines, but at a much lower rate. As shown in the profit-and-loss estimate, the convertible realizes a $21,571 loss because of the decline in the value of the stock. The short sale of stock now realizes a profit of $8,886, offsetting a large portion of the convertible's loss. The interest on the convertible provides the balance for a total loss of only $4,935, which is negligible considering the dramatic decline of the stock.

## F I G U R E   14–2

Convertible Stock Hedge Profiles

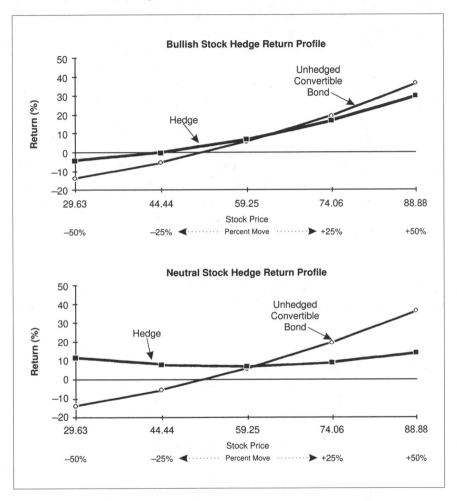

A bullish hedge trades the upside potential of the stock for increased downside safety. Figure 14–2 illustrates the profit profile of the convertible stock hedge. Notice how the hedge alters the convertible bond profit profile, providing less upside potential for greater downside safety. Varying the number of shares sold short can further modify the profit profile.

## Neutral Hedge

Figure 14–2 also presents the profit profile for a neutral hedge. The amount of stock sold short has been increased to 900 shares. This provides for a suitable return over a wide range of stock prices and does not depend on the stock either increasing or decreasing. The neutral hedge is most effective when the interest yield on the convertible is attractive and the investor is seeking protection against fluctuating stock prices.

## Bearish Hedge

For a bearish investor, the convertible stock hedge with a bearish bias can be a low-risk way to participate in declining stock prices. The investor can establish a bearish position by increasing the short sale to nearly the full amount of 1,500 shares, as shown in Figure 14–1. If the investor is correct and the stock declines by 50 percent, the position should realize a 30 percent profit because the gain on the short sale of stock more than offsets the loss on the convertible. The investor would incur a small loss if he or she was incorrect and the stock rose dramatically instead of falling in price. The profile is shown in Figure 14–3.

## F I G U R E  14–3

Convertible Stock Hedge Profiles

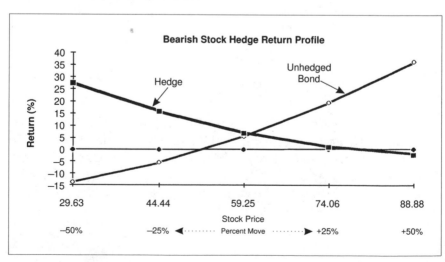

## Convertible Stock Hedge: Leveraged

Like any investment technique, how convertible hedging is used is more important than broad generalizations about its risks and rewards. Even the use of leverage can be relatively safe if done intelligently. Figure 14–4 shows the same position used earlier, but with 50 percent leverage (in this case, leverage means the investor used credit to finance the long position). The initial margin requirement for convertibles is usually the same as for stocks, and here it is assumed to be 50 percent. The initial investment becomes $56,000, with the remainder borrowed from the broker, who

**F I G U R E  14–4**

Convertible Stock Hedge: Leverage

XYZ 7.75—03/01/1996
Investment
  Long Position:
    Cash Investment        $112,000
    50% Margin                56,000
    Initial Investment      $ 56,000

  Short Position:
    Short Sale          300 shares at $59.25 = $17,750 credit
    Margin Requirement  0

| Percent Change | –50% | –25% | 0 | +25% | +50% |
|---|---|---|---|---|---|
| Assumed Stock Price | 29.63 | 44.44 | 59.25 | 74.06 | 88.88 |
| Est. Conv. Price | 90.43 | 99.65 | 112.00 | 127.48 | 146.08 |
| Total Return | –11.5% | –3.3% | 6.9% | 21.6% | 38.2% |
| *Bullish Hedge* | | | | | |
| Risk/Reward Analysis | | | | | |
| Profit/Loss on Conv. | (21,571) | (12,350) | 0 | 15,477 | 34,082 |
| Profit/Loss on Stock | 8,886 | 4,443 | 0 | (4,443) | (8,886) |
| Bond Interest | 7,750 | 7750 | 7,750 | 7,750 | 7,750 |
| Stock Dividends Paid | 0 | 0 | 0 | 0 | 0 |
| Margin Interest | (2,950) | (3,490) | (3,920) | (4,460) | (5,400) |
| Total Profit or Loss | (7,885) | (3,647) | 3,830 | 14,324 | 27,546 |
| Return on Investment | –14% | –7% | 7% | 26% | 49% |

Source: Calamos Convertible Evaluation System.

charges interest. The interest charge will vary depending on the debit balance in the account. The debit balance is affected by the mark-to-market requirement on the short position, as discussed earlier; interest costs vary due to the mark-to-market requirement. The debit balance is automatically being reduced in a declining market while it increases in a rising market. The worksheet takes this into account to arrive at the proper estimate of profit and loss of the hedge position.

Even with a leveraged position, varying the short position effectively controls downside risk. It's interesting that, on a risk/reward basis, a leveraged position using the convertible stock hedge technique has less risk than owning the stock outright on a cash basis. The cash-basis investor would receive a 50 percent increase for a 50 percent move in the stock, whereas the convertible hedger would receive 49 percent. If the stock decreases 50 percent, the cash basis investor would obviously lose 50 percent; on the other hand, the convertible position would show a loss of only 14 percent, as shown in Figure 14–5. Notice how the profit profile of the leveraged position overlaid on the cash-basis stock position shows nearly the same upside potential and less downside risk.

## F I G U R E  14–5

Convertible Stock Hedge: Leverage Profit Profile

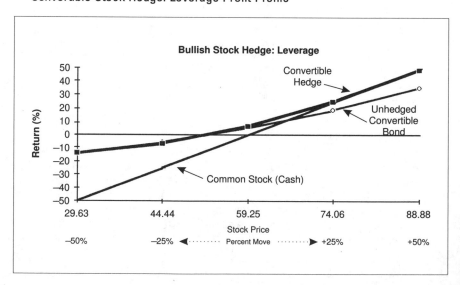

## PITFALLS OF THE CONVERTIBLE STOCK HEDGE

We have concentrated thus far on the rewards of convertible hedging. The convertible stock hedge offers flexibility in designing a profit profile to match the investor's particular objective. Unfortunately, there are also pitfalls. The convertible stock hedge profit profile is based on a number of assumptions that must be evaluated. Some of the same assumptions about convertibles that were discussed previously, including changing interest rates, changing fundamentals of the company, and other factors, all affect the price estimate of the convertible price track. In some respects, they need to be considered even more carefully with convertible hedging.

For example, if a convertible stock hedge were set up with the convertible having a reasonable conversion premium of 15 percent, and a takeover attempt on the stock ensued, the convertible hedge could show an immediate loss of the conversion premium (15 percent). This can occur because often the only way the convertible holder can participate in the takeover is to convert to the underlying common stock. The worst case for the holder of an unhedged convertible would probably be an *opportunity* loss, whereas the convertible hedge holder could have *real* losses on both sides of the hedge.

Because of its conservative nature, leverage can be applied to the convertible stock hedge to allow the investor to become more speculative. In fact, some hedge funds apply 90 percent leverage using this technique.[1] The problem with this much leverage is that a slight miscalculation can result in significant periodic losses. Hedge funds using this technique with very high margins can see their equity reduced substantially as volatility increases, bid and ask spreads widen, and conversion premiums collapse. This occurred in the fall of 1987, the stock market collapse during the recession of 1990, and the bond market correction of 1994.

Other risks include the forced buy-in of a short position and closing out the convertible hedge at a time dictated by the buy-in rather than the investor's desires. There are also costs of setting up and closing the hedge, involving not only the commissions for executing the trades but also the spread between the bid and ask prices. The spreads between securities vary greatly from issue to issue and are among the uncertainties investors must cope with. When using leverage, these costs are amortized over a smaller initial investment and become an even larger factor.

Convertibles may seem very liquid at one price level and extremely illiquid at lower prices. This is especially true of below-investment-grade securities issued by small companies. If the decreasing stock price is due to changing fundamentals of the company, the estimate of the convertible price track probably will not hold, causing a greater loss on the convertible than anticipated. Although the convertible will not decrease at a greater rate than the common stock, when using the convertible stock hedge with a bearish profile it is disconcerting to find that the short sale profit is offsetting the convertible bonds' decline in value.

Investors must view the convertible stock hedge as an intermediate- to long-term investment. It would be very unusual to realize large losses in a convertible stock hedge portfolio, even if actual portfolios varied from the estimates. Time is needed to amortize the costs of setting up the position and the spread of the securities. An important aspect of the total return is the convertibles' yield component and, obviously, time needs to pass to earn that interest. Although complex, a convertible stock hedge is an effective technique for achieving above-average returns while controlling risk—over a reasonable length of time.

## HEDGING CONVERTIBLES WITH STOCK OPTIONS

Not every convertible security can be set up as a convertible stock hedge, so the convertible hedger seeks additional ways to control risk. When the underlying common stock has listed stock options available, additional hedging techniques apply. We also assume that the reader is familiar with the basic principals and the risks and rewards of stock options.[2] Our goal here is not to detail option hedging but to show how stock options, combined with convertibles, can give an investor another means to control risk.

A call option gives the holder the right to buy the underlying stock at a specified price, called the *exercise price*, for a specified period of time, until the *expiration date*. Each contract is standardized at 100 shares of stock, and the cost of the contract is called the *option premium*.

Call options may be sold, or *written*, against stocks; this is called *covered call writing*. The option writer receives the option premium and is obligated, if and when assigned an exercise, to deliver stock according to the terms of the contract. Only the option buyer can exercise an option.

## Convertible Call Option Hedge

Many companies that issue convertibles have stock options listed on the option exchanges. Unfortunately, not every convertible can be used effectively with options. How they are used is largely determined by a worksheet analysis, which shows both the potential profit and the potential loss of the position. There are no simple rules of thumb to make this process less time-consuming.

*The Mechanics* Each convertible bond converts to a specified number of shares of the underlying common stock. As long as the number of call options written against the underlying stock represented by the convertible is no greater than the amount of shares into which the convertible can be converted, the options are considered covered. A covered option against a convertible requires no margin and can be accomplished in the cash account of the investor's brokerage account. The option premium is immediately available to the investor and can be used to reduce the initial cost of a convertible option position.

   If the option is exercised against the convertible holder, he or she can either convert to stock and deliver against the exercise or buy the stock on the exercise day to cover the sale. The decision is based on which choice offers the better economic advantage. Most often the investor would buy the stock and sell the convertible security to cover the exercise. The convertible may have accrued interest, as well as some conversion premium. Both factors should be considered before converting to deliver for an exercise.

## Convertible Option Hedge: Risk/Reward

To determine whether a convertible option hedge has a suitable profit potential, the investor can rely on the convertible option worksheet. Figure 14–6 shows an abbreviated worksheet similar to that shown with convertible stock hedging. Again, the more detailed analysis of the basic convertible is not discussed here but should not be ignored. For illustrative purposes we will cover only the hedging position and assume that the detailed analysis of the convertible has already been accomplished.

   The initial investment for the now infamous XYZ convertible bond is $103,600. This represents the purchase of the bonds for $112,000 and the option premium received of $8,400. The 100 bonds

**F I G U R E  14–6**

Convertible Call Option Hedge

XYZ—7.75% as of 03/01/1996

| | | |
|---|---|---|
| Common Stock Market Price | = | $59.25 |
| Convertible Market Price | = | 112.00% |
| Call Option Premium | = | $5.25 |
| Conversion Ratio | = | 16.44 shares |
| Expiration Date | = | 7.20 months |

*Covered Hedge:*

| | | |
|---|---|---|
| 100 @ $1,120.00 | = | $112,000 |
| 16 calls sold @ $525.00 | = | $ 8,400 |
| Initial Investment | = | $103,600 |

*Specified Hedge:*

| | | |
|---|---|---|
| 100 @ $1,120.00 | = | $112,000 |
| 10 calls sold @ $525.00 | = | $ 5,250 |
| Initial Investment | = | $106,750 |

| | –50% | –25% | 0 | Exercise | +25% | +50% |
|---|---|---|---|---|---|---|
| Assumed Stock Price | 29.63 | 44.44 | 59.25 | 65.00 | 74.06 | 88.88 |
| Estimated Conv. Price | 90.43 | 99.65 | 112.00 | 117.00 | 127.48 | 146.08 |
| *Covered Hedge:* | | | | | | |
| Profit/Loss on Conv. | (21,570) | (12,350) | 0 | 5,636 | 15,477 | 34,082 |
| Profit/Loss on Call | 8,400 | 8,400 | 8,400 | 8,400 | (6,100) | (29,800) |
| Bond Interest | 4,650 | 4,650 | 4,650 | 4,650 | 4,650 | 4,650 |
| Total Profit or Loss | (8,520) | (700) | 13,050 | 18,686 | 14,027 | 8,932 |
| Return on Investment % | (8) | (1) | 13 | 18 | 14 | 9 |
| Annual ROI (.60 years) % | (14) | (1) | 21 | 30 | 23 | 14 |
| *Specified Hedge:* | | | | | | |
| Profit/Loss on Conv. | (21,571) | (12,350) | 0 | 5,636 | 15,477 | 34,082 |
| Profit/Loss on Call | 5,250 | 5,250 | 5,250 | 5,250 | (3,813) | (18,625) |
| Bond Interest | 4,650 | 4,650 | 4,650 | 4,650 | 4,650 | 4,650 |
| Total Profit or Loss | (11,671) | (2,450) | 9,900 | 15,536 | 16,314 | 20,107 |
| Return on Investment % | (11) | (2) | 9 | 15 | 15 | 19 |
| Annual ROI (.60 years) % | (18) | (4) | 15 | 24 | 25 | 31 |

Source: Calamos Convertible Evaluation System.

represent 1,640 shares of common stock, so 16 call option contracts (each contract equals 100 shares) were sold on a covered basis.

The price range of the common stock must be estimated to properly determine the profit/loss on the position. The exercise price of the option and the price of the options at various levels are also important factors. Figure 14–6 illustrates how the option price would change at different stock prices. The profit/loss estimate of the position is calculated on the expiration date of the option, when the option contract must be closed; that becomes an important time period in which to calculate the profit/loss estimates.

The option price is a straightforward calculation. The option will be at its intrinsic value on expiration date. If the stock price is *below* the exercise price, the option will be worthless. If the stock price is *above* the exercise price, then the option will be worth the stock price minus the exercise price. With this and previously discussed convertible factors in mind, the investor can complete the profit/loss estimates. The return on investment (ROI) is calculated to the exercise date and then annualized. Both the ROI and the annualized ROI are important considerations in determining if this is a suitable hedge position. Annualized ROI for an option position allows comparison between various option positions. Since options expire at different times throughout the year, the annualized ROI will give an indication as to which position provides the better opportunity. On the other hand, the annualized number assumes that option premium levels remain the same and that the investor will be able to sell the option at the same premium level again and again—which is frequently not the case. Therefore, both ROIs become important in assessing the profit opportunity.

Notice the profit potential of the position over the wide range of stock prices. If the stock remains near its current level, the profit potential is excellent—the returns shown in this example are not unusual. Also notice how the profit is reduced if the stock increases dramatically to 88⅞. This happens because the conversion premium of the convertible decreases as the stock increases. Any conversion premium must erode as the stock increases in value; this factor is important in determining the number of calls to sell against a convertible security. If the convertible security has a high conversion premium, selling covered calls could result in an upside loss. This is another reason the convertible option worksheet is a necessity.

### F I G U R E  14–7

Convertible Option Hedge Profit Profiles

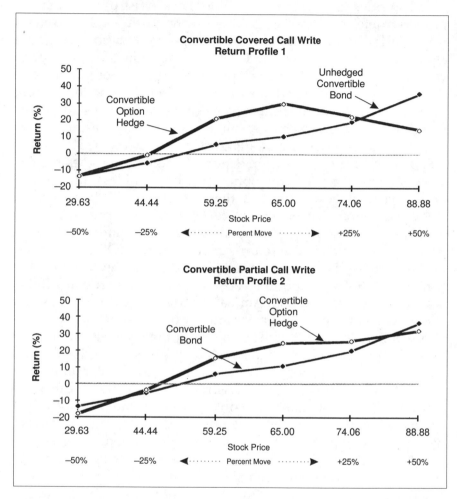

In the example shown, the return is stabilized at a stock price of 88⅞. The option hedge would show similar returns no matter how much the stock increased above 88⅞. This is shown in the profit profile graph in Figure 14–7. Notice how the profit is the maximum at the exercise price then gradually decreases as the stock varies from that point. A good measure of downside safety is provided by the option premium income, interest earned on the convertible, and the fact that the convertible declines at a lesser rate than the common stock. For a dramatic decline of 50 percent in the common stock, the convertible option hedge covered basis shows an annualized loss of only 15 percent. For a more likely stock decline of 25 percent, the convertible option hedge breaks even.

Figure 14–8 shows a worksheet using covered call writing against common stock. When comparing this situation to that of the convertible option hedge, it is evident that the convertible option hedge provides a superior risk/reward opportunity. Figure 14–9 illustrates the relationship. The upside potential is greater when using the common stock instead of the convertible bond, but there is little reduction in risk. The convertible option hedge provides a better balance between reward on the upside and additional downside safety. In addition, by varying the number of calls written (partial covered option hedge), the profit profile can be altered to provide greater upside potential.

**F I G U R E  14–8**

Common Stock Covered Call Option Hedge

XYZ—Common Stock
Covered Hedge: 1600 @ 1120 = $94,800
              16 calls sold @ 500.25 = $8,400

|  | –50% | –25% | 0 | Exercise | +25% | +50% |
|---|---|---|---|---|---|---|
| Assumed Stock Price | 29.63 | 44.44 | 59.25 | 65.00 | 74.06 | 88.88 |
| Profit/Loss on Stock | (47,400) | (23,700) | 0 | 9,200 | 23,700 | 47,400 |
| Profit/Loss on Call | 8,400 | 8,400 | 8,400 | 8,400 | (6,100) | (29,800) |
| Dividend Income | 0 | 0 | 0 | 0 | 0 | 0 |
| Total Profit or Loss | (39,000) | (15,300) | 8,400 | 17,600 | 17,600 | 17,600 |
| Return on Investment | (45.1) | (17.7) | 9.7 | 20.4 | 20.4 | 20.4 |
| Annual ROI (.60 years) % | (75.1) | (29.5) | 16.2 | 34.0 | 34.0 | 34.0 |

Note: Initial Investment: $94,800 less $8400 = $86,400
Source: Calamos Convertible Evaluation System.

Convertible Option Hedge Profit Profiles

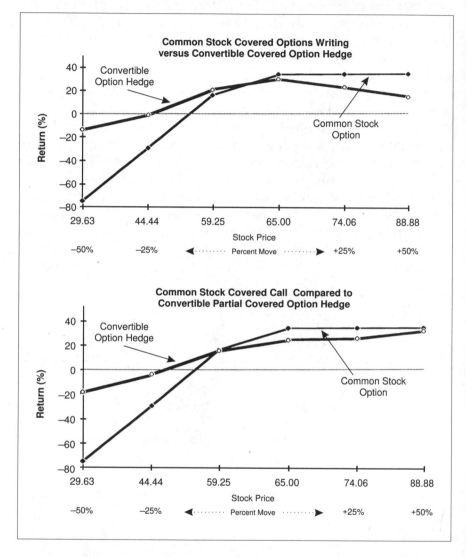

## Other Convertible Stock-Option Strategies

In addition to stock options on calls, there are also stock put options. Because puts give the investor the right to sell the stock for a specific price over a specified time period, put options increase in value as the stock decreases from its exercise price. Put options could be purchased with convertibles to provide additional downside protection., and some combination of covered calls and put purchases could provide attractive risk/reward opportunities. There are many variations of the convertible option-hedging theme, each with its own particular advantages, and these strategies are discussed in Chapter 15.

## SUMMARY

Convertible hedging with stock options provides some interesting opportunities. On the other hand, monitoring and selecting the correct investment situation is very time-consuming. Stock options are often illiquid and have wide spreads, which can cause additional frustration in executing transactions. Nevertheless, a wide variety of stock options exist, and the convertible option hedge, once discovered, can result in excellent profit opportunities.

## E N D N O T E S

1. Regulation T, NASD Rules of Fair Practice Section 30, Appendix A, Section 4 (8)(b).
2. For a basic understanding of listed stock options, consult the risk disclosure booklet titled *Characteristics and Risks of Standardized Options*, available from the Options Clearing Corporation, the options exchange, or any broker dealing in listed stock options. An excellent source for detailed information on advanced option strategies is *Option Pricing and Strategies in Investing*, by Richard M. Bookstaber.

# 15

## CHAPTER

# Convertible Hedging with Put Options

## MANAGING RISK WITH PUT OPTIONS

Chapter 14 discussed call options on stock but also introduced put options on stock. Put options can be purchased with convertibles to provide additional downside protection, and some combination of covered calls and put purchases can provide attractive risk/reward opportunities. There are many variations on the convertible option-hedging theme, each with its particular advantages.

Most investors accept the notion of call options, but put options at first glance seem confusing.

A put option gives the holder the right *to sell* the underlying stock at a specified price, called the *exercise price*, for a specified period of time, until the *expiration date*. Each contract represents 100 shares of stock, and the cost of the contract is called the option *premium*.

An investor may purchase a put option in hopes of profiting if the stock declines in value. Because a put option gives the investor the right to sell the stock for a specific price over a specified time period, the put gains in value as the stock trades below the option's exercise price. If the investor misjudged and the stock increased in value, the put option would become worthless at the time of expiration. The loss is limited to the cost of the put. A popular strategy in bull markets is to sell put options and thereby gain the option premium as the stock increases in value. This is a high-risk strategy because, as stocks decline, the put options will gain in value to create substantial losses. Our discussion will focus on the use of put options as a conservative defensive strategy to provide insurance against investment losses.

Put options can be thought of as insurance because they provide benefits if stocks decline and the insurance premium is paid for a specified period of time. The amount of protection desired by the investor is related to how much that protection will cost. Since many convertibles already have a level of protection because of their fixed-income attributes, the main benefit of using put options with convertibles is that the cost of downside protection can be reduced.

Put options with convertibles can give the investor additional flexibility to alter the profit profile of the overall investment. The purchase of put options becomes a cost factor that increases the initial investment. The cost of a put option is affected by many of the same factors that influence the convertible's price; the main difference is that the option market is much more sensitive to near-term volatility than the convertible market. Because of that, the put option can seem expensive when the stock experiences increasing near-term volatility. The investor should therefore consider carefully before using a put option.

The purchase of a convertible bond and a put on the underlying common stock illustrates how these options can be used effectively with convertibles. Again, the worksheet analysis is the best means to evaluate the risks and rewards of the strategy. Figure 15–1 under Profile A outlines the profit and loss on the purchase of 100 convertible bonds and 16 put options. The hedge ratio is equal to one because the 100 bonds represent 1,600 shares of stock and 16 puts also represent 1,600 shares of stock. (This is the same convertible bond illustrated in previous chapters.) Notice how the cost of the put seriously erodes the current yield on the convertible bond. Without the puts, the convertible's annual current yield would be 6.9 percent. If the stock remains at current levels, the current yield on the bond is reduced to an annualized rate of three percent. However, this yield does offset the cost of the puts.

**F I G U R E  15–1**

Convertible/Put Option: Hedge Ratio 1.0

XYZ Convertible Bond 7.75%—03/01/96
Put Option Expires 219 Days
Exercise Price of $55.00 and Market Price of $162.50 per Contract

| Hedge Position: 100 @ $1,120.00 per bond | = | $112,000 |
|---|---|---|
| 16 puts bought @ $162.50 per option | = | 2,600 |
| Initial investment | = | $114,600 |

*Profile A: Hedge Ratio of 1.0*

| Stock Price Range | –50% | –25% | Exercise | -0- | +25% | +50% |
|---|---|---|---|---|---|---|
| Assumed Stock Price | 29.63 | 44.44 | 55.00 | 59.25 | 74.06 | 88.88 |
| Est. Conv. Price | 90.43 | 99.65 | 108.05 | 112.00 | 127.48 | 146.08 |
| | | | | | | |
| Prof./Loss on Conv. | (21,570) | (12,350) | (3,950) | 0 | 15,480 | 34,080 |
| Prof./Loss on Put | 38,000 | 14,300 | (2,600) | (2,600) | (2,600) | (2,600) |
| Bond Interest | 4,650 | 4,650 | 4,650 | 4,650 | 4,650 | 4,650 |
| Total Profit or Loss | 21,080 | 6,600 | (1,900) | 2,050 | 17,530 | 36,130 |
| Return on Investment % | 18.4 | 5.8 | (1.7) | 1.8 | 15.3 | 31.5 |
| Annual ROI (.60 yrs) % | 30.7 | 9.6 | (2.8) | 3.0 | 25.5 | 52.5 |

Source: Calamos Convertible Evaluation System.

With this hedge, the investor is, ironically, most vulnerable to loss if the stock declines slightly and remains at the exercise price of the put option. At that level, the put expires worthless and the convertible declines from $1,120.00 to $1,085.00. Because the interest income did not overcome the price decline of the convertible and the cost of the puts, the position shows its maximum loss at an annual rate of a negative 2.8 percent. Even with the cost of the puts, the upside potential of this position remains attractive. If the stock were to increase 50 percent over the life of the option, this position would increase 31.5 percent. The value of the put is evident if the stock were to decline significantly over that same period of time. This position would gain 18.4 percent for a 50 percent decline in the common stock price. Figure 15–2 graphs the profit profile of this position. Notice that the position experiences losses if the stock declines slightly, but profits can be realized if the stock moves dramatically up or down.

**F I G U R E  15–2**

Convertible/Put Option: Profit Profile A

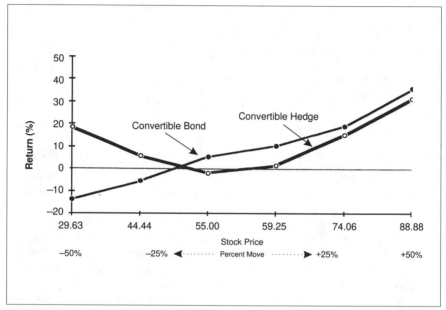

Note: Returns based on option's period of time to expiration.

This technique works well with convertibles because it provides an additional level of safety. Convertibles allow expenses to be controlled. The cost to provide this amount of safety using common stock and puts would be prohibitive. Figure 15–3 sets up a common stock position with the purchase of put options. Common stock is used instead of the convertible, but all other factors remain the same. Notice how expensive the program becomes. At the exercise price of 55, the annualized return on investment using common stock is a negative 16.1 percent, compared to a negative 1.7 percent for the convertible hedge.

Figure 15–4 lists the AROI and compares the strategies. The common stock strategy provides greater upside potential but does not provide sufficient downside safety. The convertible provides a balanced return over the complete spectrum of stock prices. Figure 15–5 illustrates the advantage of using a convertible put option hedge rather than the common stock put option position. It depicts

## F I G U R E  15–3

### Common Stock/Put Option Hedge

XYZ Common Stock—Dividend Yield  0%
Put Option Expires 219 days
Exercise Price of $55.00 and market price of $162.50 per contract

Hedge Position: 1,600 shares @ $59.25 per share       = $94,800
16 puts bought @ $162.50 per share                    =   2,600
Initial Investment                                    = $97,400

*Profile A:*

| Stock Price Range | –50% | –25% | Exercise | 0 | +25% | +50% |
|---|---|---|---|---|---|---|
| Assumed Stock Price | 29.63 | 44.44 | 55.00 | 59.25 | 74.06 | 88.88 |
| | | | | | | |
| Profit/Loss on Stock | (47,400) | (23,700) | (6,800) | 0 | 23,700 | 47,400 |
| Prof./Loss on Put | 38,000 | 14,300 | (2,600) | (2,600) | (2,600) | (2,600) |
| Dividend Income | 0 | 0 | 0 | 0 | 0 | 0 |
| Total Profit or Loss | (19,400) | (19,400) | (9,400) | (2,600) | 21,100 | 44,800 |
| Return on Investment % | (9.7) | (9.7) | (9.7) | (2.7) | 21.7 | 46.0 |
| Annual ROI /(.60 yrs) % | (16.1) | (16.1) | (16.1) | (4.5) | 36.1 | 76.7 |

Source: Calamos Convertible Evaluation System.

## F I G U R E  15–4

### Put Hedging Common Stock versus Convertible

| Stock Price Range | –50% | –25% | Exercise | -0- | +25% | +50% |
|---|---|---|---|---|---|---|
| Assumed Stock Price | 29.63 | 44.44 | 55.00 | 59.25 | 74.06 | 88.88 |
| AROI % Stock | (16.1) | (16.1) | (16.1) | (4.5) | 36.1 | 76.7 |
| AROI % Convertible | 30.7 | 9.6 | (2.8) | 3.0 | 25.5 | 52.5 |

Source: Calamos Convertible Evaluation System.

the extra advantage the convertible provides on the downside. Because the convertible declines less than the common stock, it provides a handsome profit, while the stock position shows a serious loss.

## F I G U R E  15–5

Profit Profile Put Option Hedges—Common Stock versus Convertible

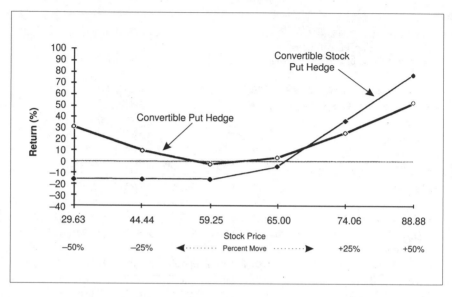

The versatility of the convertible put option hedge lies in the investor's flexibility to vary the hedge ratio. For example, instead of using a hedge ratio of 1.0, the position could be given a bullish tilt by using fewer put options. Figure 15–6 illustrates the convertible put option hedge with a hedge ratio of .63.[1] Ten put options are purchased to protect the convertible bond investment. This reduces costs in a sideways market while still retaining adequate downside protection. Should the stock decrease 25 percent, this position shows a break-even while providing significant upside gains. Figure 15–7 depicts the profit profile of the position. The convertible investor can design the hedge for his or her desired profit profile.

The convertible put option hedge can be extremely useful. It can protect a profit in a convertible that had been previously purchased. The protection can be added or removed independently of the convertible position. The drawback of the strategy is that option premium levels vary from issue to issue. Premium levels also vary due to general market volatility and can be extremely expen-

**F I G U R E  15–6**

Convertible Put Option Hedge

XYZ Convertible Bond 7.75%—03/01/96
Put Option Expires 219 days
Exercise Price of $55.00 and market price of $162.50 per contract

| | | |
|---|---|---|
| Hedge Position: 100 @ $1,120.00 per bond | = | $112,000 |
| 10 puts bought @ 4,162.50 per option | = | 1,625 |
| Initial investment | = | $113,625 |

*Profile B: Hedge Ratio of .63*

| Stock Price Range | –50% | –25% | Exercise | -0- | +25% | +50% |
|---|---|---|---|---|---|---|
| Assumed Stock Price | 29.63 | 44.44 | 55.00 | 59.25 | 74.06 | 88.88 |
| Est. Conv. Price | 90.43 | 99.65 | 108.05 | 112.00 | 127.48 | 146.08 |
| Profit/Loss on Conv. | (21,570) | (12,350) | (3,950) | 0 | 15,480 | 34,080 |
| Profit/Loss on Put | 23,750 | 8,938 | (1,625) | (1,625) | (1,625) | (1,625) |
| Bond Interest | 4,650 | 4,650 | 4,650 | 4,650 | 4,650 | 4,650 |
| Total Profit or Loss | 6,830 | 1,238 | (925) | 3,025 | 18,505 | 37,105 |
| Return on Investment % | 6.0 | 1.1 | (0.8) | 2.7 | 16.3 | 32.7 |
| Annual ROI (60 years) % | 10.0 | 1.8 | (1.4) | 4.4 | 27.1 | 54.4 |

Source: Calamos Convertible Evaluation System.

sive at times. Hedging with slightly out-of-the-money options, as illustrated in the preceding examples, can reduce costs, but close attention to premium levels is required to execute the strategy successfully. In addition, many stock options are often illiquid, with wide spreads between the bid and ask prices. This has been particularly true since the introduction of index options.

## MANAGING PORTFOLIO RISK WITH INDEX PUT OPTIONS

Index options provide an additional hedging tool for the convertible investor. In March 1983, the S&P 100 Index was launched under its original name, the CBOE 100, and many other indexes have been introduced over the years. Index options have the

## F I G U R E  15–7

Profit Profile B Convertible/Put Option Hedge Graph

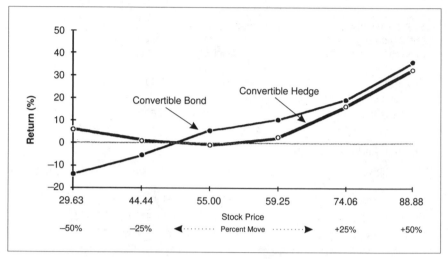

Note: Returns based on option's period of time to expiration.

standardized features of listed stock options, except that when an index option is exercised, the holder receives the cash value instead of securities. Index options can be either calls or puts.[2] Our discussion will center on the use of index puts as a means to hedge convertible portfolios.

An index put option is a contract to sell the index value at a specified price (the exercise price) for a specified period of time (up until the expiration date). Each contract is for 100 shares of the index. Therefore, if the index is at 200, each contract represents $20,000 in stock value. The index put option gains in value as the index falls below its exercise price. The market value of the index put at any specific time is called its premium.

A number of index put features make them effective vehicles for controlling market risk in convertible portfolios:

- ◆ Takeovers, tender offers, and other events peculiar to individual companies do not affect index options.
- ◆ Convertible swaps within the portfolio can be made without interfering with the desired hedge ratio.

- The index's volatility can be estimated much more accurately than that of individual stock positions. Fair value prices can be easily determined for index options.

- Because of the cash settlement of index options and the liquidity of the index option market, transaction costs are lower.

- Index options expire monthly, giving additional flexibility to hedge the portfolio; many individual stock options use a three-month cycle.

- Many index options have been introduced, allowing investors to select the one appropriate for their particular needs.

Combining index put options with convertibles is an effective way to hedge the entire portfolio. The most difficult risk factor for investors to hedge against is systematic risk. Index put options give investors a way to control the systematic risk of convertible portfolios. As with all hedging techniques, there are trade-offs that must be measured; for instance, how much do you sacrifice in potential returns for that risk reduction? Blindly buying puts without the detailed analysis needed to evaluate the accompanying costs will not produce favorable returns. Returns will most likely be based on chance rather than a systematic evaluation process. The evaluation process cannot be ignored because the associated costs with hedging portfolios can be substantial.

## Convertible Portfolio Index Option Hedge

Hedging is an attempt to avoid or lessen loss by making counterbalancing investments. The objective of the convertible portfolio index option hedge is to achieve higher risk-adjusted rates of return than might be expected if the portfolio remained unhedged. In this section, we will develop the methodology to evaluate hedged convertible portfolios. Conceptually, put options should increase in value to offset any decrease in value of the convertibles. A properly hedged position should provide good protection in the declining phase while not significantly jeopardizing the profit potential in advancing markets. Proper analysis shows that overestimating the hedge ratio can result in a stagnated portfolio; it has the effect of trading dollars, whether the market advances or declines. The consequence of such a strategy is overall poor performance.

Figure 15–8 assumes a three-month holding period over which the investor chooses to hedge a common stock portfolio. The index put option provides good downside protection, but at the expense of both the dividend yield in a sideways market and some upside potential. Figure 15–8 illustrates the advantage of using index puts and the necessary steps that must be taken to determine the amount of hedging to be accomplished.

Figure 15–9 illustrates the theory of hedging with index puts by constructing the return profile of a typical fully-hedged convertible portfolio. With the index at 264, the unhedged portfolio

## F I G U R E 15–8

### Common Stock Portfolio

| Portfolio A: Common Stock | | | |
|---|---|---|---|
| Stock Market Change | –10% | 0 | +10% |
| Index Option Value | 180 | 200 | 220 |
| Portfolio Change | –7% | 0 | +7% |
| Portfolio Dividends | +1% | +1% | +1% |
| Unhedged Portfolio Returns | –6% | +1% | +8% |
| Portfolio B: Hedged with Index Put Options | | | |
| Stock Market Change | –10% | 0 | +10% |
| Index Option Value | 180 | 200 | 220 |
| Portfolio Change | –7% | 0 | +7% |
| Portfolio Dividends | +1% | +1% | +1% |
| Cost of Index Puts | –2% | –2% | –2% |
| Value of Puts | +10% | 0 | 0 |
| Hedged Portfolio Returns | +2% | –1% | +6% |

Portfolio Characteristics:
    Assumes three-month holding period.
    Dividend yield = 4% annually.
    Portfolio beta = .70.
    Index put option cost based on 2% per quarter.

Source: Calamos Asset Management, Inc.

## F I G U R E 15–9

Convertible Securities Index Option Hedge Return Profile

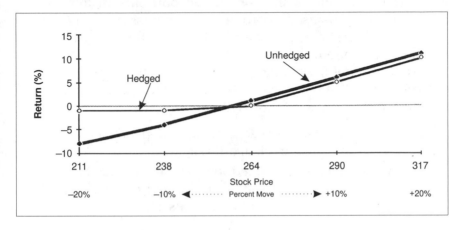

performs better than the hedged portfolio at the current level and above. The difference in the performance is the cost of the put protection. Should the index decrease in value, the hedged portfolio maintains its value except for the cost of the put premium. In practice, many steps are needed to execute the hedged strategy.

## Determining the Risk/Reward of the Convertible Portfolio

The first step is to determine the risk/reward of the convertible portfolio. The convertible portfolio summary provides needed data and conveniently measures the upside potential and downside risk of the portfolio. As discussed in previous chapters, both upside and downside betas are calculated for the entire portfolio on a dollar-weighted basis.

Projecting a portfolio's sensitivity to changes in a market index can be accomplished by calculating a weighted portfolio beta. These values can be useful in determining the effect and costs of index hedging. Figure 15–9 assumes that the upside beta of the hedged convertible portfolio is .70 and downside beta is .30. Therefore, the range of the portfolio value as compared to the market index can be easily determined. The second step is to determine the number of puts needed to protect the convertible portfolio.

Since the downside beta is .30, one has to buy only 30 percent of the puts needed for a common stock portfolio with a beta of 1.0 to offset the decline of the convertible portfolio. In this case, a hedge ratio of .30 is used to provide a near break-even, should the market index decline by 10 percent over the three-month period under consideration.

In the example illustrated in Figure 15–10, a number of assumptions must be reviewed to determine realistically the value of hedging convertible portfolios with index puts:

- The accuracy of the weighted betas depends on how the convertible price track is estimated.
- Interest rates are assumed to be stable over the three-month period, and the convertible portfolio is assumed to be well diversified to minimize unsystematic risk.

**F I G U R E  15–10**

Convertible Portfolio

| Portfolio A: Unhedged | | | |
|---|---|---|---|
| Stock Market Change | −10% | 0 | +10% |
| Index Option Value | 180 | 200 | 220 |
| Portfolio Change (Total Return) | −3.0% | 1.8% | +7.0% |
| Return on Investment | −3.0% | 1.8% | +7.0% |
| Portfolio B: Hedged with Index Put Options | | | |
| Stock Market Change | −10% | 0 | +10% |
| Index Option Value | 180 | 200 | 220 |
| Portfolio Change (Total Return) | −3.0% | 1.8% | +7.0% |
| Cost of Index Puts | −0.6% | −0.6% | −0.6% |
| Value of Puts | +3.0% | 0 | 0 |
| Hedged Portfolio Returns | −0.6% | +1.2% | +6.4% |

Portfolio Characteristics
Assumes three-month holding period.
Convertible upside beta is .70; downside beta is .30.
Index put option cost based on 2% per quarter.
Cost adjusted to provide near break-even on downside.

Source: Calamos Asset Management, Inc.

♦ Perhaps the most material assumption is the level of the put premiums. Premium levels can be measured by the implied volatility of the market.

Put premiums can vary significantly from period to period as market conditions change, making it difficult to estimate the cost of hedging the portfolio. Figure 15–11 indicates the changes in option premium levels for various indexes during 1987. Notice the extreme levels attained by these indexes over this relatively short period of time.

## Historical Perspective for Convertible Hedging with Index Puts

There is not a great deal of evidence on the performance of convertible hedging with index puts because they have only existed since early 1983. However, by backtracking we can estimate how a hedged convertible portfolio may have performed over various market cycles. Figure 15–12 traces the performance of convertibles back to the beginning of 1978. The quarterly performance on a total return basis is listed along with the Value Line Composite

**F I G U R E  15–11**

S&P 100 (OEX) Implied Volatility 1987

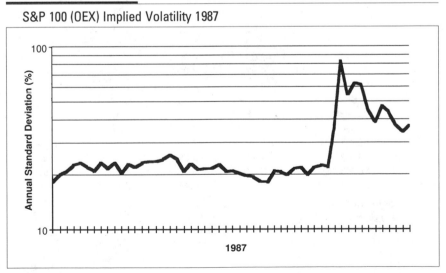

Note: Data January 1, 1987, through December 31, 1987.

**F I G U R E  15–12**

Convertible Hedging with Index Puts (quarterly percent changes)

| Year/Quarter | Convertibles (CAM)[1] | Value Line Index (XVL)[2] | Put Premium (%)[3] | Hedge Return (HDG 1) |
|---|---|---|---|---|
| 1979–4 | 4.36 | −1.00 | 2.41 | 2.59 |
| 1980–1 | −10.08 | −12.90 | 2.14 | 0.36 |
| 1980–2 | 17.50 | 16.50 | 1.74 | 15.50 |
| 1980–3 | 13.10 | 14.20 | 2.77 | 9.91 |
| 1980–4 | 1.40 | 2.10 | 2.62 | −1.61 |
| 1981–1 | 4.40 | 6.90 | 1.90 | 2.22 |
| 1981–2 | 5.00 | 0.60 | 1.66 | 3.09 |
| 1981–3 | −7.00 | −16.30 | 1.34 | 7.76 |
| 1981–4 | 8.50 | 6.20 | 1.51 | 6.76 |
| 1982–1 | −3.10 | −9.10 | 1.93 | 3.78 |
| 1982–2 | 2.10 | −3.80 | 1.70 | 3.95 |
| 1982–3 | 10.90 | 9.40 | 2.10 | 8.49 |
| 1982–4 | 12.80 | 20.50 | 2.86 | 9.51 |
| 1983–1 | 12.20 | 12.80 | 2.83 | 8.95 |
| 1983–2 | 7.40 | 14.20 | 2.56 | 4.46 |
| 1983–3 | −2.60 | −2.70 | 2.38 | −2.64 |
| 1983–4 | 0.20 | −2.40 | 2.10 | 0.19 |
| 1984–1 | −0.50 | −6.30 | 1.83 | 3.70 |
| 1984–2 | −2.70 | −5.20 | 1.83 | 0.40 |
| 1984–3 | 6.50 | 5.60 | 1.74 | 4.50 |
| 1984–4 | 3.50 | −2.40 | 1.83 | 3.80 |
| 1985–1 | 7.90 | 9.30 | 1.78 | 5.85 |
| 1985–2 | 7.10 | 1.50 | 1.91 | 4.90 |
| 1985–3 | −3.00 | −6.00 | 1.66 | 1.09 |
| 1985–4 | 9.87 | 7.60 | 2.27 | 7.26 |
| 1986–1 | 14.50 | 12.34 | 2.21 | 11.96 |
| 1986–2 | 3.40 | 2.08 | 3.54 | 1.41 |
| 1986–3 | −1.18 | −9.50 | 2.47 | 5.48 |
| 1986–4 | 2.71 | 3.93 | 5.10 | −3.16 |
| 1987–1 | 13.08 | 22.06 | 3.50 | 9.06 |
| 1987–2 | 1.16 | 5.99 | 3.90 | −3.33 |
| 1987–3 | 3.30 | 5.53 | 3.20 | −0.38 |
| 1987–4 | −12.80 | −24.48 | 2.80 | 8.46 |
| Average quarter return % | 3.94 | 2.34 | | 4.37 |
| Standard deviation | 7.12 | 10.46 | | 4.50 |
| Coefficient variation % | 180.76 | 446.91 | | 102.90 |

Notes:
[1] Convertible performance based on selected convertible portfolios.
[2] Value Line Index (XVL) has been used in this study; other indexes would show similar results.
[3] Put option premium is based on the implied volatility using the Black–Scholes option model.

Index. The cost of hedging (the put premium) is estimated using the Black–Scholes option model. Notice how these costs vary from quarter to quarter, with the lowest cost being 1.34 percent in the third quarter of 1981, rising to 5.10 percent for the fourth quarter 1986.

The data used in Figure 15–12 to estimate the put premium (cost of hedging) was prepared under the assumption that put options are purchased at the beginning of each quarter. At the end of the quarter they either expire worthless or are sold for their intrinsic value. We also assume that put options are purchased at exactly their strike price.

The convertible investor employing hedging strategies should understand that option premium levels might vary minute by minute. For example, in Figure 15–12, the fourth quarter 1987 hedging cost of 2.8 percent seemed inexpensive, considering the stock market action of October 19, but when the panic atmosphere pushed the put option premium to an exorbitant 20 percent, the costs made hedging prohibitive.

Figure 15–13 graphs these results against the Value Line Index and the unhedged portfolio. Observe how the hedged portfo-

**F I G U R E  15–13**

Index Option Portfolio Hedge Cumulative Return

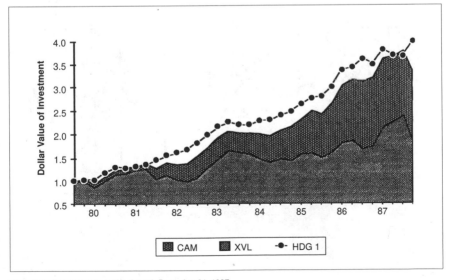

Note: Data September 31, 1979, through December 31, 1987.

lio has smoothed the returns over time. Figure 15–14 shows the returns on a quarter-by-quarter basis. The unhedged convertible portfolio reduces the peaks and troughs from the market index. The hedged convertible portfolio further reduces and eliminates many of the negative quarters.

In panel 1 of Figure 15–14, notice the high correlation between the Value Line Index (XVL) and the convertibles (CAM). Panels 2 and 3 indicate the favorable comparison of the hedged convertible portfolio (HDG 1) to both the XVL and the S&P 500.

Figure 15–15 graphs the risk-adjusted returns of the alternative investments. This illustrates the trade-off between upside potential and downside risk. The security market line is shown by the T-bill return and the S&P 500. With risk defined as the volatility of quarterly returns, the convertibles show higher returns at less risk than the stock market. The hedged convertible portfolio also reveals that the use of put options reduces risk further. It's clear that index puts allow convertible investors to fine-tune the

**F I G U R E  15–14**

Quarterly Returns

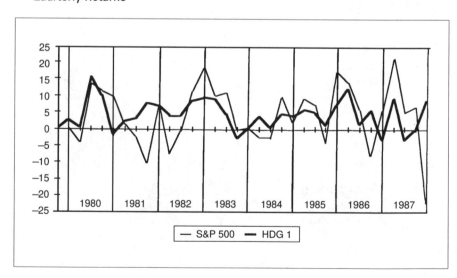

**F I G U R E  15–15**

Capital Market Line—September 30, 1979, through December 31, 1987

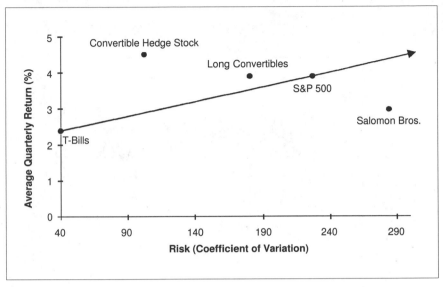

Notes:
  CAM—Calamos Asset Management, Inc.
  HDG 1—Calamos Asset Management with full hedge.
  S&P 500—Stock market proxy.
  Salomon Bros.—Bond market proxy.

risk/reward of a portfolio, control risk, and attain their investment objectives.

## SUMMARY

In the last two chapters, we have discussed the use of stock options and index options. Each has its own peculiar characteristics and can be used to control risk within the convertible portfolio. Premium levels and liquidity play an important part in whether the investor can effectively use these hedging techniques. Figure 15–16 shows the market share of both stock options and index options for all U.S. exchanges for the period 1984–87. Notice how the activity in stock options increased over that of index options during 1987. At times, writing options against convertible may not

### F I G U R E  15–16

Market Shares of Equity and Index Options—All U.S. Option Exchanges,
1987–1987

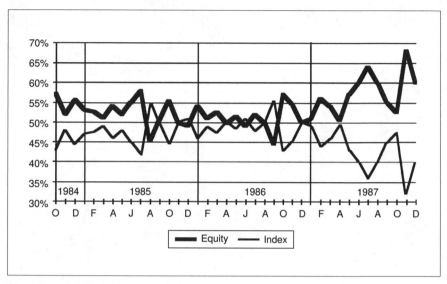

Source: The Options Clearing Corporation.

be attractive; at other times, it's extremely attractive. Market conditions play an important role in the availability of hedging opportunities, and the investor must be alert to them.

## E N D N O T E S

1. In the hedge ratio, 1 means the number of shares of stocks represented by the convertible is equal to the number of options. In this
   case, 1,000 shares/1,600 shares = .63.
2. For a basic understanding of listed stock options, consult *Characteristics and Risks of Standardized Options*, available from the Options
   Clearing Corporation, options exchanges, or any broker dealing in
   listed options.

# 16 CHAPTER

# Convertible Performance

When first introduced to convertibles, investors often feel that they are too good to be true. Convertibles provide the best of both worlds: fixed-income characteristics with stock market participation. As we have demonstrated in previous chapters, there is no doubt that a convertible provides a low-risk alternative to its underlying common stock. In particular situations, there is little question as to the value of a convertible compared to its stock counterpart. Does what seems obvious when talking about individual securities translate to the convertible market as a whole? It would be helpful for the investor to know how convertible securities have performed under different market conditions. Can convertible indexes provide such a view?

## USING INDEXES

During the 1980s, the convertible market grew dramatically; the investment community responded by introducing a number of convertible indexes to track the convertible market. Each firm that introduced an index wanted it to become the primary indicator of convertible performance, as the Dow Jones Industrial Average is the most popular quoted stock index.

Investment consultants favor indexes as a means of comparing the performance of convertible money managers. However, the problem with convertible indexes is that they are often poor benchmarks for performance. Convertibles should be selected on the basis of an individual investor's long-term objectives, especially since convertibles can be purchased as an alternative to the bond or stock market. Still, investors should examine the convertible market in detail, and the indexes are helpful to that end.

There are a number of problems with all indexes, despite their popularity, but the main problem is that most of them have a limited history. Convertible indexes were created in the mid-1980s and early 1990s, with some backtesting going back to 1982. Creating such an index after the fact is not an easy task. Indexes can be flawed simply by the way their calculations are accomplished. The indexes discussed here have been created by convertible research departments or advisory services.

## DOMESTIC INDEXES

### First Boston Convertible Securities Indexes

First Boston has introduced three convertible indexes: a general convertible index called the First Boston Convertible Securities Index, and two subindexes, the Convertible Bond Index and Convertible Preferred Index. The groundwork for these indexes was originally laid by the Harris Trust and Savings Bank of Chicago Trust, so little backtesting was required. The indexes begin in January 1982, with an initial price of 1,000. To be included in the index, domestic convertible bonds and convertible preferred stocks must have a Standard & Poor's rating of B– or better and an issue size of $50 million or more. Preferreds must have a minimum of 500,000 shares outstanding.

The index includes dollar-denominated Euroconvertibles issued by domestic companies. Those issues must also have a Standard & Poor's rating of B– or better, but the minimum size is $100 million. It consists of 328 issues with a market value of $63.9 billion as of December 1996.

At the beginning of each month, there is a new list of issues that satisfy the eligibility criteria. To be included in the index, issues must have a price at both the beginning and the end of the month. New issues in an active market have an important influence on the performance of the index, depending on when they are added or deleted.

All changes in the index are made at month end, except for issues whose call dates occur in the first 10 days of the month. In that case, they are deleted in the prior month. This may be unrealistic because calls have the near-term effect of depressing stock prices and causing an immediate loss of accrued interest. The prior month's closing price may not be an accurate measure for those few issues where the market has not anticipated the call. The indexes are capital-weighted. Each issue's price is multiplied by the dollar value of the securities outstanding.

Overall, the First Boston Convertible Indexes are well thought out and reflect available opportunities for institutional-size portfolios. Since large issues dwarf most of the issues included in the index, this may not represent how the large institutional money manger would construct a convertible portfolio, but it does demonstrate how the convertible market in general is reacting to different market conditions.

## Goldman Sachs Convertible Indexes

The Goldman Sachs Convertible 100 Index has provided continuous price and total return information on the U.S. convertible market since 1985. Performance for the Convertible 100 is calculated daily on both an equal- and market-weighted basis. Reporting both equal-weighted and market-capitalization-weighted values provides convertible investors and portfolio managers with the flexibility to choose a benchmark that best reflects their investing style.

In January 1998, the Convertible 100 Index was updated with a semiannual rebalancing methodology and fast add/delete rules to better represent the broader convertibles market in an accurate and timely fashion. The index includes the 100 largest balanced issues in the convertible universe, including bonds, preferred, and mandatory convertibles. The index is rebalanced twice a year and screens out issues with an equity market capitalization of less than $400 million, an equity premium greater than 100 percent, or parity value greater than 200 percent of the par value. From the remaining selection pool, the largest 100 securities are selected on the basis of amount outstanding. Limiting the index to 100 securities provides a statistically relevant representation of the overall market while maintaining the accuracy of the pricing information in the index. Between rebalancings, fast add/delete rules maintain the index for large new issues, redeemed securities, and convertibles that trade beyond the specified premium and parity boundaries.

Goldman Sachs publishes the index returns monthly, providing performance breakdowns by convertible type, credit ratings, and industry weightings. With its updated methodology and consideration for the changing nature of the convertible market, the Convertible 100 index provides investors with an accurate, objective and reliable benchmark for the U.S. convertible market.

## Salomon Brothers Convertible Indexes

Salomon Brothers offers an extensive set of convertible indexes, divided into two categories: the Salomon Brothers Convertible Securities Index (SBCSI) and the Salomon Brothers Broad Convertibles Index (SBBCI). The SBCSI is composed of four distinct modules: cash coupon convertible bonds, zero coupon convertible bonds, convertible preferreds, and DECS. Convertibles with limited upside such as PERCS and ELKS are included in the SBBCI along with all the modules in SBCSI. Convertible securities denominated in U.S. dollars issued by foreign corporations are currently classified as "Yankee" convertibles if their underlying stocks also trade in the United States.

The modular construction of the index increases its utility for investors with differing investment goals. Fixed-income investors can use the Convertible Bond Index, which includes cash-coupon and zero-coupon bonds, while income-oriented investors would use the Cash-Pay Convertible Index, which is SBCSI excluding zero-coupon bonds. The Salomon Brothers indexes can also provide important market information on yields, conversion premiums, and break-evens.

## Merrill Lynch Convertible Securities Indexes

Merrill Lynch first began tracking convertible performance in 1988 with its All U.S. Convertibles Index, plus a number of subindexes. This index was intended to be a comprehensive list of all U.S. convertibles, including all publicly traded U.S. issues of at least $25 million par value, and was calculated on a market-value basis. No selection criteria were used so that the index could serve as a market proxy.

Merrill expanded its indexes in 1995 in response to growth in the convertible market as well as growth in the number of different convertible structures in use. Mandatory conversion preferreds had a particular amount of influence on the market. Merrill expanded its convertible indexes again in 1997. Before 1997, indexes were constructed based on structural categories, quality classes, or liquidity grades, but the 1997 additions were based on specific performance factors such as U.S. convertibles within the first six months of issuance; U.S. convertibles with a stipulated equity capitalization size; and U.S. growth or value stock convertibles. Merrill Lynch now publishes 41 separate indexes that offer a very wide choice of criteria.

The characteristics of three of the indexes that apply to broad market segments are shown in Figure 16–1: Merrill Lynch All Qualities Index VXNO (excluding 144A); Merrill Lynch Investment-Grade Index V0A1 (excluding mandatories); and Merrill Lynch Speculative-Grade Convertible Bond Index, V0S2.

## Lipper Convertible Mutual Funds Average

In addition to the convertible securities indexes, Lipper also provides the Lipper Convertible Securities Fund Average, an index of mutual funds that manage convertibles. This index includes all types of convertible funds, including dual-purpose funds. Starting with 7 funds in 1976, it has grown to include 38 funds in 1996. Seeing as there has there been a meaningful number of convertible funds with which to create an index only since 1985, results of the years prior to 1984 may not be representative because of the small number of funds and the inclusion of a nonconvertible mutual fund in the index.

# F I G U R E  16-1

## Convertible Indexes

| | First Boston Convertible Securities | Goldman Sachs Convertible 100 Index | Merrill Lynch All Qualities Index VXNO (ex-144A) | Merrill Lynch Investment Grade Index V0A1 Ex-Mandatories | Merrill Lynch Speculative Grade Convertible bond Index V0S2 | Salomon Bros. Convertible Index |
|---|---|---|---|---|---|---|
| Beginning Date | Jan-82 | Jan-85 | Jan-94 | Jan-89 | Jan-87 | Jan-92 |
| Current Market Value | $63.9 billion | 41.3 billion | $86.5 billion | $34.4 billion | $25.9 billion | $106.1 billion |
| Number of Issues | 328 | 100 | 430 | 133 | 182 | 518 |
| Frequency of Calculation | Monthly | Daily | Daily | Daily | Daily | Monthly |
| Weighting | Market value | Both equal- and market-capitalization weighted | Market value | Market value | Market value | Market value |
| Euroconvertibles | | Must have 50% of underlying market cap in ADR form | No | Yes ??? | No | Yes |
| Convertible Preferreds | Yes, must have minimum 500K stock shares | Yes | Yes | Yes | No | Yes |
| Subjective Changes | | Rebalancings require <100% premium and <200% parity | Data screened for pricing anomalies | Data screened for pricing anomalies | Data screened for pricing anomalies | When to drop from index when mkt value drops < $50 mil |
| Capitalization Bias | large-cap | | 54% large cap | 77% large cap | Small-cap | Cap weighting results in large-cap bias; top 25 names (5%) account for 10–12% of perf. |
| Credit Quality Bias | | | 47% inv. grade; 45% spec. gr.; 8% nonrated | Only inv. grade | 100% spec. grade | Greater number of names in noninv. grade |
| Equity-Income Bias | | | | | | |
| Other Constraints | Initial price was 1,000 | | | No spec. grade/no unrated; no mandatories | No investment grade/no unrated | This is a function of the market |

Lipper also calculates a Lipper Convertible Securities Index, which includes only the top 30 funds in the convertible category. This index has an inception date of 1988. Since this index includes only the largest funds, one would suppose that those are the most successful funds. However, index results are only a few basis points higher than the average results.

Both the convertible mutual fund average and index are comprised of many different fund management styles. Many convertible funds use market timing and are not fully invested in convertibles. The mutual fund average includes a fund that for years invested only in nonconvertible, fixed-income securities, but that changed its name to include the word *convertible* because of the recent popularity of convertibles. Although it was not a convertible fund until mid-1987, this fund has been included in the average from its inception in 1976.

The index is further distorted by including funds with small initial investments on the same basis as fully invested, larger funds. The main problem with the index is its survivorship bias: If a convertible fund is eliminated from the index, Lipper takes it out of the index from its inception, grossly distorting historical returns. The funds that have been eliminated are the poorer performing funds; thus, Lipper is changing historical performance.

However, Lipper does provide many categories for comparing convertible mutual fund performance. The categories are based on size and investment objective and provide a means to compare relative performance.

## Value Line Convertible Index

The Value Line Convertible Indexes were introduced in March 1982. One index shows only price appreciation, while the other indicates performance on a total-return basis. Value Line has a long history of convertible research, and its index represents convertible performance in general. The indexes are based on the largest 585 convertibles that represent 90 percent of the convertible market *ex mandatory*.

The indexes are equally weighted and adjusted on a weekly basis. However, the index values are not calculated at the end of each month, making it difficult to compare this index with other market indexes. Individual investors could not possibly adopt the methodology used to construct this index since it would need to be adjusted weekly to reflect the equal-dollar weighting. Small issues have same weighting as large issues. The indexes are not capital-weighted.

The Value Line Convertible Indexes provide a good indication of how the average convertible is performing. They are not suitable for gauging the performance of a convertible portfolio because equally weighted issues provide a bias in favor of small issues over larger ones.

## GLOBAL INDEXES

Global indexes have features that make them even more complicated than domestic indexes. Chapter 7 discussed the wide differences between the various convertible markets around the world. Some, such as the Southeast Asian market, are very new and hence less efficient. Each has evolved separately, with widely varying norms due to the individual investment preferences of each country's investors. It would be unrealistic to try to compare market characteristics such as conversion premiums, yield to call or put, or coupon levels. Currency fluctuations can also distort performance, such as when an index is converted into U.S. dollars.

Even so, the global convertible market represents exciting investment opportunities, and several indexes have been created to try to track global performance. These indexes have short histories at the moment, but they at least provide a starting place.

### Merrill Lynch Convertible Indexes

Merrill Lynch introduced its global convertible indexes in August 1995. The Merrill series includes a world index (the Global 300) and seven subindexes (Global ex-U.S.; Global ex-US and ex-Japan; U.S.; Japan; Europe; Asia/Pacific; and Latin America). The Merrill indexes are weighted by capitalization and include both domestic markets and Euromarkets. However, the high market capitalization of the Japanese market results in a very high weighting to Japan (currently two-thirds of the Merrill Global 300 ex-U.S. index). The indexes go back to January 1, 1995 and are priced monthly.

## Jefferies Convertible Indexes

Jefferies Group, a U.S. broker, has issued the Jefferies Active Convertible Bond (JACI) World Index, a broad-based index comprising Euroconvertible bonds from around the world. The index is equal-weighted, calculated on a daily basis, and provides investors with a timely barometer of market performance. The index includes 144 of the most liquid Euroconvertible bonds out of the approximately 3,000 convertible bonds currently outstanding. All of the major regions of the world are represented in the index: Jefferies has issued other indexes that include exposure to most major convertible markets, including 10 subindexes (International; Europe and Far East; North America; Europe; Far East; Far East ex-Japan; Japan; U.S.; U.K.; and France). Data on the index are available from July 1992 to the present, although the indexes were first issued in mid-1995. They are available daily on Reuters and Bloomberg. The equal-weighted structure of the JACI makes it inappropriate as a performance benchmark. It also makes its country distribution quite distorted. For example, Japan constitutes only 14 percent of the JACI International Index, while the emerging markets account for 44 percent. It has a much shorter history than the Goldman Sachs Euroconvertible Index.

## Goldman Sachs

The Goldman Euroconvertible 75 represents the 75 largest Euroconvertibles by market cap. It includes U.S. issuers and no Japanese issuers; it also excludes domestic convertibles issued in the U.K. and Europe. It is heavily weighted towards the U.K. and France, and includes a significant weighting in southeast Asia and Latin America. Its heavy weighting in Europe (two-thirds) makes it a poor proxy for the overall international convertible market. It also suffered from being constructed as an equal-weighted index. Its big advantage is its history; it goes back to December 1987. It is priced monthly.

## Union Bank of Switzerland (UBS)

UBS introduced its global indexes in 1996 and included performance back to 1994. The UBS Global Index includes 351 issues, both domestic and Eurosecurities, bonds and preferreds, with an approximate market cap of $125 billion (versus their estimate of the world convertible market at $415 billion). Their International Index, which includes all parts of the globe except the United States, has 266 issues with an estimated market cap of $102 billion. The indexes are market-capitalization weighted.

Of all of the convertible indexes, the country weights of the UBS indexes are the most similar to those of the actual world equity markets. The UBS International index is very similar to the MSCI EAFE equity index, the most widely used international equity index. The UBS International index has a slightly lower weight in Europe than EAFE (48 versus 50 percent), a slightly higher weight in the emerging markets (11 versus 7 percent), and a very similar weight in Japan. The performance of the UBS index also tracks that of the EAFE index fairly well. The UBS results are total returns that take dividends into account.

Figure 16–2 compares three of the main global convertible indexes with the MSCI EAFE. The three convertible indexes are the Merrill lynch Global 300 ex-U.S. Index (G300, ex-U.S.); the Jefferies Active Convertible Bond World Index (JACI, which is ex-U.S.); the UBS Global Index ex-U.S.; and the MSCI EAFE. The figure shows the differences in region weights used for the indexes, as well as annual performance for 1995 and 1996.

The UBS index provides the most representative proxy of the performance of all convertible bonds around the world. However, like all the global indexes except the Goldman 75, it has a short history.

## SUMMARIZING CONVERTIBLE INDEXES

In general, convertible indexes provide a broad view of how the convertible market as a whole is reacting to various market conditions. Each index describes a particular aspect of the convertible market according to how the index was prepared. The different indexes have different index parameters and characteristics, including representation of market sectors (high- and low-cap companies), credit quality, and whether there is an equity or income bias.

The question remains whether any general convertible index, even a well-designed one like the First Boston Convertible Securi-

**F I G U R E  16–2**

Composition of Global Indexes

| | G30 Index (Ex-U.S.) | JACI Int'l | UBS Global (Ex-U.S.) | MSCI EAFE | |
|---|---|---|---|---|---|
| Developed mkts: | 89.29 | 55.78 | 88.78 | 92.60 | Europe, Japan, Australia, Canada |
| Emerging mkts: | 12.76 | 44.86 | 11.22 | 8.20 | |
| Europe | | | | | |
| Total | 28.10 | 41.03 | 48.04 | 50.10 | |
| Southeast Asia | | | | | |
| Total | 9.40 | 38.46 | 10.45 | 7.00 | |
| Latin America | | | | | |
| Total | 2.40 | 3.20 | 0.00 | 0.00 | |
| Other | | | | | |
| Japan | 60.00 | 14.10 | 40.20 | 39.50 | |
| Total | 60.10 | 17.31 | 41.51 | 42.90 | |
| Portfolio total | 100.00 | 100.00 | 100.00 | 100.00 | |

| Performance | 1995 | 1996 |
|---|---|---|
| UBS Global ex-U.S. | 14.18% | 4.46% |
| MSCI EAFE | 11.55% | 7.45% |
| Merrill G300 ex-U.S. | 12.00% | −0.90% |
| JACI Int'l | 16.94% | 9.88% |

Note: This chart shows the percentage representation of each region within each index, based on definitions used by Calamos Asset Management, Inc.

The performance comparison shows how widely the indexes can vary in results, based on index construction.

ties Index, should be used as a measure of performance for a convertible portfolio. Convertibles can be managed to achieve a particular investment objective. A random selection of convertibles does not indicate whether or not the investor was successful in achieving his or her investment goal. For example, an investor who pursues a low-risk equity strategy using convertibles may feel the objective has not been achieved when compared to a general convertible index. If interest rates and equity prices were to decline, the indexes would increase in value as the bond component of the convertibles rose as a result of lower interest rates. In all likelihood, the convertibles selected for lower-risk equity participation would increase very little and lag behind the general convertible indexes. On the other hand, this portfolio is unlikely to decline in accord with declining equity prices. In this circumstance, did the convertible investor achieve his or her objective? While the investor might regret the gains that occurred in portfolios with different structures, in fact this portfolio would have fulfilled its defensive objective.

On the other hand, the investor who constructs a convertible bond portfolio based on yield characteristics and is willing to forego much of the upside equity participation may lag behind the indexes in a strong stock market. It is more important to gear portfolio performance to the attainment of a particular investment objective rather than to a general index.

## LONG-TERM CONVERTIBLE PERFORMANCE

The definitive study of long-term convertible performance, "Convertibles Bonds as an Asset Class," a thorough analysis by Scott Lummer and Mark W. Riepe of Ibbotson Associates,[1] has helped displace many of the myths about convertible investing. This study has the additional benefit of extending over a long period of time and covering many market cycles, 1957 through 1995. None of the current indexes has that much history.

The study was sponsored by Goldman Sachs to provide an objective examination of convertible bond performance and determine whether the intuitive logic for convertible investing matched the empirical evidence. The study was updated through 1995, with the results outlined in a research publication by Goldman Sachs.[2] Their conclusions were as follows:

1. Over the period for which reliable long-run data are available (i.e., since the early 1970s), the total return performance of U.S. convertibles has virtually replicated that of the S&P 500, *but with significantly lower risk*.

2. Total return for convertible bonds has demonstrated a much higher correlation with the S&P 500 than with the corporate bond market.

3. Convertibles are useful in optimizing performance in both fixed-income and equity portfolios.

There are three possible reasons for the long-run outperformance of convertible instruments:

1. Exposure to a universe of underlying stocks with significantly higher beta than S&P 500 during a period of long-run excess returns from equities.

2. Ostensibly inefficient company timing in calling convertible instruments.

3. Attractive convertible pricing at issue.

The study dissected convertible performance over several time periods. Over the longer period of 1957 through 1995, convertibles performed in line with expectations: Convertible returns fell between those of the S&P 500 and long-term corporate bond returns. Figure 16–3 compares the performance of convertible

**F I G U R E  16–3**

Growth of $1 Invested at Year-End 1956

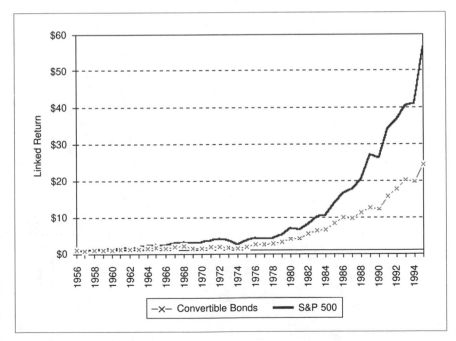

bonds and the S&P 500 over this period. However, from 1973 through 1995, convertible bond returns (11.70 percent annual average returns) were almost identical to those of S&P 500 (11.84 percent), but with a much lower risk factor; this is shown in Figure 16–4. Standard deviation was 17.27 percent for the S&P 500 and 12.4 percent for convertible bonds, making convertible securities 28 percent less risky than stock over this time period.

The study found that in recent years (1993–95), convertible performance was in line with longer-term expectations. Convertible performance at 11.35 percent fell between that of the S&P 500 (15.26 percent) and intermediate-term corporate bonds (8.79 percent). Full summary statistics are shown in Figure 16–5.

Figures 16–6 and 16–7 break out relative performance in five-year increments presented both in table and graph formats. The

**F I G U R E  16–4**

Growth of $1 Invested at Year-End 1973

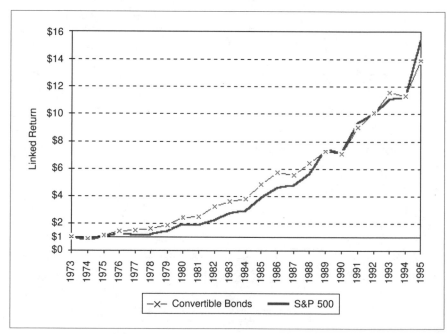

Source: Ibbotson Associates, Inc.

## F I G U R E 16–5

Summary Statistics

*1957–1995*

| Asset Class | Compound Annual Return | Wealth Index (Dec.'56—$1) | Standard Deviation |
|---|---|---|---|
| Convertible Bonds | 8.53% | $24.33 | 13.24% |
| S&P 500 | 10.89% | $56.32 | 16.37% |
| Long-Term Corporates | 7.12% | $14.62 | 10.84% |
| Intermediate-Term Corps. | 7.38% | $16.03 | 8.15% |

*1973–1995*

| Asset Class | Compound Annual Return | Wealth Index (Dec.'72—$1) | Standard Deviation |
|---|---|---|---|
| Convertible Bonds | 11.70% | $12.73 | 12.47% |
| S&P 500 | 11.84% | $13.11 | 17.27% |
| Long-Term Corporates | 9.66% | $8.34 | 12.44% |
| Intermediate-Term Corps. | 9.91% | $8.79 | 8.93% |

1970s and early 1980s were a particularly interesting time, characterized by a number of unforeseen events that would play havoc with investors' asset allocation strategies. Rising interest rates, caused by ever-increasing inflation, devastated the bond market, and a highly volatile equity market ensued. This period demonstrated the significant advantages of convertibles' hybrid nature.

Notice that between 1973 and 1977, convertible bonds performed in line with the bond market but substantially above the stock market. Between 1978 and 1982, convertibles outperformed all asset classes with returns of 16.48 percent, compared to S&P 500 returns of 14.05 percent and long-term corporate returns of 5.57 percent. Additionally, the standard deviation for convertible bonds was only 13.86 percent, compared to 18.44 percent for the S&P 500 and 15.99 percent for long-term corporates, indicating a very volatile bond market.

The study's analysis of risk factors comes to a similar conclusion. Figure 16–8 shows the risk of convertible relative to the other

# F I G U R E 16-6

Risk and Return—Five-Year Increments: 1957–1995

| Period | Convertible Bonds | | S&P 500 | | Intermediate-Term Bonds | | Long-term Corporates | |
| --- | --- | --- | --- | --- | --- | --- | --- | --- |
| | Compound Annual Return | Standard Deviation | Compound Annual Return | Standard Deviation | Compound Annual Return | Standard Deviation | Compound Annual Return | Standard Deviation |
| 1957–1962 | 3.19% | 16.08% | 8.88% | 21.33% | 4.26% | 2.99% | 4.46% | 5.01% |
| 1963–1967 | 9.36% | 12.67% | 12.39% | 13.79% | 0.76% | 2.75% | 0.30% | 3.60% |
| 1968–1972 | 0.23% | 17.65% | 7.53% | 10.70% | 6.48% | 7.59% | 5.85% | 9.87% |
| 1973–1977 | 6.79% | 10.79% | -0.21% | 17.62% | 7.81% | 6.09% | 6.29% | 8.72% |
| 1978–1982 | 16.48% | 13.86% | 14.05% | 18.44% | 7.15% | 9.81% | 5.57% | 15.99% |
| 1983–1987 | 11.45% | 14.18% | 16.49% | 21.03% | 14.30% | 6.45% | 14.06% | 11.36% |
| 1988–1992 | 12.49% | 8.86% | 15.89% | 15.48% | 11.20% | 3.89% | 12.50% | 7.01% |
| 1993–1995 | 11.35% | 7.14% | 15.26% | 9.54% | 8.79% | 4.78% | 10.47% | 7.64% |

### F I G U R E  16–7a

Risk (Standard Deviation) in Five-Year Increments, 1957–1995

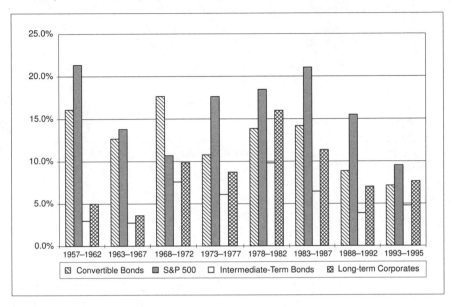

### F I G U R E  16–7b

Returns in Five-Year Increments, 1957–1995

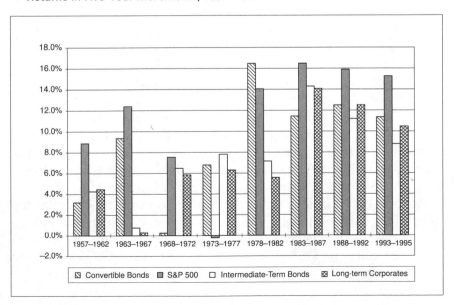

## F I G U R E  16–8

Convertible Long-Term and Intermediate-Term Bonds:
Calculation of Jensen's Alpha and Beta, 1973–1995

| Asset | Alpha | Alpha t-Statistic | Beta | Beta t-Statistic |
|---|---|---|---|---|
| Convertibles | 0.12% | 1.42 | 0.60 | 32.82 |
| Long-term corporates | 0.11% | 0.70 | 0.26 | 7.24 |
| Intermediate-term corporates | 0.14% | 1.47 | 0.18 | 8.46 |

Note: Alpha is reported in percent excess return per month. The regression is run using monthly total returns over the period 1973–1995. The regression is of the form:

$$r_i - r(\text{T-bill}) = \alpha + \beta i \, (r(\text{S\&P})) - r(\text{T-bill}) + E$$

where:

$r_i$ = monthly return on asset i
$r_{(\text{T-bill})}$ = monthly return on T-bills
$r_{(\text{S\&P})}$ = monthly return on the S&P 500

asset classes. The results indicate that convertibles and bonds had positive alphas over this period and demonstrated higher returns for the given level of risk.

Figure 16–9 again shows the hybrid nature of convertibles. Sometimes they act like the bonds they are, and sometimes they act like the stock they can be converted into. Although stocks and convertibles generally move together, as shown in the figure, yearly fluctuations tend to be lower for convertibles. The study shows that convertibles show a high correlation to stocks, with the correlation between convertibles and the S&P 500 monthly returns at 0.89.

The study uses 166 months of returns to examine the performance of convertibles relative to the S&P 500 as shown in Figure 16–10. The average return for convertibles during up months was 2.57 percent, compared to 3.70 percent for stocks. In the months that the S&P 500 declined, convertibles were off 1.44 percent, compared to 2.99 percent for stocks. Convertibles provided 70 percent of the upside of the S&P 500 and only 48 percent of the downside. This translates into a significant risk/reward advantage for convertibles. This conclusion is important because the risk/reward for individual securities that has been discussed throughout the book also characterizes the actual performance of convertibles in general.

**F I G U R E  16–9**

Convertible Bonds and S&P 500 Yearly Total Returns, 1973–1992

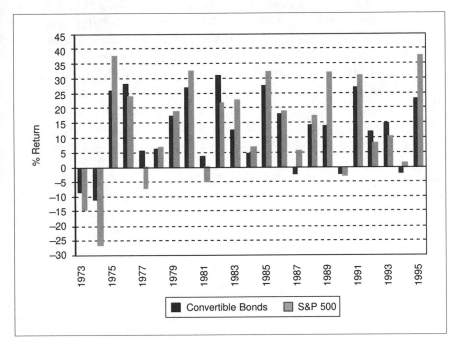

**F I G U R E  16–10**

Analysis of Monthly Total Returns in Up and Down Markets—1973-1995

| | In months when the S&P 500: | | | |
| | Increases | | Decreases | |
| | S&P 500 | Convertibles | S&P 500 | Convertibles |
|---|---|---|---|---|
| Arithmetic Mean Return | 3.70% | 2.57% | −2.99% | −1.44% |
| Standard Deviation | 2.99% | 2.17% | 3.08% | 2.35% |
| Number of Months | 166 | 166 | 110 | 110 |

The growth of the convertible market in the 1980s and 1990s has left pension fund consultants and plan sponsors debating whether convertibles constitute a separate asset class. Plan sponsors are under pressure to allocate assets properly among various classes of investment, so the Lummer/Riepe study is a welcome addition. The convertible market has advanced significantly in recent years, and it now deserves to be considered seriously in the asset allocation mix. In the past, convertible investing was not taken seriously by the large pension consultants due to the convertible market's relatively small size, sprinkled among a small number of industry groups. Not knowing whether to put convertibles in the equity or fixed-income category, many consultants placed them in the infamous "other" category. The Lummer/Riepe study should prove to be a catalyst for additional interest in convertibles by consultants and plan sponsors alike.

From an asset allocation point of view, our opinion is that convertibles can provide the much-needed protection that fixed-income portfolios lacked in the inflation of the 1970s. A significant allocation to convertibles would have provided a higher total return at less risk than that provided by comparable fixed-income portfolios.

Asset allocation is most beneficial when it uses asset classes that increase returns while reducing risk. Mean-variance optimization provides the framework by which this can be accomplished. The addition of an asset class is predicated on its correlation to other asset classes. Figure 16–11 shows the correlation of convertible bonds to other major asset classes. The results show the high correlation of convertibles to both large- and small-cap stocks and the lower correlation to fixed-income asset classes. This points to the advantage of using convertibles to further diversify a portfolio's allocation to fixed-income funds. Figures 16–12 and 16–13 provide further information on this subject. Figure 16–12 gives the expected return and standard deviation for the major U.S. asset classes, and Figure 16–13 shows the full correlation matrix for convertible bonds with other major asset classes.

The Goldman Sachs update of the Lummer/Riepe study determined that the optimal allocation of convertibles using a minimum variance portfolio was calculated as a provocative 5 percent. The update confirms the original study's high allocation to convertible bonds. The Goldman Sachs report also used model portfolios that illustrated a range from minimum variance to optimum return using standard deviations between 2 and 6 percent. These model portfolios suggested convertible asset allocations between

**F I G U R E  16–11**

Correlation of Convertible Bonds with Other Major U.S. Asset Classes

| Asset Classes | Correlation with Convertible Bonds |
|---|---|
| Large-Capitalization Stocks | 0.89 |
| Small-Capitalization Stocks | 0.85 |
| Long-Term Treasury Bonds | 0.44 |
| Intermediate Term Treasury Bonds | 0.37 |
| Treasury Bills | –0.06 |
| Long-Term Corporate Bonds | 0.47 |
| Intermediate-Term Corporate Bonds | 0.53 |
| Mortgage-Backed Securities | 0.40 |
| Real Estate | –0.08 |

Note: Correlations are generally calculated using monthly total returns over the period 1973 to 1995. The exceptions are mortgage-backed securities, which use the period 1976 to 1995, and real estate, which uses quarterly returns for the period March 1978 to September 1995.

**F I G U R E  16–12**

Estimates of the Long-Run Expected Return and Standard Deviation for Convertible Bonds and Major U.S. Asset Classes

| Asset Classes | Expected Return | Standard Deviation |
|---|---|---|
| Convertibles | 8.95% | 12.47% |
| Large-Capitalization Stocks | 13.39% | 20.42% |
| Small-Capitalization Stocks | 16.86% | 34.37% |
| Long-Term Treasury Bonds | 6.03% | 12.22% |
| Intermediate-Term Treasury Bonds | 5.76% | 7.01% |
| Treasury Bills | 4.15% | 2.75% |
| Long-Term Corporate Bonds | 6.88% | 11.80% |
| Intermediate-Term Corporate Bonds | 6.12% | 8.43% |
| Mortgage-Backed Securities | 6.98% | 10.52% |
| Real Estate | 6.71% | 15.15% |

16.2 percent and 34.1 percent. Investors may note that this is a far higher allocation than the 5 to 10 percent many analysts have traditionally recommended. The full covariance matrix is shown in Figure 16–14.

# F I G U R E  16–13

Correlation Matrix for Convertible Bonds and Major Asset Classes

| | Convs | Large-Cap Stocks | Small-Cap Stocks | Long-Term Treasury Bonds | Int.-Term Treasury Bonds | Treasury Bills | Long-Term Corporate Bonds | Int.-Term Corporate Bonds | Mort.-Backed Secs. | Real Estate |
|---|---|---|---|---|---|---|---|---|---|---|
| Convertibles | 1 | | | | | | | | | |
| Large-Cap Stocks | 0.89 | 1 | | | | | | | | |
| Small-Cap Stocks | 0.84 | 0.81 | 1 | | | | | | | |
| Long-Term Treas. Bonds | 0.62 | 0.49 | 0.21 | 1 | | | | | | |
| Inter.-Term Treas. Bonds | 0.6 | 0.41 | 0.14 | 0.92 | 1 | | | | | |
| Treasury Bills | 0.02 | −0.03 | 0.01 | −0.04 | 0.21 | 1 | | | | |
| Long-Term Corp. Bonds | 0.7 | 0.61 | 0.35 | 0.94 | 0.91 | −0.07 | 1 | | | |
| Inter.-Term Corp. Bonds | 0.73 | 0.61 | 0.39 | 0.91 | 0.95 | 0.13 | 0.97 | 1 | | |
| Mort.-backed Securities | 0.6 | 0.48 | 0.11 | 0.89 | 0.92 | 0.08 | 0.96 | 0.93 | 1 | |
| Real Estate | 0.27 | −0.03 | 0.48 | −0.07 | 0.02 | 0.24 | 0.04 | 0.12 | −0.13 | 1 |

## FIGURE 16-14

Covariance Matrix (Based on Monthly Data)

|  | S&P 500 | 5 Yr | 10 Yr | 30 Yr | Cash | Corp. | CBs | GSCI |
|---|---|---|---|---|---|---|---|---|
| S&P | 11.2 | 2.2 | 3.7 | 5.4 | 0.1 | 2.6 | 0.6 | -4.2 |
| 5 Yr | 2.2 | 1.8 | 2.6 | 3.5 | 0 | 1.7 | 0.6 | -0.7 |
| 10 Yr | 3.7 | 2.6 | 3.9 | 5.4 | 0 | 2.6 | 1 | -1.3 |
| 30 Yr | 5.4 | 3.5 | 5.4 | 8.1 | 0 | 3.7 | 1.6 | -2 |
| Cash | 0.1 | 0 | 0 | 0 | 0 | 0 | 0 | 0.2 |
| Corp. | 2.6 | 1.7 | 2.6 | 3.7 | 0 | 1.9 | 0.7 | -0.8 |
| CBs | 0.6 | 0.6 | 1 | 1.6 | 0 | 0.7 | 4.5 | -3.2 |
| GSCI | -4.2 | -0.7 | -1.3 | -2 | 0.2 | -0.8 | -3.2 | 19.7 |

Portfolio Allocations

|  | Min Var(%) | STD 2(%) | STD 4(%) | STD 6(%) | STD 10(%) | Max Return(%) |
|---|---|---|---|---|---|---|
| S&P | 0 | 9.9 | 21.6 | 50.8 | 89.4 | 100 |
| 5 Yr | 0 | 0 | 0 | 0 | 0 | 0 |
| 10 Yr | 0 | 0 | 0 | 0 | 0 | 0 |
| 30 Yr | 0 | 0 | 0 | 0 | 0 | 0 |
| Cash | 99.6 | 56.9 | 9.1 | 0 | 0 | 0 |
| Corp. | 0 | 9.1 | 17.8 | 0 | 0 | 0 |
| CBs | 0.4 | 16.2 | 34.1 | 27.8 | 0 | 0 |
| GSCI | 0 | 7.8 | 17.4 | 21.4 | 10.6 | 0 |
| Total | 100 | 100 | 100 | 100 | 100 | 100 |
| Return | 6.32 | 9.33 | 12.17 | 13.92 | 15.34 | 15.69 |
| STD | 0.62 | 2 | 4 | 6 | 10 | 11.57 |

The studies confirm our own findings that convertibles merit serious consideration for inclusion in both the stock and bond segments of the asset allocation equation.

As pointed out in the Goldman Sachs study, several factors should be kept in mind when reviewing the results. The analysis of an asset class that is small and under-researched presents difficulties in generating and assimilating data. The convertible market profile is dynamic and changes as convertibles are added and redeemed. Each separate index that attempts to track the convertible market presents difficulties. However, we believe that the study corroborates our experience as active convertible managers since the 1970s.

## Performance of Actual Convertible Portfolios

The previous section's discussion has been theoretical, based on data going back a number of years. There is always the danger that a strategy that looks good in theory may not work when actually implemented.

Calamos Asset Management, Inc., manages over $2 billion in convertible portfolios using the convertible valuation methods outlined in this book. The firm's investment process is based on managing convertible portfolios to maximum risk/reward advantage. Optimizing risk/reward is the basis for selecting, monitoring, and selling a position. Our process provides a good representation of how to manage convertibles based on their risk/reward attributes. Figure 16–15 shows two efficient frontiers, one for high-grade bond performance and one for the S&P 500. We use the Calamos Convertible Composite as a proxy for convertible market performance over these time frames. Adding convertibles to either bonds or stocks raises return and lowers risk by significant factors.

## Convertible Performance: Another View

Figure 16–16 compares the performance of the Calamos Convertible Composite to the performance of the S&P 500 Stock Index and the Salomon Brothers Long-Term Bond Index. In both indexes and the composite, interest and dividends are considered to be reinvested to provide a total return comparison.

Calamos Convertible Composite versus the S&P 500 and the Salomon
High-Grade Corporate Bond Index, October 31, 1979, through December 31, 1996

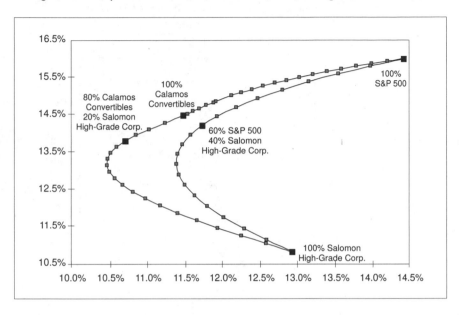

Notice how convertibles preserved capital in the early 1980s
when the bond market was in near chaos. Interest rates in 1980
alone were as high as 21 percent and as low as 8 percent. The effect
of interest-rate volatility on the nonconvertible bond market veri-
fied the benefits of convertible investing in those concerned times.
The bull market that began in August 1982 pulled convertibles and
most other financial instruments to new highs simply because all
investment strategies seem to work well in bull markets. Observe
the corrections of the stock market during this period and how the
composite retraced less, preserved capital, and stood ready to resume an upward trend from the previous plateau.

This is an important aspect of convertible investing. Convertibles actually take advantage of market volatility and, over time,
will outperform the more volatile stock market, assuming that the
investor maintains a favorable risk/reward relationship in the
portfolio. This means that as convertibles increase in price during
the bull market phase, they are sold and replaced with other con-

**F I G U R E  16–16**

Calamos Convertible Securities versus Salomon Brothers Corporate
High-Grade Bond Index & S&P 500 Index—Cumulative Growth of a $100
Investment from September 30, 1979, through December 31, 1996

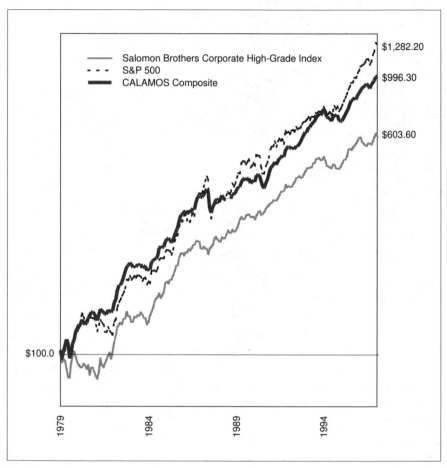

The Carmack Group. Used with permission.

vertibles possessing a favorable risk/reward relationship. The investor continually monitors the portfolio to maintain the desired risk/reward relationship.

The risk of any investment is measured by the variations of the returns on a periodic basis. Figures 16–17 and 16–18 measure

**F I G U R E  16–17**

Risk Analysis—Calamos Convertible Composite
September 30, 1979, through December 31, 1996

|  | T-Bills | S&P 500 | Salomon Brothers HGC Bonds | Lehman Brothers G/C Bonds | Calamos Composite |
|---|---|---|---|---|---|
| Cumulative Return | 242.4% | 1,196.5% | 490.4% | 448.4% | 633.9% |
| Quarterly Geometric Mean | 1.8% | 3.8% | 2.6% | 2.5% | 3.4% |
| Standard Deviation | 0.9% | 7.2% | 6.5% | 4.2% | 5.7% |
| Coefficient of Variation | 48.8% | 178.3% | 230.3% | 162.5% | 161.1% |
| Annualized Return | 7.4% | 16.0% | 10.8% | 10.4% | 14.3% |

Risk Measurement: Based on 69 quarters. The Coefficient of Variation is the standard deviation as a percentage of the mean. This produces a percentage dispersion figure used to compare the volatility of different sets of data.

**F I G U R E  16–18**

Relative Risk Analysis—September 30, 1979, through December 31, 1996

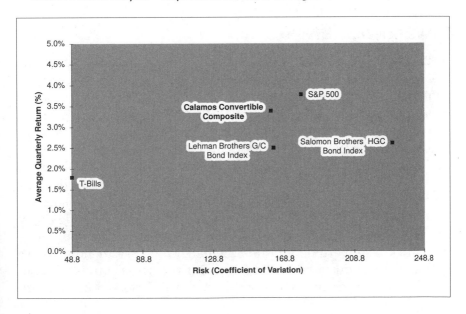

the relative risk of the Calamos composite to that of various indexes and to the no-risk investment of three-month Treasury bills. The composite exhibited less volatility and higher total returns than the bond market or the stock market.

Some view this as an aberration. In theory, the securities market is linear, bonds are not supposed to fluctuate more than stocks, and convertibles are not supposed to be the best-performing asset class. There are sound reasons why this occurred and why it should continue into the future. Convertibles as an asset class have a positive performance bias in inflationary and volatile markets. If inflation is no longer a problem and market volatility subsides, then convertibles will not outperform stocks over time. But that does not seem to be occurring: Financial markets continually exhibit alarming levels of volatility, and few investors and analysts are convinced that inflation is no longer a problem.

The Calamos Convertible Composite has provided an annualized return on investment of 14.7 percent since its inception in late 1979 through June 30, 1997. This time period covers the bull market in both stocks and bonds from the summer of 1982 to the summer of 1987 and the double-digit inflation from 1979 to 1982. Convertible investing has been tested under severe market conditions involving both inflation and deflation.

## USING BENCHMARKS

In this chapter we have discussed convertible indexes, academic studies involving convertibles, and actual results of executing a convertible strategy. The current focus on relative performance benefits investors to the extent that it provides an objective measure of whether a strategy is meeting expectations and is still consistent with the investor's investment philosophy and outlook.

When used properly, investment indexes can be helpful as benchmarks or proxies for evaluating investment portfolio performance. In some instances, benchmarks are very reasonable guidelines by which to evaluate investment results; the index may be misleading in others cases. Indexes comprising large-capitalization stock or government bonds are generally very reliable. These markets are highly liquid and represent the actual universe from which investment managers select and build portfolios. The investment results represented by these indexes are easily attainable by investment programs.

Attaining the performance of indexes that track smaller-capitalization stocks or high-yield bonds is not as easy, due to liquidity problems and large trading spreads. The securities in smaller-capitalization indexes can change quite rapidly, and the spreads in an illiquid market might be high enough to represent a month's worth of returns. Although investment managers who manage an actual portfolio might be evaluated in comparison to the index, they often cannot purchase some of the illiquid securities that are part of the index. The universe against which the investment manager is being measured does not always represent actual opportunities. Therefore, while indexes may provide some insight into a particular asset class, their use as a benchmark is less useful.

When considering the appropriateness of an index to an individual portfolio, investors should first determine if the index is constructed in a manner that is consistent with their own individual investment guidelines and overall risk tolerance. Does the benchmark represent the individual's return objective, as stated in the overall financial plan? It is very unlikely that the answer to this question will be yes. On the other hand, if the benchmark is used appropriately as a reference to monitor the manager, then deviations from the benchmark are not only possible but should be expected. The financial consultant should discuss the reasons for differences as a means to ensure that the investment manager constructs a portfolio in accordance with their expertise and their clients' objectives.

Indexes used for the convertible market are subject to some biases. While any one particular convertible index is a good proxy for the overall convertible market, it does not necessarily represent a well-constructed portfolio. Since many convertible indexes include every issue over a certain threshold size, a particular index may not be in the best interest of the investor. An index that includes all issues would include a great number of small-cap and/or non-investment-grade issues, resulting in a portfolio with a much higher risk profile than an individual investor would choose. This tends not to be a problem in bull markets, when all sectors of the market rise and even risky investments look good, but it forsakes the main advantage of convertible investing—its positive risk/reward profile. In strong markets, the result of rising stock prices is convertibles that are deep in-the-money and increasingly equity sensitive. A convertible portfolio that is well-balanced for risk as well as reward may lag equity-sensitive convertibles on the upside. The benefit will come as the market reverses and the defensive qualities emerge.

The differences between an index and a portfolio constructed to manage the risk/reward of the market are significant. In an index, market turnover is random, as are sector weights. An industry might have little or no representation in the market and then become 5 percent of the index in a matter of a few quarters. The index contains only what has been issued, regardless of the investment quality or balance-sheet risk inherent in its components.

A discussion follows of some of the factors to keep in mind when using an index as a benchmark.

## Quality

The convertible market became riskier during 1996 as many investment-grade convertible issues were replaced with below-investment-grade issues. A well-managed convertible portfolio will not allow an index to determine the riskiness of the portfolio, which should be determined in advance by the investor. The lower quality of the index could well be too low for an individual investor.

## Investment Premium

As we have discussed many times in this book, the convertible's investment value represents its value as a bond, and the investment premium is considered to be a measure of the security's downside risk. When the premium is lower, it means the market value of the bond is closer to its investment value and the bond has greater downside protection. A conservative portfolio might have an investment premium of approximately 30 percent, whereas many convertible indexes are now showing a value considerably higher than that.

## Risk/Reward

A properly managed convertible portfolio is continually monitored and adjusted to maintain a proper risk/reward profile. The risk/reward profile of an index is the result of random market process, whereas a well-constructed portfolio will have a balanced risk/reward carefully managed by the investment advisor.

## Pricing

The small, low-quality issues in the marketplace also give indexes a bias. These issues trade infrequently, and their true value is not always reflected in the index. Pricing such issues becomes an art form that is, unfortunately, best left to the same trading desks that might own the issues and have to mark them to market as a portfolio holding (and who therefore might be reluctant to mark them down but are happy to mark them higher). The true market price and volatility of these issues can easily be misrepresented.

## Volatility

What is the volatility on an issue that trades three days a month? Volatility is a poor proxy for risk, and we firmly believe the real risk is principal risk as measured by the quality of the balance sheet and the protection afforded to the investor by the convertible's risk/reward.

## Transaction Costs

An actual managed portfolio incurs significant expense with transaction costs, which can subtract one or two percentage points from performance. Since an index never really buys or sells securities, index performance is never affected by transaction costs. This makes it an unfair comparison for the money manager.

Investors should remember that good investment performance is the result of adopting a sound investment plan that considers both risk and return. Investors' obsession with indexing is a crutch used by inexperienced financial consultants who rely on indexes as the sole determinants of performance.

The next step beyond focusing on an index as a benchmark for portfolio performance is actually moving to an index strategy, that is, hiring a manager to "manage" a portfolio that has the same composition as the index. This "passive" index strategy will seem to win the performance race in a bullish market, due to its large component of riskier issues. The passive index strategy will continue to nip at the heels of an actively managed strategy during this phase of the market. The damage will show up in the declining stage of the market cycle, when the investor realizes that the allocation of risk capital was based on the performance of an index that had become riskier than his or her risk tolerance.

The larger issue is how this obsession with indexing will affect the allocation of risk capital. The efficiency of capital is based on market participants' views of valuation. Prices reflect opportunities for profit, which in turn allocate capital to achieve the highest returns. If investments are being made because certain securities are in an index, how will that eventually misallocate risk capital? This in itself can cause the market inefficiencies that indexing supposedly solves.

## Evaluating a Portfolio Manager

Most institutional investors rely heavily on benchmarks to evaluate the performance of their portfolio managers. How then can such benchmarks be used to maximum effect? The main goals are more down-to-earth than is sometimes suggested by the statistical excesses that result from such analysis. The benchmark should allow investors to relate performance to their investment goals and assist them in making rational decisions. Finally, institutional investors can help ensure maximum effort from their portfolio managers by paying them based on performance and using benchmarks as part of the criteria by which these amounts are determined.

A benchmark is not useful if a money manager is unable to duplicate its performance. Many convertible indexes include all issues above $50 million. Many managers normally purchase $50 million or more of any issue in which they have an interest, so the manager would have to buy the entire issue—which is clearly impossible. The benchmark must also be unambiguous and measurable.

The benchmark must be appropriate to the investment manager's style and the type of instruments he or she has been instructed to make. In general, managers are chosen very specifically to manage a portfolio with certain style characteristics: small- or large-cap, value or growth, high-yield or investment-grade. It makes no sense at all to compare a small-cap value manager, for example, with an index that includes issues representing all styles, sizes, and quality levels. That would perform a serious disservice to the manager. Published benchmarks will not even reflect the universe of securities from which a manager selects investments, let alone act as an investment suitable for a particular investor.

If a manager is supposed to be running an investment-grade or large-cap portfolio, most convertible indexes, with their high component of non-investment-grade and small-cap issues, would not constitute a reasonable comparison. The benchmark must reflect the manager's real investment options.

Some institutional investors suggest that a custom-designed benchmark provides the best means for measuring a portfolio manager's results, although a customized benchmark can be a complex, expensive undertaking and require significant resources to maintain. However, it is probably the fairest, most meaningful measure of an investment manager's performance.

# E N D N O T E S

1. Scott L. Lummer and Mark W. Riepe, "Convertible Bonds as an Asset Class: 1957–1992," *The Journal of Fixed Income*, September 1993.

2. *Ibid.* With updated data completed by Ibbotson Associates, as published by Goldman Sachs Global Convertible Research, 1996, "Convertibles as an Asset Class," July 1996. Figures 16–3 through 16–14 have this same source, (as do Figures 1–3 and 12–12) and are reprinted with the permission of Goldman Sachs and Ibbotson Associates. We are also indebted to Goldman for much of the discussion that follows.

# 17

## CHAPTER

# Raising Capital with Convertible Securities

**C**onvertibles are an important source of financing for many companies. More than 10 percent of all companies had ratios of convertible debt to total debt exceeding 33 percent for the period 1963-1984.[1] With the acceptance of the option-based pricing models developed in recent years and now in widespread use, we expect the use of convertible debt financing to increase.

The rationale for issuing convertible debt is not always clear. Some companies have embraced the use of convertibles; others ignore their benefits. In this chapter, we discuss the use of convertible financing to raise capital from the perspective of financial theory and real-life practice on Wall Street.

Convertibles evolved as a successful means of financing because they address the fundamental needs of both investors and issuers. This book has focused mainly on the investor's perspective, but the competitive market is an ongoing negotiation between both buyers or investors and corporate issuers. It is useful for investors to understand the decision-making process that corporate treasurers use. There are many reasons for corporate treasurers to use convertible securities as a means of financing; this chapter explores them and highlights areas of particular significance.

## CONVERTIBLES AS A MEANS OF CHEAP FINANCING

A corporate treasurer remains relentlessly focused on cost of capital, and the cost of capital for a convertible may be higher than its coupon rate because of its convertibility feature. Since a convertible is part equity and part debt, its cost of capital should be viewed as the weighted average of specific interest charges and the costs associated with issuing stock. A common misconception is that convertibles represent cheap debt. While convertibles provide an excellent means of financing, the reality of a competitive marketplace is that convertibles are closer to bringing a *fair* price than a cheap one. The notion of convertibles as cheap debt is based on their lower coupon relative to nonconvertible debt and ignores the costs associated with the convertibility feature. Only convertibles that mature or are called when the stock is below their exercise price after they become callable actually represent cheap debt financing. Convertibles may actually be more expensive to issue than they seem at first glance.

The idea that convertibles offer cheap financing is appealing. In practice, few corporate treasurers would view the cost of convertible debt financing as based on the coupon interest alone. Financial theory might not adequately take into account certain subjective factors that are important to the corporate treasurer. For example, financial analysis might consider that saving interest on a probability basis has a relatively small effect on the decision. Convertibles can save 300 to 400 basis points versus straight debt, which is significant, considering the vagaries of the business cycle. The 1990 recession was a test for many companies using convertibles. The substantial savings on interest charges meant they survived, whereas others that issued high-yield debt with coupons in the teens could not service the debt and subsequently found themselves in severe financial distress.

The argument that convertibles provide cheap financing is based on the characteristics of a convertible bond. A company issues a convertible bond at three or four percentage points below conventional straight bonds, financing at a premium of 20 to 25 percent above the current stock price. If the stock goes up and the bond is converted, the cost of financing will be 20 to 25 percent *lower* than if stock had been issued instead of the convertible bond. If the stock never attains the conversion price and the bondholders eventually redeem, then the debt financing was accomplished at an interest saving of 3 to 4 percentage points. Therefore, whether the bond is converted to stock or called for redemption, the company has benefited relative to the alternatives.

For a more complete discussion of how to calculate the cost of capital, see the appendix to this chapter.

## CONVERTIBLE ISSUANCE BASED ON COMPENSATION FOR ADDITIONAL RISK

Another academic view—one that is more positive about using convertibles—argues that convertible financing could be justified by considering the use of convertible debt as an increased cost an issuer must bear due to additional uncertainty.[2] The idea of additional uncertainty is based on the premise that the higher the risk associated with a company business, the higher the financing cost the company must bear. Convertibles protect companies with high and indeterminate risk from a prohibitive cost of straight debt financing. This makes sense because, for all aspects of the convertible market—investment grade and below investment grade—it addresses both the risks and rewards of the issuer and investor. The compensation trade-off is often more difficult to discern in larger companies with complex financial structures. However, for the speculative grade convertible market with simpler balance sheets, the logic is clearer.

In order to raise capital, companies must provide added assurance that the purchaser's additional risk is being justly compensated. A well-designed convertible provides the holder with some assurance that the increase in company risk will not adversely affect principal; additional uncertainty is accounted for with the convertibility feature.

The widespread use of convertible financing in venture capital situations uses that rationale and provides further evidence of the viability of issuing convertibles. The venture capitalist says in effect, "I will provide funds for your venture. I expect to be paid interest, and principal when it comes due, and, if your venture is successful, I expect to participate through conversion to stock." Often this cumulates with a public offering of stock. This common-sense argument may be simplistic, but it is difficult to refute. Those who invest in publicly traded convertibles securities are essentially making the same argument.

## CONVERTIBLES AS BACKDOOR EQUITY FINANCING[3]

The best way to look at a treasurer's reasoning process when considering the use of convertible debt might be to consider convertibles as backdoor equity financing. The corporate treasurer considers two aspects of convertible financing as being of utmost importance. First, convertible bonds almost always have call features that give the company the option of forcing an early conversion to common stock.[4] Second, excessive use of debt can cause severe financial problems.

The call feature is important because it gives the company the means to shift debt to equity. Most convertibles have call features that do not extend beyond three years. Some have provisional calls, allowing an even earlier call if the stock increases well above its conversion price. The call feature is a clear indication that the company views convertible financing as an equity alternative. Call terms vary, and, in some cases, companies leave convertibles outstanding well beyond the call date.

According to financial theory, the optimal point for calling a convertible bond is when the stock price is equal to the conversion price. However, in practice, companies usually wait until the conversion price is well above the call price before actually calling the issue. From the company's point of view, the important point is converting the debt to equity. If the issue is called when the bond is too close to its call price, a small decline in the stock may trigger a cash redemption rather than a conversion. Studies have determined that firms typically call convertibles when the conversion value exceeds the call price by an average of 43.9 percent.[5] Convertible bonds typically require 30 days' notice for a call—ample leeway to assure that the stock will not decline and therefore cause the conversion price to fall below the call price.

Occasionally a company will call its convertible bond issue for redemption to take advantage of changing market conditions. The typical case is when a convertible bond has been outstanding beyond its call date (in other words, it is now callable), but the common stock is trading well below its conversion price. The bond may have been issued at higher coupon rates than are now available in the current market. There may be an advantage for the company to refinance the issue by redeeming the convertible at par or, if cash is available, by simply paying down the debt. This would allow the company to lower its interest carrying cost as well as decrease fully diluted earnings. For cyclical companies, this very well may be a way to manage earnings—by calling the convertible just before an anticipated upturn in the company's business.

There is another important reason for a company to issue convertibles. Although difficult to quantify, it is of critical concern to the corporate treasurer: the possibility of the company experiencing financial distress. Managing the debt/equity balance is often crucial to survival. The financial distress that accompanies an unexpected increase in interest carrying charges or an unexpected downturn in business is no small matter. Convertibles may be helpful in relieving some of this concern. If the stock price does *not* increase beyond its conversion price, the company must be prepared to service the debt burden. In this case, the company benefits in the sense that the interest charges will be lower than if straight debt had been used instead.

Convertible financing can be helpful in managing debt if a company is relatively optimistic about its stock price. The increased leverage provided by the convertible debt can be converted to equity as the stock price increases. For companies that require capital to maintain their growth agenda, convertibles offer a means to control the debt/equity ratio. As the stock price increases, convertibles are called, thus converting debt to equity and cleaning up the balance sheet. Another convertible can then be issued to satisfy the need for additional capital. Companies such as MCI and Thermo Electron, discussed in Chapter 1, provide good examples of how some companies have been able to benefit from this strategy.

## IMPACT ON STOCK PRICE OF ISSUING CONVERTIBLES

Announcing any type of financing seems to cause a decline in the stock price. The announcement of a convertible offering benefits a company because it influences the stock price less than other alternatives. Stock performs better after an announcement of a convertible offering than after the announcement of common stock issuance. The negative impact of a stock offering is three times greater than that of a convertible offering of the same size. On average, announcing a stock issue causes a 28 percent decline, whereas announcing a convertible results in only a 9 percent decline. Studies indicating these results are illustrated in Figure 17–1.

Convertible offerings of higher-grade issues have less of an impact on stock prices than those of lower-grade issues. This makes sense in that convertible issues often constitute a much more significant percentage of total capital for a smaller company than for the typical convertible offering of larger companies. Corporate treasurers of smaller companies have the most to lose if financial distress occurs and therefore need to be optimistic about their stock price before issuing convertible debt.

Convertible debt often alleviates the negative impact of adding a large, additional supply of common stock to the market at one time. Once a convertible is callable, conversion may occur as arbitrageurs take advantage of temporary price inefficiencies. In the market-making function, convertible dealers and hedge funds may purchase convertibles to hedge with a short sale of common stock. Conversion to common stock is often accomplished slowly over a period of time and has less effect than an announcement on single day that adversely affects the stock price. Both Ford, with a $2.3 billion issue, and Chrysler, with a $862.5 million issue, had significant, large issues outstanding that were not officially called. Due to conversions, by June 1996 the issues were a reduced to $261.6 million for Ford and $32.5 million for Chrysler. Distributing stock slowly over time is most beneficial to small to mid-size companies, considering their relatively smaller daily volume.

## CONVERTIBLE FINANCING FOR GROWTH COMPANIES

Convertible financing is particularly attractive for growth companies, which are known for their appetite for capital. Even if income is rising, many growth companies have negative cash flow because the investment required to finance sales growth typically exceeds current net operating cash flow. For such companies, it is crucial to their stock price that they have access to capital. Stock valuations

## F I G U R E 17–1

Average Two-Day Announcement Impact of Common Stock and Convertible Bond Offerings[6]

---

**The Stock Market Response to Announcements of Security Offerings**

In the columns below are the average two-day abnormal common stock returns and average sample size (in parentheses) from studies of announcements of security offerings. Returns are weighted averages by sample size of the returns reported by the respective studies listed below. (Unless noted otherwise, returns are significantly different from zero.) Most of these studies appear in the forthcoming issue of the University of Rochester's *Journal of Financial Economics* 15 (1986), but full citations for all can be found in the reference section at the end of this issue.

|  | Types of Issuer | |
| --- | :---: | :---: |
| **Type of Security Offering** | **Industrial** | **Utility** |
| Common Stock | –3.14%[a] | –0.75%[b] |
|  | (155) | (403) |
| Preferred Stock | –0.19%[c,*] | +0.08%[d,*] |
|  | (28) | (249) |
| Convertible Preferred Stock | –1.44%[d] | –1.38%[d] |
|  | (53) | (8) |
| Straight Bonds | –00.26%[e,*] | –0.13%[f,*] |
|  | (248) | (140) |
| Convertible Bonds | –2.07%[e] | n.a.[g] |
|  | (73) |  |

---

[a]Asquith/Mullins (1986), Kolodyn/Suhler (1985), Masulis/Korwar (1986), Mikkelson/Partch (1986), Schipper/Smith (1986)
[b]Asquith/Mullins (1986), Masulis/Korwar (1986), Pettway/Radcliffe (1985)
[c]Linn/Pinegar (1986), Mikkelson/Partch (1986)
[d]Linn/Pinegar (19868)
[e]Dann/Mikkelson (1986), Eckbo (1986), Mikkelson/Partch (1986)
[f]Eckbo (1986)
[g]Not available (virtually none are issued by utilities)
*Interpreted by the authors as not statistically significantly different from zero.

Source: Clifford Smith, "Raising Capital: Theory and Evidence," as reprinted in *The New Corporate Finance: Where Theory Meets Practice* (New York: McGraw-Hill, 1993), p. 179.

for growth companies are based on maintaining high levels of earnings growth. Generation of positive cash flow occurs after the business reaches maturity and sales growth slows.

These companies can also be viewed in light of their need to finance the *growth option*,[7] which represents the value of the company and is rarely a tangible asset. Companies are often financed for the intellectual capital they possess. Additionally, there may be an uncertain time horizon by which the growth option may be realized.

Given all of the above factors, investors must cope with a great deal of uncertainty. A company's management team is obviously in a better position than the bondholder to evaluate the growth option, thereby adding further doubt for the investor. Investor anxiety can grow even higher as the press reports numerous cases of bondholder exploitation. It is imperative that growth companies find a means to assure bondholders that management will keep its promises.

Convertibles can reduce some of this anxiety because they align the interests of both management and debtholders. Straight debt seeks protection by placing restrictions on management; however, it is almost impossible to demand covenants strict enough to sufficiently alleviate the uncertainties to make the loan possible. Convertibles offer investors equity participation if the firm performs as promised and the downside protection of fixed-income if the firm's value drops. Management's additional flexibility of calling does not finance growth, is an added benefit, and simply gives the bondholder the choice to take a profit or become a shareholder. In-the-money convertibles that can be called will free up additional borrowing capacity to finance further growth. A well-planned convertible offering provides the means to obtain needed capital while at the same time preserving the firm's principle source of value, its growth option.

The essential benefit of issuing convertible debt—reducing the conflicts of interest inherent between bondholders and stockholders—is no small matter. In the case of nonconvertible debt, management can take action that increases shareholder value at the expense of the bondholder. Management's only limitations are specific restrictions in the bond indenture. Bond investors need to remember this extremely important point. A legal interpretation would say that it is the duty of management to take advantage of bondholders for the benefit of shareholders. There is no sense of "fairness" in this relationship, which is governed by the legal specifications spelled out in the trust indenture. The trustee hired by the company is supposed to look out for the interests of the bondholders. Protective convents are often eliminated in a strong economy when demand is high for corporate paper, and then are brought back only in times of financial distress.

A highly leveraged company may take on riskier projects that could jeopardize bondholders—as long as those projects might benefit stockholders. The leveraged buyout craze of the late 1980s offered extreme examples of this conflict. The leveraged buyout of RJR Nabisco provided a vivid example of how newly issued, investment-grade corporate bonds were suddenly relegated to junk-bond status as the corporation assumed heavy debt to effect a buyout.

Convertibles are superior to straight-debt financing, including high yield, because using them reduces management's incentive to take on very risky projects. Convertible bondholders benefit by sharing in the high returns that riskier projects might provide. Even in the extreme cases of leveraged buyouts, convertible bondholders fared much better than those who held nonconvertible straight bonds. Takeover prices were often well above conversion price, causing convertible bonds to increase in price along with the stock price. Convertible bondholders often could simply convert and tender stock to realize a profit.

## CONVERTIBLE DEBT/PREFERRED STOCK INNOVATIONS

There are many variations on traditional convertible debt financing, and more continue to be created all the time. For example, reset convertible debentures protect bondholders against a deterioration in credit standing. Puttable bonds allow an investor to put bonds back to the issuer on a specific date at a predetermined price. Other covenants provide for change in company ownership.

Convertibles issued by large companies are often designed to exploit a passing tax or regulatory quirk. These issues can quickly disappear when there are changes in the specific conditions or factors that gave rise to them. Since 80 to 90 percent of convertibles are purchased by tax-exempt entities, many issues are designed to involve a form of tax arbitrage. The exchangeable convertible preferred is a good example. Companies will issue a convertible pre-

# F I G U R E 17-2

## Selected Convertible Debt/Preferred Stock Innovations[8]

- ■ Security
- □ Distinguishing Characteristics
  - • Enhanced Liquidity
  - ○ Reduction in Transaction Costs
- ■ Year Issued
- □ Risk Reallocation
  - • Reduction in Agency Costs
  - ○ Tax and Other Benefits
- ■ No. of Issues
- ■ Aggregate Proceeds ($B)

| Security | Year Issued | No. of Issues | Aggregate Proceeds ($B) |
|---|---|---|---|
| ■ ABC Securities | ■ 02/06/91 | ■ 2 | ■ 0.4 |
| □ Non-interest-bearing convertible debt issue on which the dividends on the underlying common stock are passed through to bondholders if the common stock price rises by more than a specified percentage (typically around 30%) from the date of issuance. | | | |
| ○ If issuer converts, the issuer will have sold, in effect, tax-deductible common equity. If holders convert, entire debt service stream is converted to common equity. | | | |
| ■ Adjustable Rate Convertible Debt | ■ 04/18/84 | ■ 3 | ■ 0.4 |
| □ The interest rate on which varies directly with the dividend rate on the underlying common stock. No conversion premium at issuance. | | | |
| ○ Effectively, tax-deductible common equity. Security has since been ruled equity by the IRS. Portion of each bond recorded as equity on the issuer's balance sheet. | | | |
| ■ Cash Redeemable LYONs | ■ 06/20/90 | ■ 1 | ■ 0.9 |
| □ Non-interest-bearing convertible debt issue that is redeemable in cash for the value of the underlying common stock, at issuer's option. | | | |
| ○ If issue converts, the issuer will have sold, in effect, tax-deductible common equity. Issuer does not have to have its equity ownership interest diluted through conversion. | | | |
| ■ Convertible Exchangeable Preferred Stock | ■ 12/15/82 | ■ 129 | ■ 10.1 |
| □ Convertible preferred stock that is exchangeable, at the issuer's option, for convertible debt with identical rate and identical conversion terms. | | | |
| ○ Issuer can exchange debt for the preferred when it becomes taxable with interest rate the same as the dividend rate and without any change in conversion features. Appears as equity on the issuer's balance sheet until it is exchanged for convertible debt. | | | |
| ○ No need to reissue convertible security as debt—just exchange it— when the issuer becomes a taxpayer. | | | |
| ■ Convertible Reset Debentures | ■ 10/13/83 | ■ 8 | ■ 0.6 |

| | | | |
|---|---|---|---|
| □ Convertible bond, the interest rate on which must be adjusted upward, if necessary, 2 years after issuance by an amount sufficient to give the debentures a market value equal to their face amount. | • Investor is protected against a deterioration in the issuer's credit quality or financial prospects within 2 years of issuance. | | |
| ■ Debt with Mandatory Common Stock Purchase Contracts | ■ N/A | ■ N/A | ■ N/A |
| o Notes with contracts that obligate note purchasers to buy sufficient common stock from the issuer to retire the issue in full by its scheduled maturity date. | o Notes provide a stream of interest tax shields, which (true) equity does not. Commercial bank holding companies have issued it because it counted as "primary capital" for regulatory purposes. | | |
| ■ Exchangeable Auction Rate Preferred Stock/Remarketed Preferred Stock | ■ 11/20/86 | ■ 5 | ■ 0.1 |
| □ Auction rate preferred stock or remarketed preferred stock that is exchangeable on any dividend payment date, at the option of the issuer, for auction rate notes, the interest rate on which is reset by Dutch auction every 35 days. | □ Issuer bears more interest rate risk than a fixed-rate instrument would involve. | | |
| • Security is designed to trade near its par value. | | | |
| o Issuance of auction rate notes involves no underwriting commissions. | o Issuer can exchange notes for the preferred when it becomes taxable. Appears as equity on the issuer's balance sheet until it is exchanged for auction rate notes. | | |
| ■ Liquid Yield Option Notes (LYONs)/Zero Coupon Convertible Debt | ■ 12/18/70 | ■ 124 | ■ 17.0 |
| □ Non-interest-bearing convertible debt issue. | o If issue converts, the issuers will have sold, in effect, tax-deductible equity. If holders convert, entire debt service stream converts to common equity. | | |
| ■ Preferred Equity Redemption Cumulative Stock (PERCS)/Mandatory Conversion Premium Dividend Stock | ■ 08/16/91 | ■ 7 | ■ 4.7 |
| □ Preferred stock that pays a cash dividend significantly above that on the underlying common stock in exchange for a conversion option that has a capped share value. | □ Investor trades off a portion of the underlying common stock's capital appreciation potential in return for an enhanced dividend rate. | | |
| ■ Puttable Convertible Bonds | ■ 07/21/82 | ■ 667 | ■ 44.8 |
| □ Convertible bond that can be redeemed prior to maturity, at the option of the holder, on certain specified dates at specified prices. | • Issuer is exposed to risk that the bonds will be redeemed early if interest rates rise sufficiently or common stock price falls sufficiently. Investor has one or more put options, which provide protection against deterioration in credit quality. | | |

ferred that can be exchanged for a convertible bond at the company's option. The investor is not affected because the terms are essentially the same. Exchangeable convertible preferreds are typically issued when the company is not a current taxpayer for federal income tax purposes. When the company begins paying taxes, it would implement the option, allowing the dividend-paying preferred to be exchanged for an interest-deductible bond.

Adjustable-rate convertible debt was a passing fancy that attempted to package debt as equity. The coupon rate varied directly with the stock dividend. The IRS ruled that the security was equity for tax purposes, thus eliminating the deductibility of interest. Three issues came to the market before the IRS ruling, and none since. Convertible units that combine debt and warrants give the company a similar benefit in that the warrant is deductible over the life of the debt issue. A regulation issued in 1989 allowed interest-deductible debt with a mandatory conversion to common stock to be classified as primary capital. The various convertible innovations listed in Figure 17–2 give the corporate treasurer significant flexibility in selecting the correct structure for the particular financing project.

Zero coupon convertibles or liquid yield option notes (LYONs) are another variation. (Chapter 3 discussed their evaluation and investment characteristics.) Both interest and principal are converted to common equity, effectively giving the company a tax deduction for selling equity.

One of the most successful innovations was liquid yield option notes, or LYONs. It is also interesting to note how LYONs came into being in the mid-1980s. It demonstrates that it is possible to create securities that benefit both investor and issuer.

In 1983, Merrill Lynch's option market manager, Lee Cole,[9] combined the very risky strategy of buying call options with the purchase of the less risky corporate zero-coupon bond. From a marketing point of view, this design would attract conservative investors heavy in cash. The put option back to the issuer assured the investor that the principal could be recovered at a specified exercise price.

The corporate treasurer at Waste Management, needing capital, saw the appeal of this innovative strategy. In 1985, Merrill Lynch brought a $50 million LYON to market for Waste Management. Before this issue, institutional investors purchased 90 percent of traditional convertibles, but individual investors purchased 40 percent of this new LYON, opening up an untapped source of capital.

LYONs continue to be important source of capital for investors, appealing to both institutional and individual investors. The EuroDisney issue in June 1990 raised $965 million, and Motorola issued two LYONs, one in August 1989 and a $480 million issue in September 1993. As of December 1996, there are 37 issues of LYONs still outstanding, representing $104.1 million.

The entrepreneurial nature of Merrill Lynch was the source of this innovation. Currently, the new convertible structures of MIPS, DECS, SAILS, PERQS, and others continue to address the needs of both issuer and investors.

## MAKING CONVERTIBLES WORK TO THE COMPANY'S ADVANTAGE

The corporate treasurer has many alternatives to consider when contemplating a convertible offering. With financial engineering in full swing, constant innovation means decision making is becoming ever more complex. Here is a summary of the important factors for corporate treasurers to consider:[10]

1.  What is the advantage to the firm in terms of the borrowing itself? The finance decision is made to help support the firm's business plan; even a well-designed financing alternative will not overcome a poor business plan. A firm can always make more money by a well-implemented business plan than by a unique financing arrangement. The company needs to keep these priorities in perspective by giving the firm's business plan priority over financing.

2.  What is the probability of financial distress or embarrassment caused by a given capital structure? What would be the cost to the firm if this occurred? Consider how the advantage of lower interest costs can help alleviate concerns of unforeseen economic shocks.

3.  What are the costs associated with issuing equity, debt, or convertibles? Quantify them as much as possible, using a weighted cost of capital for debt and equity.

4. Consider the design of the corporate structure as a marketing problem. What type of investors will be attracted to the various pieces of the corporate pie?

5. When considering convertible financing, the conversion price and the price above the current stock price will be determined in relationship to the fixed-income characteristics of the offering. The conversion price can be either higher or lower depending on yield, years to maturity, and credit quality. A higher yield can compensate for a higher conversion premium.

6. It is important to model convertible securities using option pricing theory, in order to determine the best trade-off between bond and equity characteristics.

7. The issue should have a call policy that will allow the firm to advance the business plan.

8. The restrictions on dividend policy and corporate actions must be reviewed carefully for their effect on the business plan.

9. The company should take advantage of any tax implications to reduce cost of financing.

10. The company should be careful not to issue debt, equity, or convertibles simply because capital seems easy to obtain. The effect on shareholder value will not go unnoticed by the financial markets.

The growth of the convertible market demonstrates the ongoing appeal of convertible financing. Companies such as Motorola, Thermo Electron, MCI, General Motors, Ford, Chrysler, Home Depot, and many others provide ample evidence that many issuers have found it beneficial to issue convertible securities. With the emphasis on economic profit and cash flow analysis, companies are increasing the demand on corporate treasurers to increase shareholder value. Convertible financing can enhance shareholder value by controlling the carrying costs of interest and thus doing a better job than straight bonds of protecting the company from financial distress. Issuing convertible securities can provide a means for bondholders and shareholders to escape their adversarial roles, becoming instead the joint beneficiaries of a well-executed business plan.

## A P P E N D I X

# Calculating the Cost of Equity Capital
# When Using Convertibles

The cost of equity capital is often recognized by the following equation:

$$E = rf + \beta(km - rf)$$

where:
    rf = risk-free interest rate
    km = equity market required return
    $\beta$ = the stock's beta
    E = cost of equity

The cost of debt capital after tax is:

$$D = d * (1 - t)$$

where:
    d = company's weighted average interest rate on debt
        obligations
    t = tax rate
    D = cost of debt

Since a convertible is both a debt and an equity obligation, the cost of convertible financing is a function of the above equations plus an adjustment for the conversion premium above the equity value. It is important to note that the final realized cost of convertible financing is then a function of the time the convertible remains outstanding in the public marketplace.

Cost of convertible financing is:

$$CV = \frac{(1-cvp)}{[rf + \beta(km - rf)] * (1 + [cpn*(1-t)])^{n}}$$

It uses the present value of the coupon, where:
dividends = 0
        cvp = initial conversion premium
        cpn = convertibles coupon rate
        n = estimate of the outstanding life of the convertible
        CV = cost of convertible capital

It is clear that convertible financing could be more expensive than equity financing if the convertible remains outstanding for many years before being ultimately converted to stock. But this is unlikely in most cases because the present value of the after-tax cost of the convertible's coupon rate would take many years to offset the premium in dollars received for the option to convert the bond to stock.

On the other hand, should a convertible issue remain outstanding and then ultimately be redeemed at par value, then the issue was financed below the company's cost of debt or equity. The purchaser's option to convert will expire worthless, and the company will be able to provide financing at a below-market rate for fixed-income securities because of the equity option on the convertible. A number of companies have successfully issued convertibles on stock that was overpriced and therefore did not move into or remain in-the-money by the end of the convertible's call terms. Warren Buffett issued a zero coupon convertible that he ultimately redeemed for cash, thereby obtaining a cheap source of debt financing.

From the standpoint of a corporate issuer, it appears that there are four main reasons to issue a convertible security:

1. The company believes that the stock will appreciate in the next three to four years. The stock price must move above the conversion price of the convertible to ensure a conversion to common stock. This results in the company issuing equity at a cost that is less than that of a straight equity offering. The amount of the savings is a function of the cost of debt, the time the convertible remains outstanding, dividend on the stock, and the conversion premium on the convertible at issue.

2. The company believes that the stock price is overextended and, within the next three years, it will not move up to the point that conversion to stock would occur. In this case, the cost of debt capital is lower than it would have been had the company issued nonconvertible debt. For example, the company may have to issue a straight fixed-income security with an 8 percent coupon but can issue a 5 percent convertible bond because of the conversion feature. If after three years of call protection the se-

curity has run its course, the company can refinance the debt or pay it off, thereby obtaining a cost of capital below the 8 percent original cost.

3. The company finds that capital is readily available and the convertible market offers the best opportunity to get the deal done.

4. The buyer demands the convertible structure.

5. The cost of capital for financing a convertible is more likely comparable to a *combination* of debt and equity capital.

# E N D N O T E S

1. Michael J. Brennan and Eduardo S. Schwartz, "The Case for Convertibles," as reprinted in *The New Corporate Finance: Where Theory Meets Practice* (New York: McGraw-Hill, 1993), pp. 289.

2. *Ibid.*, p. 289.

3. *Ibid.*, p. 289.

4. More information about this subject can be found in Chapter 14.

5. Jonathan E. Ingersoll, "An Examination of Corporate Call Policies on Convertible Securities," *Journal of Finance* 2 (May 1977): 289–321.

6. Reprinted from the *Journal of Financial Economics*, Vol. 15, Issues 1-2, Clifford W. Smith, Jr., "Investment Banking and the Capital Acquisition Process," pp. 3–29, with kind permission from Elsevier Science S.A., P. O. Box 564, 1001 Lausanne, Switzerland.

7. The idea of growth option was introduced by Stewart C. Myers, "Determinants of Corporate Borrowing," Journal of Financial Economics, November 1977, pp. 138–147.

8. John D. Finnerty, "Financial Engineering in Corporate Finance: An Overview," *Financial Management* Vol. 17, No. 4 (Winter 1988), pp. 14-33. Used by permission of Financial Management Association International, University of South Florida, College of Business Administration, #3331, Tampa, FL 3360-5500, (813) 974-2084.

9. John J. McConnell and Eduardo S. Schwartz, "The Origin of LYONs: A Case Study in Financial Innovation," as reprinted in *The New Corporate Finance: Where Theory Meets Practice* (New York: McGraw-Hill, 1993) pp. 298–300.

10. Summarized from "The Search For Optimal Capital Structure," by Stewart Myers, as reprinted in *The New Corporate Finance: Where Theory Meets Practice* (New York: McGraw-Hill) pp. 142–50.

# 18
## CHAPTER

# The Importance of
# Long-Term Focus[1]

So far we have focused on the characteristics and behavior of convertible securities and how and why to construct investment portfolios based on those characteristics. It is now time for us to take a step back and look at some longer-term issues that affect investors. There are specific issues for specific types of investors, and we also want to point out the advantages of convertibles for corporate treasurers.

Wealth creation is about investing for the long term. There are so many conflicting forces ruling short-term investing that an investor who focuses on the short term will almost certainly be disappointed in the long term. A portfolio that can go up 20 percent in one quarter can easily go down 20 percent in another quarter. In this respect, peak short-term performance and peak short-term volatility are the same. Investing for the long term means, above all else, staying invested and managing risk. In this chapter we discuss the importance of long-term perspective.

A volatile market environment poses one of the greatest challenges an investor can face, especially when it translates into negative short-term performance numbers. Compounding the situation are the doom-and-gloom scenarios of financial "gurus," which are played up by the popular financial press. The unsophisticated investor, easily swayed by these influences and uneasy about dire media reports, can easily lose track of the importance of maintaining a long-term outlook and overreact to short-term market movements. We all know the damage a hasty response can wreak on an investment plan.

Market corrections are a normal part of the market cycle. Since 1900, the stock market has corrected by 10 percent or more 52 times, averaging about once every seven quarters. This kind of temporary deviation is what makes money management, financial planning, and long-term investing a challenge. Even worse is the fact that these corrections are unpredictable. We can tell investors to expect a correction every two years on average, but we can't tell them exactly *when* it will occur: No one can. The markets are simply too fickle.

Consider, for example, that the correction prior to early spring 1994 occurred in 1990, when the market corrected by 20 percent. By rule of thumb, we were long overdue for 1994's correction. Immediately after it occurred, however, those analysts and managers who had "correctly" predicted it were heralded as "experts" by the press. Ironically enough, many of them had been forecasting a correction for months—some for more than a year. (There are also some analysts who are perennially bearish and are recognized as being correct in their predictions every time there's a bear market.) While there had been signs of weakness and overvaluation in the market before the correction, these indicators had been around for quite a while. The investor who heeded the advice of the doomsayers and withdrew from the market at the first sign of trouble lost dearly in performance during the period of favorable markets in the interim before the market actually corrected.

Confusion and fear reign in volatile market environments. New investors often resort to market timing at the first sign of volatility, trying to beat the market and avoid the pain. Others, on the other hand, tend to make hasty decisions after a correction, pulling out of the market because of rumor, fear, and sometimes panic instead of calmly reflecting and analyzing the situation on the basis of careful research and knowledge. Such rash actions often result in a classic case of whipsaw. "As stated by one writer, being whipsawed consists of 'buying in the hope of a rise, but selling instead on a fall, then selling more, expecting a further fall, but being compelled to buy because the market goes up instead of down,' i.e., 'getting caught coming and going.'"[2] Whipsaw usually means that an investor's well-thought-out, long-term investment program is abandoned because of temporary, *unpredictable* aberrations in the financial markets.

While it is very tempting for investors to exit the market when it's rough, most investors want to get right back in when the market improves. It is as impossible to predict precisely when a correction will occur as it is to know when the turnaround will take place. Getting out and then trying to gauge the best time to get back in can spell disaster for returns. The whipsaw syndrome is costly, and it deprives investors of the potential for steady, long-term growth.

This point is clearly illustrated by a University of Michigan study that analyzed the overall effects on investment return of being out of the market for even short periods of time (see Figure 18–1). Remaining invested in the market for the full 1,276 days of the bull market period from 1982 until 1987 resulted in annual returns of 26.3 percent. Missing the 10 best-performing days during that period cut annual returns by more than 30 percent, to 18.3 percent. Likewise, being out of the market the 30 best-performing days cut the annual returns by more than 65 percent, to 8.5 percent, approximating the no-risk Treasury-bill return of 7.9 percent for the same period.

## F I G U R E  18–1

The Effects on Annual Return of Being Out of the Market—
1982–1987 Bull Market

| Period Invested in the Market | S&P 500 Annualized Return |
| --- | --- |
| Full 1,276 trading days | +26.3 percent |
| Less the 10 best-performing days | +18.3 percent |
| Less the 20 best-performing days | +13.1 percent |
| Less the 30 best-performing days | +8.5 percent |
| Less the 40 best-performing days | +4.3 percent |

Furthermore, the 40 best-performing days were scattered over 24 separate months, with several of those months containing three or four of the peak days. Because predicting the timing of these days is impossible, especially on a consistent basis, anxious investors who jump out at the first sign of turbulence may lose much more than they thought they could save in the first place.

Some investors consider shifting from one investment strategy to another rather than liquidating their portfolios. This is particularly tempting when a specific investment style goes out of favor or, more likely, when another style is doing well. But switching styles because of temporary performance patterns can also severely handicap an investment plan. Can you imagine the investment disaster that would result if an investor planned his or her fixed-income investments based on the experience of either 1979–82 or 1983–93?

One of the basic principles of sound investing is the relation of the investment time horizon to risk. Placing money in an investment program for one year or less is risky, and changing managers or asset classes on a short-term basis is a high-risk proposition, comparable to a gambling trip to Las Vegas. There are many reasons why the range of expected returns is extremely wide for such a short period: Investment styles come in and out of favor; growth opportunities present themselves in different areas all the time; the markets or managers are subject to short-term shocks; and the effects of compounding require more time in which to manifest themselves. These are only a few of the many factors that increase the risk levels of short-term investing.

Figure 18–2 illustrates the benefits of staying with an investment manager over the long term, using as its basis the Calamos performance record.[3] In addition, the chart also answers the question investors always ask: "When is the best time to invest?" As the chart shows, for the patient investor the answer is always "now."

The middle line of the graph represents the average return expectation, which, in the case of the Calamos Convertible Composite, ranges between 14 and 15 percent. (At 15 percent, the initial investment will double every five years.) The upper line in the graph depicts the best-case scenario[4] for potential returns and is based on entering the program at the market bottom with several good quarters following, which is what we all hope to do. This line

Why Long-Term Investing Works—An Illustration Using the Calamos Convertible Composite
October 1, 1979, through June 30, 1997

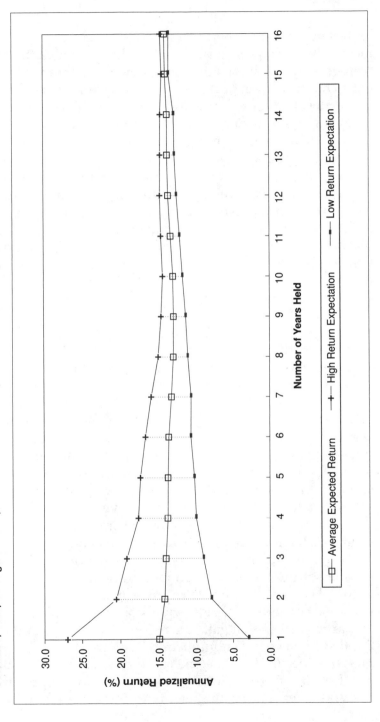

represents, in effect, perfect market timing for the initial investment. The bottom line, on the other hand, shows the worst-case scenario,[5] in which the initial investment was made at what turns out to be the market peak followed by several poor quarters.

After the first year, the investor in the best-case scenario sees an average return of almost 30 percent, whereas the worst-case scenario investor does not gain even 5 percent. After the second year in the program, the average return for the best-case scenario is still healthy, in the lower-20s range; returns for the worst-case scenario show improvement. By the eighth or ninth year, regardless of whether an investor entered the program at a market high or low, the average annual return for both scenarios begins to revert to the mean, converging toward the average return expectation. Therefore, whether the investor has the foresight to enter at a market low or the bad luck to enter at its peak, remaining invested over the long term will generate a healthy and relatively stable return.

Therefore, although the results vary widely for the three scenarios in the first two years and the *average expected return* remains the same, the longer an investor remains with a program, the narrower his or her range of *probable returns*. After five years, the probable returns for each scenario all fall in the double-digit range—from +10 to +20 percent annually, with the average return at approximately 14.5 percent. Therefore, for each year an investor stays in a program, the greater the odds of realizing the long-term return for which the investment manager or asset class was selected in the first place. Keeping the investment manager or managers for a longer period of time improves total performance.

In the particular circumstance of investing with convertible securities, the investor gets the benefit of income from the convertible's interest or dividend payments, and, very importantly, the income accrues and is compounded over time. This compounding factor plays a valuable role in investment success. Furthermore, when the convertible's underlying stock price increases, the investor participates in that gain; the holder of a straight bond does not. But these benefits are not reflected in short-term performance figures; they occur over time, the result of long-term investing.

Keeping the occasional market correction in proper perspective and safeguarding the long-term view are important components of the investment process. One way to accomplish this is to review an investment program regularly. Volatile market environments offer particularly good opportunities for such a review.

Begin with the investor's long-term investment goals. Are they still the same, or have they changed? Next, consider the investor's level of risk tolerance. Has it changed since the plan was originally developed? What has the current market environment shown the investor about his or her level of risk tolerance, since risk is an integral part of an investment program?

Review the portfolio's performance over various time periods. How has it done over the long term? Focusing on one quarter's performance will not give sufficient perspective. If an investment has been in place for less than a full market cycle of at least three to five years, the individual should remember that most investment plans are based on specific time horizons, some of which require time to "gel."

In addition to regular portfolio appraisal, investors should keep abreast of the major trends and factors—current as well as emerging—influencing the financial markets. How will they affect the markets? The economy? The social climate? Being aware of trends before they occur and envisioning their possible effects can be very rewarding from an investment standpoint. The challenge lies in getting the necessary information. Relying on the financial press can result in a narrow, short-term perspective. Investors should be searching for information on the major secular trends and economic factors affecting markets today and many years into the future.

Remaining calm in a shaky market and making decisions based on research, calm reflection, and a long-term perspective is a sound policy, although not necessarily an easy one. Staying on course has the added benefit of allowing the investor to take advantage of opportunities generated by the market situation.

Impatient or frightened investors lose sight of their goals and get badly burned in the process. Keeping long-term investment plans in focus and analyzing situations based on research and reflection serve the investor much more effectively. These are much more profitable strategies in the long run than being swayed by short-term market aberrations. It is vitally important not to let short-term market concerns impede long-term investment goals.

# E N D   N O T E S

1. The material in this chapter was originally published in an article in *Personal Financial Planning*: John P. Calamos, "Investment Risk Management: The Importance of Long-Term Focus," Vol. 7, No. 1 (January/February 1995): 58–62. Used with permission.

2. Glenn G. Munn, F. L. Garcia, and Charles J. Woelfel, *Encyclopedia of Banking & Finance* (Chicago: Bankers Publishing Company and Probus Publishing Company, 1993) p. 1080.

3. This chart was constructed using the Calamos performance record and calculating all the holding periods for the Calamos Convertible Composite since its inception on October 1, 1979, through June 30, 1997. The average return as well as the standard deviation of returns was then calculated for each holding period. The standard deviation provides the most probable range of expected returns for each holding period. The Calamos Convertible Composite is audited and conforms to the performance presentation standards set by the Association for Investment Management and Research (AIMR). For the period represented here, the annualized rate of return before deducting manager's fees (based on the actual fees charged each account comprising the Composite) for the same period was 14.7 percent.

4. Based on a one-standard-deviation move.

5. Based on a one-standard-deviation move.

# GLOSSARY

**Arbitrage.** The simultaneous purchase and sale of securities to take advantage of pricing differentials created by market conditions.

**Beta.** A measure of a stock's relative volatility in relation to the market. A beta of 1.0 represents average market volatility. A beta of 2.0 would reflect twice the market's volatility.

**Bond Value.** Also known as Investment Value. The price at which a convertible bond would sell if priced as a straight debt instrument relative to yields of other bonds of like maturity, size, and quality.

**Break-Even Time.** Bond yields typically are greater than dividend returns on the underlying common stock. The break-even measures the time it would take for the added return on the bonds to equal the conversion premium. This is also known as the payback period. Possible redemption of the bonds could invalidate the calculation.

**Busted Convert.** A convertible selling essentially as a straight bond. Assuming the issuer is "money good"—that is, can continue to meet interest obligations—such issues have very little equity participation.

**Call Feature.** A right to redeem debentures prior to maturity at a stated price, which usually begins at a premium to par (100 percent) and declines annually. Of late, new convertible issues are non-callable for at least three years, except under very limited circumstances.

**Call Terms and Provisions.** The call terms typically indicate under what circumstances the security can be called, and often involve date and price considerations. Convertible securities often have provisions that are subject to the underlying stock's price. For example, the convertible security cannot be called for three years from issuance unless the stock price exceeds 150 percent of the conversion price for 30 consecutive days. Call terms and provisions are outlined in the securities indenture and are determined at or prior to issuance.

**Convertible Debenture.** A general debt of obligation of a corporation that can be converted into common stock under the conditions set forth in the indenture.

**Convertible Debt Spread.** The difference between the convertible and the non-convertible debt yields of similar-quality securities.

**Convertible Security.** A bond or preferred stock that can be exchanged, hence converted, into the common stock of the issuing corporation.

**Convertible Preferred Stock.** A preferred stock that is also convertible into common stock. It is similar to a convertible bond, except that it represents equity in the corporation. Unlike the interest payments made on a convertible bond, the dividend income paid by the convertible preferred stock is not a pretax income item for the issuing corporations. Corporations holding convertible preferreds are entitled to a 70 percent exclusion of dividends.

**Convertible Risk Level.**   This is an indication of the broad overall risk level of the convertible, including both equity and bond risk measures. Relative risk is a means to distinguish among the various opportunities available in the market. Three levels of risk are recommended: low, medium, and aggressive.

**Cash-Plus Convertible.**   Convertible security which requires payment of cash upon exercise.

**Change-of-Control-Feature.**   Certain options available to the holder in the event of a controlling-stake change by the issuer. This usually includes the right to sell the convertible back to the issuer.

**Conditional Call.**   Circumstances under which a company can effect an earlier call. Usually stated as a percentage of a stock's trading price during a particular period, such as 140 percent of the exercise price during a 40-day trading span. Also known as a Provisional Call.

**Conversion Parity.**   The value of a bond or convertible preferred based solely on the market value of the underlying equity. Also known as Conversion Value.

**Conversion Premium.**   The amount by which the market price of a convertible bond or convertible preferred exceeds conversion value, expressed as a percentage. It is a gauge of equity participation.

**Conversion Price.**   Stated at the time of issue, the price at which conversion can be exercised. It is usually expressed as a dollar value.

**Conversion Ratio.**   The conversion ratio determines the number of shares of common stock for which a convertible can be exchanged. The conversion ratio is determined upon issuance of the security and is typically protected against dilution from stock splits, but not from secondary offerings. To determine conversion ratio, divide $1,000 par value by the conversion price.

**Conversion Value (Stock Value).**   The equity portion of the convertible bond. It is based on the conversion price set by the company at the time the bond is issued. This price in turn determines the number of shares of stock into which each bond can be converted. This can be determined by multiplying the common stock price by the conversion ratio. Conversion value represents the intrinsic value or equity value of the bond in stock.

**Current Yield.**   Stated interest or dividend rate, expressed as a percentage of the market price of the convertible security.

**Dollar Premium.**   The difference between the market price and the conversion value, expressed in number of dollars or points.

**Exchangeable Convertible Preferred Stock.**   A convertible preferred stock that can be exchanged for a convertible bond with the same terms at the option of the issuer.

**Exchangeable Investment.** Similar to a convertible bond or convertible preferred stock, but exchangeable into the common stock of a different public corporation. Can also refer to an instrument exchangeable under certain circumstances into another security of the issuing company.

**Exercise Price.** Price at which the underlying stock is either purchased or sold. Exercise prices are stated in option contracts, convertible securities, and warrants.

**Expiration Date.** Last date on which an option, warrant, or right of convertibility can be exercised.

**Forced Conversion.** To call a debenture. Companies usually will force conversion when the underlying stock is selling well above the conversion price. In this way, they assure that the bonds will be retired without requiring any cash payment.

**Hedge Ratio.** The number of underlying common shares sold short or represented by a put option divided by the number of shares into which the bonds are convertible.

**Hedging.** A trading technique involving the sale of one security or option against a purchase of another related security. The object is to minimize risk in one position while attempting to profit from inefficiencies in the market's valuation of the various securities.

**Investment-Grade Convertibles.** Those rated as investment-grade quality by Standard & Poor's (BBB or better) or Moody's (Baa or better).

**Investment Premium.** The amount that the market price of the convertible is above its investment value, expressed as a percent of the investment value.

**Investment Value (Bond Value).** The fixed-income component of the convertible. This is determined by calculating a bond value based on the assumption that the bond is not a convertible. The coupon rate and maturity date of an equivalent straight bond are used to decide this value. Over the short term, the investment value represents the investment floor.

**Investment Value Yield.** Estimated yield to maturity utilized to calculate the straight bond portion of the convertible. This can be determined by evaluating any straight debt the company may have outstanding or yield to maturity of similar quality debt in the marketplace.

**Issue Size.** Indicates the size of the convertible issue in millions of dollars for bonds and millions of shares for preferreds. Issue size can be helpful in determining the liquidity of an issue.

**Junk Bond.** Low-quality bonds issued by smaller companies. Convertibles in this category are generally rated B or below by Standard & Poor's.

**Next Call Price.**  Determined at or prior to issuance, this is the price at which the issuer may redeem the bond or preferred stock. The call price is usually above the par value of the security in order to compensate the holder for the loss of income prior to maturity. The earliest call price is most significant in evaluating a bond.

**Overvalued Convertibles.**  Since convertibles tend to trade on a fair value price track, convertibles that are overvalued, as determined by the convertible pricing model, should be avoided. Overvalued convertibles may decrease to their normal valuation without any change in the underlying stock price.

**Positive Yield Advantage.**  The convertible should enjoy a yield advantage over its underlying common stock. The short sale of stock requires the seller to be responsible for paying the dividend. The difference between the convertible's yield and the yield of the underlying stock should represent a positive yield advantage

**Put Feature.**  The right to sell the convertible back to the issuer at a predetermined price. Typically, most zero-coupon convertibles have a put feature.

**Resets.**  Convertibles featuring a reset schedule that would increase the conversion ratio if the stock were to decline over a predetermined time frame.

**Risk/Reward Ratio.**  The ratio of the potential degree of downside risk to the upside potential displayed in a convertible security. It is determined by examining various possible future market scenarios as well as by analyzing projected price movements of the underlying common stock.

**Standard Risk.**  See Volatility.

**Step-Up Convertible.**  A convertible whose original coupon payment increases, or "steps up," on a designated date. The added cash flow gained upon the coupon's increase gives the convertible an extra degree of interest-rate protection, decreasing the downside risk.

**Swap.**  To sell one security to purchase another. The aim is usually to enhance yield while maintaining equity position in a security.

**Synthetic Convertibles.**  Combining a non-convertible debt instrument with a warrant or option to create the characteristics of a convertible issue.

**Systematic Risk.**  The portion of a stock risk due to the general movement of stock prices.

**Total Risk.**  See Volatility.

**Trading Flat.**  Bonds trading flat are bought and sold without the payment of accrued interest. Income bonds and bonds in default trade flat.

**Underwriter.**  The lead underwriter for the security; useful to know because the lead underwriter often makes markets in the security and can provide information on the security and its issuer.

**Unsystematic Risk.**  Risk of a stock specific to the company's financial condition or industry group.

**Upside Beta and Downside Beta.**  This measure indicates the convertible's price sensitivity to changes in the overall stock market (not including the income portion of the convertible).

**Variance.**  See Volatility.

**Volatility.**  The standard deviation of the stock's return over a specified period of time and the measure of total risk. (Also called variance and standard risk.)

**Warrant.**  Option to buy a stock at a stated price, extending up to 10 years. Warrants themselves bear no dividend and no voting rights.

**Warrant Premium.**  The difference between the market value of the warrant and its exercise price expressed as a percentage.

**Yield Advantage.**  A convertible's yield minus the common stock dividend yield.

**Yield to Maturity.**  The rate of return on a bond, which takes into account the market price, interest payments, and time until date of maturity.

# INDEX

# ABOUT THE AUTHOR

John P. Calamos is the Founder, President and Chief Investment Officer of CALAMOS ASSET MANAGEMENT, INC.® Mr. Calamos, who has pioneered investment strategies, specializes in investment research and portfolio management of convertible securities for major institutional and individual investors throughout the country. Spanning more than 20 years, his experience includes a long and successful history of using convertibles and hedging techniques designed to control risk and stabilize the asset base during volatile market periods. Mr. Calamos received his undergraduate degree and M.B.A in Finance from the Illinois Institute of Technology.

Mr. Calamos is a member of the Investment Analysts Society of Chicago. A frequent speaker at investment seminars and conferences, he has also taught graduate level courses on finance and investment. He has written two books on the subject: *Investing in Convertible Securities: Your Complete Guide to the Risks and Rewards;* and *Convertible Securities: the Latest Instruments, Portfolio Strategies, and Valuation Analysis.* In addition to his column on investment risk management in *Personal Financial Planning,* Mr. Calamos' articles have appeared in publications such as *Pension World, Pensions & Investments, Journal of Investing,* and *Financial Executive.* He has written a chapter on convertible securities for the *Pension Investment Handbook* by Ibbotson Associates. Mr. Calamos has appeared on CNBC; he is frequently quoted as an authority on convertible securities in *Barron's, Fortune, Forbes, Pensions & Investments, Financial World, Nation's Business, The Wall Street Journal,* and on *Bloomberg Forum.*